# The Applied Law and Economics of Public Procurement



This book explores public procurement novelties and challenges in an interdisciplinary way. The process whereby the public sector awards contracts to companies for the supply of works, goods or services is a powerful instrument to ensure the achievement of new public goals as well as an efficient use of public funds. This book brings together the papers that have been presented during the 'First Symposium on Public Procurement', a conference held in Rome last summer and to be repeated again yearly.

As public procurement touches on many fields (law, economics, political science and engineering) the editors have used an interdisciplinary approach to discuss four main topics of interest which represent the four different parts in which this book is divided:

- Competitive dialogue and contractual design fostering innovation and needs analysis;
- Separation of selection and award criteria, including exclusion of reputation indicators like references to experience, performance and CVs from award criteria;
- Retendering a contract for breach of procurement rules or changes to contract (contract execution);
- Set-asides for small and medium firms, as in the US system with the Small Business Act that reserves shares of tenders to SMEs only.

The recent publication of the European Commission Green Paper, with a strong reformist approach of the previous laws, underlines how Procurement Directives are subject to a constant process of change and improvement, requiring expertise to bring to the forefront of the debate the main sensitive points that affect the capacity of firms and procurement operators to work effectively toward mutual satisfaction. The purpose of the project is to, through dialogue and discourse, bring together economists, engineers, lawyers and specialists in the field of public procurement, in search of reducing their language barriers and cultural diversities, reaching a joint wider understanding of specific issues, fulfilling the ambitious task of suggesting reform for better acquisition for public administrations.

**Gustavo Piga** is Professor of Economics, University of Rome Tor Vergata, Italy.

**Steen Treumer** is Professor of Public Procurement Law and Privatization Law, University of Copenhagen, Denmark.

**The economics of legal relationships**
Edited by Nicholas Mercuro
and
Michael D. Kaplowitz
*Michigan State University*

1 **Compensation for Regulatory Takings**
*Thomas J. Miceli and Kathleen Segerson*

2 **Dispute Resolution**
Bridging the settlement gap
*Edited by David A. Anderson*

3 **The Law and Economics of Development**
*Edited by Edgardo Buscaglia, William Ratliff and Robert Cooter*

4 **Fundamental Interrelationships Between Government and Property**
*Edited by Nicholas Mercuro and Warren J. Samuels*

5 **Property Rights, Economics, and the Environment**
*Edited by Michael Kaplowitz*

6 **Law and Economics in Civil Law Countries**
*Edited by Thierry Kirat and Bruno Deffains*

7 **The End of Natural Monopoly**
Deregulation and competition in the electric power industry
*Edited by Peter Z. Grossman and Daniel H. Cole*

8 **Just Exchange**
A theory of contract
*F. H. Buckley*

9 **Network Access, Regulation and Antitrust**
*Edited by Diana L. Moss*

10 **Property Rights Dynamics**
A law and economics perspective
*Edited by Donatella Porrini and Giovanni Ramello*

**11 The Firm as an Entity**
Implications for economics, accounting and the law
*Edited by Yuri Biondi, Arnaldo Canziani and Thierry Kirat*

**12 The Legal-Economic Nexus**
*Warren J. Samuels*

**13 Economics, Law and Individual Rights**
*Edited by Hugo M. Mialon and Paul H. Rubin*

**14 Alternative Institutional Structures**
Evolution and impact
*Edited by Sandra S. Batie and Nicholas Mercuro*

**15 Patent Policy**
Effects in a national and international framework
*Pia Weiss*

**16 The Applied Law and Economics of Public Procurement**
*Edited by Gustavo Piga and Steen Treumer*

* The first three volumes listed above are published by and available from Elsevier.

# The Applied Law and Economics of Public Procurement

Edited by Gustavo Piga and Steen Treumer

Routledge
Taylor & Francis Group
LONDON AND NEW YORK

First published 2013 by Routledge

2 Park Square, Milton Park, Abingdon, Oxon OX14 4RN
711 Third Avenue, New York, NY 10017, USA

*Routledge is an imprint of the Taylor & Francis Group, an informa business*

First issued in paperback 2016



*British Library Cataloguing in Publication Data*
A catalogue record for this book is available from the British Library

*Library of Congress Cataloging in Publication Data*
A catalog record has been requested for this book

ISBN: 978-0-415-62216-5 (hbk)
ISBN: 978-1-138-68643-4 (pbk)

Typeset in Times New Roman
by Wearset Ltd, Boldon, Tyne and Wear

# Contents

# Contributors

**Robert Ågren** is a doctoral student at the Faculty of Engineering, Lund University.

**Gian Luigi Albano** is Head of R&D, Consip Ltd.

**Alessio D'Amato** is Assistant Professor at the Department of Economics and Finance, University of Rome "Tor Vergata".

**Andrea Appolloni** is Research Fellow at the Department of Business Government Philosophy Studies, University of Rome "Tor Vergata".

**Timothy Bates** is Professor of Economics at Wayne State University.

**Chris Bovis** is H.K. Bevan Chair in Law and Professor of European Business Law at the University of Hull.

**Giacomo Calzolari** is Professor of Economics at the Department of Economics, University of Bologna.

**Wenjuan Cheng** is a Phd student in Environmental Economics and Law at the Department of Economics and Finance, University of Rome "Tor Vergata".

**Mario Comba** is Professor of Public Comparative Law and President of the School of International Studies of the Political Sciences Faculty at the University of Torino.

**Paul Davis** is Lecturer in Procurement in Dublin City University, University of Enterprises.

**Nicola Dimitri** is Professor of Economics at the Department of Economics and Statistics, University of Siena and Research Associate at Maastricht School of Management.

**Marta Fana** is a Phd student in Economics at Sciences Po - L'Institut d'études politiques (IEP) de Paris.

**Pedro Maia Graça** is Co-Founder and Managing Director of Eway Systems.

**Jan M. Hebly** is Partner and Procurement Lawyer at Houthoff Buruma, Netherlands.

**Paul Heijnsbroek** is Associate and Procurement Lawyer at Houthoff Buruma, Netherlands.

**Anne Landin** is Professor at the Department of Construction Sciences, Faculty of Engineering, Lund University.

**Fernand A. Lavallée** is Partner at DLA Piper US LLP.

**Philip Lee** is Managing Partner at Philip Lee Solicitors.

**Torstein Fjeldet Lunde** is Project Manager at Inventura AS.

**Dag Thomas Nybø-Sørensen** is Partner at Inventura AS.

**Gustavo Piga** is Professor of Economics at the Department of Business Government Philosophy Studies, University of Rome "Tor Vergata".

**Hans-Joachim Prieß** is Partner at Freshfields Bruckhaus Deringer.

**Stéphane Saussier** is Professor of Economics at Insitut d'Aministration des Entreprises, University of Paris I Panthéon Sorbonne.

**Luìs Valadares Tavares** is Full Emeritus Professor of IST Technical, University of Lisbon.

**Pedro Telles** is Procurement Law Specialist at Bangor Law School, Bangor University.

**Steen Treumer** is Professor of Public Procurement Law and Privatization Law at the Faculty of Law, University of Copenhagen.

**Elvira Uyarra** is Research Fellow at the Manchester Institute of Innovation Research, Manchester Business School.

**Christopher Yukins** is Associate Professor and co-director of United States' leading public procurement law program at the George Washington University Law School.

**Roberto Zampino** is Economist at the R&D Unit, Consip Ltd.

# An introduction to four fundamental aspects of EU public procurement law from the point of view of an economist and a lawyer

*Gustavo Piga and Steen Treumer**

Public procurement is an activity that primarily has been regulated in detail in the EU in order to achieve an economic goal: the free movement of goods and services with regard to public contracts. As the topic is closely linked to the internal market the relevance of economic analysis is evident. Legal research is equally important as the primary tool for achieving the objective is a legal regime that ensures a high degree of equal treatment of tenderers and transparency with regard to tender procedures covered by the regime. However, it is remarkable that academic research only to a very limited extent has combined law and economics and that economists and lawyers typically are not aware of the ongoing research in other fields than their own. The purpose of the 1st Interdisciplinary Symposium on Public Procurement held in Rome in June 2011 and the current publication was to open up a fruitful dialogue between the disciplines and thereby to make a difference by establishing a forum for dialogue, orally and in writing.

We chose four themes to be debated, which we considered to be of general interest. The consideration of these issues in the recent proposal for a directive on public procurement forwarded by the Commission 20 December 2011 confirms the actuality and relevance of the topics considered in the current publication.[1] The themes were:

1 competitive dialogue and contractual design fostering innovation and needs analysis;
2 separation of selection and award criteria, including exclusion of reputation indicators like references to experience, performance and CVs from award criteria;
3 retendering a contract for breach of procurement rules or changes to contract;
4 set-asides for small and medium firms, as in the US system with the Small Business Act that reserves shares of tenders to SMEs only.

These issues will be further commented and introduced below.

The first theme, 'competitive dialogue and contractual design fostering innovation and needs analysis', is linked to one of the most important challenges in public procurement: balancing the need for dialogue and flexibility with the need to ensure that the principles of equal treatment of tenderers and of transparency are observed, while fostering at the same innovation within the public sector demand. It is a well-known fact that the EU public procurement rules have established a very high standard of equal treatment of tenderers and of transparency. This implies that access to flexible tender procedures that allows dialogue on fundamental aspects of the contract is the exception. The contracting authorities normally have to apply either the open procedure or the restricted procedure and must therefore observe the so-called ban on negotiations.

The tender procedure competitive dialogue was introduced in 2004 in response to the criticism of many stakeholders that the EU public procurement regime did not allow enough room for negotiations, which is particularly relevant for complex or innovation-driven contracts. However, the European legislator did not grant contracting authorities a free choice between the open procedure, the restricted procedure and the competitive dialogue and the conditions for application of competitive dialogue have to be fulfilled. It is far from obvious how the conditions should be interpreted even though many consider that they point towards a very limited scope for the procedure.[2]

The chapters of Steen Treumer and Elvira Uyarra focus on competitive dialogue and consider the field of application and its application in public procurement practice. Steen Treumer submits that the field of application clearly appears to be broader than what follows from a literal interpretation of the Public Sector Directive. Elvira Uyarra and Steen Treumer also comment on the uneven use of the procedure and on the possible explanation for this phenomenon. The United Kingdom and France are very frequent users of the procedure whereas the procedure is hardly applied in several of the other Member States, including Germany. Another aspect that is considered in the chapters that follow, including Chapter 2 on experiences with competitive dialogue in Spain, is 'the models' for the development of the project during the dialogue. The Public Sector Directive essentially does not regulate how this dialogue is to be structured even though certain approaches of doing so are of obvious relevance ('the models') and can been seen in public procurement practice. The chapters also address the consequences of the so-called ban on cherry picking in Art.29(3) of the Public Sector Directive. As Elvira Uyarra points out, the model based on non-disclosure of confidential information is more likely to hinder knowledge-sharing by preventing participants from coming up with innovative solutions. It can be added that in Chapter 2 Pedro Telles points out that there was a clear preference for one particular model in Spain in the medical sector. The preference was for the application of a model where the participants contribute to a common solution during the dialogue stage, resulting in a common technical specifications document at the end of the dialogue phase. In Chapter 3, Ågren and Landin focus on a case study of procurement in a highly complex research facility, for which it would be very demanding and expensive to specify in detail the needs and requirements. A key finding is that the research facility exhibits high asset specificity, which creates the need for special consideration of how the property rights are distributed. It also suggests where and how competition through the use of competitive dialogue would improve the delivery of good quality. In Chapter 4, Nicola Dimitri, focusing on the Lisbon strategy and Europe 2020 where innovation is considered a fundamental force by the European Union to promote economic growth and increase citizens' well-being, argues that while competitive dialogue to procure complex projects is usually meant to elicit solutions already available on the market, the Communication by the European Commission COM(2007)799 (COM henceforth) introduced Pre-Commercial Procurement (PCP) as a legal instrument to introduce innovative products when not yet available on the market, or when the existing solutions are particularly unsatisfactory.

Theme 2, separation of selection and award criteria, including exclusion of reputation indicators like references to experience, performance and CVs from award criteria, is another highly relevant theme because of recent case law from the Court of Justice of the European Union[3] and for its implications for the final quality of the delivered goods or services to the public sector so as to generate an effective outcome for citizens. This case law could be interpreted as *in principle* ruling out the use of award criteria and evidence relating to experience, CVs, references and relative risk of non-performance in the *award* stage. This is remarkable and problematic for various reasons. One of these reasons is that contracting authorities frequently consider the above to be of obvious relevance for the award of services contracts. Another reason is the fact that the approach of national courts and review boards prior to and also *after* the *Lianakis* ruling typically is based on a fundamental acceptance of the use of such criteria and evidence also in the award stage even though under certain conditions.[4] It should be stressed that the flexible approach in the majority of the Member States has not been supported by the European Commission that until recently has insisted on a restrictive approach to the issue.

However, the attitude of the European Commission appears recently to have undergone a fundamental change as the draft proposal for a new public procurement directive allows contracting authorities to take into consideration 'the organisation, qualification and experience of the staff assigned to performing the contract in question' as award criteria under certain conditions (see Art.66(2)(b) of the Draft). This exception is intended to apply only to services contracts and contracts involving the design of works and it is a condition that such staff may only be replaced with the consent of the contracting authority which must verify that replacements ensure equivalent organization and quality. This change of point of view is to be welcomed and it is noteworthy that the suggested provision corresponds to the dominant trend in European procurement practice as accepted in the public procurement case law at national level before and after the *Lianakis* case. The clear majority of cases in which the flexible approach has been accepted by national courts or complaints boards concerns *services* and in particular services of a complex nature where there is an obvious link between the organization, qualification and experience and the economic value of the tenders and a close connection between these factors and the likelihood of non-performance.[5] The flexible approach has also been accepted in national case law concerning works even though the acceptance appears in general to be more a matter of principle for these contracts.[6]

In light of the above it is not surprising that several of the chapters on this theme essentially question and criticize the development in the case law of the Court of Justice outlined above. In Chapter 6 Philip Lee is very blunt in his criticism as he points out that the Court of Justice in its recent case law on the issue 'has made a fundamental mistake' and an error 'that is causing great difficulty right across Member States'. As noted above it now appears that the European legislator will remedy this with the introduction of new legislation based on a flexible approach to the issue. Chapter 9, by Torstein Fjeldet Lunde and Dag Thomas Nybø-Sørensen, considers the possible consequences of a restrictive approach and the trend in the case law – with emphasis on the case law in the Nordic countries – after the *Lianakis* case. These authors' concern is that a restrictive approach results in less quality and innovation with regard to public contracts and that it could decrease the possibilities of ensuring that the tenderer with the most economically advantageous tender actually is awarded the contract. They also consider whether it is relevant with a particular approach for high-tech services and to take things one step further by also allowing an evaluation of the ability of the company to recruit and maintain personnel with at least the same competence as the ones offered for the performance of the contract. They submit that this is the case. It can be added that the Draft of the Commission implicitly accepts this line of reasoning and even takes it a step further by making it a condition that staff may only be replaced with the consent of the contracting authority which must verify that replacements ensure equivalent organization and quality.

In Chapter 5 Chris Bovis elaborates on the interests of the various stakeholders in the EU tender procedures and rightly points out that also the service providers want expertise and esteem factors to be taken into consideration in the award stage as they consider this to reflect a relevant competitive advantage. He also points out that the Commission on the other hand will 'dogmatically support any policy and legal effort to narrow the application of award criteria to what is literally provided for in the public procurement Directives, with a neo-classical stance view'. It should be noted that the economist Giacomo Calzolari fully agrees with the statement that the Commission seems dogmatically to support the narrowing of the set of award criteria to be used even though he cannot understand why this 'short-sighted interpretation' should be attributed to a 'neo-classical stance view' as stated by Chris Bovis.

Giacomo Calzolari introduces his paper with the thought-provoking statement that in the economic analysis of tender procedures (auctions in the terminology of economists) there is no distinction between selection and award. He furthermore points out that this is not because the theory on this point is marginal or underexplored. Instead it is one of the most developed and sophisticated areas of economic analysis. Giacomo Calzolari also mentions that it is possible that 'the relevance of this exoteric distinction' might be overemphasized and goes on to stress that selection, if it has a meaning, should be devoted to identifying those who can deliver. However, he also states that the indicator of past experience is not particularly convincing for an economist as it may represent a barrier to entry and thus hinder competition. Finally, he pinpoints that there is a clear borderline between expertise and esteem and that we lack a mutual and common understanding of these terms, which has fundamental consequences on the way we interpret and consequently design selection and award.

Pedro Maria Graça and Luis Valadares Tavares delve into the extremely important issue of the weights to be given to evaluate offers with economically advantageous tender award criteria. How important is each criterion for the decision maker? How can the decision maker be helped to realize how important each criterion is? How should such procedure and its protocol be built to be used as a tool for the learning process of the decision maker? The authors argue that most methods do not consider such issues enough. The proposed method is based on a structured approach using pairwise comparison to help the decision maker to develop a progressive, interactive and iterative learning process to improve his assessment about each weight, without aspiring to achieve a precise, accurate and unique value, but rather to identify the most appropriate range of acceptable values.

Theme 3, retendering a contract for breach of procurement rules or changes to contract, is actually not one theme but two themes that to some extent are closely linked. The main emphasis in the current context has been placed on the subtheme of changes of concluded contracts leading to a duty to retender. The disregard of such a duty to retender is a breach of the procurement rules that can lead to a duty to terminate the concluded contract (that often will be followed up by a retender of the contract).

The regulation in the EU Public Procurement Directive is essentially focused on the actions of the contracting authority until the conclusion of the contract.[7] It is therefore not surprising that possible consequences of the EU public procurement rules after the conclusion of the contract have been overlooked or denied by many. However, it is now certain that substantial changes of concluded contracts can imply that a contracting authority has a duty to retender the contract and thereby to ensure a new competition for the contract. This problem has received considerable attention in the EU context after a recent landmark judgment in the Pressetext case[8] from the Court of Justice of the European Union. The culmination of this development is that the Commission in its draft proposal for a new public procurement directive has inserted a new important and elaborate provision on modifications of contracts during their term in Art.72.

Nevertheless, the issue has only to a very limited extent been considered in public procurement disputes in the EU context, be it in the case law of the Court of Justice or in the case law of national courts or complaints boards.

The issue can easily be overlooked by contracting authorities because they focus their attention on contracts tendered out for competition. It can also be inconvenient and controversial to handle a duty to retender a contract before its expiry as the contractual partner of the contracting authority for obvious reasons often will object to a renewed competition for the contract before its expiry.

These objections might be followed up by a claim for damages if the contracting authority eventually decides to retender before the anticipated time. As a consequence contracting authorities will be reluctant to opt for a retender and will instead tend to presume that the public procurement rules allow for the changes in question even though this is not necessarily the case. If this leads to a violation it has been – and still is – the exception that the violation is challenged by a complaint or lawsuit. The competitors will typically not know of the breach of the public procurement rules because it takes place after the competition for the contract when their attention is elsewhere. It is often also very difficult to obtain exact insight into the details of the contract and the subsequent changes to the contract which will discourage most competitors from complaining.

If a competitor by chance becomes aware of such a breach it will still be unlikely that it is challenged, mainly because in reality it was previously impossible, and still is very difficult, to force the contracting authority to terminate the contract. However, the ruling in C-503/04, *Commission* v. *Germany*,[9] made it clear that there are situations where a contracting authority has the duty to terminate a contract concluded in breach of the EU public procurement rules and it is a requirement in the new Remedies Directive 2007/66 that the Member States ensure that concluded contracts in specific circumstances can become ineffective.[10]

In Chapter 10, Hans-Joachim Prieß covers both retendering as a consequence of a breach of the EU public procurement rules and the duty to retender due to contract changes with emphasis on the case law of the Court of Justice of the European Union. He also touches upon the reaction and interpretation in Germany to these recent developments and challenges a number of suggestions made by Stéphane Saussier as mentioned below.

The economist Stéphane Saussier's main message is that there is need for a flexible approach concerning both the procedures leading up to the conclusion of the contract and the limitations on changes of the concluded contract. The background for this is that contracts are often complex agreements signed in an uncertain environment by contracting parties with limited abilities. Saussier suggests that interacting with a limited number of suppliers increases the actualized value of the relationship and therefore that more bidders are not always good and supports his argumentation with a couple of concrete examples.

Hans-Joachim Prieß is not entirely convinced by this argumentation and comes up with critical remarks to the two examples provided by Saussier. Saussier also clearly seems to put higher emphasis on the need for flexibility than Prieß. Likewise the incomplete contract theory even suggests that changes (labelled 'renegotiations' in economic theory) are unavoidable. Prieß is also sceptical of this assertion as he rightly points out that renegotiations are not necessarily unavoidable because a well-drafted contract will provide for an adaptation mechanism that can ensure that the contract does not have to be retendered. Even though the argumentation of Prieß is compelling on this point it must not be forgotten that unforeseen circumstances in many instances will make it necessary or unavoidable to make changes to the contract. Admittedly, however, a diligent drafter of the public contract will be able to steer clear of many pitfalls in practice.

In Chapter 11, Jan Hebly and Paul Heijnsbroek concentrate on the main theme of changes of a concluded contract, that lead to the ending of the contract and retendering, shedding more light on what constitutes a material change. In addition they examine Dutch case law on the issue and elaborate on what they perceive to be the most serious obstacles from the point of view of a practitioner. It is interesting to note that the ruling in the Pressetext case seldom has been cited and that the criteria it established rarely have been applied in Dutch case law. These authors also consider the possibilities of insertion of contract clauses that ensure scope for change, an issue that was also touched upon in Chapter 10 by Hans-Joachim Prieß. Finally, they advocate for increased scope for making changes.

In Chapter 13 Mario Comba addresses a specific scenario that frequently arises in public procurement practice from an EU and comparative perspective – a scenario that still is surrounded by considerable legal uncertainty: do you need to retender the contract in case of the bankruptcy of the contractual partner or can the trustee of the bankrupt firm sell the contract to a third party? A first reading of the Pressetext case leads to the conclusion that the contract should be retendered.[11] However, the answer to this question is complex and it has recently been argued by the undersigned that 'the legality of such a sale cannot be ruled out as a matter of principle and that such a sale will not be a violation of the EU public procurement rules in several instances'.[12]

Mario Comba considers the issue from a public procurement law, state aid law and bankruptcy law perspective and concludes that 'one can argue that a distortion of the market does not occur and therefore that the transfer of the contract after bankruptcy should be allowed under EU law'.[13]

It is important to be aware that the Commission in its draft proposal for a new public procurement directive addresses the replacement of the contractual partner in case of bankruptcy and suggests that such a change shall not be considered substantial and thereby not lead to a duty to retender the contract.[14] This presupposes according to the draft that the new economic operator fulfils the criteria for the qualitative selection initially established, that this does not entail other substantial modifications to the contract and that the replacement is not aimed at circumventing the application of the directive.[15]

In Chapter 12 Gianluigi Albano and Roberto Zampino take advantage of an important dataset to understand what happens when contract award and contract management are handled by different public authorities, as is the case for framework agreements done by an Italian Central Purchasing Body in Italy. Data reveal a very weak level of contract enforcement. They run a regression analysis to assess to what extent contract mismanagement may depend upon the intrinsic characteristics of the contracts and/or the nature of the public authority using the contract itself. Their empirical findings raise serious concerns. Not only does contract mismanagement imperil the principle of competition of the whole procurement process, but when correctly anticipating the lack of contract enforcement competing firms may 'rationally' react by submitting more 'aggressive' price-quality schedules in order to get the contract, and then recover extra profit margins at the execution stage. As a result, seemingly abnormally low bids might just reveal to the awarding authority – a central purchasing body in our case – that, at least to some extent, firms fight ruthlessly to 'buy the option' of implicitly renegotiating contracts at a later stage, thus undermining the whole purpose of selecting the highest value-for-money tender at the selection stage. Whether this is due to incompetence or corruption remains to be seen.[16]

Theme 4 touches upon the important issue of participation and equal opportunities in public procurement,[17] by looking into set-asides for small and medium firms, as in the US system with the Small Business Act that reserves shares of tenders to SMEs only. In the dialogue of Chapter 14, Yukins and Piga explore alternative rationales and potential weaknesses of procurement mechanisms meant to bridge the competitive gap between large and small firms. Looking at the US experience, Yukins notices that US preferences do not work merely through rigid set-asides since agencies tend to act in a more ad hoc and outcome-oriented manner, steering contracts to small businesses on an opportunistic basis in order to meet the 23 per cent annual goals, which are set and judged on an agency-by-agency basis. Yukins worries that the small business preference is, in the eyes of many foreign observers, a domestic preference and, while he agrees with Piga that such US small business programmes are probably founded on the notion that large businesses tend to dominate public procurement, he disagrees with the term 'subsidy' proposed by Piga, as it would have explosive political consequences. Indeed, Yukins warns of both the highly political content of small business programmes, where politicians' desire to build political support by nurturing small businesses in their political districts runs high, and its bureaucratic costs.

Piga, taking a European perspective, notices that several countries characterized by a substantially market-oriented approach to industrial policy subsidize small and medium firms in government procurement while the European Union does not, being either considered contrary to the current EU directives or even against the principles of the European Treaty itself. Beside enhancing competition by forcing larger firms to bid more aggressively, there are other advantages to helping small firms. The first is related to making less effective and also, as a consequence, making corruption between bureaucrats and firms less profitable and harder to sustain. Second, insofar as the lack of competitiveness of small firms with respect to large firms is due to discrimination in credit markets (including as a consequence of delays of payment by governments), inefficiencies from price preferences for SMEs are reduced. Third, dynamic competition may make these inefficiencies vanish over time as preferences today – that encourage small firms to sustain fixed costs and try to enter the public market by participating in tenders – increase the likelihood of entry tomorrow by stronger candidates (SMEs that have become large/successful firms). For which compelling purpose 'should (we be) helping SMEs in procurement'? If such a compelling purpose was the EU principle of 'equal treatment (non-discrimination/fairness)' of equals and different treatment for different situations it is evident that SMEs deserve to be 'subsidized' to a certain extent in procurement: SBA studies point out that 'at the aggregate level, regulatory compliance costs per employee appear to be at least 36% higher in small firms than in medium size and large firms'. Credit market imperfections biased against small firms have similar implications. How could anyone argue that today's tenders in the EU provide for equal treatment (yes) of equal situations (no)?

In Chapters 16 and 17, Lavallée and Bates expand and document, in a complementary manner, some key issues of the American social experiment that was made through the Small Business Act.

While Lavallée reminds the reader of the 'sophistication of US small businesses … individuals who are typically highly educated and skilled, such as scientists, engineers and other high technology workers' who demonstrate that 'small businesses have the human resources to deal with complex technical challenges and are a substantial source of employment for highly skilled individuals', Bates focuses on minority-owned businesses and the history of procurement set-asides, depicting a fascinating excursus which started from an array of mostly Afro-American business in the 1970s, with limited capacity and with most enterprises in the wrong line of business, lacking the necessary expertise, working capital and bonding capacity contractors needed to complete successfully all but the smallest government procurement tasks. Eventually, serving government clients has enabled many minority-owned businesses to expand their penetration of mainstream markets, and sales to businesses, including major corporations, now account for greater aggregate sales revenues than minority-owned business (MBE) sales to government clients.

Lavallée and Bates seem to agree on the basic fact that, when it comes to socio-economic preferences, the government must be vigilant to ensure that the appropriate groups are targeted for eligibility in the programmes, avoiding fraud, and that a well-defined and meaningful system for protests and challenges to the government's solicitation and evaluation process and decisions is crucial but also that, ultimately, to be successful, the benefits and value of the socio-economic preferences must give due consideration to the non-economic objectives of the nation.

Davis adds another dimension to the issues of preferences for firms, showing the development in Ireland of a public procurement innovation framework attentive to SMEs. It was through the development of a single model in Ireland that a framework was developed to link public procurement and innovation together.

## Notes

* Our thanks for the publication of this volume go to Routledge and their precious team of editors. Also, Roberta Marta provided fantastic support during the conference and Elena Innocenzi was outstanding in maintaining order in the difficult process of keeping in touch with each author and helping with sorting out the various editorial changes that were needed.

1 Proposal for a Directive of the European Parliament and of the Council on Public Procurement, COM(2011)896 final of 20 December 2011.

2 For an in-depth analysis of competitive dialogue based on law, case law and practice in ten selected Member States see Sue Arrowsmith and Steen Treumer (eds), *Competitive Dialogue in EU Procurement*, Cambridge University Press (forthcoming).

3 See in particular C-532/06, *Lianakis* [2008] E.C.R. I-251.

4 See the Special Issue of the *Public Procurement Law Review* with seven articles on the Application and Implications of the ECJ's Decisions in Lianakis on the Separation of Selection and Award Criteria from 2009, pp. 103–64 (ed. Steen Treumer) and in particular section 3 of the article by Steen Treumer, 'The Distinction between Selection and Award Criteria in EC Public Procurement Law: A Rule without Exception', 18(3), p. 103 (pp. 106–9 on trends in national case law).

5 See the Special Issue of the *Public Procurement Law Review*, op. cit., note 4 and in particular p. 107 of section 3 of the article of Steen Treumer, op. cit., note 4.

6 See Steen Treumer, op. cit., note 4, p. 107.

7 An important exception can be found in Art.31(4) of the Public Sector Directive.

8 C-454/06, *Pressetext* [2008] E.C.R. I-4401. See the case note of Adrian Brown in *Public Procurement Law Review*, 2008, NA253. See also the article by Christina Tvarnø, 'Does the Danish Interpretation of EC Public Procurement Law Prevent PPP?', *Public Procurement Law Review*, 2010, p. 73 (especially section 3, p. 81 with emphasis on the Pressetext case).

9 C-503/04, *Commision* v. *Germany* [2007] E.C.R I-6153. See Steen Treumer, 'Towards an Obligation to Terminate Contracts Concluded in Breach of the EC Public Procurement Rules: the End of the Status of Concluded Public Contracts as Sacred Cows', *Public Procurement Law Review*, 2007, p. 371.

10 An analysis of this new remedy and the approach to ineffectivness in a range of Member States can be found in Steen Treumer and François Lichère (eds), *Enforcement of the EU Public Procurement Rules*, Copenhagen: DJØF Publishing, 2011.

11 See paragraph 40 of the Pressetext case, according to which:

> As a rule, the substitution of a new contractual partner for the one to which the contracting authority had initially awarded the contract must be regarded as constituting a change to one of the essential terms of the public contract in question, unless that substitution was provided for in the terms of the initial contract, such as, by way of example, provision for sub-contracting.

12 See Steen Treumer, 'Changes of Concluded Contracts and its Implications in the EU Context: Sale of Contracts after Bankruptcy', in *Papers for International Public Procurement Forum II* (2010) hosted by the Central University of Finance and Economics (Beijing, China) and Xinjang University of Finance and Economics (Xinjiang, China), pp. 149–53.

13 This conclusion is more cautious than the one of Steen Treumer, op. cit., note 12.

14 See Art.72(3) of the Draft proposal, op. cit., note 1.

15 These conditions were listed by Steen Treumer, op. cit., note 12, as conditions for the legality of a sale to a third party in the context of bankruptcy. However, it should be noted that this author claims that this is the current state of law and that this appears to be in accordance with the dominant trend in the administrative practice of the European Commission on the issue. Mario Comba also makes his conclusion conditional and presupposes that the 'economic conditions of the contract are not materially changed'.

16 See for this matter O. Bandiera, A. Prat and T. Valletti, 'Active and Passive Waste in Government Spending: Evidence from a Policy Experiment', *American Economic Review*, 99(4), 2009, pp. 1278–308 and G. Piga 'A Fighting Chance Against Corruption in Public Procurement?', in *International Handbook on the Economics of Corruption*, vol. 2, edited by Tina Soreide and Susan Rose-Ackerman, Cheltenham: Edward Elgar, 2011.

17 For a general view on this issue and others related to the economics of procurement see N. Dimitri, G. Piga and G. Spagnolo (eds), *Handbook of Procurement*, New York: Cambridge University Press, 2006.

# Part I

# Competitive dialogue and contractual design fostering innovation and needs analysis

# 1 Dialogue

*Steen Treumer and Elvira Uyarra*

## 1 Argument by Steen Treumer

### *1.1 Introduction*

Competitive dialogue is one of the most important novelties in the EU public procurement regime. It is well known that the objective of the introduction of the procedure of competitive dialogue was to achieve procedural simplification and to make the EU public procurement regime more flexible.[1] This is also spelled out in the Explanatory Note on Competitive Dialogue from the European Commission[2] where it is mentioned that the procedure was introduced in the Public Sector Directive 2004/18/EC in response to the finding that the 'old' Directives, Directives 92/50/EEC, 93/96/EEC and 93/37/EEC, did not offer sufficient flexibility with certain particularly complex projects due to the fact that the use of negotiated procedures with publication of a contract note is limited solely to the cases exhaustively listed in the Directives.

The introduction of the procedure should therefore allow increased dialogue fostering innovation and a much better needs analysis than what has been feasible according to the classical public procurement procedures. However, this presupposes that the procedure can be used where it is relevant which leads to the analysis of the field of application of competitive dialogue in the second section of this chapter. Furthermore, it is relevant to consider the limits following from EU public procurement law to the contractual design fostering innovation and needs analysis. This issue is considered in the third section of this chapter with emphasis on the so-called 'ban on cherry picking'.

### *1.2 The field of application of competitive dialogue*

The field of application of competitive dialogue is considered in several provisions and a recital in the Public Sector Directive. It follows from Article 28 of the Directive that contracting authorities may award their public contracts by means of the competitive dialogue in the specific circumstances expressly provided for in Article 29. The latter article provides that in the case of particularly complex contracts Member States may provide that where contracting authorities consider that the use of the open or restricted procedure will not allow the award of the contract, the latter may make use of the competitive dialogue in accordance with that Article. 'Particularly complex' is defined in Article 1(11)(c) of the Public Sector Directive to mean where the contracting authorities are not objectively able to define the technical means in accordance with Article 23(3)(b)(c) or (d) capable of satisfying their special needs or objectives, and/or are not objectively able to specify the legal and/or financial make-up of a project. A part of Recital 31 in the preamble to the Classic Directive reads as follows:

> Contracting authorities which carry out particularly complex projects may, without this being due to any fault on their part, find it objectively impossible to define the means of satisfying their needs or of assessing what the market can offer in the way of technical solutions and/or financial/legal solutions.[3]

The formulation of the below-mentioned provisions and the quoted recital from the Public Sector Directive clearly indicate that the access to the procedure is limited to special circumstances. This is noteworthy but it is important to stress that this is only one of several elements which has to be taken into consideration when determining the field of application.

The Court of Justice of the European Union has not considered the field of application of competitive dialogue in its case law. This is remarkable as the procedure was introduced several years ago and has been used thousands of times in the Member States of the EU. There do not appear to be pending cases on the issue that would lead to a clarification of the state of law in the near future. However, it is important to stress that the Court is known for its *purpose-oriented* and *dynamic* interpretation of EU law and that the background for the introduction of the competitive dialogue procedure was to ensure a more flexible approach for complex public contracts. So even though the wording in the Public Sector Directive clearly points towards a restrictive interpretation of the competitive dialogue procedure the legislative history and the purpose of the introduction of the procedure obviously points in the opposite direction.

As a consequence it has to be expected that the approach of the Court of Justice will be more flexible and pragmatic than the one that is reflected in the wording of the Public Sector Directive. It can be added that the current tendency in the case law of the Court of Justice of the European Union is to interpret the public procurement rules in a more flexible and pragmatic manner than previously. The field of application of competitive dialogue is therefore presumably broader than what follows from a literal interpretation of the Public Sector Directive.

The European Commission is 'the guardian of the Treaties' and for this reason it is of obvious relevance to consider the Commission's interpretation and approach to the enforcement of the rules on competitive dialogue. Again it is remarkable that there is a general lack of case law. I have looked in vain for references to concrete cases where the Commission has questioned the application of competitive dialogue procedures. It would therefore appear that the Commission implicitly has accepted the experimental approach in the Member States.[4] This is noteworthy as you get the impression that the grounds for application is interpreted fairly flexible at least in some Member States and in particular in the United Kingdom and France where the procedure has been applied in more than 3,000 instances.

As the contracting authorities in some Member States appear to interpret the conditions for the use of the competitive dialogue procedure in a flexible manner one could expect that there would be several challenges of the use of competitive dialogue at national level. However this is absolutely not so and it appears surprisingly enough that Denmark actually is the only Member State with case law of this type.

To summarize, the field of application of competitive dialogue therefore clearly appears to be broader than what follows from a literal interpretation of the Public Sector Directive.

### *1.3 Limits on the contractual design fostering innovation and needs analysis*

It follows from Article 29(3) that the contracting authorities may not reveal to the other participants solutions proposed or other confidential information communicated by a candidate participating in the dialogue without his/her agreement. This provision has to be read in conjunction with Article 29(6) according to which the contracting authority shall ask the participants in the procedure to submit their final tenders on the basis of the solution or solutions presented and specified during the dialogue. From this follows that the so-called 'cherry picking' is not allowed unless the participant agrees and that each participant must submit a bid based on their own proposal for a solution.

The background for the ban is that the Commission's first proposal for the procedure[5] met strong objections from trade and industries because it allowed cherry picking as the proposal made it possible for the contracting authority to define the final technical specifications either by retaining one of the solutions presented by one of the participants or by combining the solutions presented to it. The adopted rule was inserted in order to strike a better balance between the interests of the contracting authority and the participants in the procedure.

For obvious reasons the approach of the legislator in this respect is likely to be challenged in practice. Many contracting authorities will surely be tempted to set aside the ban on cherry picking in order to obtain value for money. However, there appears not to be case law on the issue yet competitive dialogue has in general been the object of very few public procurement disputes at the national level.

As mentioned above there is an important exception to the ban on cherry picking as the participants in the procedure can agree that their solutions or other confidential information can be revealed and applied by the contracting authority (see Article 29(3)). The contracting authorities can specify prices and payments to the participants in the dialogue (see Article 29 (8)), which is likely to make it easier to get the agreement of the firms involved. It appears that this opportunity is not frequently applied in the practice of the Member States which is rather surprising.

It is not clear if a contracting authority can insert a *tender condition* in the contract notice or descriptive document to the effect that the participants must accept that the contracting authority may share its solution with the other participants in the competitive dialogue. One point of view is that this is excluded as it is inconsistent with the set up of the competitive dialogue procedure as a systematic use of such tender conditions could completely undermine the effect of the ban on cherry picking. However, it is submitted that a contracting authority can insert such a condition in the tender conditions as the participants are made aware of the foreseen procedure when they enter the competition and before they have submitted their solution. The contracting authority using such a tender condition from the very outset of the procedure risks that the procedure becomes a failure as the potential tenderers in general might oppose the idea of sharing their solutions and know-how.

Finally, it should be mentioned that it can also be questioned whether variant bids can be authorized in competitive dialogue procedures. The state of law is unclear and the issue is of interest because authorization of variant bids occasionally is seen in practice and has been disputed in a case at national level.

## 2 Argument by Elvira Uyarra

### 2.1 Introduction

Public procurement accounts for a significant proportion of overall demand for goods and services (17 per cent of EU GDP) and as such it is increasingly seen as an attractive and feasible instrument for furthering the goals of innovation policy. While the interest in the use of procurement as an industrial and technology policy tool is by no means new[6] there has been a renewed focus on this underexploited 'demand side' policy tool in recent years.[7]

A range of specific policy initiatives have been launched, both at European and at national level, to encourage the use of public procurement in support of innovation. The Europe 2020 strategy sees public procurement as one of the market-based instruments that should be used to achieve the objectives of smart, sustainable and inclusive growth.[8] A recent Green Paper by the European Commission[9] states that existing procurement tools and methods should be modernized in order to make them better suited to deal with the evolving political, social and economic context. This includes increasing efficiency of public spending and support of common societal goals such as protection of the environment, higher resource and energy efficiency and combating climate change, promoting innovation and social inclusion, and ensuring the best possible conditions for the provision of high quality public services.

Challenges associated with taking this agenda forward include regulatory complexity, potential conflict between policy objectives, and capacity and resource constraints in contracting authorities. Difficulties also arise in defining what constitutes innovation in procurement terms, and in relation to measuring the extent and impact of such innovations. The policy and academic debate has all too often focused on 'buying innovations', implicitly overlooking innovation effects beyond the initial purchase, and on radical (new to the world) innovations, paying less attention to other categories of innovation.[10] Innovation cannot be confused with novelty, indeed novelty may not necessarily be a good thing. As Geroski notes, 'using procurement policies to encourage firms to develop new capabilities does not imply that one ought to uncritically encourage them to generate something new'.[11] Procurement decisions will always have innovation impacts via their influence on intermediate outcomes such as competition, industrial structure and network effects. The key question is therefore not whether but *how* innovation impacts take place.

This brief section looks at some of the mechanisms recently encouraged to favour innovation, particularly the competitive dialogue procedure, highlighting key issues around their use and some key challenges, and finally stresses the need to keep a broad and flexible framework that reflects the diversity of situations in which innovation is enabled through procurement whilst providing better guidance on their application.

## 2.2 Procedures to promote innovation procurement

The current EU Directives on public procurement incorporate a number of mechanisms that enable contracting authorities to encourage the market to find innovative solutions. For instance under the design contest procedure participants can propose ideas outside of the strict terms of reference and that may be used in a future procurement procedure. 'Pre-commercial procurement' has been introduced[12] to enable the procurement of research and development services for the development of new solutions, with a view to their possible purchase at a later stage through a normal public procurement procedure. Pre-commercial procurement has been taken up mainly by innovation promotion agencies in a number of Member States, which have introduced their own scaled down versions of the US SBIR programme, linked to national innovation policy objectives.

One key challenge, however, is to connect the development of new products through pre-commercial procedures with commercial (normal) procurement. At the moment there are no clear mechanisms to link commercial procurement with pre-commercially procured goods or services so that they can compete with their off-the-shelf counterparts.

In the case of complex contracts the directive allows for the use of competitive dialogue procedure. As suggested by Lundvall,[13] user–producer interaction is key for the production of innovations. The procedure enables contracting authorities to engage in a dialogue in which participants' ideas and solutions are discussed. By allowing discussions between contracting authorities and suppliers, competitive dialogue introduces greater flexibility to develop innovative solutions.

One difficulty associated with the use of the procedure is that it necessitates more careful management and more time and resources than other processes. In addition there is a danger of cherry picking of intellectual property rights or innovative solutions, since participants may see their ideas or solutions revealed to their competitors. Even though proposed solutions and confidential information must be kept confidential, it may be difficult to avoid the disclosure of some information.

The use of competitive dialogue is still limited across member states. Directives did suggest a quite restrictive application (in highly complex contracts) and gave Member States the choice to use this procedure nationally. Poor uptake may also be due to authorities being unaware of it, unsure of how to use it or uncertain about its legal implications. There is an issue of insufficient awareness and lack of clarity surrounding these procedures, and therefore a risk that they may be underutilized or misused.

In order to enable procurement to foster multiple goals, the Green Paper on the modernization of public procurement suggests that further efforts could be directed to:

1 providing contracting authorities with the means to take into account those objectives under procedural public procurement rules ('how to buy'); or
2 imposing mandatory requirements on contracting authorities or provide incentives to steer their decisions as to which goods and services should be procured ('what to buy').

The latter could introduce obligations in relation to the characteristics of goods/services/works that contracting authorities should purchase. The former could mean more refined guidelines in relation to the pursuit of different procurement objectives, which could imply a more strict separation of normal procurement regulations from procurement serving other policy objectives such as innovation. Caution should be exercised in relation to mandatory requirements and targets, except perhaps minimum requirements for a core set of products and services, as they may restrict flexibility for contracting authorities. More strict guidelines on how to buy in relation to different policy objectives may also be too rigid given the diversity of procurement situations and risk establishing an artificial divide between innovation procurement and normal procurement.

In order to encourage contracting authorities to make more and better use of procedures such as competitive dialogue, directives could reduce legal uncertainty through further clarifying their use and provide better guidance on their application together with examples of their successful applications.

## *2.3 Diversity of innovation impacts*

Procurement is a multi-objective, dynamic, activity, where decisions need to be taken on a case-by-case basis and with a focus on the future dynamics of the demand–supply relationship. As Dimitri *et al.* note:

> there is not a one-size-fits-all measure for effective procurement design: the variety and complexity of situations in which procurement decisions are made means that appropriate purchasing procedures must take into account many aspects, and be tailored to each single situation.[14]

The interplay between supply and particular demand effects brings to the fore the characteristics and dynamics of product markets. As Murmann and Frenken[15] point out, 'successful innovation is in essence a coupling process focusing superior technological competencies in products and processes to meet the specific needs of users'. Such coupling processes involve a balance between technological exploration and exploitation, and between scale of demand and need specificity. Indeed, the successful introduction of an innovation may be dependent upon a group of experimental customers, or on untapped needs of potential users. This demand may subsequently 'pull' innovation if it guarantees a significant level of production and a reduction in uncertainty that allows firms to benefit from economies of scale and technological investment. Demand side dynamics can give rise to network effects leading consumers to gravitate towards a particular design or standard.

Procurement can be associated with all the above demand effects.[16] Public procurers can influence innovation through shaping the size, specificity, technical sophistication or standardization of demand. They can do so through pooling requirements, aggregating contracts, opening or restricting competition through tendering procedures, setting standards and defining specifications, and through engaging with users and suppliers.

Procurement decisions should be made on a case-by-case basis depending on the good or service being procured, demand–supply relationships, capacity and financial constraints and policy objectives. The choice of what procedure to follow is one of many aspects influencing innovation.

## 3 Reply by Steen Treumer

### *3.1 Introduction*

The first section of Elvira Uyarra (hereafter 'the Section') touches on several issues and I have chosen to focus on those related to key issues and key changes relating to competitive dialogue.

### *3.2 The field of application of competitive dialogue*

The first section submitted by the undersigned considered to a large extent the field of application of the competitive procedure. The following is therefore essentially limited to remarks on the Section. It is stated in the Section that 'the use of competitive dialogue is still limited across member states'. The reality is more diverse as the procedure is used very frequently in a few Member States and relatively frequent in some other Member States.[17] The procedure has been used in the United Kingdom and France in more than 3,000 instances. It has also been used relatively frequent in other Member States, for example Poland and Denmark. However, the procedure has been applied only in a limited number of cases in some Member States, such as Portugal and Italy, and in relatively limited numbers as in Germany.

It is suggested in the Section that the limited use is due to the regulation of the field of competitive dialogue in the Public Sector Directive and that it may be 'due to authorities being unaware of it, unsure of how to use it or uncertain about its legal implications'. It is correct that the formulation of the relevant provisions and recital 31 of the Public Sector Directive clearly indicate that the access to the procedure is limited. Furthermore, there is considerable uncertainty on how to run a competitive dialogue. I therefore fully agree that this presumably has a significant bearing on the limited number of applications in many Member States. Nevertheless, it should be noted that this does not at all seem to have inhibited the users of the procedure in the United Kingdom and France. However, it is questionable whether contracting authorities in a larger number are unaware of the procedure. The procedure has received so much attention and been discussed repeatedly over the years that this would appear to be highly unlikely.

It is furthermore suggested in the Section that

> In order to encourage contracting authorities to make more and better use of the procedures such as competitive dialogue, directives could reduce legal uncertainty through clarifying their use and provide better guidance on their application together with examples of their successful applications.

These suggestions are highly relevant and merit some remarks. The current regulation of competitive dialogue in the Public Sector Directive is fragmented and clearly points towards a very limited scope for the application of the procedure. This is not consistent with the motivation for the introduction of the procedure and with the need for increased flexibility in public procurement practice. The guidance on competitive dialogue is limited both at supranational and national level and it would surely be beneficial to change this situation. Nevertheless, guidance from the European Commission does exist as the Commission issued an Explanatory Note on the procedure. It is therefore a pity that many practitioners appear to overlook this important Note or at least to be unaware of its content in more detail. The national authorities responsible for giving guidance on public procurement will frequently hesitate to give more elaborate guidance on the field of application and on how to run the procedure due to the considerable legal uncertainty. Researchers in the field could therefore provide a valuable input to practitioners by analysing regulation, case law and practice in the Member States.

### *3.3 Limits on the contractual design fostering innovation and needs analysis*

As outlined in my first section the contracting authorities running a competitive dialogue procedure must respect the so-called 'ban on cherry picking' as they normally may not reveal to the other participants solutions proposed or other confidential information communicated by a candidate participating in the dialogue without his/her agreement. Even so 'it may be difficult to avoid the disclosure of some information' as pointed out in the Section. For obvious reasons the approach of the legislator in this respect is likely to be challenged in practice. Many contracting authorities will surely be tempted to set aside the ban on cherry picking in order to obtain value for money. Alternatively contracting authorities will attempt to obtain the agreement of the tenderers to cherry picking. One way of doing this could most likely be insertion of a tender condition to the effect that the participants must accept cherry picking if they wish to participate in the dialogue (see the discussion of this approach in the first section of the undersigned).

It should be pointed out that the interests of the tenderers are fundamentally different depending on the model of contracting chosen by the contracting authority. If the contracting authority has decided to opt for a model (hereafter model 1) where each tenderer submits a tender strictly based on development of its own solution the tenderers will be concerned that the contracting authority respect the confidentiality. However, the interest of the tenderers takes a complete turn when it comes to the alterative model based on cherry picking – the sharing of ideas and innovation – ending up with a common solution as the basis for the bids of all tenderers (hereafter model 2). In this case the tenderer has an interest in getting as much influence on the drafting of the common solution as possible as this presumably will give the tenderer in question a clear competitive advantage. So in the latter situation the tenderer can be expected to be willing to submit highly detailed information on its preferred solution.

In this respect the scenario is completely different from the situation where model 1 is applied where the tenderers will tend to hesitate to submit detailed information on their solution prior to the bid. The background for this is that the tenderers typically will fear that the contracting authority passes on their innovative ideas to one or more of their competitors to their own competitive disadvantage. Model 2 – bidding on a common solution – will presumably be preferred by the contracting authorities. I would also presume that this model is preferable from the point of view of the society. *Is model 2 the best model of contracting for the promotion of innovation from the perspective of an economist?* It can be added that it frequently will be illegal to run the competitive dialogue procedure according to model 2 as this would violate the ban on cherry picking presupposing that the tenderers have not given their consent to cherry picking.

## 4 Reply by Elvira Uyarra

### *4.1 Introduction*

The first section by Steen Treumer deals mainly with the field of application of competitive dialogue. The present paper looks at some issues pertaining to the application of the procedure, particularly in relation to the UK context. The section by Steen Treumer makes the case that, despite the wording in the public sector directive, which points to a restrictive interpretation of the procedure, its field of application appears to be broader and more flexible. It is noted how the Court of Justice of the European Union has not considered the field of application of competitive dialogue in its case law. Furthermore, the section argues that there have been no challenges of the use of competitive dialogue, despite it being used thousands of times in the Member States of the EU.

The section mentions 3,000 instances altogether in which competitive dialogue has been applied. Indeed, since 2006 more than 1,200 procurements have been undertaken using this procedure in the UK alone and the UK and France account for 80 per cent of the total procurements using competitive dialogue in Europe. We could then speak about an uneven rather than a poor uptake of the procedure, given the large number of cases and its concentration in a small number of countries. It would be interesting to inquire why this is the case and to compare the different types of uses of the procedure in different countries.

Competitive dialogue was introduced in the Public Sector Directive 2004/18/EC in response to the finding that the 'old' Directives did not offer sufficient flexibility with certain particularly complex projects. According to Art. 29 of the Directive, the procedure is confined to particularly complex contracts. Complex procurement is defined by the UK Office of Government Commerce as:

> one where the specification is difficult to define or is complex or innovative, the procurement is high risk, the competition is restricted to a limited market, the contract will be based on unusual commercial models (PFI or a PPP variant) or where the procurement involves spend in a number of categories.[18]

The extent to which competitive dialogue has been applied to large and complex projects in the UK is questionable in the light of a recent review of the use of the procedure by HM Treasury.[19] The review showed that 44 per cent of the procurements using competitive dialogue were for contracts of five years or less and 52 per cent had a capital value of £5m or less (41 per cent with a services value of £5m or less). Even though project value is not necessarily an indication of complexity, these figures give pause for thought.

It is suggested in the review that contracting authorities in the UK may view competitive dialogue as the default process (except for straightforward procurements) rather than utilize the full range of procurement procedures. Authorities may be unsure of how to use competitive dialogue, or what is allowed under the open, restricted and negotiated procedures. Furthermore, different types of contracting authorities use the procedure differently: whereas local authorities in the UK used competitive dialogue extensively but with little repeated experience of its application, central government bodies appeared not only to have more capacity to deliver the dialogue but also tended to consider a range of alternatives rather than a blanket use of the procedure.

On the other hand, the use of the procedure may have the effect of changing the size and structure of contracts when compared with negotiated procedure. At least this is what emerges from a recent research on municipal waste management in the UK.[20] A consultant involved in a large, integrated, waste PFI conducted under negotiated procedure during 2005–9 and interviewed in the context of this research noted that:

> This project was so large and so complex with so many sites, it poses the question of whether you could run a project of this size effectively under competitive dialogue. [Under competitive dialogue] ... it would have had a very different structure. Now with the use of CD what is happening is that rather than an integrated project like this one, it would be split into parts. So you never see large integrated projects now.

One problem is the increased costs associated with the use of competitive dialogue. The same interviewee noted that 'because it is such a big project, how do you run two negotiations side by side?... the cost would be enormous for both the bidders and the authority'.

Private sector representatives in the UK estimate an increase in cost from 2–3 per cent of the contract size under negotiated procedure to 5–6 per cent under competitive dialogue.[21] These are costs that previously they only had to meet if they reached preferred bidder status. The UK government policy is not to cover those costs. It would be interesting to understand whether this is an issue in other countries and whether and how it is dealt with. Costs would naturally be higher if the procedure is not used appropriately, for instance in relation to down-selecting solutions and in terms of timescales, namely if too many bidders are taken into dialogue and for too long. It is remarkable that almost 15 per cent of respondents to the survey to public sector individuals conducted on behalf of the HM Treasury had taken at least six bidders through to final bid submission.

The directive allows for considerable flexibility in terms of how the dialogue is conducted. However, issues remain about how it is carried out in practice, and whether it helps secure value for money. For instance contracting authorities often use the dialogue phase as an opportunity for free consultation with the market rather than using it to clarify and refine solutions.

But the use of competitive dialogue cannot be a substitute for adequate preparation and proper early market testing. While the pre-procurement phase is key to drive innovative solutions onto the market, this is often neglected and poorly executed.[22] Contracting authorities are often tempted to enter the procurement process too early and without sufficient preparation.

In relation to the issue of cherry picking, there is a perception in the UK that this is an issue of significant concern; however it appears that contracting authorities are giving due care to respecting confidentiality, the level of objection therefore being low. This is in line with the point made by Steen Treumer in his section in relation to the low level of dispute surrounding this issue. Interestingly, the HM Treasury finds that bidders often wait until relatively late in the process to introduce their most innovative ideas.

## 5 Conclusions by Steen Treumer

The following section comments on the second section of Elvira Uyarra (hereafter the section) that essentially related to the field of application of competitive dialogue.

As pointed out in the second section and by the undersigned it is appropriate to speak about an uneven rather than a poor uptake of the competitive dialogue procedure. It is stated in the section that 'it would be interesting to inquire why this is the case and to compare the different types of uses of the procedure in different countries'. The background for the very different approaches to the procedure will surely vary from Member State to Member State and many circumstances can and will influence the approach. However, it is relevant to highlight a few factors that have not already been mentioned in the previous sections. It is highly likely that contracting authorities in United Kingdom have been more inclined to use the procedure due to the relatively low risk of legal challenge in the field of public procurement. The United Kingdom has little litigation and case law in comparison with other Member States.[23] In other Member States the high risk of litigation has surely inhibited the use of competitive dialogue. Even more important is probably the fact that procedures very similar to competitive dialogue had been applied for years in the high users of competitive dialogue, the United Kingdom and France, prior to the implementation of competitive dialogue. The approach in competitive dialogue mirrors an approach that had previously been applied in the United Kingdom under the government's Private Finance Initiative[24] and a procedure in France designed and applied for complex procurement.[25] The section also points out that the increased costs associated with the use of competitive dialogue is a problem. The Directives opens up for the possibility of payments to the participants in the dialogue, (see Art.29(8) of the Public Sector Directive). It is stressed in the section that UK government policy is not to cover those costs. It follows from a comparative analysis of competitive dialogue in ten selected Member States that it is a clear exception that participants in competitive dialogue procedures receive any payment for their efforts.[26] This is rather surprising as the costs of participation are very high and it is also contrary to what appears to have been anticipated by the European legislator. The expectation was that the payment for participation in the procedure would facilitate that the participants agreed that their solutions could be revealed and applied by the contracting authority (see Art.29(3) of the Public Sector Directive).

## 6 Conclusions by Elvira Uyarra

The current EU Directives on public procurement incorporate a number of mechanisms that enable contracting authorities to encourage the market to find innovative solutions. One of those key mechanisms is competitive dialogue, which allows contracting authorities to engage in a dialogue in which participants' ideas and solutions are discussed.

The section by Professor Treumer makes the highly relevant point that the field of application of the procedure is a lot broader than what can be expected from a literal interpretation of the directive. The grounds for application appear to be interpreted fairly flexibly considering the large number of instances in which the procedure has been used. The general lack of case law and the very few disputes that have resulted from it – especially considering the initially contentious issue of cherry picking – seem to provide further evidence in this direction.

The HM Treasury review on the use of competitive dialogue in the UK[27] concluded that 'where it is used *appropriately*, both the public and private sectors believe the Competitive Dialogue procedure has been a positive addition to the procurement spectrum'. In such instances, the application of the procedure has succeeded in maintaining competition, enabling greater discipline, establishing good working relations between the public and private sector and delivering improved solutions. However the flexibility and extended use of the procedure could also mask instances where its use may be neither appropriate nor good value for money. Its wide use and its application in projects that are not particularly complex suggests a blanket use of competitive dialogue and therefore a need for better guidance at national level about the appropriate use of the different procedures. Further, in some instances contracting authorities seem to lack the resources, capabilities, leadership and prior preparation needed for the delivery of the procedure, resulting in delays and unnecessary costs. However many of these issues (lack of resources, capacity, leadership, preparation) are common pitfalls in procurement, irrespective of the procedure used.[28] Indeed, as the HM Treasury notes: 'the outcome of a procurement will be influenced as much by the capacity and capability of those party to the process as by the nature of the contract to be delivered'.[29]

However one element emerges which is specific to competitive dialogue, namely the higher costs associated with the procedure. Particularly in the current economic climate, this may deter firms, especially small ones, from participating in procurements which adopt the procedure. This could potentially have a detrimental effect on competition and innovation. Also specific to competitive dialogue is the 'ban on cherry picking' which Professor Treumer discusses in his first and second sections. A model in which cherry picking was allowed (model 1) would presumably allow a more fluid dialogue and lead to a better combined solution than a model based on non-disclosure of confidential information (model 2). The latter is more likely to hinder knowledge-sharing by preventing participants from coming up with innovative solutions. Indeed in the UK, where confidentiality appears to be duly observed (model 2), bidders admit that they only introduce their most innovative ideas later on in the process. Such an outcome may not be ideal from the point of view of stimulating innovation.

## Acknowledgements

Elvira Uyarra would like to acknowledge the input of Jakob Edler and the funding from the UK Economic and Social Research Council Grant R111539, with contributed support from the Department of Business Innovation and Skills, NESTA and the Technology Strategy Board.

## Notes

1 This was already stressed in the Commission's Communication 'Public Procurement in the European Union' of 11 March 1998, COM (1998) 143 Final, section 2.
2 The Explanatory Note 'Competitive Dialogue-Classical Directive' corresponding to document CC/205/04_rev 1 of 5 October 2005.
3 It is also specified in recital 31 that 'This situation may arise in particular with the implementation of important integrated transport infrastructure projects, large computer networks or projects involving complex and structured financing the financial and legal make-up of which cannot be defined in advance'.
4 There are also other indications in written material from the European Commission supporting a more flexible approach to the field of application than what seems to follow from the wording of the Classic Directive.
5 COM (275) 275. The adopted version corresponds to a very high degree to the second proposal from the European Commission.
6 See e.g. R. Rothwell (1984) 'Creating a Regional Innovation-Oriented Infrastructure: The Role of Public Procurement', *Annals of Public and Cooperative Economics* 55(2): 159–72; P.A. Geroski (1990) 'Procurement Policy as a Tool of Industrial Policy', *International Review of Applied Economics* 4(2): 182–98.
7 See J. Edler and L. Georghiou (2007) 'Public Procurement and Innovation – Resurrecting the Demand Side', *Research Policy* 36(7): 949–63.
8 Within the Europe 2020 strategy, the communication 'Innovation Union' – SEC(2010) 1161 highlights the strategic use of public procurement to promote research and innovation.
9 Green Paper on the modernisation of procurement policy: towards a more efficient European Procurement Paper. Brussels, 27.1.2011 COM(2011) 15 final.
10 E. Uyarra and K. Flanagan (2010) 'Understanding the Innovation Impacts of Public Procurement', *European Planning Studies* 18(1): 123–43.
11 Geroski, op. cit., p. 192.
12 Commission communication 'Precommercial Procurement: Driving Innovation to Ensure Sustainable High Quality Public Services in Europe', COM(2007) 799.
13 B.A. Lundvall (1992) 'User-producer Relationships, National Systems of Innovation and Internalization', in B.A. Lundvall (ed.) *National Systems of Innovation* (London: Pinter).
14 N. Dimitri, G. Piga and G. Spagnolo (2006) 'Introduction', in N. Dimitri, G. Piga and G. Spagnolo (eds) *Handbook of Procurement* (Cambridge: Cambridge University Press).
15 J.P. Murmann and K. Frenken (2006) 'Toward a Systematic Framework for Research on Dominant Designs, Technological Innovations, and Industrial Change', *Research Policy* 35(7): 925–52, at 947.
16 See Uyarra and Flanagan (2010), op. cit.

17 See Sue Arrowsmith and Steen Treumer (eds) (2011) *Competitive Dialogue in EU Procurement* (Cambridge University Press, forthcoming): Chapter 2.
18 www.ogc.gov.uk/procurement_documents_complex_procurement_.asp.
19 HM Treasury (2010) Review of Competitive Dialogue (London: HM Treasury).
20 S. Gee and E. Uyarra, 'The Role of Focal Organisations in System Transformation: A Case of Municipal Waste Management', paper presented at the 2nd International Conference on Sustainability Transitions, University of Lund, June 2011.
21 HM Treasury (2010), op. cit.
22 HM Treasury (2010), op. cit.
23 This has increased from only one or two cases a year to around 15–20 a year at present. See Sue Arrowsmith, 'Implementation of Competitive Dialogue in the UK', paper presented at the conference Public Procurement: Global Revolution V, Copenhagen, 9 September 2011.
24 Sue Arrowsmith, fn. 23 above.
25 See Sylvia de Mars and Frédérique Olivier (2011) 'Competitive Dialogue in France', in Sue Arrowsmith and Steen Treumer (eds) *Competitive Dialogue in EU Procurement* (Cambridge University Press, forthcoming).
26 See Sue Arrowsmith and Steen Treumer (2011), op. cit., Chapter 1.
27 HM Treasury (2010), op. cit., p. 6 (my emphasis).
28 E. Uyarra (2010) 'Opportunities for Innovation through Local Government Procurement: A Case Study of Greater Manchester', NESTA research report, May 2010.
29 HM Treasury (2010) op. cit., p. 7.

# 2 Competitive dialogue and innovation

## The case of the Spanish health sector

*Pedro Telles*[1]

### 1 Introduction

Competitive dialogue was introduced by Directive 2004/18 as a means of facilitating the award of particularly complex contracts. These are contracts where open and restricted procedures were deemed inappropriate due to their lack of flexibility. Regarding potential areas of application, the Commission suggested that competitive dialogue would be particularly suited for public–private partnership (PPP) projects.[2]

The procedure was transposed in 2007 into Spain through the Law on Public Sector Contracts. In this law, competitive dialogue is mainly regulated in Book III, Title I, Chapter I, Section 5, in articles 163 through 169.[3] As a general note, Spanish regulation of competitive dialogue has amounted to copying the content found in Directive 2004/18. Most provisions are simply direct transpositions. The only remarkable novelty of the Spanish law is making competitive dialogue the default procedure for the award of what it calls 'public–private cooperation contracts', described in further detail in Section 2.[4]

The decision by Spanish law makers to simply copy the content of articles and recitals of Directive 2004/18 leads to the replication of the same questions and issues that had been pointed to in the competitive dialogue's European draft. As issues identified by academics, one can mention the grounds for use of the procedure,[5] how to deal with confidentiality and equal treatment of candidates,[6] 'cherry picking',[7] the use of successive stages to eliminate solutions or candidates,[8] the degree of completeness of final tenders[9] and the scope for post-tender changes and negotiations.[10] Furthermore, although the Spanish law has for the most part copied the Directive, the local version adds some extra issues of its own, such as the exact scope of public–private cooperation contracts[11] or the composition of the procedure's jury.[12] In addition, one can say that the Spanish legal draft of competitive dialogue makes it so well adapted (or not) to the procurement of innovation as in Directive 2004/18.

In Spain, out of a total of 73 competitive dialogue procedures initiated, 33 have been for public–private cooperation contracts, with 13 in the health sector. All but one of these 13 were public–private cooperation contracts. This represents only a very small percentage of the total contracts in the health sector, as since 2008 over 1,000 open procedures were initiated in this sector. This should be expected, as the competitive dialogue is to be used only for the award of particularly complex contracts and is not a standard procedure in the sense that open and restricted procedures are.

In this chapter the interplay between public–private cooperation contracts and innovation in the health sector will be analysed, covering the models adopted by contracting authorities, the practice in the health sector and lessons that can be learned from the Spanish experience.

## 2 Public–private cooperation contracts in Spanish law

Public–private cooperation contracts are relevant for the purposes of this chapter for two reasons. First, as mentioned in the introduction, according to article 164(3) of the Law on Public Sector Contracts, competitive dialogue is the default procedure for the award of public–private cooperation contracts.[13] Second, not only they have been used in the health sector they have also been used for the innovation relevant contracts.

Public–private partnerships are considered to be an umbrella term in EU law.[14] However, Spain opted for a slightly different expression of public–private cooperation contracts.[15] The approach to the definition of this legal concept is not entirely clear in article 11 of the Spanish law,[16] but these appear to be the contracts where a private entity is mandated to perform certain tasks necessary to satisfy the general interest for a period of time, with payments to be made during the performance in certain situations. Similar figures such as public works[17] and services[18] concessions were extensively used in the country[19] and kept in the current law in a heavily regulated form.[20] Therefore, the scope of public–private cooperation contracts will depend on the exact boundaries separating them from the other types mentioned.

## 3 Models of competitive dialogue

Before getting into the analysis of the actual practice of competitive dialogue in the health sector in Spain, it is relevant to explain the distinct ways contracting authorities are organizing the dialogue stage in Spain, according to the research the author conducted in 2010 for the purposes of his PhD thesis.[21] In his research the author discovered that contracting authorities were organizing the dialogue in different ways, developing approaches that can be synthesized into three models.[22] These models are:

1 own solution;
2 common specifications;
3 crowd-sourced or common trunk models.[23]

The three models can be distinguished by the existence of a common solution (common and crowd-sourced) or not (own solution) and, if the common solution exists, whether it is developed during the dialogue stage (crowd-sourced) or not (common solution).[24]

### *3.1 Own solution model*

In this model, candidates present tenders that are revisions of the solution developed during the dialogue stage. As no common technical specifications are drafted at the end of the dialogue stage, tenders have to be assessed through outputs or else assessing them may prove difficult. When one reads the competitive dialogue rules on article 29 of Directive 2004/18 this is the first organizational model that springs to mind as the way of running the dialogue stage.

### *3.2 Common specifications*

Under the common specification model, contracting authorities draft a common set of technical specifications at the end of the dialogue stage. Candidates then submit tenders based on these specifications and not the solutions developed in the dialogue. The common specifications are not developed during the dialogue but merged by the contracting authority only at the end of the dialogue stage. In addition to the use in Spain, this is the default and (apparently) only model for conducting competitive dialogue procedures in Portugal.[25]

### *3.3 Crowd-sourced or common trunk model*

This model is defined by the appearance of a common development trunk during the dialogue stage. During this stage, participants contribute changes to this trunk solution that then end up in a common technical specifications document. Since the actual development of the common solution is shared among candidates during the dialogue, each contributing some elements, the development process is similar to what can be found in crowd-sourced projects such as Wikipedia.

One can describe the model as follows. The contracting authority has either a preconceived idea about a solution that needs confirmation or develops enough capabilities during the dialogue to better understand what it needs. During the dialogue stage it then proceeds to request changes to the solutions presented by the candidates to fit its conception. These changes amount to an extreme situation of cherry picking, as candidates are in reality contributing to a common solution and not developing their own. The common solution under development is thus a much better match for the needs of the contracting authority than the original solutions. This progressive unifying development may take some iteration where the candidates end up developing ever more similar solutions. In reality, they are contributing to the development of the 'master solution' without knowing it.

The author identified this model first in the procurement of innovative products. In that case, the contracting authority was asking companies to develop a new bespoke dual-use product that could fulfil two different tasks. It was clearly observed that the contracting authority was prompting candidates to making changes to their products during the development that rendered them progressively more similar.

This is also the model seen in practice by the author for the procurement of innovation in the health sector in Spain, associated with public–private cooperation contracts. Knowing the existence and features of this model is key to understand the way the health sector is using the competitive dialogue in the country.

## 4 Health sector practice

As mentioned in the introduction, competitive dialogue was used in the health sector for the award of 13 contracts, all but one of which were public–private cooperation contracts. Ten contracts were tendered in the Balearic Islands by the same contracting authority, one in Murcia and another in Catalonia. In addition, in the Basque country a new health tender for a services contract was put up in May 2011.

### *4.1 Balearic Islands*

The contracts tendered in the Balearic Islands were for equipment and service provisions for a single new hospital. The construction work itself was not tendered through a competitive dialogue. The tenders covered radiotherapy, imaging, monitoring, IT systems, endoscopy, critical services, surgical equipment, lab equipment, incubators and analytics. All of them are public–private cooperation contracts expected to last between 48 and 84 months.

Of the mentioned contracts, the most important ones for the purpose of this chapter are the first three mentioned: radiotherapy, imaging and monitoring. Their relevance is due to the updating clause included in all of them. The contracting authority wanted not only to be served with current technology but to make sure the equipment was updated during the life of the contract. This included not only updates already in the market but deemed too expensive, but also updates yet to be made commercially available.

A major reason for the adoption of public–private cooperation contracts where the equipment being supplied is upgraded during the execution of the contract is that this allows the contracting authority to classify the cost as a running expense and not as capital expenditure. This accounting change ensures the contracting authority that the money needed to pay for the equipment will always be available and not subject to potential budget cuts. As we are talking about a form of renting of equipment it has the added benefit of taking out the depreciation cost from the public entity as well.

### *4.2 Murcia*

In Murcia, the regional health authority put out to tender all the equipment and its maintenance for a newly built hospital. Unlike the situation in the Balearic

Islands, this contracting authority considered that having a single integrator would facilitate management tasks, as it would deal with a single point of contact. They have thus used a single public–private cooperation contract to equip, manage and maintain equipment for a period of around ten years.

### *4.3 Catalonia*

The competitive dialogue procedure was used in Catalonia for the award of a contract to supply, manage and maintain image equipment to the various hospitals and services covered by the regional health authority.[26] As before, this was a public–private cooperation contract (five years long) and not a traditional supply contract. However, as pointed out in the Balearic Islands example, the defining element of this project for the purposes of this chapter is the fact the contract included an equipment upgrade clause. That is, it was agreed that the machines delivered at the start of the programme would be the most advanced available in the market *and* that they would be upgraded during the life of the contract.

### *4.4 Basque country*

In May 2011 a Basque contracting authority initiated a competitive dialogue for the creation of a global solution to provide remote assistance to patients. At this time it is unclear if the contract includes any innovation component but there is a hint that it may since the contracting authority is asking for the creation of a global solution. It should be noted as well that it is a traditional services contract for 18 months and not a public–private cooperation contract.

## 5 Innovation in the health sector

From the cases described above it is apparent that Spanish contracting authorities are not engaging in the procurement of innovation in its strictest sense. That is, they are not going to market specifically asking for something yet to be developed. They are, however, *indirectly* fostering innovation and the development of new equipment in two ways. First, they are looking for cutting-edge technology available today, ensuring that previous developments made by private companies are actually used in the market. Second, due to the relatively long duration of the public–private cooperation contracts and the equipment upgrades required over the duration with as yet unreleased technology, companies can keep pushing the boundaries because they have the obligation of delivering new technology in the coming years. Furthermore, it allows companies to plan their developments with a certain degree of certainty regarding when their new technology is needed.

It can be said that the long nature of these contracts with an equipment updating clause are a form of *indirect procurement of innovation*. On the one hand, the contracting authority wanted to make sure that developments still in the pipeline would be made available. On the other hand, the company receives assurances for investing in new technology, as it knows that there are buyers willing to pay for upgrades to its current kit.

This is not to say that the approach undertaken by Spanish contracting authorities is foolproof, since there are some risks attached to this approach. First and foremost, they are locking themselves out of future technologies developed by other companies for the duration of the contract, effectively handing a monopoly to a single supplier. Second, that supplier may take the opportunity not to push as hard as it would since during the execution of the contract there is no prospect of competition, thus potentially impairing the bringing to the market of new advances.

## 6 Relevance of competitive dialogue

It is apparent that the current use of competitive dialogue for the procurement of innovation in the health sector in Spain is more of an 'accident' derived from the fact it is the default procedure for public–private cooperation contracts and not a specific choice undertaken by procurers. In other words, they choose the contract type beforehand and then adopt competitive dialogue due to its default nature.

However, practice in Spain is showing that competitive dialogue is an appropriate procedure for the *indirect procurement of innovation*. From the author's research, it is clear contracting authorities are happy with the procedure in itself and the results it produces in this sector. Due to the discussions with companies before defining the technical specifications, Spanish contracting authorities are reporting being able to get more up-to-date technology and for a cheaper price than if an open or restricted procedure had been used.

Outside the health sector, the author saw during his research a contracting authority using competitive dialogue to procure a new piece of equipment that was not available in the market at the time, thus entailing the traditional procurement of innovation. This contracting authority ended up using competitive dialogue on two more occasions where it needed to have new products developed from scratch.

## 7 Best practices identified

One can point to some best practices identified in the current Spanish practice regarding the use of competitive dialogue in the health sector, such as the design of the dialogue stage, internal controls and lack of discussions after the submission of tenders.[27]

The way the contracting authority designs the dialogue stage is of paramount importance for producing the outcome it wants to achieve (e.g. more up-to-date technology, better price), be it on a general or health sector competitive dialogue procedure. From the author's research, adopting a crowd-sourced model of organization has consistently given good results in the health sector. This is not to say that the other models have not produced good results, but that there is a clear preference (almost organic) from contracting authorities to adopt this model even without being aware it.

Although this model perhaps does not bring a specific benefit for the procurement of innovation in the sense of the *indirect procurement of innovation* discussed above, its overall characteristics are appropriate for deployment in cases of regular procurement of innovation. The example outside the health sector mentioned in the last paragraph of Section 6 was a clear-cut case of a contracting authority using a competitive dialogue procedure with a crowd-sourced stage[28] to procure a new piece of equipment that was not available in the market at the time. During the dialogue stage, the contracting authority chose the best parts of different candidates and had them iterate various versions of prototypes that were progressively similar since they were following the same instructions. At the end of the dialogue the contracting authority put out a common set of specifications with candidates submitting tenders based on them.

The second best practice worth mentioning is the need to ensure the existence of internal controls and strict adherence to deadlines and milestones. As all of the contracts identified in the health sector were expensive (from hundreds of thousands of euros to hundreds of millions) the ability to impose sound project management internal controls is important to avoid any cases of 'discussion creep', where the dialogue stage drags on without any real achievements.

The third best practice identified is an overall lack of discussions after tenders are submitted. Although Spanish law allows for the existence of post-tender discussions with tenderers on the exact same terms as the Directive article 29(6) and 29(7),[29] contracting authorities in the health sector are refraining from adopting them. In all the scenarios mentioned above, the most that has been discussed have been the brand of equipment (irrelevant for the actual functionality) or clarifications to check if the tender submitted was compatible with the technical specifications. One of the contracting authorities involved explained that this ensured companies did not try to claw back concessions made in the final tender or 'move the goalposts in their favour'. As a consequence, companies are forced to discuss all relevant issues during the dialogue and to submit very detailed tenders. This option for very detailed tenders may have the drawback of increasing transaction costs for the parties involved, especially if one bears in mind the preference for Spanish contracting authorities not to limit the numbers of participants in the dialogue in advance or to conduct exclusions during the dialogue stage.

## 8 Lessons learned

Some insights may be drawn from the author's research on competitive dialogue in Spain, in particular related to the procurement of innovation in the health sector. First, competitive dialogue was used only 13 times and not once for pre-commercial procurement, that is for the development of products or solutions not already on the market.[30] The reasons are not known at this stage, but one can speculate that the since 12 out of those 13 contracts are public–private cooperation contracts that are to last a long period, perhaps contracting authorities want to make sure the equipment to be acquired at the start of the contract is already available in the market and being used. In other words, this may be due to risk mitigation factors.

However, this does not mean that such authorities are not interested in using new technology during the execution of public–private cooperation contracts. It is clear that indeed they are interested in making sure that their equipment will stay up-to-date through whatever innovations are developed by the contractor during the life of the contract. In other words, contracting authorities are trying to make sure companies keep investing in new technologies through indirect pre-commercial procurement.

The preference for lengthy public–private cooperation contracts can be seen in a not so positive light as well. It may be true that they entice the contractor to keep investing in new technology to bring to the market during the duration of the contract, however it may also be seen as an opportunity to extract rent from the contracting authority since it is not facing any competition.

There is also a preference for crowd-sourcing the development of the common set of specifications in Spanish procurement of innovation. Contracting authorities are defaulting into the crowd-sourced model of organizing the dialogue stage. This model allows them to develop a bespoke solution for their needs and have all candidates tender based on that same solution, potentially increasing competition at the tender stage. This model, however, collides with the safety feature of article 29(3) paragraph 3 on the protection of confidential information. The said paragraph excludes the possibility of the contracting authority passing information from one candidate to another if it has been classified as confidential by the first.

From the practice analysed by the author it is questionable if confidentiality is relevant in the terms exposed by the Directive.[31] It is clear that in other situations – where candidates tender based on their own solutions – every bit of information passed around can potentially improve another candidate's solution and, in consequence, its tender. The industry's strong stance on defending confidentiality may draw upon their interpretation that competitive dialogue has to follow the own solution model, where someone's profit equals someone else's loss. This does not appear to happen in the crowd-sourced model.

But is confidentiality protecting the candidates' best interests when they tender based on common technical specifications? The author would argue that, for the most part, it does not. Having the information circulate during the dialogue stage and convincing the contracting authority that something should be part of the technical specifications is more beneficial than keeping it cloaked under the veil of confidentiality. The reasons for this opinion are the same as those that lead companies to try to influence technical specifications in open procedures, for instance. If a company can influence the technical specifications, then it will have a better chance of putting up a competitive tender further down the line. The same is happening in crowd-sourced competitive dialogues, with the difference that the influencing is being carried out in front of the competition. The bigger input a candidate can have on the specifications, the more competitive it may be on the final tender stage. In this model, it is in each company's best interests to have more information in the common specifications, which are inherently public anyway. This leaves the pressing question of what should Spanish contracting authorities do if candidates insist on parts of their solutions remaining confidential during the dialogue stage? There are two alternatives. On the one hand the contracting authority could make it clear in the descriptive document that confidential information would be protected but its content could not be part of the technical specifications. On the other hand, such information could be used indirectly as a desirable feature of the equipment being bought, that is, as a feature that would accrue extra marks to the companies able to offer it.

Finally, no issues surrounding intellectual property (IP) were identified in the health sector practice. No company has raised any questions regarding IP in health sector competitive dialogues. This may be due to the fact that none of the situations described consisted of pure procurement of innovation and companies were discussing products currently in the market to supply at the start of the contract's performance. This does not mean IP is not a thorny issue in relation to competitive dialogue, especially if paired with the crowd-sourced model described, where different companies contribute to the overall solution. Who owns the IP of that solution then? As a cautionary position, contracting authorities shall make clear in the descriptive document that they will own any and all IP from the solution.[32] They may also compromise themselves to license the IP back either to all candidates or only the winning candidate, for instance. In the long run, dealing with the IP arising from the solution developed in crowd-sourced models – more than protecting confidentiality during the dialogue – appears to the author to be one of the most pressing questions regarding the use of competitive dialogue for the procurement of innovation.

## 9 Conclusion

We have seen that in the Spanish health sector, competitive dialogue has been used essentially as a means for awarding public–private cooperation contracts. In some of these contracts it can be argued that contracting authorities engaged in the indirect procurement of innovation and a case is still to be found where traditional pre-commercial procurement took place.

When paired with public–private cooperation contracts, competitive dialogue has been able to give Spanish health contracting authorities enough flexibility and adaptability for them to be able to get up-to-date technical specifications and also the possibility of having the equipment upgraded with yet to be commercially available new versions.

Contracting authorities are organically running the dialogue stage in the crowd-sourced model described above and this model has enabled them to extract up-to-date equipment and better prices.

No problems have been identified relating to confidentiality or intellectual property, and although the relevance of the first is questionable if paired with crowd-sourced competitive dialogues, the importance of the second remains to be seen in pre-commercial procurement tenders. It may depend on how contracting authorities draft their descriptive documents and any safeguards there included.

Finally, it is obvious that the body of evidence of competitive dialogue use in the health sector for the procurement of innovation in Spain is small at present, especially when compared with the much larger number of contracts tendered through the open procedure, but in the situations analysed by the author, contracting authorities have considered themselves happy with the results it has produced.

## Notes

1 PhD, lecturer and public procurement law specialist at Bangor University, Wales.

2 M. Burnett, 'Conducting competitive dialogue for PPP projects – towards an optimal approach' (2009) 4 *EPPPL*, pp. 190–1; S. Arrowsmith, 'Implementation of the new EC procurement directives and the Alcatel ruling in England and Wales and Northern Ireland: a review of the new legislation and guidance' (2006) 3 *PPLR*, p. 86 and Commission, *Green Paper on public-private partnerships and Community law on public contracts and concessions COM (2004) 327 final*. Stating that, however, the procedure may not be as useful for these projects as anticipated, see M. Farley, 'Directive 2004/18EC and the competitive dialogue: a case study on the application of the competitive dialogue procedure to the NHS LIFT' (2007) 2 *European PPLR*, p. 68; S. Arrowsmith, *The law of public and utilities procurement* (2nd edition, Sweet & Maxwell, 2005), p. 630.

3 A number of other articles scattered across this law are also relevant, either directly or indirectly, to the regulation of competitive dialogue in Spain, such as articles 11(1), 26, 45(1), 64, 65, 66, 67, 68, 73, 75(5), 93(3), 101(3)(b)(c) and (d), 118, 119, 120, 122(2), 129(2), 130, 135(3), 147, 148, 149, 150(2)(3)(4) and (5), 154(a) and 296.

4 Article 164(3) of the Law on Public Sector Contracts.

5 Defending a restricted interpretation of those, S.E. Hjelmborg, P. Jakobsen and S.T. Poulsen, *Public procurement law: the EU directive on public contracts* (Djøf Pub, 2006), p. 283; S. Treumer, 'The field of application of the competitive dialogue' (2006) 6 *PPLR*, p. 313. Arguing for the exceptional nature of the competitive dialogue according to French law, P. Delelis, 'Le dialogue compétitif' (2007) 3 *Revue du Tresor* p. 280. With a more liberal view, M. Farley, 'Directive 2004/18EC and the competitive dialogue: a case study on the application of the competitive dialogue procedure to the NHS LIFT' (2007) 2 *European PPLR*, p. 62 and S. Arrowsmith, *The law of public and utilities procurement* (2nd edition, Sweet & Maxwell, 2005) pp. 632–5. Considering competitive dialogue as a 'special procedure' and not an exceptional one such as the negotiated procedure, Commission, *Explanatory note – competitive dialogue – classic directive* (2005), p. 2.

6 S. Arrowsmith, *The law of public and utilities procurement* (2nd edition, Sweet & Maxwell, 2005), pp. 647–8.

7 S. Charveron, 'Competitive dialogue threatens PFI' (2007) 18 *Construction Law*, p. 29; A. Brown, 'The impact of the new procurement directive in large public infrastructure projects: competitive dialogue or better the devil you know' (2004) 4 *PPLR*, p. 173; and S. Treumer, 'Competitive dialogue' (2004) 13 *PPLR*, p. 178.

8 A. Brown, 'The impact of the new procurement directive in large public infrastructure projects: competitive dialogue or better the devil you know' (2004) 4 *PPLR*, p. 174; S. Arrowsmith, *The law of public and utilities procurement* (2nd edition, Sweet & Maxwell, 2005), pp. 646–7; S. Treumer, 'Competitive dialogue' (2004) 13 *PPLR*, p. 181.

9 S. Arrowsmith, *The law of public and utilities procurement* (2nd edition, Sweet & Maxwell, 2005), p. 649.

10 S. Arrowsmith, *The law of public and utilities procurement* (2nd edition, Sweet & Maxwell, 2005), pp. 655–6 and S. Treumer, 'Competitive dialogue' (2004) 13 *PPLR*, p. 183.
11 This will be discussed in more detail in the next section.
12 At least a third of the jury's members have to be 'especially qualified' on the topic of a competitive dialogue and may be external to the contracting authority. In the remaining procedures, the jury may only be composed of internal members. In practice, contracting authorities are not composing the jury differently.
13 Which raises the question of knowing if either all public–private cooperation contracts have a 'particularly complex' nature or if the Spanish law makers extended the grounds for use outside what anticipated by Directive 2004/18.
14 S. Arrowsmith, 'The entity coverage of the EC procurement directives and UK regulations' (2004) 2 *PPLR*, paragraph 2.16.
15 On cooperation contracts in general, L.M. Macho, 'Las formas de colaboración público-privada en el Derecho español' (2008) 175 *Revista de administración pública*, p. 157; N. Salom, 'El contrato de colaboración entre el sector público y el sector privado' (2008) 18 *Revista General de Derecho Administrativo*; and C. Chinchilla Marín, 'El nuevo contrato de colaboración entre el sector público y el sector privado' (2006) 132 *Revista española de derecho administrativo*, p. 609.
16 This article was recently amended by Law 02/2011, which clarifies only the entities that can adopt this contract without providing new insight on its characteristics.
17 Article 7 of the Law on Public Sector Contracts.
18 Article 8 of the Law on Public Sector Contracts.
19 For instance, during 2009 Spain launched 71 public works concessions tenders, 24 services and only 11 public–private cooperation contracts of any kind, according to data collected on the Tenders Electronic Daily website.
20 On articles 223 through 250 and 251 through 265.
21 The thesis, *Competitive dialogue in Portugal and Spain*, was supervised by Prof. Sue Arrowsmith of the University of Nottingham and successfully defended in December 2010. The author conducted qualitative analysis of the implementation of competitive dialogue in Spain, through 27 semi-structured interviews with contracting authorities, lawyers and public procurement advisory bodies between March and August 2010.
22 Racca and Casalini (2010) 'Implementation and application of competitive dialogue: experience in Italy' (paper presented at the Global Revolution V conference in Copenhagen, September) have come up with a similar classification based on the research they carried out in that country.
23 The author does not argue that these are the only ways competitive dialogue has been or can be used in practice.
24 The issues surrounding the legality of these approaches are debated in Section 8.
25 In this country, competitive dialogue was used only five times, with one of these instances in the health sector. However, this contract was unrelated to innovation.
26 This procedure was not concluded as after the end of the dialogue stage and before the submission of final tenders, the new Regional Government did not authorize the expenditure.
27 These and other best practices were discussed in more detail by the author in Chapters 10 and 11 of his PhD thesis, see note 21.
28 It was this situation that made the author re-analyse different procedures and identify the pattern that led to the three-pronged classification.
29 Thus meaning the same limitations apply.
30 Not withstanding the fact that the contract put out to tender in the Basque country may include an innovation component.
31 Companies have not challenged the treatment of confidentiality in relation with the health sector in Spain.

32 On the example of pre-commercial procurement outside the health sector cited in this chapter, that is what the contracting authority ended up doing. However, one must be aware of the costs and risks associated with this option. The contracting authority must be prepared to support the costs of registering the IP and eventually defend it if challenged down the line.

# 3 Contract design for procuring complex projects

*Robert Ågren and Anne Landin*

## 1 Introduction

The difficulties facing a procurer procuring just about any construction project ought to be almost self-evident. The delicateness of specifying the scope of the construction project, the level of quality demands on the building and, in some cases, level of quality for services being required after handover is often daunting and time consuming. The process sets high demands on the procurers' expertise and experience. Not surprisingly, this area has been thoroughly investigated by various researchers (Donohoe and Brooks, 2007; Kumaraswamy and Dulaimi, 2001; Brown, 2004; Öztas and Ökmen, 2004; Wang and Wang, 2010). This is a case study of the procurement of a highly complex research facility.

The term 'highly complex research facility' may need some clarification. The building will be housing many research instruments and tools many of which yet to be developed. The complexity in the project is multifaceted. One characteristic present in the procurement of 'highly complex facilities' is that the technical scope of the project is hard or impossible to define sufficiently and has much in common with procuring innovation. It is not a matter of skill or knowledge of the procuring authority, but rather when the procured object is hard to describe no matter who is describing it. On another level contractual aspects may also add complexity. Pricing and reimbursement schemes may be quite difficult to describe as when there are difficulties to produce a specification only at the time of the procurement. It is also hard to know what the market will accept, and it is difficult to predict the market reaction towards risk allocation and liability. If the project is also a public–private partnership the financial situation adds another dimension to the procurement process (Chowdhury *et al.*, 2011). Highly complex construction projects are generally capital intensive and run perhaps over 20–30 years. The long contract period adds another challenge, the inherent inability for a procuring authority and the contractor to predict the future. This definition of highly complex construction projects resonates with a proposed complexity test for competitive dialogue put forward by Michael Burnett (Burnett, 2010).

In order to understand what contractual provisions a procuring authority might perceive as important and how the authority offsets those obstacles in the contract, this case study was conducted. Information for the case study was gathered through interviews with procurement staff in the project. Documents were collected from the procuring authority and these included the contract notice, contract documents, signed contracts, received bids and information between the authority and tenderers. There might be additional contracts and scope of work signed after the procurement. Information arising after the contract award has not yet been collected and thus is not included in this chapter. The analysis of the gathered documentation went through a three-step coding process, similar to the one suggested by Juliet Corbin and Anselm Strauss (1990). As the first step the texts were coded by their similar intentions or effect. This included conceptual codes as possibilities for the client or contractor to exit the contract. Renegotiation points were allocated one code; if liability for a task or performance was placed upon the client or the contractor this was allocated in two different codes. In a second step categories were formed from different coding schemes. Cases which provided benefits for the client were grouped together, and the same was done for those beneficial to the contractor. Another set of categories was created if something gave the client or contractor unilateral decision-making power regarding a situation or event as opposed to joint decisions. Not all codes were included in categories; only repeated occurrences and codes which had clear contrasts were placed into emergent categories. The third step brought categories together according to what can be regarded as themes. The themes constituted a desire to handle problems with high asset specificity, immeasurability of contractor's execution of the contract and the immeasurability of the results. Finally, one theme covered issues concerning the long contract lifespan. One theme that was missing from the data, and which the authors did however expect to find, was some form of lateral communication regarding contract provisions and their effects on cost estimations and risk premiums.

The conclusion is that the procuring authority did prefer to abstain from safeguards concerning the performance of the facility, thus creating an incomplete contract. The long timespan was countered with milestones where the procuring authority unilaterally could leave the contract. Furthermore the contractual arrangement leaves out provisions of contractual liability for time and performance requirements and resorts to indemnity liability in case of disputes in order to escape from defining contractual requirements. Even though the contract risk is mostly held by the contractor, the contract can, prima facie, be interpreted to be in a Nash equilibrium (Nash, 1950, 1951). A Nash equilibrium exists when a player in a non-competitive game cannot gain by changing its strategy unilaterally. Thus, in many cases, the player would gain in changing strategies together with other players. In such state the design would encourage the parties to cooperate during contract execution. However, the implemented approach might have created higher price levels due to the fact that the procuring authority did not have any information regarding the risk premiums potentially added because of the risk allocation. It is suggested that this could have been remedied by using a participatory approach under a competitive dialogue.

The theoretical framework representing the themes which were identified during the coding of the documentation; immeasurability of outcomes and efforts, asset specificity and long contract lifespans are presented first. A description of the procedure for competitive dialogue within the European public procurement framework is provided as background on a practice that would permit lateral communication. The object of the case study is described in order to illustrate the context in which the procurement was undertaken. Themes within the contract are identified. Finally, the results are discussed and conclusions are drawn that highlight the absence of lateral communications between the parties during the procurement.

## 2 Contractual designs

The procurement of highly complex facilities is characterized by a sequence of complicated decision-making. Selecting a suitable project delivery method (Al Khalil, 2002), for example design-bid-build (Ling, 2004), design-build (Ling and Lau, 2002), build-operate-transfer (McCarthy and Tiong, 1991), can be difficult. Different project delivery methods have different influences on risk attitude, motivation and behaviour. Then there is the issue of contract design and the matter of allocating risk through the project and between the parties. For instance who takes responsibility for what works and when, and who has decision-making rights. Three dominant areas were identified in the study. First, there is the problem of lack of an adequate scope definition at the time of contract award. Hence there are a lot of different criteria regarding the quality of performance being defined at a later stage of the project and thus being immeasurable with regard to the contract award. Second, there is the long timespan of the contract itself. Unforeseen events will affect the implementation of the contract to some extent, changing the balance in the contract. Last, there is a high degree of asset specificity in actual execution of the contract.

### *2.1 Immeasurability of outcomes and efforts*

Contracting which is based on unobservable or immeasurable variables is inherently difficult. When procuring complex construction projects they are nevertheless almost always present at the first point of contract. There have been several suggestions on how to deal with the issue. Cost-plus contracts (Bajari and Tadelis, 2006), allow for quality to be negotiated without the need to renegotiate the entire contract and thus reduce the costs of repeated contracting (Aghion *et al.*, 1994). It should be noted that such an *ex post* renegotiation would be carried out from a position different to the one of the *ex ante* negotiation (Hart and Moore, 1988), not the least with regard to different pressures of competition (see Bolton and Dewatripont, 2005, for a game theory approach). A common complaint levelled at cost-plus contracts is that they do not motivate the contractors to keep costs down. Additionally, these contracts do not reduce the likelihood of time overruns. Not even a build-operate-transfer project would motivate the contractor to keep costs down since the costs are transferred to the client in one way or another. The regular advice usually is that by some means one uses incentives or contractual language to encourage cooperation between the parties (Phifer, 2003) or provoke a Nash equilibrium (Nash, 1951) where both parties would gain on using a non-competitive strategy. Another path around the problem is to use schedule of rates contracts, though this has been shown to be less satisfactory when there is high uncertainty as to actual costs *ex ante* (Pfeiffer *et al.*, 2011). Cost-plus contracts thus deal with situations where outcomes are at least observable; however the effort being made by the contractor is not observable and consequently leads to the possibility of moral hazard. One solution is to allow for the punishment of the contractor during the lifespan of the contract, and as a result counteract risks of moral hazard (Zhao, 2007). It has also been suggested that contracts with immeasurable or uncertain variables should be made in a flexible manner, allowing them to be adjusted whenever new information becomes available (Sommer and Loch, 2009). Making a contract more flexible might open a door to moral hazard from one of the parties or to a need for complete negotiation (Hart and Moore, 1988; Morasch, 1995), thereby increasing contracting costs. Immeasurability at the contracting stage could be avoided if the client spent enough time and effort on trying to specify exactly what was required. Incomplete or relaxed contracting would according to this view be an option if the costs were higher than the risk of using incomplete contracting. In the construction industry, this situation could be compared to the design-bid-build strategy. A game theory approach has shown that the transaction cost of designing the facility might not be significant to the total cost (Maskin and Tirole, 1999b) if the contract lives under an assumption of symmetric information between the parties. In fact, it has been shown that the cost of designing might be irrelevant even if information during the production phase is asymmetric, as long as the information in the contracting phase is symmetric (Kunimoto, 2010). The choice of delivery method, and contract completeness, would in that case be governed by other factors.

## *2.2 Asset specificity*

Asset specificity refers to a situation where a supplier needs to make large investments in order to accommodate a specific procurer's needs, for example specialized manufacturing equipment. It might also be some other asset specific to a given client. The problem with a high level of asset specificity in a contract is that it increases the likelihood for a hold-up or, some would suggest, even increase the prospect of market failure (Klein, 2000). Hold-up is a double-edged sword; the buyer can hold up the supplier if the asset for the production of goods or services cannot be used for other customers. Hence the buyer can demand a non-market price for its purchases. Alternatively, the supplier can hold up the buyer, if the latter is not able to procure the goods or services from another contractor. The supplier can then demand excess prices based on the hold-up. Coase (1937, 1988, 2000) argues that a hold-up due to high asset specificity can be resolved through long-term contracting. In the world of construction contracts this could be seen as an argument for build-operate-transfer contracts. Klein objects (2000) arguing that asset specific hold-ups are generally solved with vertical integration arising from lower contracting costs associated with repeated contracting. We suggest this approach would translate to at least a design-bid-build method in the construction industry. This view is reinforced by Williamson's transaction theory (Williamson, 1985) which states that when asset specificity is a problem then the transaction cost of securing risks is high and requires a strong organizational effort and unified governance in order to cope with the risks, which steers the relationship towards vertical integration.

Oliver Hart has made a major contribution to the field of asset specificity with his property rights approach. These rights refer to the extent which a party can determine how a specific asset is used (Hart, 1995). An owner of an asset can contractually transfer control over the asset, but when a contract is incomplete, the original owner of the asset has residual control rights of the asset. In this the owner has control over everything that is not governed by the contract or by law (Hart, 1995). Hart describes the position thus:

> [S]uppose that you rent my house, and that a friend of yours moves in who hates the colour of the bedroom. The decision to repaint would presumably be mine, not yours. That is, you would have to persuade me to repaint the room; you could not force me to do so (so in this example, I possess the residual rights of control). On the other hand, if the paint began to peel or an effluent of a neighboring factory reacted with it, it would probably be within your rights to insist that I repaint the room.
>
> (Hart, 1988, p. 124)

The notion of residual rights together with an incomplete contract would in itself incur transaction costs, due to the renegotiations which have to take place due to those aspects which are silent within the contract, forcing those contracts towards vertical integration. Furthermore it could be argued that investments made by a firm into a specific asset are correlated with the amount of control which the firm obtains from that specific investment (Grossman and Hart, 1986). In the case of a specified contract lifespan, this would lead to underinvestment in the later stages of the lifespan due to risk aversion. The firm cannot expect a return on investment due to the loss of control over property rights (Hart, 1995).

### *2.3 Contract lifespan*

The question has to be how one succeeds in securing a long-term contract when relying on asset specificity in the construction industry. A specialized facility such as the one in the case study can often reach high asset specificity quite early in the life of the contract. This is because costs are incurred and cumulate once construction starts. There is no prefabrication, no repeated design possibility. On the other hand the client often starts to pay the contractor fairly early if there is no long-term contract, already in the design or construction phase. Additionally, there are possible time constraints and effects of time overrun. Moreover there is the prospect of the contractor's ability to hold up the client on the notion that an exit would create too large transaction costs. Returning to Coase (1988), there seems to be a mutual desire to at least do a long-term contract within the construction industry. If one were to make a 25-year contract, then one should at least decrease the costs of repeated contracting (Williamson *et al.*, 1989). Although there is a point worth making with regard to the average lifespan of a facility; the lifespan of a facility is usually projected at around 80–100 years and would entail at least some repeated contracting during its life. The complexity of the contract can require some additional negotiation 'along the way' as the project moves between different phases of operation, for example switching between design and construction then operation. This would no doubt incur costs. A 25 year or longer contract will need some organizational effort in order to deal with the contract's execution and follow up on goals and requirements in the contract; both from the contractors' and the clients' side. In the contract this situation is typically dealt with through a series of required meetings (Harris and McCaffer, 2001). It has in the past proved at times to be somewhat insufficient. As a consequence the practice of partnering has become quite popular in the last few years. Partnering is a process covering a wide field of activities, and concepts, not all necessarily present at every partnering project. It could be team-building, setting joint objectives, conflict resolution mechanisms, concurrent engineering or joint selection of subcontractors (Eriksson, 2010).

In order to deal with Hart's property rights approach the contractual design has to deny, or at least restrict, the opportunity to underinvest in the project during the contract execution. This requirement is problematic for the construction industry since major investments are made at the start of the contract. If the contractor is allowed to underinvest in the early part of the contract life the consequences will be felt throughout the contract lifespan. One has to assume, if theories about market behaviour are correct, that the contractor will invest as much as necessary in order to fulfil the contract. In terms of quality, there will be the matter of immeasurability of quality in many cases. Since we are talking about long-term contracts there is of course also the question of periodic maintenance and upgrades as time passes. There have to be provisions in place in order to negotiate this risk. The client has to be able to put some form of pressure on the contractor in order to keep the investment at a reasonable and appropriate level through the contract's life. Those provisions should not allow the client an opportunity for unilateral hold-up against the contractor.

To sum up, if Coase is right in his statement that dangers with asset specificity can be resolved through long-term contracts, there remain some issues to be resolved. First, there has to be some safeguard concerning the increased cost of repeated contracting. There also needs to be some mechanism providing unified governance to deal with the complex contract arrangements needed for long-term contracting and, in addition, there needs to be some protection against underinvestment.

## 3 Competitive dialogue

Competitive dialogue was one of the new additions in the European Commission's public procurement directive. It was put into place between the open and negotiated procedures in an attempt to allow for more innovative and complex procurement (European Commission, 2005) while adhering to the fundamental principles of the public procurement legislation package (Burnett, 2009). There are several approaches to how one could employ competitive dialogue in order to procure highly complex facilities. One way is to launch a consultative approach based on a reference facility or a proposed preferred project. The contracting authority would then be able to compare and contrast suggestions from contractors (Burnett, 2009). This would probably require a relatively low level of immeasurable variables in order to allow for comparison. At the very least it requires a high degree of knowledge on the part of the contracting authority. On the other hand it is possible to simply remove the immeasurable features from the competitive dialogue, and state that the intention is to procure something that is largely undefined, and highly immeasurable. A sample contract, for example a cost-plus contract, is put forward for comparison. The other route is to launch an investigative approach based on a problem definition by the contracting authority, with the solutions more or less driven by the bidders (Burnett, 2009). This does however require that the scope of the project is detailed enough to create a definition that is clear enough for the bidders to actually offer a solution. If one removes the immeasurability aspect in this approach we end up with the question: how should the contract be written? The contracting authority would then stand with an unspecified project procured under an unspecified contract. It is fairly clear that if competitive dialogue should be actualized in a case such as the one in hand, it ought to be through the first alternative mentioned. Otherwise one would end up in a de facto negotiated procedure.

There have been some concerns about the tension between transparency and confidentiality (Treumer, 2004; Hoezen *et al.*, 2010) within the competitive dialogue process. This could lead to a lowering of competitive pressure due to hesitation to participate in a competitive dialogue because of lack of confidentiality and protection of business secrets. If one were to procure a contract and allow for the contractual framework to evolve through competitive dialogue there ought to be little tension between transparency and confidentiality, since most of the framework will concern the forms of contracting, and not their execution.

During competitive dialogue, there seems to be ample room for changes and extending of the scope, as long as the fundamental principles of the Union are followed. Here, competitive pressure can be upheld and bidders can compete by offering the best conditions for the contract or accepting more risk on a given scale. It will also allow for bidders to shape their own risk management during the contract performance, since they will be able to suggest change in the way the contracts are written to make them more comfortable with the risk they have to manage. The alternative, to be handed a document, applies a procurer-inspired method of dealing with risk. It is important that this is explained to the bidders during the dialogue. After the dialogue is closed, there is little room for the bidder to alter the offer or its risk balance (Verschuur, 2006). Consequently, there is no room for the contracting authority to even out the bids after the dialogue has been closed. There does not seem to be much room to manoeuvre after the preferred bidder has been selected (Kennedy-Loest, 2006).

## 4 The research facility

The facility is being constructed for the purpose of generating synchrotron light. In this machine electrons are accelerated at high speed in order to emit light. The light is then used to X-ray objects in the study of different materials, for example metals, medical compounds or archaeological artefacts. To accelerate the electrons one uses very large and powerful magnets, which also steer the position of the electron beam, thus it is highly sensitive to vibrations. If two magnets placed next to each other vibrate at different frequencies, the electrons tend to hit the wall of the tunnel thus reducing speed and lowering their resolution. This has led to the need for a very stable non-vibrating building. The exact specifications are not yet established and there are still discussions on how to define and measure actual vibrations. The allowed difference between two adjoining magnets is 20–30 nanometres. To visualize how small this is, one could use a strand of hair, and split it lengthwise 2,000 times. To put it in a construction perspective, a 1 metre thick concrete plate will displace down 200 nanometres when an average man stands on that plate. The facility is supposed to be built upon 17 meters of soil of varying density before hitting the bedrock. Tests have shown that the soil above the bedrock acts like water in transporting waves from vibration sources, such as cars and people walking. Additionally, one has to take account of vibrations from cooling systems inside the facility, people walking inside the facility and wind loads on the building itself.

Neither at the time of the procurement nor today is there an understanding of what properties the facility has to exhibit. There were however indications of the magnitude of the vibration requirements. Yet, the density of the soil where the facility is supposed to be built was unknown. The scope of the project was therefore largely undefined for the client as well as for the contracting tenderers in the tender process. As mentioned before the project is far from finished, and there has already been a proposal for additional work on the facility, to make room for a new set of instruments with similar vibration demands, but for different types of research. There is also something to be said about the character of research funding for these kinds of projects. Funding is provided according to politically motivated projects, and even though, in the case of this particular project, operating costs have to some extent already been awarded, there are therefore no provisions for additional funding, or funding compensating for unexpected cost overruns. Extended funding requires a renewed political process to cover contingency costs.

## 5 The procurement scheme

The procurement process was governed by a few important objectives. The procurement body saw them bound by the public procurement regulations and there was no intention of using the research exemption in the legislation. Additionally the procurement had to lead to a lease/operate contract, since the current national legislation forbids the contracting authority from owning buildings or land, even if it should be noted that it is possible for the government to make an exemption in individual cases. The procurement process was not allowed to delay the project timetable. In other words there was no time for arguing about the procurement process in the courts. The procurement process had to apply some form of competitive pressure to keep the prices down. The established budget could not be exceeded. And the facility should be able to be used for its intended purposes.

In terms of documentation there were some drawings, there were lengths of tunnels, there was a conceptual design report detailing the workings of the research instruments and an estimation of the total floor area. There was no completed design, nor were there any established specifications regarding the research equipment at that time. The contracting authority chose a negotiated procedure with prior publication of a contract notice. The choice of procurement methodology was made due to uncertainty as to whether it was at all possible for tenderers to prepare an offer based on the tender documentation. The criteria for qualitative selection included financial standing in the form of demands on turnover of approximately 40 per cent of the estimated project cost and an appropriate credit rating. Technical ability considered total floor area currently being managed, as well as experience of similar construction projects. The procedure included a selection phase limiting the number of contractors to five. The selection criteria were based on some vague formulation of suitability and views on contractors' profit margins. Only four companies, all qualified, requested to participate, leaving the selection criteria unused.

At the time of procurement the procedure for competitive dialogue was not implemented in the national legislation. The procurer stated in interviews that during the planning stage of the procurement they visualized a negotiated procedure similar to that of competitive dialogue. Once the process started, the need for a competitive dialogue or negotiations proved to be quite small. There was some communication between the contracting authority and the contractors during the tendering stage, however, this communication was more in the nature of questions and answers, than negotiations. There was an attempt by one contractor to attach a liability clause put upon the procuring authority regarding deconstruction costs after the lease was terminated. This move was rejected because the procurer perceived it to be against national legislation. There was a suggestion to change the buyout options during the lease lifespan, and it was accepted as a possible negotiation point; but the procuring authority rejected another attempt to remove those options on the same day. There were also several attempts to change the index clause in the proposed lease agreement, because one contractor claimed that the clause was driving costs up, and that the contractor would have to be compensated in the tender. Another contractor stated that the profit margin would be lower than the possible margin decrease in accordance with an incentive clause, thus wanting to remove or limit this clause. Also, there was an attempt to add a renegotiation regarding cost depletion and calculation of the residual value when all costs had been identified. This was rejected, and the contractor withdrew the suggestion. Additionally, there was a statement that the procuring authority, in the event of it taking over the facility management, would follow the maintenance instructions from the contractor. These are implemented in the lease agreement but it is unclear from the documents and interviews whether or not this was because of the contractor's statement. The sole accepted qualification was that a change regarding the index and interest rates, as proposed by the client, were dependent on the contractor's ability to renegotiate its refinancing contracts. Furthermore, a statement that the client will be a procuring authority was made in the documentation in order for the contractors to procure a more favourable interest rate in their refinancing negotiations. In hindsight, the procurement could probably have been conducted as an open or restricted procedure, with identical results.

Three qualified contractors submitted tenders; it is not known why the fourth qualified contractor did not submit a tender. The tenders were submitted using provided documentation, and could not contain any qualifications. Contractors were allowed to suggest further qualifications after the tender had been submitted. However, no changes were made to any bid or to the contracts once the tenders were submitted. The offers were evaluated against different cost parameters: margins on invested capital into the project, margins put on additional work, required fees facility management (per square metre). The parameters were then entered into a model based on an assumed cost for the project, assumed level of additional works and assumed levels of annual index increase. The total cost over 25 years was then calculated and the lowest bid was selected. The award decision was not challenged in court.

## 6 The contract

### *6.1 Handling of immeasurability in the contract*

The design of the contract was built on a design-build-operate-transfer model. The contract design consists of three consecutive contracts governing different phases in the relationships between the contracting parties: the design stage, the construction phase and the operating stage. During the contract lifetime the stated intention is that the parties should govern the project in the spirit of partnering (see Morledge *et al.*, 2006, for an overview of the term partnering in the construction industry), though this form of cooperation naturally is more present in the design and construction stage than in the operating phase. The contract notice states:

> The Client has the intention to implement the project through partnering both in the design and in the construction stage, with the explicit intention to reach higher quality, cost efficient construction and a greater level of commitment and interest by all parties involved
> [...]
> The Client intends to use partnering as a tool for the execution [of the contract]. The exact details for the implementation of partnering in the current project will be outlined in cooperation with the selected tenderer and jointly selected contractors.
>
> (Authors' translation)

Furthermore, the contract document states that the design stage shall be performed in consultation with the client, and that the client shall respond to specific questions about the specifications in a timely manner.

One key feature of this form of cooperation is the practice of open books, allowing for the contracting authority to audit actual costs in the project. Any significant cost not previously planned should, before they are incurred, be subject to a joint decision during project meetings. During the design phase the contractor is allowed to invoice incurred costs up to a level of approximately 1–2 per cent of the total project cost. There are no such provisions during the construction phase. But rent can be raised when a part of the project has passed final inspection and is ready for use. Such rent is based on the completed part's percentage of the total estimated cost.

There was an outline schedule sent out together with the contract notice. The notice stated that the contracting parties shall together create a final schedule for the project, which was also clarified in communications during the procurement process. Nevertheless, the suggestion put forward was to be seen as guidance and the authority did not intend to accept major adjustments as to when the construction would be completed.

The rent is based, as implied above, on an annuity interest on actual cost of construction with the addition of a fee for facility management. The actual cost is described as all costs incurred as a result of the design and lease contracts, and includes all costs related to subcontractors. The margin of profit should also include costs for insuring the facility. Interest is based on a published index with the addition of a margin of profit. At the end of the design stage, the contractor is obliged to specify the value of all work predicted during the construction phase, and request quotations from subcontractors in competition. According to the partnering scheme being employed the contracting authority would have access to those quotations. The sum total of these quotations will be used as a reference price when calculating an incentive. For every million crowns (SEK) that the actual cost is below the reference price, the margin on the annuity interest is increased by 0.003 per cent. On the other hand the margin is decreased by the same percentage for every million the actual cost is above the reference price. If actual cost exceeds 10 per cent of the reference price, 50 per cent of the surplus cost is allowed to be used as a base when calculating actual cost.

### *6.2 Contract lifespan and asset specificity*

Between the design stage and the construction stage there is an exit clause for the procuring authority. If the latter does not feel that its goals and requirements could be met if they were to execute the construction project, it can exit the contract. However, the procuring authority is required to pay the contractor's direct costs up to that point. The lease time of the facility is fixed for 25 years with a residual value specified as a percentage of the original investment in the bid. There is an option clause to purchase the property from the contractor in years 15, 20 and 25. Additionally there is a pre-emption clause if the contractor wants to sell the property to another company. The price of using the clauses is the current residual value of the property with the addition of a 'fair' profit margin. At the end of the 25-year lease, there is an automatic extension with five years, and a three-year provision on cancelling the lease. There is also an option for the contracting authority to terminate the facility management agreement from year five, without payment of compensation for costs incurred. During the procurement process the following exchange took place:

CONTRACTOR: The tenant wants to be able to acquire the property for 'at the current time residual value with the addition of a fair profit'. We consider this qualification to acquire the property with mentioned conditions to be unreasonable and that a future sale of the property should be carried out with regard to current market value, based on the variables governing the prices in the real estate market at that point.

PROCURING AUTHORITY: It is a common practice in a tenant lease to establish an option to acquire the property when the lease agreement has a financial characteristic and when the nature of the property is highly specialized and of considerable importance to the tenant and its operation. (Authors' translation)

When analysing the contract four emergent trends seem to appear. A fair amount of effort had gone into defining the high-level scope of the project; however, any detailed provisions regarding the scope could not be found within the contract. Most statements are more declarations of intentions and goals rather than contractual provisions. Excluding the facility management agreement, the dominant trend in the contract is to place the responsibility for actions, building soundness and documentation upon the contractor. There are only a few sections where the contracting authority assumes responsibility for something. A small number of provisions allocate explicit liability for damages, almost all of them fall on the contractor. Most decision points in the contract put the authority of the decision either on a joint process or on the procuring authority. The contractor has few possibilities to reject a request or demand made by the procuring authority.

## 7 Discussion

The contract has a long lifespan, altogether over 30 years. Nevertheless, there are issues regarding repeated contracting to discuss. First, the set-up based on three consecutive contracts will automatically incur contracting costs. Regarding the first renegotiation, there are some provisions as to the form they take. Even so, the client has a unilateral exit clause, but it has to make cure payment (for a fair profit margin) to the contractor. Second, the contractor is supposed to obtain quotations using competitive pressure and, according to the partnering principle, those requests and answers should be presented to the client. It is these which form a base for the renegotiations. The second scheduled renegotiation will take place when the facilities have passed final inspection. The contract states 'The third lease agreement will be signed after completion and the approval of all buildings' (authors' translation) but it does not provide any forms for this purpose. It does not state any situations when either the contractor or the procuring authority could refuse to sign the third lease contract. This ought to mean that the procuring authority can refuse to sign the contract only if the facility does not meet the specifications set for the final inspections. In turn, it would suggest that the specifications set at the first renegotiation five years earlier have to be final. Every change request made after this renegotiation should be seen as additional work, thus subject to separate negotiations. The contractor does not seem to have any right to refuse to sign the contract either, though due to the high asset specificity there might not be any incentive for such refusal anyway. Nonetheless, there does not seem to be any reason for the contractor to hold up the client at the second renegotiation. There are no provisions covering failure of final inspection, nor is there any provision regarding legal remedies for time overrun. Further disputes are assigned to national courts. Those disputes have to be solved with indemnity liability, an intrinsically difficult and expensive process.

There are four implicit negotiation points in the contract. Starting at year five and onwards of the last lease agreement, the procuring authority has a unilateral opportunity to cancel the part of the agreement containing the facility management service. Consequently the client has a continuous right to renegotiate the facility management contract. There is no exit point until year 25 for the contractor and as a result the only possible exit before year 25 is for the contractor to refuse the procuring authority renegotiation terms regarding the facility management.

At years 15 and 20 the procuring authority has an exit clause giving some room for the client to initiate renegotiations. There are provisions made for such exits. The client has to pay the current annuity cost plus a fair profit margin. The annuity cost is specific and defined, but the fair profit margin is not defined. In consequence, the only counter-argument available to the contractor is to argue for a higher fair profit. Again, disputes are passed over to the public courts; it is not obvious if a fair profit margin refers to the profit that usually would be taken when selling an identical facility at the same time or if fair profit refers to what the contractor should have earned if the contract were to continue until year 25. Despite the seemingly long-term contracting there are a few, but significant, renegotiation points through the contract; although some of these can only be activated by the procuring authority. From the contractor's point of view there are several renegotiation points which will or could occur, creating a high risk for contracting costs. The danger would therefore be that the project could suffer from high contractual costs.

High contracting costs have a counterbalancing factor in the employment of a partnering cooperation. The partnering process should not only establish trust, but should also serve as facilitator of continuous communication. The organizational set-up as of today is a joint project management team. Each party then has a supporting project management team feeding information and specifications through the joint team. The contracting authority has tied researchers within each identified problem area in order to check and control solutions provided by the contractor and thus to secure quality. This process ought to reduce risks and costs incurred by the renegotiations. It should also reduce the problem for the client of immeasurable quality variables, since they could be set in cooperation and understanding with the contractor. Thus, the partnering provisions would act, to a certain extent, in the same fashion as a unified governance approach.

Despite potentially high contractual costs, the number of renegotiation points could presumably serve as a force against underinvestment tendencies with high asset specificity contracts. If the quality of the services were to decline it is likely to be because of underinvestment in the required assets. Those would themselves serve as counteractions against underinvestment. While the unilateral nature of many of the renegotiation points does remove the ability of the contractor to hold up the client due to underinvestment threats, it does not provide any safety for the contractor. Most specifications will come from the procuring authority. Still, those specifications will in this case be exclusively controlled by the procuring authority as these are established by the research equipment being installed in the facility. This results in the contractor depending on the clarity of the communication of those specifications, and their timely delivery. The procuring authority does of course want a good contract execution, but once the reference price is set there is a potential margin where the procuring authority would actually gain from shifting costs on the contractor.

The object of the contract does contain a high level of asset specificity, since the facility cannot be used for anything else. The procuring authority deals with the risk of a hold-up by assuming almost all property rights within the contract. The residual control left to the contractor is facility maintenance beyond regular facility management. Furthermore, there seems to be a degree of control left to the contractor with regard to expansion and rebuilding. Nevertheless, the degree of control left is quite small. There are exit clauses in the contract, while the consequences concerning compensation are unclear; those exit clauses might result in underinvestment due to unpredictable return on investment. They can nonetheless also be seen as an opportunity for the procuring authority to reduce the likelihood of underinvestment, since the contractor would actually want to extend the contract, securing another five years of payments. This duality might actually prove to be a Nash equilibrium, where both parties would earn on non-competitive behaviour, and remove risk of moral hazard altogether.

The second conclusion is that there are many renegotiation points during the contract lifespan. This will inevitably lead to some transaction costs and adjoining risks. The contract decision to move from the design stage to construction phase is a safeguard in order to not be liable for an amount greater than the actual cost up to that date, in case the project proves to be too complicated, or even impossible. And it is unilateral in favour of the public authority. The other contract points do have some contractual relevance, but they could also be seen as unnecessary. Given the other exit points and a Nash equilibrium, there is probably no theoretical reason for the partnering process not to work. More importantly, if the partnering process should go badly with one abusive party there are no liability clauses in the contract to handle this situation, and the renegotiation points do not provide such clauses. Any wrongdoing would thus be left as a matter of indemnity liability. What the renegotiation points do incur is additional costs added by a risk-averse contractor. This conclusion is in the line of the theoretical reasoning of Maskin and Tirole (1999a).

Normally, one would be using a negotiated procedure under the public works directive (2004/18/EC) for this kind of public procurement which indeed was the case with this example. In fact, little negotiation took place and the tenderers were not allowed to make changes with regard to risk allocation or price estimations. They had to tender on the stated conditions. The effect is to ensure that information between the different tenderers is symmetric and it suggests that the information between tenderer and the procuring authority is also symmetric. This may be wrong. The public authority has no information on the structure of the refinancing contracts each tenderer would have to negotiate. The procuring authority has no information on the impact of the refinancing contracts due to each renegotiation and exit clause. It would be possible for the public authority to attain such information under a negotiated procedure if it were done with a structured method. Under the public procurement regulations this has to be done in an open and transparent way, whilst protecting trade secrets of the contractors. By using a couple of steps of competitive dialogue one might be able to achieve this if one sets up a regimen where the price of the total project was evaluated in the same way as in our example. During each step in the competitive dialogue the tenderers were allowed to submit a tender based on the previous contract, and one bid depending on a removal of a perceived risk. The procuring authority would then be able to evaluate if it would want to hold the suggested risk, or if it would rather pay the risk premium. If the risk was consumed by the procuring authority, a new round would be sent out, giving every tenderer the option to bid on the new suggestion. This procedure would be done in two or more steps, giving the procuring authority information regarding the risk premia in the suggested contract. The repeated auctioning scheme would potentially lead to an increased competitive pressure because the tenderers would gain some knowledge regarding their competitive strategy and so every step would lead towards optimal bidding strategies.

## 8 Conclusion

A case study of the procurement of a highly complex research facility has been presented. An analysis of the documentation covering the procurement procedure for the facility has identified three themes: immeasurability, asset specificity and contract lifespan. Those themes have been discussed from the perspective of law and economics. It is clear that a complex project such as the case study would be very demanding and expensive to specify in detail. It is expensive because of the frequency of immeasurable variables in these types of projects. Instead of using many short-term contracts, the public authority chose a long-term contracting solution thus reducing contracting costs associated with repeated contracting. In order to keep control over the result of the project, the procuring authority has established a form of unified governance. This was achieved through partnering, as well as through joint decision points during the currency of the contract. The process allows for details to be specified throughout project execution. A key finding is that the research facility exhibits high asset specificity, which creates the need for special consideration of how the property rights are distributed. Property rights for the research facility fall heavily on the procuring authority, leaving the risk of underinvestment in the later stages of project execution. In those later stages, the procuring authority has the option to exit the contract by purchasing the facility. The relevant contract clauses can be seen as a counterweight to a desire to underinvest in the facility. However, using the exit clause would be costly for the procuring authority, so acting as a counterweight is to hold up the contractor by threatening to invoke the exit clause. The arrangement could create a setting where the parties would gain from cooperation instead of maximizing their own results without regard to the other party. Using these types of exit clauses could lead to a high risk premium being added to the tender. Under normal circumstances the procuring authority would not have any information on the size of those premia. It is, therefore, suggested that those premia are to be subject to competition through the use of competitive dialogue.

## References


Aghion, P., Dewatripont, M. and Rey, P. (1994) Renegotiation design with unverifiable information. *Econometrica: Journal of the Econometric Society*, 62: 257–82.

Al Khalil, M.I. (2002) Selecting the appropriate project delivery method using AHP. *International Journal of Project Management*, 20: 469–74.

Bajari, P. and Tadelis, S. (2006) Incentives and award procedures: competitive tendering vs. negotiations in procurement. In N. Dimitri, G. Piga and G. Spagnolo (eds) *Handbook of procurement*. Cambridge: Cambridge University Press, pp. 121–39.

Bolton, P. and Dewatripont, M. (2005) *Contract theory*. Cambridge, MA: MIT Press.

Brown, A. (2004) The impact of the new procurement directive on large public infrastructure projects: competitive dialogue or better the devil you know? *Public Procurement Law Review*, 13: 160–77.

Burnett, M. (2009) Conducting competitive dialogue for ppp projects – towards an optimal approach? *European Public Private Partnership Law Review*, 4: 190–8.

Burnett, M. (2010) Developing a complexity test for the use of competitive dialogue for PPP contracts. *European Public Private Partnership Law Review*, 5: 215–23.

Chowdhury, A.N., Chen, P.-H. and Tiong, R. (2011) Analysing the structure of public-private partnership projects using network theory. *Construction Management and Economics*, 29: 247–60.

Coase, R.H. (1937) The nature of the firm. *Economica*, 4: 386–405.

Coase, R.H. (1988) 1. The nature of the firm: origin, meaning, influence. *Journal of Law, Economics, & Organization*, 4: 3–47.

Coase, R.H. (2000) The acquisition of Fisher Body by General Motors. *Journal of Law and Economics*, 43: 15–31.

Corbin, J. and Strauss, A. (1990) Grounded theory research: procedures, canons, and evaluative criteria. *Qualitative Sociology*, 13: 3–21.

Directive 2004/18/EC of the European Parliament and of the Council of 31 March 2004 on the coordination of procedures for the award of public works contracts, public supply contracts and public service contracts.

Donohoe, S. and Brooks, L. (2007) Reflections on construction management procurement following Great Eastern Hotel Company v. John Laing. *Construction Management and Economics*, 25: 701–8.

Eriksson, P.E. (2010) Partnering: what is it, when should it be used, and how should it be implemented? *Construction Management and Economics*, 28: 905–17.

European Commission (2005) Explanatory note – competitive dialogue – classic directive, CC/2005/04.

Grossman, S.J. and Hart, O. (1986) The costs and benefits of ownership: a theory of vertical and lateral integration. *Journal of Political Economy*, 94: 691–719.

Harris, F. and McCaffer, R. (2001) *Modern construction management*. Oxford and Malden, MA: Blackwell Science.

Hart, O. (1988) Incomplete contracts and the theory of the firm. *Journal of Law, Economics, and Organization*, 4: 119–39.

Hart, O. (1995) *Firms, contracts, and financial structure*. Oxford: Clarendon Press.

Hart, O. and Moore, J. (1988) Incomplete contracts and renegotiation. *Econometrica*, 56: 755–85.

Hoezen, M., Van Rutten, J., Voordijk, H. and Dewulf, G. (2010) Towards better customized service-led contracts through the competitive dialogue procedure. *Construction Management and Economics*, 28: 1177–86.

Kennedy-Loest, C. (2006) What can be done at the preferred bidder stage in competitive dialogue? *Public Procurement Law Review*, 6: 316–26.

Klein, B. (2000) Fisher-General Motors and the nature of the firm. *Journal of Law and Economics*, 43: 105–41.

Kumaraswamy, M. and Dulaimi, M. (2001) Empowering innovative improvements through creative construction procurement. *Engineering Construction & Architectural Management*, 8: 325–34.

Kunimoto, T. (2010) Indescribability and its irrelevance for contractual incompleteness. *Review of Economic Design*, 14: 271–89.

Ling, F.Y.Y. (2004) Key determinants of performance of design-bid-build projects in Singapore. *Building Research and Information*, 32: 128–39.

Ling, Y.Y. and Lau, B.S.Y. (2002) A case study on the management of the development of a large-scale power plant project in East Asia based on design-build arrangement. *International Journal of Project Management*, 20: 413–23.

McCarthy, S.C. and Tiong, R.L.K. (1991) Financial and contractual aspects of build-operate-transfer projects. *International Journal of Project Management*, 9: 222–7.

Maskin, E. and Tirole, J. (1999a) Two remarks on the property-rights literature. *The Review of Economic Studies*, 66: 139–49.

Maskin, E. and Tirole, J. (1999b) Unforeseen contingencies and incomplete contracts. *Review of Economic Studies*, 66: 83–114.

Morasch, K. (1995) Moral hazard and optimal contract form for R&D cooperation. *Journal of Economic Behavior & Organization*, 28: 63–78.

Morledge, R., Smith, A. and Kashiwagi, D.T. (2006) *Building procurement*. Coventry: Blackwell Science.

Nash, J. (1950) Equilibrium points in n-person games. *Proceedings of the National Academy of Sciences of the United States of America*, 36: 48–9.

Nash, J. (1951) Non-cooperative games. *Annals of Mathematics*, 54: 286–95.

Öztas, A. and Ökmen, O. (2004) Risk analysis in fixed-price design-build construction projects. *Building and Environment*, 39: 229–37.

Pfeiffer, T., Schiller, U. and Wagner, J. (2011) Cost-based transfer pricing. *Review of Accounting Studies*, 16: 219–46.

Phifer, W. (2003) Ending the pricing paradox: moving away from a zero sum IT world. *Engineering Management Conference, 2003. IEMC '03. Managing Technologically Driven Organizations: The Human Side of Innovation and Change*, 91–5.

Sommer, S.C. and Loch, C.H. (2009) Incentive contracts in projects with unforeseeable uncertainty. *Production and Operations Management*, 18: 185–96.

Treumer, S. (2004) Competitive dialogue. *Public Procurement Law Review*, 4: 178–86.

Verschuur, S. (2006) Competitive dialogue and the scope for discussion after tenders and before selecting the preferred bidder – what is fine-tuning etc? *Public Procurement Law Review*, 6: 327–31.

Wang, F. and Wang, S. (2010) Study on steel bar management of construction project. *International Conference on Measuring Technology and Mechatronics Automation*, 3: 645–7.

Williamson, O.E. (1985) *The economic institutions of capitalism: firms, markets, relational contracting*. New York: Free Press.

Williamson, O.E., Johanson, J. and Sjöstrand, S.-E. (1989) *Perspectives on the economics of organization*. Lund: Lund University Press.

Zhao, R.R. (2007) Dynamic risk-sharing with two-sided moral hazard. *Journal of Economic Theory*, 136: 601–40.

# 4 Some law and economics considerations on the EU pre-commercial procurement of innovation

*Nicola Dimitri*

## 1 Introduction

According to the Lisbon strategy and Europe 2020 innovation is considered a fundamental force by the European Union to promote economic growth and increase citizens' well-being. In particular, since it is estimated that about 16–18 per cent of European Gross Domestic Product is transacted by the public sector (Dimitri *et al.*, 2006), procurement activity in such sector can represent a crucial driver to pursue the above goals (Geroski, 1990). Consistently with this view, in recent years the EU has made available to the system of public administrations some new legal instruments, suitable to purchase complex and innovative 'projects'. In particular, while the Directive 2004/18/EC has introduced the 'Competitive Dialogue' to procure complex projects, however typically with solutions already available on the market, the Communication by the European Commission COM(2007)799 (COM henceforth) enacted pre-commercial procurement (PCP) as a legal instrument to introduce innovative products not yet available on the market, or when the existing solutions are particularly unsatisfactory.

This chapter focuses on PCP as originally proposed by a group of ICT experts (Report IST, 2006), and subsequently implemented by the EC in COM. Indeed PCP, if appropriately and efficiently used, could allow public administrations to solicit and promote even radical innovation. For this reason, PCP could be considered as a complementary instrument to the 2004 Directive on public procurement.

The idea underlying COM concerns R&D investments for goods and services that must be undertaken before commercialization, and that may characterize the public system as 'first purchaser' of a certain solution, for the development of which it could share risks and benefits with partnering firms. It must be pointed out however that, according to the current legislation, the public sector may not buy directly at the end of a PCP procedure, but rather subsequently through a procurement procedure specified in the Directive. Indeed PCP is conceived separately from commercialization, as procurement for R&D services only, a filtering phase to test the feasibility of innovative solutions.

Therefore, in this sense, PCP differs meaningfully from more standard purchasing procedures since it does not procure already existing products, but may support R&D investments sustained by the partners in the explorative phases of the project and prototype building, up to producing a limited number of units that are needed to test their characteristics and properties.

Therefore PCP locates at an intermediate stage of the innovation process, between curiosity driven research and commercialization. It is a stage where a promising idea, if not adequately supported, may fail to develop and materialize its own economic potential and social benefits.

Since the public sector already supports fundamental research, as well as purchasing of commercialized technological innovations, PCP represents the missing link in the chain of activities that public administration may entertain to sustain new solutions.

Clearly, the public system may be interested in a PCP initiative developing a new product only if the potential commercialization and diffusion of the idea could benefit the public sector and, in general, the society.

Since in the R&D phase where PCP operates intellectual property rights (IPR) may not be completely defined, PCP could potentially take the form of a public–private partnership (PPP), within which partners decide how to share risks and benefits, included IPR. Indeed, the PCP Communication appears to have a degree of flexibility on this.

As interesting as PCP could be, COM raises a number of economic questions that are not fully answered, and which shall be addressed in this chapter.

## 2 'Pre-commercial procurement' of innovation

A PCP initiative is competitive and concerns R&D services only. It is typically based on three main stages:

*Stage 1*: The request by a public administration (PA henceforth) to potentially interested suppliers of a first, explorative, proposal.

*Stage 2*: For those proposals selected after the first stage the PA may request the presentation of a prototype.

*Stage 3*: Test of the prototypes selected by the PA after the second stage.

From an economic point of view, a PCP initiative is characterized by the following two main points. As already mentioned the first is risk sharing, hence investments and possibly also revenues sharing, between the selected suppliers and the promoting PA while the second is state aid. The two points may be partly linked.

In our view risk allocation is the most important conceptual aspect. Indeed, the PA is not simply the promoter of the initiative, namely the part posing the issue and soliciting potential suppliers to propose a solution, but also a subject sharing partly or fully the risk of failure underlying R&D activities. As we shall argue later, risk sharing can take various forms: it could be based on patents, royalties, prizes and subsidies, also in favour of those companies that won't be selected.

On the issue of state aid the EU is particularly sensitive (Article 87, EU Treaty) for the possible distortionary effects that might negatively affect the correct functioning of the market. If a particular PCP initiative might run the risk of being interpreted as state aid for R&D investments, then the PA should make it explicit from the very start of the procedure and refer to the specific EU rules to explain the reason of such choice. If for PCP state aid is the case when the compensation by the PA to the selected firm is larger than the market price, then there could be a main difficulty in defining the market price of genuine innovations.

### *2.1 A first explorative proposal*

In this first phase, after having defined the problem and formulated the terms of the initiative, by publishing a call and then organizing a competition the PA solicits the companies that can potentially provide a solution to submit a preliminary proposal.

Since this very first set of initial projects, the definition of IPR plays an important part for the success of the initiative. Among others, the following scenarios could be envisaged (Ramboll, 2008):

1 If a participant does not own the patent rights related to his proposal, then the PA will have to specify in the call how IPR will be shared between the PA and the company. Such choice can clearly affect the final outcome of the initiative since IPR can be a fundamental incentive for the companies to invest in R&D. For this reason, should the PA be interested in owning the IPR related to the selected proposal, it will have to contemplate a prize for the winner, compensating for the forgone earnings that the potential commercialization of the solution protected by IPR might generate. If instead the PA would not want to own the IPR then, conditional on its development, it could ask for free use of the product and, perhaps, require that the winner would license the IPR according to the FRAND (Fair, Reasonable and Non Discriminatory) principle (Layne-Farrar *et al.*, 2007; Salant, 2007).
2 If instead some of the participants would already own IPR related to some/all components of their proposal, then the PA should specify in the call if it intends to acquire them, or alternatively if it simply would offer a reward without purchasing them, or some other indication. Again, the final outcome may be affected by the type of incentive chosen (that is whether IPR will be purchased or simply rewarded, etc.).

Finally, for both points (1) and (2) the PA will have to specify in the call who will own the IPR related to non-selected proposals and at what conditions.

Indeed, more in general, the assignment of IPR will crucially shape the incentives for the participants to invest in highly innovative proposals, and/or to disclose the relevant details in the exploratory phase. If participants would not be certain of the IPR ownership structure then, for example, knowing that competitors may have access to the details of their proposal, and freely imitate it or improve it, they may decide not to participate or cautiously submit incomplete, less innovative, ideas. Such circumstance may clearly damage the PA, which might receive fewer ideas, of lower quality, than otherwise.

Certainty of IPR assignment may be crucial for the PA to be able to manage situations such as the following example. Suppose, in the first stage, that the PA receives proposals from four companies: A, B, C and D. Moreover, suppose the PA thinks of selecting the proposals of C and D for the second stage, but that the PA wishes to insert some elements of the proposal made by B into those of C and D, that would much improve them. If the IPR ownership structure is well defined and legally enforceable, then the PCP call could explicitly contemplate the possibility that the PA may purchase some components of the received proposals that are not selected for the second and third stage.

A further important element in the first phase (as well as in the second and third phase) that might meaningfully affect the final outcome of PCP is the possibility that the PA might reward participants, to compensate for expenditures afforded for that project. Here too, the presence of such reward may give rise to different behaviour and outcomes with respect to when such compensation is unavailable. Indeed, without rewards it may be that only financially strong companies could submit a proposal while financially weaker, but potentially creative, firms may not be able to afford the risk of investing in a very specific initiative, without being at least partially compensated in case they would not win the competition. Discouraging smaller, financially weaker but creative, firms bears analogies with the well-known 'hold-up' problem, which arises when for the fear of economic losses a company may decide not to take the risk of making specific investments, even when they could be socially beneficial.

Indeed, without a system of rewards competition would be like a so-called 'all-pay' Tullock contest (Tullock, 1980; Konrad, 2009), that is a contest where only the winner is compensated while all participants pay their efforts, in the case of PCP the costs of their specific investment. Due to the presence of sunk costs it is well known how the outcome of such all-pay competitions can be characterized by high uncertainty (formally, the only Nash Equilibria of the game are in mixed strategy) both as far as the number and the quality of submitted offers are concerned.

More explicitly, the problem emerges if investments are specific to the project, so that in case a proposal would not be selected they could not be profitably used for other initiatives. Should such investments enjoy instead a mild degree of specificity then hold-up would certainly be less of a problem. However, in general it is reasonable to suppose that the PA may not typically possess full information on the degree of the investment specificity that companies have to face to enter the competition.

For this reason the presence of a reward scheme could mitigate, if not fully solve, such uncertainty by eliminating sunk cost issues. In fact in this case participants would be guaranteed to cover all, or part, of their costs with the possibility for them to focus their effort only on the quality of the proposed solution, since also non-selected companies would receive some compensation.

It is clear however that companies may, in principle, try to behave opportunistically by inflating costs, and/or asking to be reimbursed for non-specific investments, that were made for other projects, already financially covered.

Therefore, except for the last considerations, it should be clear that a system of rewards may enhance social welfare if the following hold. First, without them some potentially interesting proposals may not be submitted. Therefore, second, this may mitigate the degree of competition among participants, and as a consequence worsen the overall quality of the proposals.

For example, if the PA would not contemplate a scheme of rewards then it might receive proposals from companies A and B but not from C and D, who would have participated only if they received some financial compensation. Such adverse effect on participation may also negatively affect the overall quality of the submitted projects.

Still related to the role of a reward scheme, it is useful to discuss an aspect characterizing 'all-pay auctions', where all participants pay what they offer. In such competitions the so-called 'exclusion principle' may hold, that is the principle suggesting that under certain conditions the PA may prefer to exclude the best competitors (Hillman and Riley, 1989; Baye *et al.*, 1993, 1996; Konrad, 2009; Siegel, 2009). The underlying intuition is simple. For example in the standard case of sale auctions awarded to the highest price if the contest is 'all-pay', and because of this the auctioneer maximizes the sum of all the offers, then he should not design a contest to maximize the highest price.

Indeed to pursue such goal, when some of the bidders may be willing to submit particularly high prices and this information is known to all participants as well as to the auctioneer, the auctioneer may find it convenient to exclude those bidders who, in principle, are willing to offer the best prices to prevent the other competitors from being discouraged and decide not to compete actively.

For a better illustration of the point consider the following numerical example. Suppose that in a sealed-bid sale auction there are three potential participants, A, B and C, competing for an object. A is willing to offer up to 100€ for the object, B up to 60€ and C up to 50€. Suppose further that they are all informed about each other's maximum willingness to pay. Hence, since B and C know that A can offer much more than they could, in any case a price above 60€, various scenarios can be envisaged. For example, B and C may decide to compete aggressively to try to win the contest but they may also decide not to participate, or to propose a very low price, since they will have to pay anyway.

More specifically, imagine that A is interested in purchasing the object, that B competes aggressively hoping that A would not offer above 60€ and that C instead thinks he has no chance and decides not to compete to avoid certain loss. Therefore A would propose 61€ while B could offer 59€, just below his maximum willingness to pay. In this case the auctioneer would obtain 61 + 59 = 120€. To the other extreme, suppose instead that also B, anticipating that A will obtain the object, decides to offer 0€ to avoid costs that could not be recovered. In this case the auctioneer would only obtain 61€. If the auctioneer is a priori uncertain on the degree of competition that would unfold when A participates, then he may evaluate the benefit from inviting A to participate by considering an average of the two rewards. In this case the auctioneer might expect to receive 90.5€.

Suppose instead that should A be excluded from the competition the auctioneer thinks that B will submit a price just enough to win and that C will compete aggressively, offering a price just below his maximum willingness to pay. In this case B would offer 51€ while C will propose 49€, for a total of 100€. If, when A is not invited to compete, the auctioneer considers this as the most plausible outcome, then he would prefer to exclude A from the competition.

Hence, it is interesting to ask whether this intuition, valid for sales auctions, may be plausible also for PCP and, if so, how it could manifest itself in this context? That is, would it be appropriate to exclude some of the participants to increase the level of competition in a PCP contest? The issue is interesting theoretically but, even more so, for decision-making in contest design, just because admitting or excluding from the competition candidates with higher potential may give rise to very different outcomes.

To try answering such a question it is important to point out an element, namely that PCP contests are not always a pure version of 'all-pay auctions' in the sense that not all of the proposals submitted, including those which will not be selected, can necessarily provide benefits to the PA in terms of ideas, etc. From this point of view the difference with sales auctions should be clear, since in those contests the costs afforded by participants (that is their submitted prices) are directly beneficial for the auctioneer.

Finally, in general it seems plausible to imagine that the PA would be more interested in receiving at least a good project with the potential to solve the problem posed rather than a high number of projects, all containing some interesting elements, but none of which with the desirable potential.

This said, the following two scenarios could be envisaged:

> If the PA thinks that at least one participant will submit a proposal with the potential of solving the problem then the PA should not exclude them from the competition. In this case, even if some of the interested firms would be discouraged from participating the loss of interesting ideas could be minimized. If instead the PA thinks that no participant, on his own, has the potential to submit a proposal that could solve the problem, then the PA may consider excluding those firms with higher chances of winning if their presence could discourage participation. Indeed, though the best firms do not have the ability to solve the problem the PA may still be interested in receiving a certain number of suggestions and ideas, that otherwise would not be submitted if some of the interested companies were acknowledged as very likely to win.

To summarize, it seems like that a system of rewards to cover (partially or completely some of) the costs may encourage participation and, moreover, mitigate the dilemma of the PA as to whether to exclude the best participants.

### 2.2 Request of a prototype for the proposals selected in the first phase

After having received the first set of proposals, in a second phase the PA may request to present a prototype to those firms with potential. Also at this stage ownership and management of IPR, as well as the possibility of introducing a reward scheme, would play an important role to encourage companies to submit a prototype. However, unlike the first phase, from the second phase onward companies have already undertaken some investments, and related costs, to enter the first phase. Therefore, deciding not to participate in the second phase would not be costless.

### 2.3 Testing the prototypes selected after the second phase

If the previous observations concerning the importance of the IPR and the rewards remain valid also in this phase, there are some considerations specific to this case that we now want to make explicit.

Should the proposed prototypes be sufficiently interesting for the PA, it would be desirable to test at least two of them (Anton and Yao, 1992; Fullerton and McAfee, 1999; Che and Gale, 2003; Lyon, 2006), to compare the relative advantages of the two solutions. Furthermore, since until the PCP contest was performed the market offered no solution to the problem, the possibility of inducing two substitutable technologies may not just provide a solution but also prevent the risk that by selecting a single firm the newly created market may turn out to be monopolistic, at least initially, with possible undesirable socio-economic effects.

### 2.4 Financing PCP

In this section we briefly discuss the issue concerning the financial requirements for a PA to support a PCP procedure. In particular, we ask whether the PA could implement a PCP initiative without absorbing resources from its budget.

Clearly, the amount of financial resources needed to compensate participants in the three phases depends upon the nature of the problem. In case a relatively large amount of financial means would be needed, and yet the PA has a strong interest in developing an innovative solution, then a way for the PA to save or collect resources could be that of sharing with the winner part of the future revenues generated by commercializing the product. This would occur upon having protected it with IPR, possibly after having regulated the price and deciding to cover only the costs of non-selected firms.

Therefore the PA could conduct a PCP in financial equilibrium by covering expenses with future earnings, without taking resources away from the current budget. In this case, from a social point of view, the costs of innovation would not be paid by all taxpayers (as when innovation is funded from the PA's fiscal budget), rather only by those end users adopting the new technology.

The outcome of a PCP would then be socially efficient, since thanks to the initiative a new technology would now be available to society that was not available before. Costs would be paid only by those adopting the innovation, whose welfare would then increase after the adoption.

If obtaining resources from product commercialization could be difficult for a public institution, then the PA could ask to buy the product at a convenient price, 'funding' the costs of PCP by future savings accruing to the PA through a more efficient, and modern, functioning of the administration.

## 3 Some final considerations

Within the EU agenda emphasizing the role of innovation as a main driver for the social and economic progress of the Union, PCP represents a particularly interesting opportunity for the public sector to be effective in promoting new, socially desirable, technological solutions not yet commercialized. Now that the first main step in this direction has been taken, and a legal instrument is available, a further crucial role for effectively introducing beneficial innovations will be played by the professional competence and skills of civil servants in charge of conducting the initiative.

## References


Anton, J. and Yao, D. (1992) 'Coordination in Split Award Actions', *Quarterly Journal of Economics*, 1077: 681–707.

Baye, M.R., Kovenock, D. and de Vries, C. (1993) 'Rigging the Lobbying Process: An Application of the All-Pay Auction', *The American Economic Review*, 83(1): 289–94.

Baye, M.R., Kovenock, D. and de Vries, C. (1996) 'The All-Pay Auction with Complete Information', *Economic Theory*, 8: 291–305.

Che, Y.-K. and Gale, I. (2003) 'Optimal Design of Research Contests', *American Economic Review*, 93: 646–71.

Communication 2007/CE, no. 280. *Guide on Dealing with Innovative Solutions in Public Procurement. 10 Elements of Good Practice.*

Communication 2007/CE, no. 1668. *Pre-commercial Procurement. Driving Innovation to Ensure Sustainable High Quality Public Services in Europe.*

Dimitri, N., Piga, G. and Spagnolo, G. (2006) *Handbook of Procurement*, Cambridge: Cambridge University Press.

Directive 2004/18/EC of the European Parliament and of the Council of 31 March 2004 on the Coordination of Procedures for the Award of Public Works Contracts, Public Supply Contracts and Public Services Contracts.

Fullerton, R. and McAfee, P. (1999) 'Auctioning Entry into Tournaments', *Journal of Political Economy*, 107: 573–605.

Geroski, P. (1990) 'Procurement Policy as a Tool of Industrial Policy', *International Review of Applied Economics*, 4: 182–98.

Hillman, A.L. and Riley, J.G. (1989) 'Politically Contestable Rents and Transfers', *Economics and Politics*, 1: 17–40.

Konrad, K. (2009) *Strategy and Dynamics in Contests*, Oxford: Oxford University Press.

IST. Report of Experts (2006) *Pre-Commercial Procurement of Innovation. A Missing Link in the European Innovation Cycle.*

Layne-Farrar, A., Padilla, J. and Schmalensee, R. (2007) 'Pricing Patents for Licensing in

Standard-Setting Organizations: Making Sense of Frand Commitments', *Antitrust Law Journal*, 74(3): 671–706.

Lyon, T. (2006) 'Does Dual Sourcing Lower Procurement Costs?', *The Journal of Industrial Economics*, LIV: 223–52.

Ramboll Management Consulting (2008) *Opportunities for Public Technology Procurement in the ICT-related Sectors in Europe*, Rapporto Finale per la DG Information and Society, CE.

Salant, D. (2007) 'Formulas for Fair, Reasonable and Non-Discriminatory Royalty Determination', *Munich Personal RePEc Archive*.

Siegel, R. (2009) 'All-Pay Contests', *Econometrica*, 77: 71–92.

Tullock, G. (1980) 'Efficient Rent-seeking', in J. Buchanan, R. Tollison and G. Tullock (eds), *Towards a Theory of the Rent-Seeking Society*, College Station: Texas A&M University Press, 97–112.

# Part II

# Separation of selection and award criteria, including exclusion of reputation indicators like references to experience, performance and CVs from award criteria

# 5 Dialogue

*Chris Bovis and Giacomo Calzolari*

## 1 Argument by Chris Bovis

### *1.1 Rationale*

The relevant provisions of the public procurement Directives relating to the qualitative selection and qualification criteria refer to the technical ability and knowledge of tenderers, where proof may be furnished by evidence of educational or professional qualifications, previous experience in performing public contracts and statements on the contractor's expertise. The references, which the tenderers may be required to produce, must be specified in the notice or invitation to tender.

Selection and qualification criteria underpin the procedural foundation of public procurement. Selection and qualification criteria focus on financial and economic standing of undertakings and their respective technical capacity to perform a public contract. They produce direct effect and serve the principle of non-discrimination in public procurement by allowing the supply side (industry) to offer its price and performance solutions to the demand side (public sector).

Award criteria underpin the contractual subject matter of public contracts. They limit the choice of the demand side to either economic factors (lowest offer) or a combination of qualitative and economic factors (most economically advantageous offer) for justification of awarding public contracts. Award criteria serve the principle of objectivity in public procurement.

### *1.2 The legal treatment of selection and award criteria*

Fusion of selection and qualification criteria with award criteria in public procurement is not permitted. The Court has recognized their independent and autonomous function from each other, though it concurred that the two processes could run in parallel during public procurement procedures. The Court also maintained[1] that the examination of a contractor's suitability based on its technical capacity and qualifications and its financial and economic standing may take place simultaneously with the award procedures of a contract.[2] However, the two procedures (the suitability evaluation and bid evaluation) are totally distinct processes, which shall not be confused.[3]

### *1.3 Market dynamics and the selection process in public procurement*

In public services procurement, features relating to expertise and esteem could clearly be factors of selection and qualification of providers. But could they feature again during the procurement procedures as award criteria of the relevant public contracts?

The inability of fusion of selection and qualification criteria with award criteria is justified on the grounds of possible dilution of the direct link of the latter with contractual subject matters, which at all times bear an economic dimension.

This justification targets any discretion of contracting authorities to deviate from the exclusive (lowest offer or most economically advantageous offer) yet non-exhaustive parameters for the award of public contracts. Even if the most economically advantageous offer is utilized as award criterion, the weighted factors which comprise the assessment of contracting authorities must economically relate to the subject matter of the relevant contract. So, the non-exhaustive character of the most economically advantageous offer exerts relative discretion to the demand side of public procurement.

In public services contracts, expertise and esteem could co-relate with the projected outputs in an economic dimension which is directly linked to the subject matter of the relevant contract. They could demonstrate dimensions of quality, innovation, security of completion and could also indicate factors which are relevant to design and know-how or intellectual property rights.

### *1.4 Who is afraid of expertise and esteem being part of award criteria?*

The Court has been reluctant to disrupt previous precedent in relation to the fusion of selection and qualification criteria with award criteria and sees the insertion of expertise and esteem factors as a contamination exercise which undermines the integrity of the process by duplicating into two distinctive and separate procedural segments of public procurement which cannot be *de lege lata*.

The Commission will dogmatically support any policy and legal effort to narrow the application of award criteria to what is literally provided in the public procurement Directives, with a neo-classical stance which corresponds to public procurement serving as a conveyer belt of competition in the relevant markets.

Member States relish flexibility and freedom to procure services, works and supplies and they welcome any discretion in the application of the public procurement *acquis* recognized by the Court.

The supply side (service providers) wish to utilize expertise and esteem factors as competitive advantage in securing public contracts, alongside any economic factor legitimately allowed by the public procurement Directives.

### *1.5 The inevitability of expertise and esteem being part of award criteria*

The Court held in *Lianakis*[4] that tenderers must be aware of 'all the elements' to be taken into account by the authority for identifying the most advantageous offer, including their relative importance. The contracting authority cannot apply weightings or sub-criteria that it has not previously brought to tenderers' attention. The weightings and sub-criteria related to the evaluation procedure leading to the award of a contract cannot be established or changed after the submission of tenders. In *Lianakis*, the specific issue in question was the fusion of selection and award criteria, an issue already clarified by the Court. The Court has maintained[5] that the examination of a contractor's suitability based on its technical capacity and qualifications and its financial and economic standing may take place simultaneously with the award procedures of a contract. However, the two procedures (the suitability evaluation and bid evaluation) are totally distinct processes, which shall not be confused.

In *Lianakis* the contracting authority specified the bidder's experience on projects in the last three years, as well as the bidder's manpower and equipment and the bidder's ability to complete the project by deadline as award criteria. The Court reiterated that award criteria cannot be 'essentially linked to the tenderer's ability to perform the contract in question', pointing that the criteria used by the contracting authorities were in fact selection criteria in order to establish suitability of interested tenderers, and they must relate to financial standing and technical capability of interested tenderers. The Court concluded that the public procurement Directives prohibit selection criteria from being used as award criteria and reminded contracting authorities the selection and award processes are two independent and separate process in a public procurement and that a fusion of selection and award criteria is infringing public procurement rules.

The Court in *Commission* v. *Greece*,[6] examined the procurement process of a railway utility which advertised a contract for engineering services whereby non-Greek engineers were excluded since they submitted qualifications different from those required for the relevant contract. The Court ruled that the utility had confused selection and award criteria and applied the *Lianakis* ruling *verbatim*.

For public services contracts, expertise and esteem would inevitably appear as factors in both selection and qualification and award procedures.

The battle of CVs could have implications in making the relevant market more concentrated and prone to barriers to entry. Furthermore, the degree of objectivity in assessing expertise and esteem as award criteria could be compromised, as the relevant weighting of factors which has to be determined in advance of the commencement of the procurement process cannot be known until after the lapse of selection and qualification process.

## 2 Argument by Giacomo Calzolari

Let us start by being provocative. In most legislations, selection is intended to identify those suppliers who are *capable* to procure the good or service of interest with regard to firms' financial, technical and professional characteristics, whilst award is the truly competitive part of procurement in which suppliers are *compared* so as to identify the best offer.

Well, in the economic analysis of auctions there is no such distinction between selection and award. I am not referring to a marginal and underexplored subfield, actually auction theory is certainly one of the most developed and sophisticated areas of economic analysis. On the other hand, we are here discussing the importance of separating these two phases in public procurement and the EU 2011 consultation on the modernization of public procurement asked questions such as 'Would you be in favour of a more flexible approach to the organization and sequence of the examination of selection and award criteria as part of the procurement procedure? If so, do you think that it should be possible to examine the award criteria before the selection criteria?'

Then either economists are missing something important in their analysis, as sometimes happens, or we are overemphasizing the relevance of this rather exoteric distinction between selection and award. With respect to the second possibility, this distinction has been a hot topic for public procurement in the EU since a couple of cases involving the European Court of Justice in which, among other things, it has been ruled that criteria normally used for selection, such as technical ability and past experience, should not be confused and used also for award criteria. These decisions spurred a debate (where economists have been absent, at least to my knowledge) with many advocating further distinctions such as the 'quality of the bidder' and the 'quality of the bid' or maintaining that since experience is a useful measure of quality of the bidder and since the quality of the bid depends on the quality of the bidder, then experience must be counted both in selection and award which is in fact a non sequitur. I will try to describe why I think we are in such state of affairs.

What is the rationale for selection or pre-qualification? The idea is that the public buyer wants to avoid the risk of identifying and awarding a firm which is then not capable of delivering what is needed. Since normally the payment by the public buyer is not provided upfront, the main risk here is really not that the supplier 'takes the money and runs' but rather that it does not deliver or does not deliver as contractually contemplated. The parallel, in case you want to sell something, such as when a government wants to sell radio frequencies of a new spectrum, is that you really want to first select and then deal with buyers who are in a financial condition to pay if they win. This is simple as it is. Well actually it is not that simple.

Continuing with the parallel of selling, there is a telling story which is worth mentioning. In 1996, the US Federal Communications Commission (FCC) auctioned off licenses for radio frequencies which totalled record winning bids ($810.2 billion). However, actually only a few of the winners eventually paid. Most of them instead declared bankruptcy so that the FCC collected almost none of the pledged payments and had to re-auction most of the licenses (obtaining a meagre $8,400 for some licenses).

Now, nobody wants to sell to someone who cannot pay, because it is at minimum wasting your time and it could even be very costly in terms of litigation (most of the defaulted firms and the FCC were involved in litigations of bankruptcy and appeals which lasted more than five years), but it happens. Similarly, nobody wants to buy from someone who cannot deliver what has been promised, but it happens, as many eBay buyers know very well.

Selection should then 'simply' guarantee that participants in a market are 'real' and not 'fake' buyers and sellers: they are in a position to pay and deliver what has been promised. That is why, probably, economists haven't paid much attention to the distinction between selection and award in auctions.

For economists, individuals populating demand and supply in a market are simply 'real' buyers and sellers by definition. In the real world, instead, this is not necessarily the case primarily because the real world is plagued with asymmetric information: we do not know all the details of the thousands of firms available for procurement. My previous discussion has also highlighted the main issues that may emerge when encountering a 'fake' counterpart: wasting time, undue payments (if the buyer pays in advance), additional costs (for example to re-auction) and litigation costs. All these pertain to the category of what economist have named transaction costs, i.e. the costs of using and participating in a market. Hence, selection from an economist's viewpoint should be devoted to restrict the market to 'real' players, those who *can* deliver what is expected, and exclude fakes, those who *cannot* deliver (the emphasis on the words 'can' and 'cannot' is important and will be clarified in the sequel) what the public buyer or seller want to obtain. Here, quality really does not matter to the extent that what should be delivered has been clearly stated (we will also come back to this). A first consequence of this simple reasoning is that some of the criteria which are currently used in selection are meaningless. Think for example of the claim that the ability criterion of specialized labour force should be measured in relative terms since otherwise large firms are at an advantage and small firms risk being excluded. This reasoning is totally flawed at the selection phase: what matters is whether the counterpart can or cannot deliver and if, say, five specialized workers are needed to deliver, it does not make sense to state that the supplier share of specialized workers should be 2 per cent of total labour force. The problem on selection should thus only refer to the difficulty to overcome the issue of asymmetric information of the public agency and to infer counterparts' capability to deliver, on the basis of some incomplete information or indirect indicators (such as the number of specialized workers for specific tasks).

I incidentally notice that the indicator of past experience is not particularly convincing for an economist's viewpoint since it may represent a terrific barrier to entry and thus hinder competition. Is a firm capable of delivering what it is contractually expected to even with no experience? It depends, I think, in some standard cases yes, in other cases no. But still let me re-emphasize that selection, if it has a meaning, should be devoted to identifying those who can deliver and not those who, being capable of delivering, are also willing to deliver. The former issue should be addressed with the type of procurement (e.g. restricted) and with the award procedure. Hence, the public agency should identify a set of conditions which are necessary to the capability to deliver so that counterparts not fulfilling any single such condition are not capable and must then be excluded. In this respect, then, whether selection and award are temporally separated seems to me irrelevant although the two phases are and must be clearly logically separated. Furthermore, if the administrative burden associated to selection is significant, it may make sense to postpone even during the awarding phase, although clearly before its execution. This would also have the merit to increase competition since more firms would be admitted to bid. Is this good? It sounds so at least for an economist, as I will discuss later.

Now, it is clear that almost in any case, all the indirect measures that can be conceived and used in the selection phase, although hopefully necessary, will not be sufficient to guarantee deliver and some uncertainty would still remain. Were all the selected buyers of spectrum licenses financially sound, robust to default and thus able to pay what they had to? Hopefully yes, in reality no. This brings us to the award phase. Here I will not enter into the details of the many different awarding procedures and the underlying rationales. What matters here is twofold: first whether the counterpart may default, and, second, whether the counterpart does want to deliver.

Consider first the risk of default that is left, after all reasonable and conceivable indicators have been applied at the selection phase. In some countries this risk is at least partially dealt with by third party guarantees (which however tend to cover costs to the public agency up to the awarded price). In several countries this risk is addressed with laws that allow to exclude from the award procedure those bids that are abnormal (i.e. either too low in procurement or too high in the case of auctions to sell, such as for spectrum licenses). The precise mechanisms differ but they all share the idea that abnormal bids are a symptom of risk of default and then the awarding price should stay away from those bids, thus being higher in case of procurement and lower in case of auctions to sell. Here economics has recently provided some interesting insights. First, indeed the risk is real since those firms, which are more at risk of default, tend to be more aggressive and, if not limited by some properties of the auction mechanism, tend to win. Second, if the cost for the public agency of no delivery is very high (as it can be the case for small municipalities or for highly sensible procurement such as in the health sector), then an optimal procurement mechanism should contemplate some randomness in the allocation of the contract. The idea is that the public buyer should pay a sufficiently high price (which could be partially recovered with fees that competing firms could be asked to pay to participate in the auction process) and then randomly allocate the contract with equal probability.[7] This may seem the typical economist's wired and naive idea but it is actually not (although a straight implementation of this mechanism may be problematic). Indeed, the many different mechanisms frequently used to eliminate abnormal bids actually generate randomness in the allocation (but also, suboptimally, on price). Incidentally, I am asking why public procurement does not use some participation fee in those overcrowded auctions in which hundreds of firms participate? I personally have no answer for this.

This brief discussion of the risk of default illustrates the difference between selection and award phases which are logically distinct, although not necessarily in time, since they both can help in coping with the risk of default.

We are now left to deal with the possibility that, instead, the firm that has been chosen with the award procedure, actually *decides* not to deliver what is expected, which can be either no delivery at all, or delivering something different than promised. I think that the responsibility for this issue should be attributed to the award phase and not to the selection phase which, I reiterate, should be devoted to the selection of those who *can* deliver. Here the problems can be of two types. Either the public agency cannot fully state and express what it wants and its own needs, since for example they are still partially uncertain at the auctioning stage, or some dimensions of what it is seeking to procure are not contractible in the sense that cannot be explicitly stated in the contract. The first issue can be dealt with by the type of procurement process (for example with competitive dialogue procedures), the second should instead rely on reputation. In both cases a key ingredient is the possibility for the public agency to exercise some discretion which is the counterpart of the impossibility to specify all that should be relevant in the procurement contract. It is important to notice that I am not referring here to the fact that in some cases procuring at the lowest price is not the optimal choice since there are quality dimensions that are also important to take into account. This instance should be 'simply' addressed with what economists name multi-dimensional auctions, that is with the choice of the most economically advantageous offer that weighs the price together with other relevant factors, such as quality, which can be contracted upon.

In case of non-contractible dimensions instead it is useful that the public agency has the discretion to decide possibly also on the basis of good or bad past experience, not simply on whether a firm has some past experience. The idea is that the public agency should be able to discretionarily reward high and or punish low non-contractible quality so that suppliers face the right incentives to deliver what is expected, although not held immediately liable for contract infringement if they don't do so (since we are dealing here with non-contractible dimensions). A typical punishment which is often used in the private sector, but can also be implemented in public procurement with restricted procedures for example, is exclusion from future procurement procedures. However, notice that there should be again a strict logical distinction between the use of past experience as for capability in the selection phase and (negative) past experience for exclusion in the exercise of discretion by the public agency in the award phase. It is still past experience used in both cases, but for different reasons. Incidentally we notice that economic analysis has also illustrated that an alternative to the threat of exclusion based on poor past performance could be the promise to (again discretionary) deliver bonuses to well performing suppliers. However, we see very limited actual use of bonuses in the public sector (actually I know of none), which are instead significantly employed in the private sector. A possible but not completely convincing reason could be that bonuses are at risk of corruption in the public sector (but why should this not be the case for a manager in a corporation?). As stated, reputation is something which a firm can really put at stake in contracting with a public agency and I think that current procurement procedures are too timid in (actually not) using this element explicitly. Again the tension is clearly that of the risk of corruption of the civil servant in charge of the procedure when exercising discretionary power.

However, in many cases reputation can be based on the 'voice' of the many final users of the goods or services, i.e. the citizens, so that the risk of corruption is definitely diluted.

## 3 Reply by Chris Bovis

Both economists and lawyers agree that procurement and auction processes are based on two fundamental concepts:

First, the concept of 'due diligence', where the seller or the buyer, as the case may be, are deemed to pass certain standards/benchmarks in relation to their suitability to sell to or to buy from the public sector. The ultimate rationale of due diligence is risk management.

Second, the concept of 'performance', where contractual engagement between public and private sectors is based on price or price related considerations. The ultimate rationale of performance is accountability.

Due diligence appears as a precondition of performance. Without it, performance is deemed implausible, risky or susceptible to corruption or impropriety.

Due diligence is achieved by the process of selection and qualification.

The European procurement legal system uses criteria which appear to provide a degree of comfort and security to the public sector in relation to the potential engagement of private sector operators (sellers or buyers). These criteria are generic in character; qualitative criteria focusing on the technical capacity of economic operators in addition to financial criteria related to the economic standing of operators. Here comes the first wave of uncertainty: how could contracting authorities differentiate between economic operators based on their technical capacity? The information required by the public procurement Directives is evidential, which means it leaves a great deal of discretion to contracting authorities to select and qualify the economic operators which will be invited to compete. Along the same lines, qualification of economic operators based on financial information supplied by them bring a second wave of uncertainty, in as much as evaluation of such information is subjective to the views of the contracting authority.

Performance is accomplished by the process of award of public contracts, which is based on criteria related to the consideration (price) of the envisaged demand or supply requirements on the part of the public sector or on criteria which bring into the equation qualitative features which are contractually related to the subject matter of the demand or supply requirements of the contracting authorities. Discretion to contracting authorities is also evident, particularly in setting and evaluating the factors of the most economically advantageous offer criterion. However, discretion, and the surrogate uncertainty, is limited to the most economically advantageous offer. The lowest offer, as award criterion, appears as a rigid and structurally objective criterion which limits the discretion of contracting authorities and eliminates uncertainty, save for abnormally low (or high in cases of auctions) offers or predatory pricing, which contracting authorities can discard.

The uncertainty over the evidential character of selection and qualification criteria could be spilled over to the award criteria if a fusion occurs.

What would be the implications of such fusion?

First, an apparent dilution of contract-related factors to the weighted criteria comprising the most economically advantageous offer will emerge. If reputation and esteem are factors which are part of the 'due diligence' process and are allowed to appear again during the award process, an element of double-counting occurs, which undermines the award process.

Second, an apparent contraction of competition of the supply side would occur, if public contracts are awarded on the basis of reputation and esteem factors. Evaluation of reputation and esteem is also highly subjective and conducive to abuse on the part of contracting authorities.

Third, if a mix-and-match approach between selection and qualification criteria and award criteria occurs, the principles of public procurement law and policy are significantly weakened, as subjectivity and discretion on the part of the contracting authorities takes priority over economic justification of public expenditure.

## 4 Reply by Giacomo Calzolari

I found the document very useful and happily realized that we, economists and lawyers, can speak a common language. My comments are mainly clarifications on interesting themes for discussion.

The first point does not refer only to the pages I am commenting on but it is more general and I think it may refer to my own ignorance on how to interpret the law. What is it the common distinction between *financial* and *economic* standing of firms (in addition to technical capacity) as for the section and qualification phase? It would be useful to elaborate, since I clearly see the meaning of financial solidity and technical ability, but I think the economic dimension is less clear for the selection and qualification phase. Isn't it that we are already alluding to 'esteem' or reputation (see also below)? On this I have my own idea that I have illustrated in my document.

It would be also interesting to elaborate on the fact that the general opposition to mixing selection with award is based on the 'risk of dilution' of the connection between the award criteria and the 'contractual subject matter' (i.e. what in the end we want to procure). If I understand well, the idea is that it is upfront important that there is a clear logical connection between award (the method and related approach) and what one is trying to procure (the contractual subject matter). There are then two points to be identified. First, any discretion applied at the level of award is somehow 'dangerous' since it makes this connection fuzzy, unclear and may even break it. Second, one example of this discretion is precisely the mixing of selection and award that could take place by allowing the same information to be repeated both for selection and award. Although I understand the first point, I do not understand the second.

Expertise and esteem are very often presented together as economic types of information relevant for the contractual subject matter. In the document it is stated that they should then certainly be used (within the constraints of the procurement method) to award the contract. But I would like to emphasize the intrinsic logical difference between expertise and esteem. At least to me, expertise refers to the ability to perform what is indicated in the subject matter (the good or service we want to procure). It is an objective measure of ability to perform based on past experience. Esteem is a completely different concept that, again to me, refers to the subjective valuation by a party of a relationship with another party. Esteem is the party's perception of the other party's reputation based on past interactions that took place with the involvement of the two. I think it would make sense to separate the two. In my document I take the position of clearly attributing to the two logically different phases of selection and award. In this respect I fully agree with the idea that we should not be afraid of esteem being part of the award criteria, but I think expertise pertains to selection for the motivations illustrated here and in my document.

I also fully agree with the statement that the Commission seems to dogmatically support the narrowing of the set of criteria to be used in the award criteria as contemplated in a strict interpretation of the procurement Directives. It may be just a matter of terminology, however I do not understand why this short-sighted interpretation of the Commission should be attributed to its 'neo-classical stance which corresponds to public procurement serving as a conveyer belt of competition in the relevant markets'. In most European countries (probably more on the continent) I think a strong reference to competition as an essential ingredient for market economies to work well is never undue and always worth stressing, also in the case of public procurement which is responsible for a very large part of European economies. I am not personally keen on classifying theories and schools of thought, but I personally think that what is normally named the neo-classical economic theory did a lot of good in clarifying how important competition is for the functioning of markets. On the other hand I agree, as I also stated in my document, that procurement is matter of competition and discretion and the right blend of the two is a difficult task which is very often overlooked.

Finally, I think the theme of clarity and *ex ante* selection of criteria for award discussed in the last paragraph is important and should be further elaborated. With this respect I simply notice that if it makes sense to leave some dimension of discretion and associated responsibility in the award phase, and I think it does make sense, then discretion cannot be codified *ex ante* almost by definition.

## 5 Conclusions by Chris Bovis

Economic and legal discourse is in conceptual alignment in the issue of separation of selection and award criteria in public procurement

Selection and qualification criteria underpin the procedural foundation of public procurement. Award criteria underpin the contractual subject matter of public contracts.

Selection and qualification criteria focus on financial and economic standing of undertakings and their respective technical capacity to perform a public contract. Award criteria limit the choice of the demand side to either economic factors (lowest offer) or a combination of qualitative and economic factors (most economically advantageous offer) for justification of awarding public contracts. Selection and qualification criteria produce direct effect, whereas award criteria do not seem to produce direct effect.

Selection and qualification serve the principle of non-discrimination in public procurement by allowing the supply side (industry) to offer its price and performance solutions to the demand side (public sector). Award criteria serve the principle of objectivity in public procurement.

The inability of fusion of selection and qualification criteria with award criteria is justified on the grounds of possible dilution of the direct link of the latter with contractual subject matters, which at all times bear an economic dimension.

In procurement for public services contracts, features relating to expertise and esteem could clearly be factors of selection and qualification of providers, but they could feature again during the procurement procedures as award criteria.

Expertise and esteem could co-relate with the projected outputs in an economic dimension which is directly linked to the subject matter of the relevant contract. They could demonstrate dimensions of quality, innovation, security of completion and could also indicate factors which are relevant to design and know-how or intellectual property rights.

The Court has been reluctant to disrupt previous judicial precedent in relation to the fusion of selection and qualification criteria with award criteria and has viewed the insertion of expertise and esteem factors undermining the integrity of the process by duplicating into two distinctive and separate procedural segments of public procurement which cannot be *de lege lata.*

The law on EU public procurement needs to address the schism between the legal treatment of fusion of selection and qualification criteria with award criteria in public procurement and align its regulatory thrust with market dynamics currently prevailing in public markets.

## 6 Conclusions by Giacomo Calzolari

It has been interesting and reassuring noticing that economists and legal scholars, although often using different languages, share a common view on the main components and the logical steps that altogether constitute the complex process of procurement.

Interacting with legal scholars is an important source of knowledge for economists particularly in terms of policy design, and this also true for procurement. Economists may have a tendency to reset the environment and, if needed, to start anew with no reference to constraints that instead may make sense and may be justified with reasonable considerations.

In my opinion the theme that probably would benefit more from a close interaction between economists and legal scholars is that of discretion in procurement. On this subject it seems that the two disciplines have a lot to learn from joint reasoning and a lot to profit from each respective stock of knowledge. In particular, in the context of selection and award it would be fundamental to indentify when discretion could and should performed and clearly identify its boundaries. A better understanding of all the associated details would allow to first obtain a better understanding of pros and cons of the actual and different procurement modes that we already know and, second, it would allow a better, more efficient and effective design of procurement. I see the analysis of discretion in selection and award as a very interesting area for interdisciplinary work. Indeed I think that the common perception about public procurement still fails to see it as a complex blend of competitive forces, discretion and accountability. With this respect economists and legal scholars seem to agree that dogmatic positions and restrictive interpretations of the law may not allow to identify the best procurement practices.

An open issue, at least to me, is the one pertaining to the possibility to clearly and neatly separate the role of selection and award in identifying those suppliers which, although they can procure what the public agency requests, they actually plan not to honour the agreement. Is it possible and efficient to attribute the responsibility of this identification to the award phase or should one also make use of selection? A deeper interaction among economists and legal scholars may be particularly fruitful for the substance of this issue.

Another theme which in the end should be better investigated with the contribution of both the disciplines, economics and legal studies, is the one pertaining the distinction between experience and esteem. Here I think we still lack a mutual and common understanding of these terms. It is important to notice that it is not simply a matter of terminology. Indeed, the definition of these two important ingredients in procurement has fundamental consequences on the way we interpret and consequently design selection and award, the two cornerstones of public procurement. Clearly, this also relates back to the identification of the boundaries of discretion.

## Notes

1 See case 31/87, *Gebroeders Beentjes B.V.* v. *State of Netherlands* [1988] ECR4635.

2 See case C-27/86, *Constructions et Enterprises Indusrtielles S.A (CEI)* v. *Association Intercommunale pour les Autoroutes des Ardennes*; case C-28/86, *Ing.A. Bellini & Co. S.p.A.* v. *Regie de Batiments* and case C-29/86, *Ing.A. Bellini & Co. S.p.A.* v. *Belgian State*, [1987] ECR3347.

3 See case C-71/92, *Commission* v. *Spain*, judgment of 30 June 1993. Also, in *Beentjes*,

op. cit. at paragraphs 15 and 16, where the simultaneous application of selection of tenderers and award procedures is not precluded, on condition that the two are governed by different rules.

4 See case C-532/06, *Emm G. Lianakis AE* v. *Alexandroupolis* [2008] E.C.R. I-251.

5 Case 31/87, *Gebroeders Beentjes B.V.* v. *State of Netherlands* [1988] ECR4635.

6 See case C-199/07, *Commission* v. *Greece*, judgment of 12 November 2009.

7 The mechanism must be random since, otherwise, again, risky bidders tend to outbid the others. Increasing participation is still desirable since selecting from a larger pool of firms guarantees increased efficiency.

# 6 Implications of the *Lianakis* decision

*Philip Lee*

## 1 Introduction

The Public Procurement Directives (the 'Directives') not only promote the principles of free movement and equal treatment but also encourage the importance of delivering value for money for the taxpayer. As regards the latter assertion, the Directives do not differ from private procurement which is also aimed at delivering the best value for money for the purchaser. They do of course also have the objective of deepening the internal market. While these two should lie comfortably together, the public sector may not always be able to follow all developments pursued in the private sector. Since 1993, procurement law has developed at an extraordinary pace, perhaps more so than any other area of European law. It has generated much work for lawyers. It has not generated much work for economists and has possibly frustrated public procurement specialists originating from the private sector who feel they are more constrained than is necessary in seeking to deliver value for money. The European Court of Justice (the 'Court') has been exceptionally proactive in pushing the Directives beyond where the Member States had perhaps originally envisaged them travelling. The early landmark decisions such as the *Storebealt Bridge* decision,[1] the *Universal Bau* decision[2] and the *Teleaustria* decision[3] have by and large been understood and perhaps even welcomed by lawyers, as the purpose that these decisions sought to achieve was not difficult to understand. The concepts of transparency, proportionality and equal treatment are certainly ones with which we lawyers are very familiar. This chapter seeks to demonstrate that the *Lianakis* decision[4] is not supported by any of the above rationales. It is not supported by any substantive jurisprudence, nor is it supported by the texts of the Directives,[5] and is incompatible with sound commercial and economic reasoning.

The Court in the *Lianakis* decision, prompted by the Legal Services of the European Commission, has made a fundamental mistake. It is an error that is causing great difficulty right across Member States.

For the purposes of this symposium, I have updated a previous paper published in the *Public Procurement Law Review* (*PPLR*) in February 2010, in which I argued that a fresh approach to this question of the distinction between selection and award criteria would be greatly welcomed. The paper, reproduced here in part, pointed out that the *Lianakis* decision drew conclusions from the *Beentjes* decision,[6] and from the wording of the Directives which are dubious at best, and also drew attention to the amendments introduced by the most recent Procurement Directives which presented the Court with the freedom to orchestrate a dignified requiem for *Lianakis*. Sadly, whilst a small opportunity arose in the recent decision of *Commission* v. *Greece*,[7] the Court has failed to face up to its error. The Advocate General in this case did however at least throw some cold water on the Commission that there should always be a distinction between the qualification stage and the award stage. In the *Commission* v. *Greece* case, the Commission challenged the Greek authorities on the basis of their failure to distinguish between selection and award criteria in an open procedure. The Advocate General dismissed this as of any relevance as there are not in any event two stages in an open procedure. Both the selection and the award are combined and therefore he did not think that it was appropriate to even comment on the use of experience at the award stage. Though subtle, this could be interpreted as a critical swipe at the jurisprudence emanating from the *Lianakis* decision.

Since the publication by the *PPLR* of my examination of *Lianakis*, the Commission has published a green paper on public procurement (the 'Green Paper')[8] inviting submissions on the separation of pre-selection and award criteria. The Green Paper is somewhat helpful as the Commission alludes to some of its concerns should the distinction created by *Lianakis* be removed. Unfortunately, the Commission's explanations are far from lucid. However, this discussion is the only source from which some rationale for the distinction might be found, as the *Lianakis* decision itself provided insufficient reasoning for its findings and the subsequent *Greece* decision did not serve to clarify the issue. In fact, the Court in that case merely recites *verbatim* the mantra stated in *Lianakis*.

## 2 Experience and skills of the project team

It appears from the survey of procurement practices in Europe that the procurement departments of public bodies in many Member States are applying what is known as a 'flexible' interpretation of the *Lianakis* decision.[9] Not only is this the modus operandi of many procurement departments but it can presently be seen in appeal cases before tribunals who also support this 'flexible' approach. The flexible approach appears to suggest that the experience of the 'project team' offered in the tender bid, as opposed to the general experience of the firm, may be used as award criteria if the experience is relevant to the subject matter and (possibly) also to the terms of contracts. Whilst I support the logic and sense of such an approach, it is not supported by the facts in *Lianakis* nor does it appear to be supported by the Commission. However, it is clear that the flexible approach needs to be facilitated by either an amendment to the Directives or by a reversal of *Lianakis* at a European Court level. Indeed the Commission has taken into account the need for this flexible approach with the recent publication of the proposal for new Procurement Directives which I will go on to discuss later.

It is regrettable that the Commission's Green Paper did not 'call it as it is' and identify this as the core issue. The Commission identifies two concerns. First, it identifies a concern that Member States wish to consider selection criteria once the successful tender has been identified based on the award criteria. This of course is possible in practice under the open procedure and the *Beentjes* decision specifically reiterates that selection and award criteria can be assessed simultaneously in the open procedure.[10] However, it would seem a strange request to ask that the selection criteria be applied at the award stage under the restricted or negotiated procedure since the very purpose of having a two-stage procedure is to reduce the burden on the public body and to 'cull' or reduce the numbers that submit full bids. Such a request would in effect suggest that some of the selection criteria might be applied at the first stage but some of the selection criteria would not be applied until after the successful bidder under the award criteria was identified.

The second concern raised by the Commission's Green Paper relates to the following:

> some stakeholders present more far reaching proposals that would call into question the separation in principle between selection and award criteria. They claim that the possibility to take into account bidder related criteria, such as experience and qualification, as award criteria might help to improve procurement outcomes.[11]

In relation to this point, the Commission states the following:

> However, one has to be aware that creating such a possibility would result in a major change in the procurement system set out in the Public Procurement Directives. The separation between selection and award criteria guarantees fairness and objectivity in the comparison of tenders. Allowing the inclusion of bidder related criteria such as experience as contract award criteria could undermine the comparability of the factors to be taken into account and ultimately infringe the principle of equal treatment. The reliance on bidder related criteria could thus potentially also lead to distortions of competition. Proposals in that direction should therefore be envisaged, if at all, in limited circumstances only e.g. for specific types of contracts, in which the qualifications and CV's of available staff are particularly relevant.[12]

The Commission paper states that taking into account bidder related criteria such as experience would 'result in a major change in the procurement system set out in the Public Procurement Directives'.[13] Is this correct? Prior to *Lianakis*, experience and qualification would have been common award criteria (at least for services contracts) and generally applied without difficulty. Is it not correct to say that it was *Lianakis* that represented a change, in fact a major change, to this practice? For over 30 years prior to this judgment, the inclusion of 'experience' as an award criteria (particularly when it related to the experience of the team offered) would have been considered as consistent with the Directives and thus it cannot be correct to say that going back to this approach would now represent a 'major change' in the procurement system.

The Green Paper states that the separation between selection and award criteria 'guarantees fairness and objectivity in the comparison of tenders', and that allowing bidder related criteria such as experience at award stage could 'undermine the comparability of the factors being taken into account and ultimately infringe the principle of equal treatment'.

Taking the example of using 'experience of the project team' as an award criteria, one must ask how this might 'undermine the comparability of the factors', whatever that means. Experience can and is taken into account for the firm as a whole at the selection stage. One might question why the project team could not be considered at the award stage. The Green Paper suggests that such methods of evaluation could serve to undermine the principle of 'equal treatment'. Regrettably, the Green Paper offers no explanation as to why the use of 'experience' at award stage would undermine the principle of equal treatment. In practice quite the contrary is the case: where a superb and experienced team is offered in a tender bid, but the offer is rejected at the award stage and the tenderer is defeated on (for example) an insignificant price difference, then in fact the principle of equal treatment has not been adhered to and the tenderer who offered a superior team but a marginally higher price, has, in my view, been unfairly discriminated against. One must question whether the Commission's position is justifiable given their failure to provide any rational explanations to support that position.

It is perhaps salutary to look at the UNCITRAL Model Law on Procurement[14] (the 'UNCITRAL Model Law'). Article 39 of the UNCITRAL Model Law deals with the criteria for the evaluation of proposals for service contracts and lists the following as the limited criteria that may be used:

a The qualifications, experience, reputation, reliability and professional and managerial competence of the supplier or contractor and of the personnel to be involved in providing the services and;
b The effectiveness of the proposal submitted by the supplier or contractor in meeting the needs of the procuring entity.

It should be a matter of concern that the Commission and the Court have pursued a policy which is neither supported by the 1996 Agreement on Government Procurement ('GPA') nor by the United Nations in relation to best practice for procurement.

The guidance notes to the UNCITRAL Model Law discuss the inspiration behind Article 39:

> in reflecting the importance of the skill and expertise of the suppliers and contractors in the bulk of the cases of procurement of services, paragraph

> 1(a) lists as one of the criteria the qualifications and abilities of the personnel who will be involved in providing the services. *This criterion would be particularly relevant* in the procurement of those services that require a high degree of personal skill and knowledge on the part of the services providers, e.g. in an engineering consultancy contract [emphasis added].
>
> By establishing the effectiveness of the proposal in meeting the needs of the procuring entity as one of the possible criteria paragraph (1) (b) enables the procuring entity to disregard a proposal that has been inflated with regard to technical and quality aspects beyond what is required by the procuring entity in an attempt to obtain high ranking in the selection process, thereby artificially attempting to put the procuring entity in the position of having to negotiate with the proponent of the inflated proposal.

Such further criteria would of course also be available under the European Public Procurement Directives and would facilitate, where appropriate, the awarding of the top quality scores to several tenderers all of whom provided more than adequate technical or professional experience.

Since this is a multi-disciplinary symposium, I have also taken the opportunity to examine the leading textbooks on private sector procurement as recommended by procurement experts. I can find no reference within these texts to support the refusal to consider criterion such as the quality of the project team at the final stage of the tender selection process. Czerniawska and Smith explain that firms shortlisted for the award stage should be required to clarify 'who will be working on the assignment and why they have been chosen'.[15] It seems to be (not surprisingly) standard practice to assess the quality of the personnel appointed to provide the services under the contract when differentiating between different shortlisted firms at final selection stage.

Thus, not only is the *Lianakis* decision running counter to best international practice as reflected in the UNCITRAL Model Law, the GPA and private sector practices, but also does not represent a decision based on a solid legal foundation as I seek to explain below.

The facts of the *Lianakis* case have been covered extensively in my previous article but in brief they concerned proceedings issued by a consortium of consultancy firms against the municipality of Alexandropoulis in connection with the award of a contract by the municipality to carry out a town planning project. The budget for the consultancy project was €461,733.

The question posed by the Greek court concerned the entitlement of a contracting authority to stipulate, at a later date, the weighting factors and subcriteria to be applied to the award criteria referred to in the contract documents. However, the European Commission, in making its written submissions, suggested that before replying to that question it was necessary to consider whether Directive 92/50 (the applicable services Directive at that time) precluded the contracting authority from taking into account as 'award criteria' rather than as 'qualitative selection criteria' the tenderer's experience, manpower and equipment, or its ability to perform the contract by the anticipated deadline. The Court agreed with the Commission's request to firstly examine what criteria could properly be considered as award criteria.

In examining the criteria which could be considered as award criteria, the court stated that:

> 31 In the case in the main proceedings, however, the criteria selected as 'award criteria' by the contracting authority relate principally to the *experience, qualifications and means of ensuring proper performance of the contract* in question. Those are criteria which concern the *tenderers' suitability* to perform the contract and which therefore do not have the status of 'award criteria' pursuant to Article 36(1) of Directive 92/50.
>
> 32 Consequently, it must be held that, in a tendering procedure, a contracting authority is precluded by Articles 23(1), 32 and 36(1) of Directive 92/50 from taking into account as 'award criteria' rather than as 'qualitative selection criteria' the tenderers' experience, manpower and equipment, or their ability to perform the contract by the anticipated deadline [emphasis added].

Here the Court made it clear that it considers 'experience, qualifications, and means of ensuring proper performance of the contract' to be criteria which concern 'the tenderer's suitability' to perform the contract and therefore to be selection criteria and not award criteria.

The judgment does not help us understand whether the municipality was evaluating the entity which had been selected or the project team proposed by the entity to work on the contract. Thus the findings do not explicitly rule out a distinction being made between 'tenderer's' experience and experience of the 'project team'. For example, an awarding authority seeking management consultancy services is likely to find that the global consultancy firms have the capacity and manpower to carry out almost any given management consultancy project. However, it is self-evident that the success of the project will depend not on the capacity of the firm but on the specific resources made available by that firm for the project.

A literal interpretation of this judgment suggests that the experience of the team proposed to carry out a contract could not, in any circumstances, be evaluated, nor indeed could that team's ability to perform the contract by the anticipated deadline be evaluated at award stage. While such a conclusion is not unsupported by the wording in the judgment, given the decision's consequences it is important to examine in more critical detail its findings, and consider whether the distinction between the 'tenderer' and the 'project team' exists and how the Court might respond to a subsequent case which turned on such a distinction.

## 3 'Tenderer' versus 'team' offered by the tenderer?

In *Lianakis*, the Court correctly pointed out that the *Beentjes* case indicated that there are two separate stages in a procurement procedure, namely the selection stage and the award stage, but that both stages are governed by 'different rules'. However, in *Beentjes* the Court did not rule out the possibility that at selection level it was appropriate to evaluate the capacity of the 'tenderer', and at the award stage to evaluate the particular skills of the members of the 'project team'.

The Court in *Lianakis* refers to the inappropriateness of treating as award criteria '*evaluation of the tenderer's ability to perform the contract in question*' (emphasis added). The wording does not clarify whether the experience of the members of the 'project team' could be a valid award criterion.

## 4 *Lianakis* factual matrix

To understand the *Lianakis* judgment it is necessary to look at the factual matrix in which the case arose. The contract notice in *Lianakis* prescribed 'the proven experience of the design team and its leader' as the first award criterion. This unfortunately suggests that this criterion was not evaluating the 'tenderer' but the project team. However, the actual method of evaluation painted a different picture. This criterion was to be evaluated by reference to the 'value of completed projects'.

The methodology chosen was that for experience on projects worth up to €500,000, a tenderer would be awarded 0 points; for experience on projects valued at between €500,000 and €1 million, six points; and for projects between €1 million and €1.5 million, 12 points and so on, up to a maximum of 60 points for projects worth over €12 million. This method is not consistent with evaluating 'team members' but arguably reflects an evaluation of the 'tenderer'. In *Lianakis* the project was worth only €461,000. Thus designing an evaluation system in which 60 points are awarded to a firm (or a team) with experience on projects worth in excess of €12 million is not consistent with evaluation of individual design team members. Such an exercise would require an examination of the individual team members. It is, however, the method one might expect in evaluating a firm at the selection stage. It appears, from the methodology used, that the Municipality of Alexandropoulos may not have examined the experience of the team proposed, but the firm. Are the findings of the Court a reflection of this reality?

The evaluation criteria used for the assessment of the firm's manpower and equipment, the second award criterion, was assessed by reference 'to the size of the project team'. The scoring mechanism was based on a different number of points, depending on whether the team offered one to five persons, six to ten persons and so on up to a maximum score of 20 points for a team of 45 persons. The project concerned town planning for a town of fewer than 2,000 inhabitants, and the value was under €500,000. It must be questioned whether this method was appropriate to evaluating a team for such a small-scale project for a town of fewer than 2,000 inhabitants. The range (up to 45) makes little sense for a project of such a small scale. Thus, while the phrase 'project team' has been used in paragraph 15 of the judgment, the facts of the case go some way to undermine the contention that the municipality genuinely examined the project team rather than the firm's size. Nevertheless the fact that the contract notice referred to the design team and its leader is a concern for those that wish to take a more liberal interpretation of this, perhaps unfortunate, judgment.

To critically review the judgment it is necessary to go beyond the findings and factual matrix, and examine:

- the findings of the *Beentjes* case relied upon in *Lianakis*, on the question of selection and award criteria;
- whether the wording of the old and new Services Directives precludes examining the experience of a 'team' at the award stage;
- decisions of the General Court which immediately preceded and proceeded the *Lianakis* case.

## 5 Does the *Beentjes* case support a prohibition on examining the 'project team' at award stage?

The Court in *Lianakis* specifically relies on paragraphs 15, 16, 17 and 18 of *Beentjes* case, which read as follows:

> 15 According to the structure of the Directive, in particular Title IV (Common Rules on Participation), the examination of the suitability of contractors to carry out the contracts to be awarded and the awarding of the contract are two different operations in the procedure for the award of a public works contract. Article 20 of the Directive provides that the contract is to be awarded after the contractor's suitability has been checked.
> 16 Even though the Directive, which is intended to achieve the coordination of national procedures for the award of public works contracts while taking into account, as far as possible, the procedures and administrative practices in force in each Member State (second recital in the preamble), does not rule out the possibility that examination of the tenderer's suitability and the award of the contract may take place simultaneously, the two procedures are governed by different rules.
> 17 Article 20 provides that the suitability of contractors is to be checked by the authorities awarding contracts in accordance with the criteria of economic and financial standing and of technical knowledge or ability referred to in Articles 25 to 28. The purpose of these articles is not to delimit the power of the Member States to fix the level of financial and economic standing and technical knowledge required in order to take part in procedures for the award of public works contracts but to determine the references or

> evidence which may be furnished in order to establish the contractor's financial and economic standing and technical knowledge or ability (see judgment of 9 July 1987 in Joined Cases 27 to 29/86 CEI and Bellini (1987) ECR 3347). Nevertheless, it is clear from these provisions that the authorities awarding contracts can check the suitability of the contractors only on the basis of criteria relating to their economic and financial standing and their technical knowledge and ability.
> 18 As far as the criteria for the award of contracts is concerned, Article 29 (1) provides that the authorities awarding contracts must base their decision either on the lowest price only or, when the award is made to the most economically advantageous tender, on various criteria according to the contract: e.g. price, period for completion, running costs, profitability, technical merit.

The *Beentjes* case merely clarified that award criteria must be related to evaluation of which tender is the most economically advantageous. It also clarified that the experience of the tendering entity is a valid selection criteria.

## 6 Does the wording of the Services Directive preclude evaluation of project team experience at award stage?

*Lianakis* was based on the old Services Directive 92/50,[16] now replaced by Directive 2004/18.[17] Article 36 of the old Services Directive deals with award criteria and lists a non-exhaustive set of award criteria. Included in this list are 'quality and technical merit'.

The criterion 'technical merit', when applied to the assessment of a services contract, invites the awarding authority to look at the merit of the service being offered. It is difficult to avoid the assumption that an important element of such an assessment must include the skills of the team being made available by the tenderer. Similar arguments arise in relation to the criterion 'quality'. Is it possible to evaluate the quality of the skills of the team or resources offered without evaluating their experience?

Article 23 of the old Services Directive dealt with the interaction of selection and award criteria. The wording of Article 23 merely provides that award criteria are applied 'after the suitability of the service provider's … has been checked by the contracting authorities in accordance with the criteria referred to in articles 31 and 32'. Articles 31 and 32 of that Directive refer to proof of the service provider's financial and economic standing and the evidence that can be relied upon to show the ability of the service provider to supply the services. There is nothing explicit or implicit in the wording of the Directives that leads to the conclusion that the experience of the project team cannot be, or should not be, evaluated at the award stage. Indeed, while various decisions, commencing with *Beentjes*, confirm that selection and award procedures are governed by different rules, that is not to say that there could not be similar criteria, or even identical criteria, but applied to different facts, namely the entity at selection or the project team at award. Unfortunately, neither in

*Beentjes* nor in *Lianakis* is there any rationale offered to explain the harm that could arise if 'experience' were considered at both stages, in particular where at selection, 'experience' is examined at the level of the entity and at award stage it is the 'experience' of the project team that is scrutinized. As explained below, the the General Court specifically confirms that the quality of the team can have an impact on costs and delays to a project. In a construction project, a poor design is likely to lead to additional costs from the contractor. The experience of the design team is critical in ensuring the highest economic advantage to the client.

There is also nothing that can be derived from the fundamental principles underlying the Directives which supports a more conservative interpretation of *Lianakis*. The core principles of transparency, equal treatment, non-discrimination, mutual recognition and proportionality are not in any way inconsistent with evaluating 'experience' of the project team at award stage. Thus, if this prohibition derives neither from core principles nor from the text of the Directives, its authenticity might be questioned.

## 7 The new Public Services Directive

As outlined, *Lianakis* interpreted the provisions of Directive 92/50, the old Services Directive. This Directive has now been changed and is replaced by Directive 2004/18. Recitals have been introduced which deal with award criteria in more detail. Recital 46 provides:

> Contracts should be awarded on the basis of objective criteria which ensure compliance with the principals of transparency, non-discrimination and equal treatment and which guarantee that tenderers are assessed in conditions of effective competition. As a result, it is appropriate to allow the application of two award criteria only, the lowest price and most economically advantageous [...]
> Where the contracting authorities choose to award a contract to the most economically advantageous tender they shall assess the tenders in order to determine which one offers the best value for money.
> In order to do this they shall determine the economic and quality criteria which, taken as a whole, must make it possible to determine the most economically advantageous tender for the contracting authority. The determination of these criteria depends on the object of the contract since they must allow the level of performance offered by each tenderer to be assessed in the light of the object of the contract, as defined in the technical specifications and the value for money of each tender to be measured.
> In order to guarantee equal treatment, the criteria for the award of the contract should enable tenderers to be compared and assessed objectively.

The recitals in the old Directives were silent regarding award criteria. This legislative change clarifies that where criteria are relevant to assess the 'performance offered' by each tenderer, it is an appropriate and valid award criteria. Recital 46 of Directive 2004/18 changes the emphasis that might have existed in the old Directives, and clarifies that criteria, where they assess the 'level of performance', must be valid criteria regardless of whether it was also a selection criterion. How else is the anticipated level of performance in a services contract to be evaluated? Does the experience of the specific personnel offered not become a necessary evaluation criterion? Perhaps the anticipated level of performance and the mere ability to perform are different. A League One soccer player has the ability to 'perform' in a soccer match, but the anticipated level of performance would be significantly different from that of a Premiership player.

The new Directives also differ with regard to the criteria that may be used for pre-selection. Whereas in the old Directives the criteria for pre-selection were exhaustively laid down in the Directive, this is not the case under the new legislation. The new Directive provides that where there is the intention not merely to pre-select all qualified candidates, but to compare the candidates and to limit the number to a particular range (which might therefore exclude candidates that would otherwise be capable of performing the contract), the awarding authorities may do so by applying other criteria, providing they are objective and non-discriminatory. Could indicative pricing be used? If so, this would clearly necessitate a re-examination of that criterion at award stage.

This important change to the potential selection criteria and the new recital on award criteria provide comprehensive grounds for distinguishing *Lianakis* and ensuring a departure from its worst implication.

## 8 Judgments of the General Court[18]

*Lianakis* was a judgment of the European Court of Justice, superior to the General Court. There was no opinion from the Advocate General, which may suggest the judgment carries somewhat less weight. The views of the General Court provide a starkly different approach to similar questions.

The *Renco*[19] judgment was delivered by the General Court in February 2003, several years before *Lianakis*. The case concerned the award of a contract by one of the European institutions, the Council of the European Union. The governing legislation for the award of public works contracts by the Council is the Financial Regulation[20] which provides that each institution shall comply with the same obligations as those imposed upon bodies in the Member States under the Directives on public works contracts, when concluding contracts for which the amount involved is equal to or greater than the threshold provided for by those Directives.

A contract notice was published by the Council inviting tenders for general renovation and maintenance works in the Council buildings in Brussels. The procedure was to result in the conclusion of a five-year framework contract renewable for 12-month periods. One of the award criteria included 'the experience and technical competence of the undertaking'.

The applicant, Renco, claimed that issues such as the competence of the contractor or its sub-contractors were too vague, and that the awarding authority was obliged to avoid value judgments which were difficult to justify. The Commission legal services were not involved in the case and it does not appear that Renco made specific arguments claiming the invalidity of the other than their vague nature.

The Court, in its judgment, pointed out that award criteria do not have to be of a purely economic nature because 'it cannot be excluded that factors which are not purely economic may influence the value of a tender'.

The Court then went on to state at paragraphs 68 and 69:

> 68 It follows that Article 30(1)(b) of Directive 93/37 cannot be interpreted as meaning that each of the award criteria used by the Council to identify the most economically advantageous tender had necessarily to be either quantitative or related solely to the prices or rates contained in the summary. Various factors which are not purely quantitative may affect the execution of work and, as a result, the economic value of a tender. For instance, the experience and technical competence of a tenderer and its team, the familiarity with the kind of work covered by the contract in question and the quality of the sub-contractors proposed are all qualitative factors which, if they do not reach the level required by the contract, may cause delays in the execution of the work or make additional work necessary. It follows that, even if some of the criteria mentioned in the contract documents for assessing a tenderer's competence to carry out the works are not expressed in quantitative terms, they may be applied objectively and uniformly in order to compare the tenderers and are clearly relevant for identifying the most economically advantageous tender.
>
> 69 In the present case, as the Council has stated … the eight criteria referred to in the contract documents, apart from the first criterion concerning the conformity of the tender, are qualitative and quantitative … the Court considers that although those six criteria, amongst them the experience and technical competence of the company and the quality of any subcontractors proposed, are not absolute or quantitative like the first two, they are nevertheless not vague and can all be evaluated objectively and specifically. Furthermore it should be pointed out that criteria like the experience and technical competence of the company and the quality of any subcontractors proposed are factors which may affect the value of the tender and, contrary to what the applicant claims, it is appropriate that they should appear amongst the criteria of the contract documents.

The findings of the General Court in this decision are not reconcilable with that of the Court in *Lianakis*.

A similar issue arose six months subsequent to the *Lianakis* decision, in the July 2008 case of *AWWW GmbH ArbeitsWelt–Working World* v. *The European Foundation for the Improvement of Living and Working Conditions*.[21]

In this case the three principal award criteria were:

1 knowledge and experience [55];
2 ability to deliver the specified services [25];
3 quality control [20].

Under the first heading, 'knowledge and experience', the sub-criteria included the 'quality of the proposal' and 'the understanding of relevant policy issues and developments at national level in the requested areas of work'. Arguably, therefore, the title 'knowledge and experience' is misleading when viewed in light of the sub-criteria.

A query in relation to providing CVs during the award stage arose, and the awarding authority pointed out that the capacity of tenderers was checked during the first stage, and that the CV of any additional personnel would not be taken into consideration. However, this was undermined by a letter from the awarding authority stating that the possibility of using additional persons not mentioned in the first stage could be dealt with by showing resources as evidence of how the tenderer was going to fulfil some of the award criteria.

The applicant challenged the decision on the grounds that the award criteria were based mainly on a criterion which does not appear in the invitation to tender. It claimed that it was the particular experience of the successful tenderer in co-ordinating international projects, which was the main ground for the award of the contract and that this had not been clearly stated. The awarding authority, in its defence, stated that it did not evaluate the knowledge and experience of the applicant, 'in isolation from the quality of its proposals, but in the light of its particular proposals'. The awarding authority had stipulated in its tender documentation that if the knowledge and experience of the tenderer is taken into account under the award criterion, such information 'may only concern the way in which those aspects apply for the purposes of this contract'.

In its judgment, the General Court approved this approach. It said that the awarding authority, when it referred in its evaluation report, to the ability to deliver the specified service,

> the Evaluation Committee did not go back on the selection stage but … assessed the quality of ability in the light of the specific proposals put forward by the applicant for carrying out the services.

Thus the Court approved of the qualification inserted by the awarding authority regarding experience suggesting that the awarding authority could go back on the information contained at the selection stage such as experience and expertise, provided it evaluated these 'in the light of the specific proposals put forward by the applicant for carrying out the services'. This suggests that if in the methodology, an awarding authority referred to the CVs of particular persons mentioned at the selection stage setting out how those persons would devote a significant proportion of their time to this project, that that would be considered appropriate for the requirements of the Directive.

The Court specifically stated:

> Experience in coordinating international products was not, in itself an award criterion. Nevertheless there was no reason why the Foundation could not have regard to such experience in assessing the quality of the tenderer's ability to cover the three required areas of work.

The General Court was clearly trying to reconcile its earlier positions with the more recent decision in *Lianakis*, but with some difficulty. Nevertheless, it concludes that CVs from the selection process can be relied upon, and experience can be relied upon in assessing the quality of a tenderer's ability to cover particular areas of work. Such a ruling, delivered only a few months after *Lianakis* is supportive of the interpretation that a distinction does indeed exist between experience of the tenderer and the 'project team'.

## 9 Conclusion

The *Lianakis* case clarifies that to evaluate tenderers under the heading 'experience', based on the value of completed projects using a very simplistic method whereby points are awarded depending on the value of the completed scheme, is not acceptable. This is quite different from taking into consideration the individual experience of a particular team proposed, and assessing that experience in light of its relevance to the particulars of an individual contract being awarded. However, the wording chosen by the Court would also seem to rule this out.

Thus, *Lianakis* will lead awarding authorities to follow an interpretation that an awarding authority is precluded from taking into account 'the project team's experience' as an award criterion. While that is not unreasonable, a public policy issue must be considered: namely, the most economically advantageous tender must be awarded, not just because that is required by the purpose of the Procurement Directives, but because it is essential in order to achieve value for money. It is difficult if not improbable to do this without considering the qualities of the tenderer, including the experience of the 'project team'.

However the newly published Commission proposal for new Procurement Directives provides for a more flexible interpretation of the distinction between the selection of tenderers and award of the contract and effectively renders the decision in *Lianakis* redundant. The proposal allows for contracting authorities to examine award criteria before selection criteria and in the case of service contracts and contracts involving the design of works, allows contracting authorities to use the organisation, qualification and experience of the staff assigned to performing the contract in question as an award criterion, as this may affect the quality of contract performance and ultimately the economic value of the tender.

I regret to say, as Cato the Elder, the Roman statesman said, … Lianakis delenda est.

## Notes

1 Case C-243/89 *Commission of the European Communities* v. *Kingdom of Denmark*, Judgment of the Court of 22 June 1993.
2 Case C-470/99 *Universale-Bau AG*, Judgment of the Court of 12 December 2002.
3 Case C-324/98 *Telaustria Verlags GmbH and Telefonadress GmbH* v. *Telekom Austria AG*, Judgment of the Court of 7 December 2000.
4 Case C-532/06 *Emm. G. Lianakis AE* v. *Dimos Alexandroupolis, Planitiki AE.*, Judgment of the Court of 24 January 2008.
5 See subsequent comments on recital 46 to the Public Service Directive.
6 Case 31/87 *Gebroeders Beentjes BV* v. *State of the Netherlands*, Judgement of the Court of 20 September 1988.
7 Case C-199/07 *Commission* v. *Hellenic Republic*, Judgment of the Court of 12 November 2009.
8 European Commission Green Paper on the modernisation of EU public procurement policy towards a more efficient European Procurement Market, 27 January 2011.
9 Steen Treumer, 'The distinction between selection and award criteria in EC public procurement law – a rule without exception?', *Public Procurement Law Review* 2009, p. 103.
10 Case 31/87 *Gebroeders Beentjes BV* v. *State of the Netherlands*, Judgement of the Court of 20 September 1988.
11 European Commission Green Paper on the modernisation of EU public procurement policy towards a more efficient European Procurement Market, 27 January 2011, p.17.
12 Ibid.
13 Ibid.
14 1994 UNCITRAL Model Law on Procurement of Goods, Construction and Services with Guide to Enactment.
15 Fiona Czerniawska and Peter Smith, 'Buying professional services: how to get value for money from consultants and other professional service providers', *The Economist*, 2010.
16 Council Directive 92/50/EEC of 18 June 1992 relating to the coordination of procedures for the award of public service contracts.
17 Directive 2004/18/EC of the European Parliament and of the Council of 31 March 2004 on the coordination of procedures for the award of public works contracts, public supply contracts and public service contracts.
18 The General Court was known as the Court of First Instance until November 2009.
19 Case T-4/01 *Renco SpA* v. *Council of the European Union* [2003] E.C.R. II-171.
20 Financial Regulation applicable to the general budget of the European Communities [1977] OJ 1977 L356/1. 21 Case T-211/07 *AWWW* v. *EFILWC* [2008] E.C.R. II-106.

# 7 OPTIONCARDS

## An interactive approach to elicit qualification and award criteria weights

*Pedro Maia Graça and Luis Valadares Tavares*

### 1 Introduction

The procurement of goods, services or works by public sector bodies is ruled by the EU treaty, by the EU Directives (Directive 2004/18/EC of the European Parliament and of the Council of 31 March 2004 and Directive 2004/17/EC of the European Parliament and of the Council of 31 March 2004 and Directive 2007/66/EC of the European Parliament and of the Council of 11 December 2007) and by case law. The aim of the EU procurement rules is to create a single market by removing all discrimination against or in favour of tenderers. The EU procurement rules impose the respect for principles through the procurement process on all public contracts, including those which fall below the relevant thresholds, namely, the principles of transparency, equal treatment, non-discrimination, mutual recognition and proportionality. Therefore, public sector bodies cannot simply adopt common sense or arbitrary processes when selecting tenderers or evaluating tenders. The EU Directive text and case law on award criteria tries to clarify how the Contracting Authority (CA) should meet the needs of the public concerned and achieve value for money, without disrespecting the above-mentioned principles.

In the case of the most economically advantageous tender (MEAT), articles 55 and 53, of the 2004/17/CE and 2004/18/CE Directives respectively, state that 'various criteria linked to the subject matter of the public contract in question' shall be defined and that 'the contracting authority shall specify … the relative weighting which it gives to each of the criteria chosen'. According to the Directives and case law CAs are to disclose, in advance, award criteria, sub-criteria and the respective weighting, either in the contract notice or in the contract documents. If the contract is being awarded using the competitive dialogue procedure, the weightings must be stated in the descriptive document.

Decision sciences have developed a large number of methods to support decision-making in problems characterized by multiple criteria (MCDA) [1, 2, 3]. Some models are particularly adequate to be applied to public procurement processes, in particular the multi-attribute utility theory additive model (MAUT)

[4]. The application of the decision models is usually straightforward but the definition of criteria weights is one of the most controversial processes within MCDA [5]. Underlying this discussion there is a quest to search for the best weight elicitation method. Accuracy, vulnerability to biases [6], results interpretation [5] and user-friendliness [7] are just some of the issues raised when discussing weight elicitation methods.

Many studies has been made on the comparison of method's outcomes [e.g. 8, 9, 10], but there is no agreement on the methods that produce more adequate results. Some authors, e.g. Barron and Barret [11], suggest that one reason for this debate is that the 'target' is itself not clearly understood. Several works have defended, however, that the purpose of decision support is not to discover the absolute truth [12] but to constructively build up the knowledge to support better decisions. A good example of this debate is the paper of Figueira and Roy [13], commenting on the paper of Wang and Triantaphyllou [14].

Another common issue when discussing elicitation methods is the potential need for quantification of the weight parameters. It has been demonstrated that decision-makers have problems judging precise values [17, 7]. Tversky and Kahneman [18] provided sound demonstrations that the heuristic principles that people rely on to reduce the complex task of predicting values to simpler judgemental operations, may lead to severe biases and errors. Direct quantification is prone to error and biases so the methods should take this into consideration and, if possible, elicit weights indirectly. This leads to the debate of what results should be expected from the decision-makers. On the one hand, decision-makers have problems judging and quantifying their preferences and views in precise values and some authors [11] have reported the underlying problems of precise weights elicitation.

Decision support models should help to reveal the decision-maker's conviction and help to build a clearer assessment of the factors that interfere in the decision-making process and allow for a gradual reduction of the uncertainty about the values of the parameters. Moreover, these model should not be a 'black box' but easy to use, understand and implement. But, this simplicity should not lead to ambiguities in the interpretation of the parameters or the results. A good illustration of these ambiguities is the case of the interpretation of criteria weights in AHP models [5]. The ambiguity of the question 'how much more important is this criterion compared to another?' is well exemplified by the comparison of cities presented by Saaty [15].

The purpose of this chapter is to present a method (OPTIONCARDS) to elicit the decision-maker's weights based on a learning interactive and iterative process that does not require direct quantifications of weights, trade-offs, swings or preferences by the decision-maker. The weights parameters are well defined as swing weights as the base model in question is the additive MAUT. The weights [5] are elicited from a sequence of pairwise comparison of predefined dummy alternatives that, gradually, will reduce the uncertainty about the swing weights. Starting with the initial accepted complete domain for all weights to be elicited, the process, at the end, will result in a much more refined and detailed sub-space for each weight based on the decision-maker's pre-order relations instead of creating the illusion that a single and precise value for each weight is discovered. Such sequential process has a tree structure on its base to accommodate the possible answers given by the decision-maker at each stage and it is built to provide a similar level of uncertainty reduction at each stage. The results of the method may be a set of precise weights or a sub-space of weights for the particular criteria under study that are consistent with the revealed preferences.

## 2 A multi-criteria model for the most economically advantageous tender award criteria

The Public Procurement and Utilities Directives, 2004/18/EC and 2004/17/EC respectively, are particularly clear about the decision-making principles that should be adopted by a contracting authority to award a contract:

> Contracts must/should be awarded on the basis of objective criteria which ensure compliance with the principles of transparency, non-discrimination and equal treatment and which guarantee that tenders are assessed in conditions of effective competition. As a result, it is appropriate to allow the application of two award criteria only: 'the lowest price' and 'the most economically advantageous tender'.
>
> (Directive 2004/17/EC Paragraph 55 and Directive 2004/18/EC Paragraph 46)

Obviously, 'the lowest price' is only adequate for procuring simple or standard goods or services. Regarding the most interesting rule, 'the most economically advantageous tender', these Directives state:

> To ensure compliance with the principle of equal treatment in the award of contracts, it is appropriate to lay down an obligation – established by case-law – to ensure the necessary transparency to enable all tenderers to be reasonably informed of the criteria and arrangements which will be applied to identify the most economically advantageous tender. It is therefore the responsibility of contracting authorities to indicate the criteria for the award of the contract and the relative weighting given to each of those criteria in sufficient time for tenderers to be aware of them when preparing their tenders.
>
> [...]
>
> The determination of these criteria depends on the object of the contract since they must allow the level of performance offered by each tender to be assessed in the light of the object of the contract, as defined in the technical specifications, and the value for money of each tender to be measured. In order to guarantee equal treatment, the criteria for the award of the contract should enable tenders to be compared and assessed objectively.
>
> (Directive 2004/17/EC Paragraph 55 and Directive 2004/18/EC Paragraph 46)

These principles imply the adoption of a decision model to evaluate alternatives – tenders or qualifying candidates. To fulfil the Directives requirements this model should be defined and announced before the delivery of tenders and should help rationalize, justify and quantify the decisions taken.

One of the most acceptable multi-criteria models to be applied to this procurement process is the multi-attribute utility theory additive model. This is a simple model, widely studied in decision sciences that is based on:

1 score functions to convert criteria units (for example euros or weeks) to partial scores (e.g. on a scale of 0 to 10); and
2 criteria weights to balance the several criteria scores to a single final score.

### *2.1 Alternatives evaluation*

Procurement decisions can be formulated in terms of selecting one alternative from a list of alternatives previously proposed as feasible alternatives.

This formulation can be exemplified by a CA selecting the best tender from a set of $N$ submitted tenders on a public procedure.

Thus, the list of alternatives results from the market response to a notice or to an invitation from the decision-maker. This is the case of any open or restricted procedures to allow a public CA to select the best tender.

In the case of the open procedure, the public contracting authority accepts tenders presented by any company complying with the defined general conditions. The selection of the best tender out of this set is then required.

In the restricted procedure, only those passing through the qualifying stage are invited to present tenders. The Directives state that in restricted procedures, contracting authorities may limit the number of suitable candidates they will invite to tender, to negotiate or to conduct a dialogue with, provided a sufficient number of suitable candidates are available. This qualifying stage can be based on yes/no economic and technical conditions (simple model) or be based on the selection of the $K$ best candidates according to specified scoring rules expressed in terms of such economic and technical conditions (complex model), requiring a multi-criteria evaluation model for the candidates.

Lastly, the selection of the tender can be made in terms of the minimal price criterion if there is no other criterion subject to competition but, in most cases, the selected tenders should be the most economically advantageous tender requiring a multi-criteria evaluation model for the tenders.

In addition to candidate's qualification and tender evaluation, the multi-criteria models can also be applied to perform ongoing or *ex-post* evaluations of the contract performance. In this case, the model's outputs would be criteria-based and global measures of the supplier's performance.

In any of these cases, the selection of an alternative from a list of alternatives requires the specification of a multi-criteria model including:

1 Formulating the $N$ evaluation criteria ($j = 1,\ldots, N$)

The formulation of each criterion, $j$, requires the specification of how it is measured for each alternative $i$, $i = 1,\ldots, M$, i.e. the definition of the descriptor $Xj(i)$, and how it is scored, $Vj(i)$, in terms of $Xj(i)$.

For instance, $T(i)$ can be the duration of a project proposed by tender $i$ and $Vj(i)$ a scoring function that converts the duration units into scores (see Figure 7.1).

In this case $T'$ is the minimal credible duration (with score 10) and $T''$ is the maximal accepted duration (with score 0). Any duration between $T'$ and $T''$ is given a score between 0 and 10.

## 2 Defining the mathematical model to aggregate N criteria

The determination of which tender is the most economically advantageous from the point of view of the contracting authority implies the use of an aggregation method like the weighted sum. This method is implicitly referred to in the EU case law on public procurement and is certainly the most widely used. Therefore, the tender evaluation model may be mathematically represented as follows:

$$V(i) = \sum_{i} w(j)y(i,j)$$

where $V(i, j)$ is the overall score of criterion $j(j = 1,\ldots, N)$ due to the outcomes (partial scores) of alternative $i$ $(i = 1,\ldots, M)$ and where $w(j)$ is the compensatory weight associated to $j$. According, to this model the contract should be awarded to the tender with the highest overall score ($V$).

Directives 2004/17/EC and 2004/18/EC require the presentation of the evaluation model with their weights when the notice is published in order that competitors can understand, when preparing the tenders, how they will be evaluated.

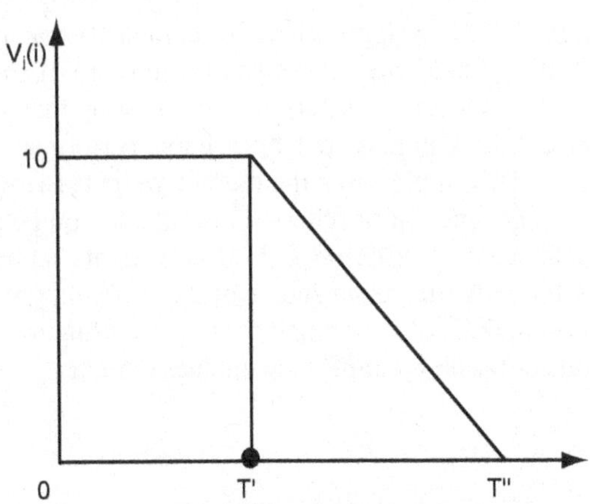


*Figure 7.1* Scoring function for criterion T.

Thus, public contracting authorities should specify the presented model to award a contract and they may also use this type of model to rank candidates and to select the best M candidates from the qualifying stage (complex model) of a restricted procedure.

### 2.2 Criteria trees

The evaluation of any alternative implies considering its ability to satisfy the decision-maker according to multiple perspectives such as quality, cost, time, etc. Unfortunately, the elicitation of such perspectives frequently tends to generate list of concerns that are incomplete or overlapping.

Therefore, a special effort has to be made to help the decision-maker to formulate the relevant areas of concern avoiding any forgotten perspective and avoiding double coverage through overlapping concepts. The list of major criteria will be based on such concerns.

Obviously, each criterion, for instance, quality, can be branched down into sub-criteria (e.g. reliability, durability, resistance). One way to structure this information is to build a criteria tree with nodes representing criteria and branches representing the hierarchical relationships between criteria.

Usually, the number of criteria branching from each node should not be high because, if so, the interpretation and allocation of weights by the decision-maker might become a hard task. This means that grouping several sub-criteria into a few criteria will be better than a longer list of such sub-criteria.

Therefore, having a multi-layer tree is better than adopting a one-level tree. Those criteria that are not branched down into other sub-criteria, usually named elementary criteria, are the criteria subject to evaluation and scoring. The others are mere instruments to organize the criteria information.

### 2.3 Criteria weights

In the additive value function model, the weights are mere coefficients that allow transforming partial scores of the defined criteria into an overall score. It should be noted that the mentioned model is a compensatory model, meaning that a bad performance in one criterion can be compensated by a good performance in another criterion, and vice versa. This implies that the ratio of weights ($wi/wj$) is equal to the increment on the score function of criterion $i$ needed to compensate a loss of one unit on the value scale of criterion $j$. That is, weights represent replacement rations or trade-offs between partial scores of the different criteria. This trade-offs allow the determinations of how much the CA is willing to compensate a score reduction in one criterion by improving another criteria.

### 2.4 Alternatives ranking

The ranking of alternatives is easily computed after specifying the model and after introducing the descriptors of each elementary criterion for each alternative.

The final scores can be computed by multiplying the partial scores by the respective criteria weights and adding up these scores for each alternative.

## 3 The OPTIONCARDS method

Many methods have been developed, within decision sciences, to elicit precise weights from the decision-makers: the direct rating and point estimation [9]; the trade-off method [2], the swing method [19], SMART [19], SMARTER [20], rank-based methods [10, 11] and AHP [15], and from these many variations have risen. Generally, these methods imply either the difficult task of quantifying weights, swings or trade-offs, or the direct ranking of the criteria and both approaches can lead to inconsistent and erroneous results due to several already studied reasons.

### *3.1 Proposed approach*

The method proposed by the authors, OPTIONCARDS, is based on a set of pairwise comparisons of predefined dummy alternatives and on the pre-order relations of these alternatives stated by the decision-maker. This process allows the elicitation of precise weights or weights intervals without the need either for direct quantification of any parameters or to rank criteria. At the same time the OPTIONCARDS method works on comparisons of alternatives and elicits the weights from the underlying preferences of the decision-maker which avoids the mentioned pitfalls of measuring criteria relative importance. Moreover the method is based in an iterative and progressive approach that helps the decision-maker to build up knowledge about the parameters and gradually reduces the uncertainty of these parameters.

### *3.2 Pairwise comparison as a weight elicitation approach*

The base hypothesis of the OPTIONCARDS method is that the decision-maker is able to compare pairs of alternatives characterized by a set of discrete scores (from 0 = worst to 30 = best) and say which alternative is preferred or if they are indifferent (pre-order relation).

The approach based on pairwise comparison of alternatives plays a classical and key role in economic models since their very historical beginning (e.g. Edgeworth indifference curves in [21]) and MCDA models [22]. On the latter, this technique has been applied to eliminate demonstrably inferior alternatives [23], determine preference 'strength' [5, 15] or to build up pre-order relations between alternatives [12]. Strangely enough, the alternatives pairwise comparison hasn't been used in a structured way to elicit swing weights. When comparing (pre-order relation) two alternatives, the decision-maker is using the notion of swing weights and expressing valuable information about these parameters. If the right alternatives are subjected to comparison, in a structured process, then it is possible to elicit criteria weights from the revealed preferences.

The key step of the OPTIONCARDS method is the provision of several sets of pairs of dummy alternatives that are contrasting in some criteria and constant in the remaining criteria so that, when the decision-maker specifies the pre-order relation between this pairs, information about the criteria trade-offs is being given and, from there, a set of swing weights that are compatible with this preferences can be found.

For example, on the case of three criteria, when the decision-maker is asked to compare a pair of alternatives expressed in the discrete scale above indicated, e.g. $X = [10, 0, 0,]$ and $Y = [0, 10, 0]$, from the specified pre-order relation, one can extract information about the underlying weights, specifically:

1 If the decision-maker is indifferent between $X$ and $Y$ then $w_1$ and $w_2$ are the same (or sensitively the same if as range is being considered);
2 if $X$ is preferred to $Y$ than $w_1$ should be greater than $w_2$; and
3 if $Y$ is preferred to $X$ than $w_2$ should be greater than $w_1$.

This reasoning, when applied to particular weight sets, will give valuable information about the decision-maker's weights of the criteria.

It should be noted that, although this method uses pairwise comparison of alternatives and a discrete scale, its principles are quite different from AHP – Analytic Hierarchy Process. The OPTIONCARDS method works with the concept of trade-offs and not relative importance and it does not use importance ratios but the trade-offs between criteria. Also, the discrete scales do not carry the problems of semantic scales and their quantification [5]. In the OPTIONCARDS method the weights domains is reduced to a discrete set of weights (as many as the enabler wishes) and the alternative scales are used merely to indicate on which side of the weight sub-space the decision-maker is in each step.

### 3.3 The method

The OPTIONCARDS method is based on the TRIDENT framework [24] which works within the weights space. The possible weights space is the geometric area that contains all possible combinations of weights subject to given restrictions, usually, that the sum of the weight equals 1.

The continuous weight space is transformed into discrete possible weights through indifference lines. The space is divided by indifference lines such as, for two alternatives $X$ and $Y$, the final scores of these alternatives are the same for the given weights:

$$V(X) = V(Y) \Leftrightarrow \sum_j w(j).v(x, j) = \sum_j w(j).v(y, j)$$

On the intersections of the indifference lines reference points are set (A, B, to Q, in Figure 7.2 and Table 7.1) which correspond to the discrete sets of weights with which the method will work. There is no limit on the number of reference

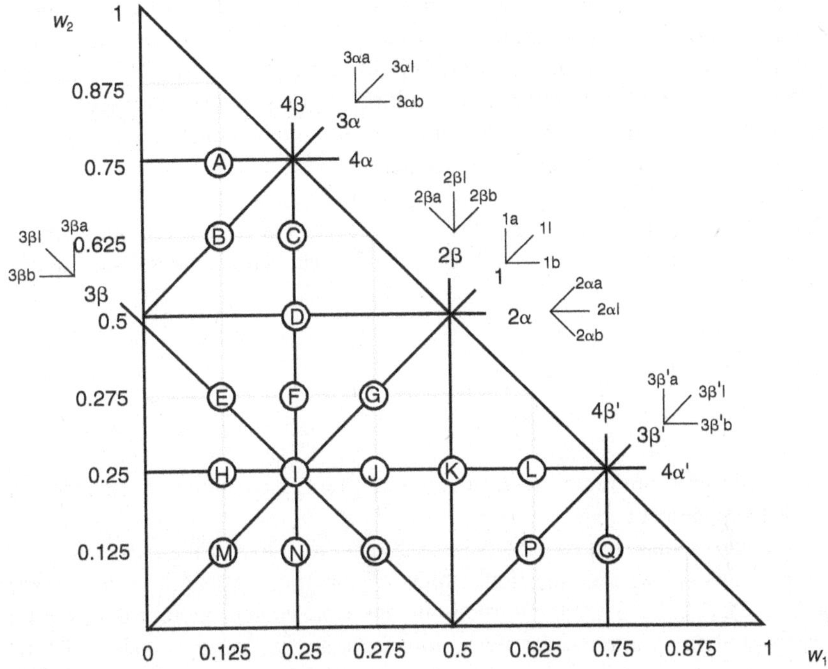


*Figure 7.2* Weights, sub-spaces and indifference lines (three criteria).

*Table 7.1* Reference points coordinates

| *Point* | *[w1; w2]* |
|---|---|
| S | [0.50; 0.50] |
| A | [0.125; 0.750] |
| B | [0.125; 0.620] |
| C | [0.250; 0.625] |
| D | [0.250; 0.500] |
| E | [0.125; 0.375] |
| F | [0.250; 0.375] |
| G | [0.375; 0.375] |
| H | [0.125; 0.250] |
| I | [0.250; 0.250] |
| J | [0.375; 0.250] |
| K | [0.500; 0.250] |
| L | [0.625; 0.250] |
| M | [0.125; 0.125] |
| N | [0.250; 0.125] |
| O | [0.375; 0.125] |
| P | [0.625; 0.125] |
| Q | [0.750; 0.125] |

points and indifference curves to consider but the more segmented the weight space is, the more sensibility and awareness is required of the decision-maker and the more steps are required to define each set of weights. The authors have opted for a set of 18 reference points (ten indifference curves and 8 × 0.125 sections on the domain of each weigh resulting in 16 weight sub-spaces). This choice results from the several applications of the method, and it is revealed to be an adequate compromise between accuracy and required information and workload.

For each pair of criteria, e.g. criteria 1 and criteria 2, the definition of the weights starts with the assessment of the relation between $w_1$ and $w_2$, specifically if:

1 $w_1/w_2 = 1$;
2 $w_1/w_2 > 1$; or
3 $w_1/w_2 < 1$.

These possibilities are represented by *a*, *b* or *I* (the last character on the index of the indifference lines).

This analysis does not require either the quantification of the parameters, or the direct answer to the question which of the three possibilities are more adequate. The choice is made indirectly by the expression of a pre-order relation between predefined alternatives that allow withdrawing the conclusion of how $w_1$ relates to $w_2$ in the mind of the decision-maker. Using the reasoning presented previously the alternatives to be subject to comparison should allow for this answer to be given.

For each indifference line, it is possible to build pairs of dummy alternatives so as their comparison will allow knowing which weight sub-space or indifference line is being implicitly selected by the decision-maker and, from there, elicit the set of weights for the criteria in question. Starting from an initial selected point the OPTIONCARDS process will narrow the weight possibilities through alternatives comparison until it converges to the final weight set. This last set will depend on all the pre-orders relations built in that round. When the answer indicates that one alternative is preferred to the other the process will continue but, from then on, considering the weight sub-space that is coherent with those preferences. When the answer indicates indifference between two alternatives the available weights from that point on will be within the indifference line. So, on each iteration, depending on the answers of the decision-maker, further constraints will be added, narrowing the sub-space of available weights and reducing the uncertainty about the weight parameters.

The pre-order relation between *X* and *Y* will dictate the results for the weights:

1 if *X* is indifferent to *Y*, $w_1/w_2 = 1$;
2 if *X* is preferred to *Y*, $w_1/w_2 > 1$; or
3 if *Y* is preferred to *X*, $w_1/w_2 < 1$.

The process can continue with a similar reasoning to the other indifference lines and other points, but additively considering the previous result as constraints.

The comparisons are made through a sequence of queries (Figure 7.3), each query being the comparison of two alternatives (pre-order relation). As each query results in an additional constraint the next query has to take this constraint into account and so it is possible to construct a query structure compatible with this framework (Figure 7.3). A set of queries will result in the definition of exact weights for the criteria under analysis. The process has to be applied for each group of sibling criteria, i.e. criteria which descend from the same aggregative criterion (node) in the value tree, so for each node in the value tree there is a set of queries that will result in the definition of the weights of the descendant criteria.

The process, for each node, can start at any of the reference points in the indifference lines. The authors opted for the reference point $S = [w1, w2, w3] = [50, 50, 0]$ so that the weights in question are $w_1$ and $w_2$. The OPTIONCARD containing the first alternatives to be compared is then presented (Figure 7.3). Depending on the given answers the base coordinate will move reflecting the implicit weights. The answer to the first query will define in which direction the decision-maker is moving (1a, 1b or 1I, Figure 7.2 and Figure 7.4) and that will determine what reference point, indifference line and OPTIONCARD is used in the following step. The number of nodes in the criteria tree determines the number of sets of queries. The number of queries within each set depends on the number of criteria in each node and then on the answers given.

At the end of each set of queries, the results will be one reference point. The weights to consider in the decision model can be those given exactly by the reference point coordinates or by the coordinates of any other point belonging to that weight sub-space.

The OPTIONCARDS method does not require the definition of the scoring function as it is based on the weights space and the scale used to present the alternative scores is the same for every criterion. The number of indifference lines and reference points will determine the level of uncertainty about the weights and the number of questions the decision-maker has to answer.

1 Comparing

X = [ 0 ; 20 ; 20 ] with Y = [ 20 ; 0 ; 20 ]

a) Indifferent – OptionCard 2 [1I]

b) Prefer X to Y – OptionCard 3 [1a]

c) Prefer Y to X – OptionCard 4 [1b]

*Figure 7.3* Example of an OPTIONCARD.

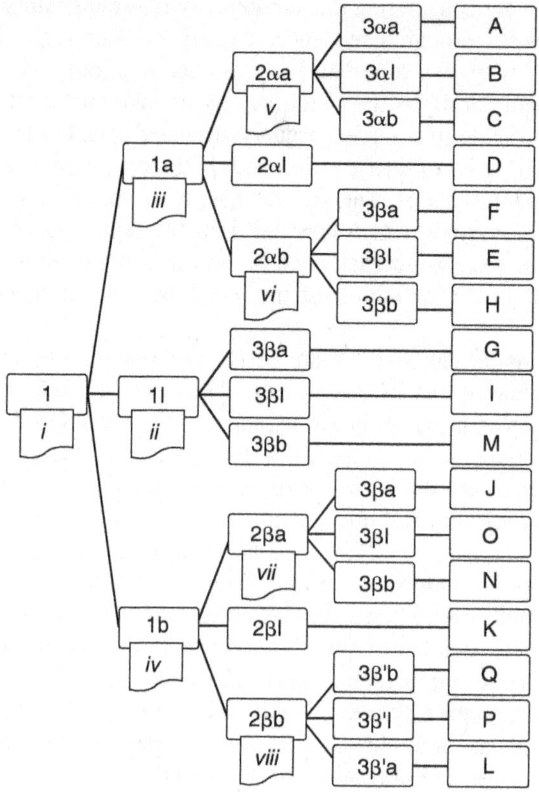


*Figure 7.4* Sequence of elicitation questions.

## 4 Conclusions

The concept of weight has been a pillar of the most challenging issue of MCDA: how important is each criterion for the decision-maker? However, this interrogation has shown to be more a source of further questions than answers. What is the meaning of importance? How can the decision-maker be helped to know how important is a criterion? How should such procedure and its protocol be built to be used as a tool for the learning process of the decision-maker? This explains the wide variety of proposed methods, but, unfortunately, most of them either ignore the complex nature of that basic interrogation or assume that the decision-maker is fully aware and clear about the answer.

Actually, such denial may produce equivocal or misleading conclusions inducing less rational behaviours. On the other hand, the adoption of the 'illuminated' assumption is in clear contradiction with the studies concerning real decision-makers. Moreover, if such assumption would be valid, MCDA would most likely be superfluous as the decision-maker would be able to rationalize the process of decision-making without additional support.

In this chapter, a new position is adopted, neither denying the complex and uncertain nature of the interrogation nor believing that the decision-maker is fully 'illuminated' about the issue.

The proposed method is based on a structured approach using pairwise comparison to help the decision-makers to develop a progressive, interactive and iterative learning process to improve his assessment about each weight, without aspiring to achieve a precise, accurate and unique value, but rather to identify the most appropriate range of acceptable values.

## References


[1] H. Simon (1969) *Science of the Artificial*, Cambridge, MA: MIT Press.

[2] R.L. Keeney and H. Raiffa (1976) *Decisions with Multiple Objectives*, New York: J. Wiley and Sons.

[3] J. Figueira, S. Greco and M. Ehrgott (eds) (2005) *Multiple Criteria Decision Analysis*, Springer.

[4] P.C. Fishburn (1970) *Utility Theory for Decision Making*, New York: Wiley.

[5] V. Belton and T. Stewart (2002) *Multiple Criteria Decision Analysis: An Integrated Approach*, Kluwer Academic Publishers.

[6] K. Borcherding, T. Eppel and D. von Winterfeldt (1991) Comparison of weights judgments in multi-attribute utility measurement, *Management Science*, 37(12): 1603–19.

[7] M. Riabacke, M. Danielson, L. Ekenberg and A. Larsson (2009) A Prescriptive approach for eliciting imprecise weight statements in an MCDA process, *Algorithmic Decision Theory*, 5783/2009: 168–79.

[8] F.H. Barron and B.E. Barret (1996) The efficacy of SMARTER: simple multi-attribute rating technique extended to ranking, *Acta Psychologica*, 93: 23–36.

[9] P.A. Bottomley, J.R. Doyle and R.H. Green (2000) Testing the reliability of weight elicitation methods: direct rating versus point allocation, *Journal of Marketing Research*, 37: 508–13.

[10] P.A. Bottomley and J.R. Doyle (2001) A comparison of three weight elicitation methods: good, better and best, *Omega*, 29: 553–60.

[11] F.H. Barron and B.E. Barret (1996) Decision quality using ranked attribute weights, *Management Science*, 42(11).

[12] B. Roy (1996) *Multi-criteria Methodology for Decision Aiding, Nonconvex Optimization and its Applications*, Dordrecht: Kluwer Academic Publishers.

[13] J.R. Figueira and B. Roy (2009) A note on the paper, 'Ranking irregularities when evaluating alternatives by using some ELECTRE methods', by Wang and Triantaphyllou, *Omega* (2008), *Omega*, 37: 731–3.

[14] X. Wang and E. Triantaphyllou (2008) Ranking irregularities when evaluating alternatives by using some ELECTRE methods, *Omega*, 36: 45–63.

[15] T.L. Saaty (1980) *The Analytic Hierarchy Process*, New York: McGraw-Hill.

[16] V. Mousseau (1992) Are judgements about relative importance of criteria dependent or independent of the set of alternatives? An experimental approach, Cahier du LAMSADE 111, Université de Paris Dauphine.

[17] Z. Shapira (1995) *Risk Taking: A Managerial Perspective*, New York: Russell Sage Foundation.

[18] A. Tversky and D. Kahneman (1981) The framing of decisions and the psychology of choices, *Science*, 211: 453–8.

[19] D. von Winterfeldt and W. Edwards (1986) *Decision Analysis and Behavioral Research*, Cambridge: Cambridge University Press.

[20] W. Edwards and F.H. Barron (1994) SMART and SMARTER: improved simple methods for multi-attribute utility measurement, *Organizational Behavior and Human Decision Processes*, 60: 306–25.

[21] W. Edwards and A. Tversky (1967) *Decision-making: Selected Readings*, Harmondsworth: Penguin.

[22] P.C. Fishburn (1977) Multi-criteria choice functions based on binary relations, *Operations Research*, 25: 989–1012.

[23] C.W. Kirkwood and R.K. Sarin (1985) Ranking with partial information: a method and an application, *Oper. Research*, 33: 38–48.

[24] L.V. Tavares (1984) The TRIDENT approach to rank alternative tenders for large engineering projects, *Foundations of Control Engineering*, 9(4): 181–93.

# 8 Is public procurement going green?

## Experiences and open issues

*Andrea Appolloni,*[1] *Alessio D'Amato*[2] *and Wenjuan Cheng*[3]

### 1 Introduction

Since the 1992 Conference on Environment and Development of the United Nations in Rio de Janeiro, sustainable development has been considered as a common goal for human beings by many countries throughout the world. Green Public Procurement (GPP) has been brought up for its remarkable potential contribution to such a goal. Green Public Procurement/Purchases encompasses all activities that aim to integrate environmental concerns into the purchasing process of public entities, which in turn impacts the whole production chain.

GPP means that purchasing agencies take into account environmental aspects when purchasing goods and services (Nissinen *et al.*, 2009) and, as a subset of sustainable procurement, it is considered as one of the key policies to promote changes of unsustainable consumption and production patterns (Tukker *et al.*, 2008; Clark, 2007).

Public purchasing is indeed a promising tool to boost the development of green procurement, as public authorities are at the same time responsible for environmental policy design and significant actors in green markets. In the latter respect, public purchasing accounts for around 16 per cent of the EU's GDP, with much larger shares in specific sectors, such as, for instance, IT, energy-efficient buildings and public transportation. Turning to single countries, in 2006 the Swedish authorities purchased goods and services totalling between 450 and 535 billion SEK, which corresponds to 15–18 per cent of annual GDP (Brännlund *et al.*, 2009). GPP development has another striking example in Germany where practical GPP guidelines have existed for almost 20 years (Gunther and Scheibe, 2006).

The European Commission (EC) is encouraging the deployment of cost-efficient GPP (European Commission, 2008a) and, in compliance with the EU's Integrated Product Policy (IPP), Member States have been encouraged to develop national action plans. As a result, the role that authorities play in procurement has grown in importance, at both national and EU levels. Nowadays, many countries have already adopted (at least preliminary) steps in the direction of greening public purchases (Li and Geiser, 2005). Crucial research questions arise:

1 Is GPP indeed an effective environmental policy rule?

2 How to shape GPP institutions in the broader public procurement setting?
3 How to measure the degree of 'greenness' of public procurement?

Starting from these questions we aim to provide food for thought on the design of public procurement and, where possible, to identify the relevance of such questions in the application of GPP by Italian authorities. Our focus cannot be on a comprehensive and detailed analysis of what is green and what is not in Italy. However, we will make a preliminary step in this direction, by summing up some desirable GPP experiences in the EU and in Italy and by highlighting some crucial open issues.

## 2 The legislation status

### *2.1 At the European Union (EU) level*

In 2001, EU published the Green Paper on Integrated Product Policy (IPP) and raised interest towards product-oriented environmental focus (European Commission, 2001). The aim of IPP is to reduce the environmental impacts of products throughout their life cycle, taking into consideration also the market and competitiveness concerns (European Commission, 2001, p. 6). Increased demand for greener products by GPP, in competition with the more traditional products, is well suited to this market oriented approach of IPP. Environmentally responsible public procurement can also be seen as a driving force in the integration of environmental policy instruments in the purchasing process (Li and Geiser, 2005). The preparation of new related directives in the EU between 2001 and 2004 fostered active debate regarding the possibility to use environmental grounds in public purchasing, and also the Organization for Economic Cooperation and Development provided a recommendation on GPP in 2002 (OECD, 2002), according to which the OECD member countries agreed to improve the environmental performance of public procurement.

In 2004, Directives 2004/17/EC and 2004/18/EC were approved by the European Parliament and the European Union Council of Ministers, with the aim of simplifying and modernizing procurement procedures, increasing competition and transparency, and explicitly including environmental criteria in the public purchases procedures. The very recent EU Public Procurement Directive Proposal (European Commission, 2011), which is expected to replace the 2004 Directives, reinforces the role of GPP as a key part of the Europe 2020 strategy and as one of the market-based instruments aimed at supporting a shift towards a resource efficient and low-carbon economy.

Also relevant to GPP is the publication of the Communication on Public Procurement for a Better Environment (European Commission, 2008a), which sets out to 'provide guidance on how to reduce the environmental impact caused by public sector consumption and to use GPP to stimulate innovation in environmental technologies, products and services'. Such Communication established, in particular, an ambitious (though indicative) target according to which 50 per cent of all public tendering procedures should have been compliant with core EU GPP criteria by 2010.

After such Directives and Communications, the EU renewed the Sustainable Development Strategy in 2006, and in 2008 the Sustainable Consumption and Production and Sustainable Industrial Policy Action Plan was published, aiming at improving the energy and environmental performance of products and at increasing the demand for more sustainable goods and production technologies. Along with the EU 2020 strategy, the Action Plan has set specific goals for the GPP in terms, for example, of energy saving and energy efficiency. More generally, the EU legislation on environmentally sustainable consumption and production has evolved rapidly in the last few years, together with the related (explicit or implicit) obligations for the public sector. Relevant examples include:

- energy end-use efficiency and energy services Directive (2006/32);
- waste Directive (2008/98), explicitly underlying the role played by public purchasing authorities in waste reduction and management;
- Directive on the promotion of clean and energy efficient road transport vehicles (2009/33);
- COM (2011) 109, setting out an energy efficiency plan explicitly accounting for a key role to be played by public purchasing authorities and with a particular focus in public building restructuring and adoption of sustainability enhanced criteria.

Besides the guidelines, which aim at instructing the practices of GPP, in 2006 Public Procurement Remedies Directives (Directives 89/665/EEC and 92/13/EEC) have been revised, in order to improve the effectiveness of national review procedures for the award of public contracts. Directive 2007/66/EC provides for rules aiming at obtaining a clear and effective procedure for bidders who consider contracts have been unfairly awarded to seek redress. The Directive gives to the rejected bidders the opportunity to start an effective and timely review procedure, when unfair decisions can still be corrected, and also seeks to combat illegal direct awards of public contracts, considered as the most serious infringement of EU procurement law.

Clearly, a crucial issue in the process of reshaping public purchases is related to the assessment of what can be considered good or acceptable under an environmental perspective (Larsen and Svane, 2005) and to the evaluation of whether such assessment should be expanded to other relevant dimensions. Significant complications would indeed arise as a result of a wider focus, taking into account a broader set of objectives. The tools to be developed are expected to vary, for example, if we somewhat limit our attention to issues related to environmental consciousness in public purchases or if, more broadly, we choose to also account for other social and ethical problems, such as deprivation, human health etc.

The appropriate definitions as well as the optimal degree of integration of environmental issues in the more general development strategies of countries are outside the scope of this chapter. We only point out that the more ambitious the definition, the more difficult the related implementation. Indeed, we can expect that a broader set of objectives might be related to a larger complexity and to the possibility of several trade offs arising.

Although we recognize that the environment is not the only crucial dimension to be accounted for in discussing the desirable design of public procurement procedures, we deem the achievement of an overall rethinking of public purchases as a long-term objective, and we will focus our attention on the 'narrower' concept of GPP in the rest of our work.

## *2.2 Domestic laws and regulations*

In Italy, the Public Procurement Code (approved by Legislative Decree April 12, 2006, no. 163, which entered into force on July 1, 2006 – hereinafter referred to as the 'Code') governs public procurement. The Code has put together the previous Italian pieces of legislation on public procurement into one single text. As far as its scope is concerned, the Code covers public works contracts, public supply contracts and public service contracts.

Coherent with the EU legislation, a National Action Plan (NAP) on GPP has been adopted in 2008; this plan is being implemented by an inter-ministerial committee and is being supported by an advisory board, consisting of a body of representatives which includes scientists and stakeholders from all the involved sectors. The NAP establishes three main goals for GPP in Italy:

- efficient usage and saving of natural resources, especially energy;
- waste reduction;
- reduction in hazardous substances use.

Also, it requires that at least 30 per cent of goods purchased by public administration comply with ecological criteria and at least 30–40 per cent features reduced electricity consumption. The NAP defines strict core criteria for GPP, leaving however space for adjustment through specific requirements concerning single issues (tender design, minimum requirements, etc.). Subsequent decrees by the Italian government introduce explicit provisions concerning tender design issues.

Relevant examples in this respect include:

- D.P.R. n. 205/2010: art. 6 amends the Code by introducing art. 180 bis concerning the role of public administrations in promoting initiatives to boost reuse and recycling of waste.
- D.P.R. n. 207/2010: art. 120 introduces the obligation for public purchasers to include environmental criteria in evaluating the most economically advantageous offer (see below).

Other decrees were also approved between 2009 and 2011, to ratify existing EU Directives as well as to regulate specific issues (for example in October 2010 and in February 2011 minimum requirements concerning specific goods and services were introduced).

## 3 Is GPP an effective environmental policy tool?

A first broad question which is somewhat in the background of our chapter is related to the effectiveness of GPP in obtaining environmental policy objectives (energy savings, waste and pollution reduction, etc.) As Brännlund *et al.* (2009) underline, though generally regarded as an effective means to secure environmental improvements, GPP has been little studied within a framework of welfare economics. From this perspective the authors assess GPP as an environmental policy tool and compare it to other tools, such as taxes. Effectiveness and efficiency of environmental policy instruments is the subject of a substantial amount of literature (see, among others, Tietenberg and Lewis, 2009). Brännlund *et al.* (2009) show that the standard cost-effectiveness argument (equalization of marginal costs of environmental care) is likely to be violated by GPP procedures, while other instruments (pollution permits, environmental taxation) are, at least theoretically, capable of achieving an efficient (i.e. least cost) outcome, for a given environmental target. An example in this respect can be based on the uniformity of environmental requirements across potential tender participants. As a result of such uniformity heterogeneities across participants are not exploited and marginal costs are not equalized. Such inefficiency is however somewhat reduced if we focus on awarding criteria: giving the same weight to environmental performance implies that firms featuring smaller marginal costs of environmental protection will be able to offer, *ceteris paribus*, a better deal, improving the efficiency of the tendering process.

Turning to the impact of GPP on market competition, Brännlund *et al.* (2009) have underlined that it is a purely empirical question. The net outcome is in fact difficult to establish theoretically, and it is likely to be market specific. Also, the impact on price can be counterintuitive, i.e. a larger competition might be coupled with higher prices, due, for example, to adjustment costs by bidding firms. Reverting again to the environmental requirements example, stricter environmental conditions will imply more or less competition depending on the number and size of firms that gets out of the tendering process (as they do not meet the required standards) or choose to participate (as they are capable of complying with the standards).

Finally, in the reduction of the environmental impact of public purchases the authors show that GPP can be linked in a very weak way to environmental improvements, as procurement procedures are likely to account for such improvements in an 'indirect way'.

These considerations suggest that further theoretical and empirical research is needed to investigate the proper role of public procurement in coping with environmental issues. As Walker and Phillips (2006) underline, the majority of sustainable supply research has been conducted in the private sector, though (mainly empirical) literature on the greening of public purchase is growing.[4]

A general conclusion would suggest that GPP is more likely to be an efficient policy choice in sectors where standard environmental policy instruments are difficult to be implement and/or are in their very early stages. Also, we can expect it to be fruitful when it is introduced in sectors characterized by relatively new technologies (recycling, renewable energy), where the exploitation of economies of scale and scope is necessary to improve the competitiveness of firms operating in such sectors. On the other hand, we deem as very unlikely the chance for GPP to be an effective policy tool in sectors where public intervention is already well established. However, as the judgment of GPP as an effective and efficient policy tool is necessarily based on a case-by-case analysis, we can conclude that a first open issue arising from our chapter is related to the need of assessing welfare effects of existing and future GPP practices in Italy.

## 4 Green practices in the EU and in Italy

### *4.1 Good environmental GPP practices in the EU*

Several examples of GPP implementation in the EU suggest that a significant effort is being devoted to progress along the GPP pathway.

The EU Commission has published a guidebook in several languages (European Commission, 2004), and national guidebooks have also been published (e.g. in Finland in 2004).

Also, the EC with Communication 400 in 2008 focuses on the removal of obstacles to a full implementation of GPP procedures in the EU. Several hurdles are identified under this respect, including:

- limited established environmental criteria for products/services as well as the absence of publicity mechanisms;
- insufficient information on life cycle costing of products and the relative costs of environmentally friendly products/services;
- low awareness of the benefits of environmentally friendly products and services;
- uncertainty about legal possibilities to include environmental criteria in tender documents;
- lack of political support and resources.

The Communication then sets out objectives, funding as well as core sectors. In targets setting, a major role is acknowledged to several Member States who took the lead in promoting GPP practices. For example, the Dutch government has set a 100 per cent Sustainable Procurement target to be reached by 2010; the Austrian government has identified ambitious targets to be met by 2010 for relevant sectors, such as IT, electricity and paper. France has set equivalent, though apparently less ambitious, targets in terms of ‘clean’ vehicles. Finally, the Sustainable Procurement Action Plan in the UK aims to reduce the government’s carbon emissions by 30 per cent by 2020.

Significant guidance is provided by the EU. We do not go into details.[5] However, it could be useful to provide additional details on the actual implementation status in the EU as well as to exemplify how green criteria are currently integrated into the public procurement procedures (see Table 8.1).

*Table 8.1* Priority sectors and green criteria in selected sectors

| | *Product group* | *Product* | *Core criteria* | *Comprehensive criteria* |
|---|---|---|---|---|
| 1 | Cleaning products and services | Cleaning services (including cleaning products) | • Use of cleaning products without hazardous substances | • Training of employees<br>• Use of reusable microfibre clothing and/or dry-cleaning techniques |
| 2 | Construction | New buildings and offices | • Consideration of energy – saving measures in design and usage phase of building<br>• Water-saving technologies in kitchen and sanitary facilities<br>• Use of material without hazardous substances<br>• Use of timber from legal sources | • Use of localization renewable energy sources |
| 3 | Electricity | Electricity | • 50% or higher electricity from renewable energy sources | • 100% electricity from renewable energy sources |
| 4 | Catering and food | Catering services (including food) | • Organic production of food products<br>• Use of seasonal fruit, vegetable and fish | |
| 5 | Gardening | Gardening services and machinery | • Fuel type use of gardening machines<br>• Use of soil improvement without peat and sewage sludge | |
| 6 | Office IT equipment | Computers (desktops and laptops) and monitors | • Energy star standards<br>• Accessibility and changeability of memory hard disks and/or CD/DVD drives | |
| 7 | Paper | Copying and graphic paper | • Production from recovered paper fibres<br>• Use of ECF/TCF paper<br>• Pulp production from sustainable managed forests for paper based on virgin fibres | |
| 8 | Textiles | Clothing | • Oko–Tex Standard 100 | |
| 9 | Transport | Passengers cars and light duty vehicles | • Maximum $CO_2$ emission per vehicle segment<br>• Euro 5 standard | |
| 10 | Furniture | Office furniture | • Use of wood from legally sources timber and sustainably managed forests | |

Source: PricewaterhouseCoopers *et al.* (2009).

Table 8.1 sums up core and comprehensive criteria related to a selected set of sectors and green environmental targets. Core targets address the most significant environmental impacts, and are relatively easily verifiable, while comprehensive targets are related to the achievement of more ambitious objectives which require more effort and more difficult verification. Such targets are coherent with the GPP training toolkit developed by the EU.

PricewaterhouseCoopers *et al.* (2009) provide details on the status of actual implementation of GPP practices in the so-called Green-7 countries (Austria, Denmark, Finland, Germany, the Netherlands, Sweden and the UK). Figures 8.1 and 8.2 represent the relative relevance of core and comprehensive criteria in terms of value and the number of contracts respectively.

As it clearly emerges, the Green-7 countries accounted, on average, for around 45 per cent of the total value and 55 per cent of the total number of contracts in 2006/7.

The same report underlines how GPP procedures in the Green-7 have generated significant environmental gains, at least in terms of $CO_2$ emissions, that on average have been reduced by 25 per cent with a maximum of -47 per cent in the Netherlands (see Figure 8.3).

Also, we can conclude that the evaluated GPP procedures have made win-win improvements in several cases, i.e. they also generated significant financial gains in terms of cost reduction.

Finally, PricewaterhouseCoopers *et al.* (2009) focus on the combination of $CO_2$ and financial impact, and conclude that transport, construction and electricity

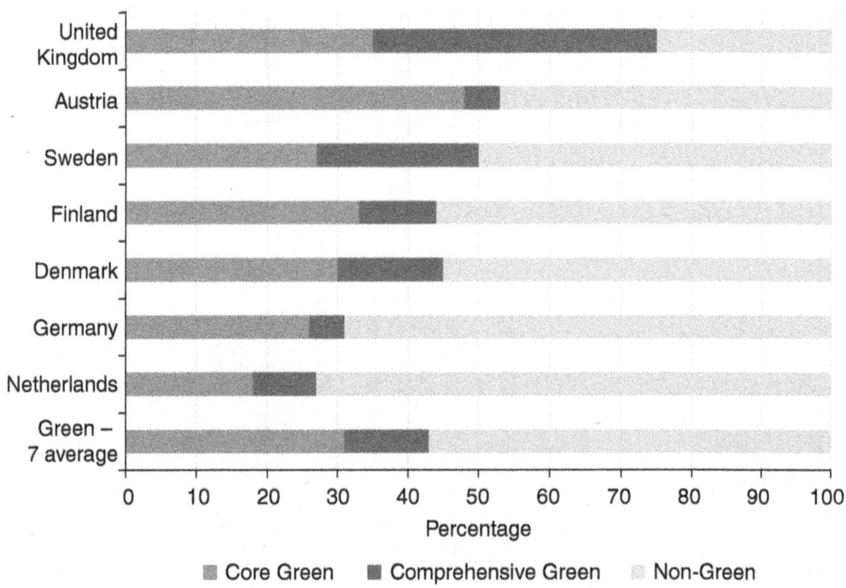


*Figure 8.1* Relevance of GPP on total public procurement in terms of value (source: PricewaterhouseCoopers *et al.*, 2009).

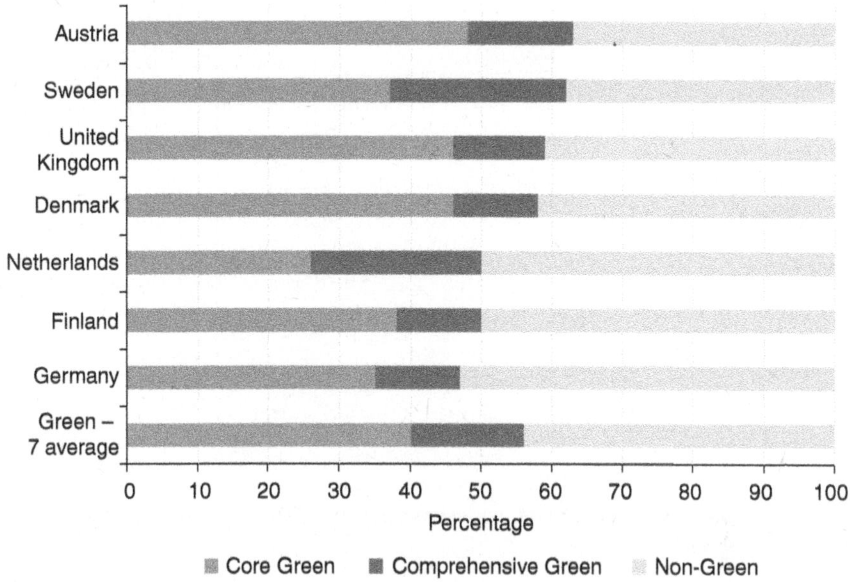


*Figure 8.2* Relevance of GPP on total public procurement in terms of the number of contracts (source: PricewaterhouseCoopers *et al.*, 2009).

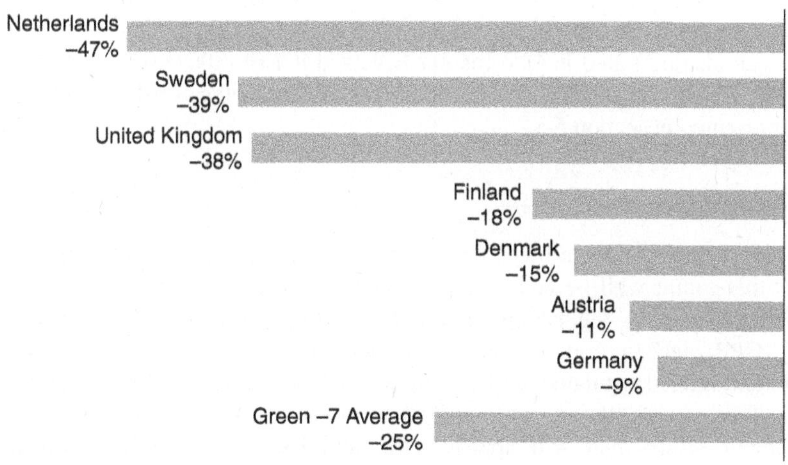


*Figure 8.3* $CO_2$ impact of GPP per country (source: PricewaterhouseCoopers *et al.*, 2009).

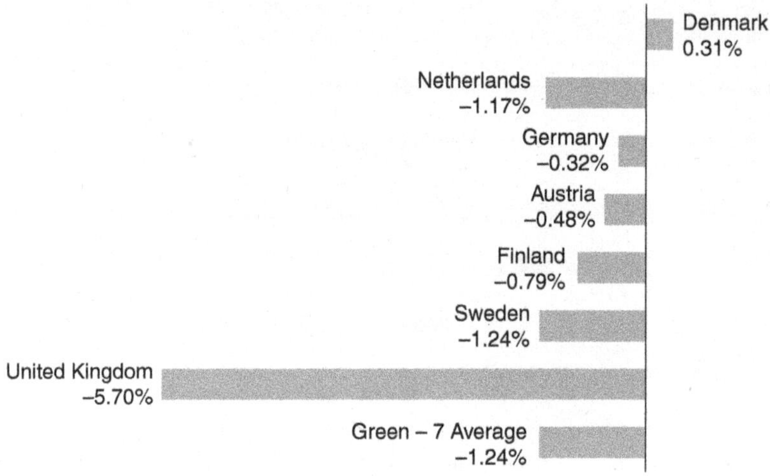


*Figure 8.4* Financial impact of GPP per country (source: PricewaterhouseCoopers *et al.*, 2009).

are sectors that deserve attention from the public procurement authorities, as they appear to be the most cost-effective in terms of the reduction of environmental impact per euro spent. Additional, more detailed assessments of the status of GPP implementation in the EU are out of the scope of this chapter, and can be found, among others, in AEA (2010), while a detailed analysis of the related costs and benefits can also be found in Öko-Institut E.V. and ICLEI (2007) with reference to 2006/7.[6] Also, additional evidence, mainly referring to the Nordic countries, will be presented in section 5.3.

### *4.2 GPP implementation in Italy*

As the last section has clarified, GPP brings about significant environmental benefits that might well be coupled with financial gains to contracting authorities. Turning to Italy, legislation has progressed towards a larger implementation of GPP, and several aspects of public purchases are now subject to environment related regulation and incentives. The current status of GPP in Italy appears, however, scattered, with several virtuous cases but compliance and management efforts that still appear weak and lacking a kind of national coordination. As a result, it is difficult to provide a comprehensive idea of the development of GPP in Italy. However, several examples can be provided, to give a flavour of how matters are developing.

Consip S.p.a. is a first significant example; Consip is a public stock company owned by the Italian Ministry of the Economy and Finance (MEF) that operates on behalf of the state, within the framework of the strategic guidelines and tasks given by MEF itself.[7]

Consip has no profit goals and deals with two main fields of action:

1 consultancy on technical and organizational projects;
2 set up, diffusion and support on e-procurement system and tools.

Under an environment/sustainability point of view, several specific initiatives have been undertaken over time by Consip, including IT and energy efficiency related projects. Table 8.2 shows an application of environmental criteria to IT procurement according to Consip strategies. As it clearly emerges, sustainability criteria are accounted for in the whole life cycle of IT machineries, from the design and the production phase, down to the end of life and the management of the related waste.

The estimated environmental impact and cost savings are significant. For example, improved energy efficiency is expected to bring about around €1,575 million in terms of cost savings.[8]

Another example might be found in the framework contract on 'Integrated Energy Management Services' (heating services including improvement of energy efficiency, consumption reduction and $CO_2$ emissions avoidance) launched by Consip[9] in 2006. The tendering process was an open procedure with 12 lots awarded to five different suppliers; the framework was awarded on the basis of the most economically advantageous tender (MEAT), with 70 per cent of marks allocated to price and 30 per cent to quality. Significant effects have been obtained both in terms of cost savings (27 per cent, involving approximately 5,000 buildings) and in terms of energy savings (around 6,000 tonnes of oil equivalent).

Several other GPP initiatives have been implemented in Italy. These include, among others:

- The ARPAT (Agenzia Regionale per la Protezione Ambientale della Toscana, the Environmental Protection Agency in Tuscany), where a pilot GPP project for cleaning services for two of its 19 offices was introduced in 2004. Due to the results, in March 2009, the procedure was replicated on a broader scale to encompass all of its offices. The procurement was an open procedure for a three-year contract worth €2.2 million – 11 bids were submitted.

*Table 8.2* Consip approach to GPP in IT public procurement

| Design | Production |
|---|---|
| • Increase of energy efficiency<br>• Cost reduction<br>• Environmental impact reduction | • Reduction/elimination of use of hazardous substances<br>• Decrease of environmental impacts<br>• Optimization of carriage packaging |
| • Correct energy use management<br>• Information management on environmental impacts<br>• Use of alternative sources of energy | • Reuse<br>• Recycling<br>• Disassembly of equipment<br>• Recycling of consuming materials |
| Use | End of life |

Source: Capparelli (2011).

- The Municipality of Rome, in 2001, began a programme called 'Sustainable Food Procurement for Schools in Rome' in 2001 which aimed to support organic agriculture and organic food chains, and its most recent call for tender for the school food service covers the period September 2007 to June 2012 and has a base value of approximately €355 million. This programme has improved the market in terms of sustainability by procuring organic agriculture products and in turn has reduced the environmental impact of food production and the related activities.[10]

All the above pieces of evidence, though not exhaustive, have the merit to show that GPP is increasingly adopted in Italy.[11] On the other hand, several issues have yet to be addressed.

## 5 GPP: open issues

### *5.1 The degree of centralization*

#### *5.1.1 GPP and functional centralization*

Accord to Martimort (1996), the allocation of jurisdictions across governmental agencies can be analysed by means of models dealing with multiple principals in the presence of asymmetric information.

Indeed, government authorities cannot be viewed as a unique body pursuing a common objective but, rather, as a set of entities with different and somewhat diverging objectives. Also, the design of regulatory tools must be implemented in the real world, where there are significant informational asymmetries between regulated firms and government bodies.

In this respect, the example of GPP is straightforward: price reduction and environmental quality of tender outcomes are competing objectives that might be potentially pursued by competing authorities. It is therefore meaningful to investigate the costs and benefits related to the separation of duties among several regulators and/or the integration of functions in a single authority.

Baron (1985) models a regulatory setting close to the US framework, where a Public Utility Commission is interested in the welfare of an individual state's consumers and taxpayers but is also interested in the profit of the regulated firm(s) located in the same state, while a Federal Environmental Protection Agency is interested in welfare effects related to the environmental impact of regulated firms' activity at the whole country (i.e. federal) level. In Baron's setting an institutional ordering of jurisdictions is assumed, so that the Environmental Protection Agency is capable of free-riding on the regulatory design (and costs) imposed at a state level by the Public Utility Commission; as a result, environmental protection is stronger when the two authorities act in an independent way. Opposite results are obtained by Martimort (1996), where no ordering of jurisdictions is introduced: in a hidden information (i.e. adverse selection) context, both regulators design their intervention in order to free-ride as much as possible on the capability of the other regulator's contribution to guarantee that a socially desirable project is indeed undertaken, leading to suboptimal equilibria and a lower likelihood that the beneficial project is performed.

D'Amato (2006) models a GPP setting (including also the possibility of moral hazard), where the environmental quality of public purchases changes under two possible institutional frameworks: a centralized one, where a single regulator is in charge of both production efficiency and environmental quality, and a decentralized one, where two separate bodies operate, namely an environmental agency securing environmental quality and a procurement agency pursuing efficiency. The main conclusion is that decentralization results in a downward distortion in environmental quality as compared to the case of a single integrated authority.

A conclusion stemming from the above papers is, again, that more applied research is needed. Indeed, the institutional scenario might change across countries and sectors, so that countries like the United States feature a federal-level EPA and state-level public utilities regulation while in other countries such as Italy no such ordering exists. Further, some of the standards for environmental quality in GPP might be set at a EU level while other environmental as well as non-environmental requirements might be set by Italian and other Member States government bodies. The assessment of the optimal regulatory setting can therefore be expected to be country and sector specific, and the theoretical analysis presented can be deemed only as a starting point towards a full understanding of the needed steps to achieve the best possible integration of powers in GPP management and design.

### *5.1.2 GPP and 'demand' centralization*

Demand centralization/decentralization is another hot issue in the shaping of the Italian procurement procedures that might have a significant impact in terms of environmental quality. Currently, there is no constraint for public purchasers to act in a cooperative way. As a result, several local bodies might be in charge of public procurement to satisfy local needs.

According to Albano and Sparro (2010), the main economic justification for public purchases centralization can be found in the need to reduce the related costs. It is a fact that several countries feature government level procurement agencies (the United States and the UK being two important examples). Cost savings are mainly related to the ability to reduce the buying price as well as to the reduction in transaction costs.

Under the first respect, a major role is played by the possibility to exploit the significant economies of scale that tender participants are likely to experience due to a larger production level, as well as the increased bargaining power the contracting authority would get by holding a sort of monopsony power.

On the other hand, the reduction in costs might also be related to the achievement of transaction cost reductions related to 'optimal' procurement process via specialization, investments in infrastructures (for example e-procurement tools), etc.

The impact of public procurement centralization can be significant also in terms of innovation. Indeed, public procurement might 'correct' the market outcome by internalizing positive externalities stemming from innovation, in a kind of 'market pull' approach. Such an approach would have the merit of providing firms developing new products and processes with less uncertainty in their potential market, therefore reducing the risk related to R&D investments. In this respect, environmental innovations and the reduction in the related risk are an important example. Also, in the presence of network effects, green purchases might boost a 'new' and/or environmental market by sustaining a learning by doing process on the demand side. More generally, as already suggested, centralizing public purchases might make it more likely that minimum production scales are reached in innovative sectors.

Another impact of public procurement centralization in innovative sectors is related to the expenses in financing R&D as well as educational programmes, which needs substantial budgets to be properly implemented.

Other significant reasons that might affect the way in which GPP translates into a better environmental quality are linked to the degree of positive or negative externalities stemming from public purchases. A first consideration under this respect suggests that a local authority might be willing to internalize pollution damages only to a very limited extent when the pollution problem at hand is of a regional or global nature (such as $CO_2$), i.e. it mainly generates damages far from the source. This raises significant free-riding incentives, leading to too little weight potentially given to environmental quality in the awarding criteria and too weak environmental requirements to access the tendering process.

Another important issue has to do with the time horizon of procurement authorities and to the weight assigned to future benefits and costs (as measured by the discount rate). Consider the example of the functional obsolescence of the objects of a tendering process. A small purchasing authority is very likely not to have the specialized and highly qualified know-how that would be needed to account for the proper discount rate to perform a rigorous analysis of the costs and benefits related to obsolescence. Also, we can expect a smaller authority to have a smaller time horizon with respect to a larger authority. This is likely to lead smaller authorities to choose a suboptimal obsolescence and to put an inefficiently small weight on the duration of the procured good, leading to a larger than efficient impact on the environment. A straightforward example is related to IT purchases. A too large discount rate (a larger impatience) and a smaller time horizon would lead to buying cheaper computers featuring a quicker obsolescence, implying larger impacts on virgin material as well as a larger waste production.

Of course, procurement centralization also features significant difficulties, including the possibility of larger tenders to exclude smaller firms and, above all, the risk of lock-in related to the repeated nature of the procurement process. Also, a centralized procurement design might imply a lower capability of public purchasing authorities to account for local specificities in demand. Costs and benefits must therefore be carefully evaluated. However, the environmental benefits of centralization might be worth the effort of designing procurement procedures in such a way to avoid lock-in or 'excess scale' problems, for example through the adoption of multiple lots tenders and limits to the number of contracts that can be awarded to each winner.[12]

## *5.2 How to put the environment in public procurement strategies?*

According to Piga and Zanza (2004), the design of public procurement involves several steps, including the number of lots, the length of the contract as well as participation requirements and awarding criteria.

We will focus in this section on two crucial parts of the tendering process design in the shaping of GPP procedures, namely requirements and award criteria.

### *5.2.1 Selection of participants*

As Palmujoki *et al.* (2010) point out, a first possibility for public contracting authorities to include environmental quality in tendering processes is by setting it as a prequalification of bidders, as mandatory requirements for the contract, or as contractual terms. Some examples in this respect include:

- the exclusion of companies that have acted against environmental legislation or regulations;
- the inclusion of green considerations in the technical capacity criteria in terms of the past experience of companies and of the professional qualifications of their personnel;
- the inclusion of environmental management systems, such as EMAS, or other eco-labels, such as the EU Ecolabel, as a means of proof for that technical capacity.

More generally, the selection of participants is an important albeit complex phase of GPP design. Indeed, several difficulties can be identified. First of all, according to EU legislation, mandatory requirements cannot be discriminatory, so that if, for example, the technical specifications imply that the EU Ecolabel is enough to guarantee technical capability, potential participants must be admitted also on the basis of other, equivalent, proofs of the same capability.

The following table represents a good example of 'green tenders' design using the EU Ecolabel. As it clearly emerges from the table, the use of an Ecolabel must guarantee that no discrimination takes place among bidders based exclusively on the Ecolabel itself.

Also, important trade-offs are involved at this stage, the most relevant being tight requirements vs. competition; for example, stricter technical specifications might imply that potential bidders are excluded from the tender, reducing the number of potential participants and, therefore, the degree of competition. This is why, in some cases, the tendering process can introduce mild environmental

*Table 8.3* Using the European Ecolabel in GPP

| *Using the European Ecolabel in GPP* | | |
|---|---|---|
| | *Right* | *Wrong* |
| Specification | All offered cleaning must meet the ecological criteria of the European Ecolabel | All offered cleaning products must carry the European Ecolabel |
| Verification | Products carrying the European Ecolabel will be deemed to comply. Any other appropriate means of proof will also be accepted, such as the technical dossier of the manufacturer or a test report from a recognized body | The products must carry a European Ecolabel |
| Award criteria | Additional points will be awarded to products that meet the ecological criteria of the European Ecolabel | Additional points will be awarded to the products that carry the European Ecolabel |

Source: EC (2008b).

prerequisites and choose, instead, to use stricter environmental standards in the awarding criteria. This has been the case in the design of recent IT tenders held by the Italian public purchasing agency CONSIP.

### *5.2.2 Awarding criteria*

Turning to awarding criteria themselves, they are indeed viewed as a crucial step in the design of any public procurement tender, and they can be very fruitfully used to address environmental issues. The existing public procurement Directives clarify that contracts awarding might be based on two main options, i.e.:

- the lowest price;
- the most economically advantageous tender (MEAT).

The first one only awards the contract to the bidder that succeeds in making the least costly offer, while in the second case a 'scoring rule' can be implemented, including criteria other than the price in the score according to which the contract is awarded.

Clearly, if the environment is an issue, using the lowest price as the only awarding procedure requires the other phases of the tender to be properly designed (for example in terms of technical specifications), while the MEAT implies that bidding can be left open to competition while the environment can be judged in the awarding procedure. On the other hand, the MEAT appears to leave discretionary power in setting the scoring rule, with the risk of not accounting for the environment properly. As a result, there is no one-size-fits-all solution under this respect.

If the environment is included in the awarding criteria according to the MEAT, then the contracting authorities have to set out both the environmental characteristics and their scores in the call for tenders. Such scores must be publicly available and transparent; also, they have to be objectively quantifiable. Though such goals make it clear how difficult setting awarding criteria can be, commonly used procedures exist. Indeed, as the EC (2008a) suggests, a widely used methodology is Life Cycle Costing (LCC), properly including:

- purchase and all associated costs (delivery, installation, commissioning, etc.);
- operating costs, including energy, spares and maintenance;
- end-of-life costs, such as decommissioning and removal.

The adoption of LCC and, more generally, a life cycle approach to GPP can lead to significant cost savings in the public procurement procedures, a higher energy efficiency of buildings and IT equipment being two possible examples.

An evaluation of the relevance of awarding criteria in environmentally related public procurement procedures can be found in Kippo-Edlund *et al.* (2005). Using data collected in spring 2003, the authors conclude that 58 per cent of the Swedish tender calls included some kind of environmental criteria, but only 36 per cent included environmental award criteria. Environmental aspects were considered also in selection criteria (36 per cent of tender calls), technical specifications (39 per cent) and contract clauses (12 per cent). Another contribution, more focused on the role played by environmental considerations in MEAT, is the one by Parikka-Alhola *et al.* (2006); using data collected in the period 21 July–29 September 2005 in three Nordic countries (Denmark, Finland and Sweden), the authors find that the total price of the purchase accounts (on average) for 50 per cent of the awarding scores whereas quality accounts for 37 per cent of the scores. In addition, delivery and contractual terms are worth 7 per cent of scores and the environment is weighted on average 3.3 per cent of the scores. This suggests the interesting result that a bidder that accounts properly for environmental criteria can on average charge a price that is 3.3 per cent larger than a bidder that does not achieve good environmental scores. This is relevant information, as it suggests that some (although limited) gain can be obtained from making a greener bid.

Other examples confirming the tendency of GPP to focus on awarding criteria as one of the tools to provide incentives to environmentally friendly bids can be found in examples already reported in Section 4.2. Having said of the relative weight of energy efficiency in the Consip framework contract on 'Integrated Energy Management Services', it is also interesting to note that in the GPP example related to sustainable food procurement for schools in Rome, the awarding criteria specify that slightly less than half of the score (49 points) is supposed to be assigned according to quality, including environmental criteria. An even clearer example can be found in the copying paper procurement framework contract designed in the Lombardy region in Italy. Award criteria include in this case the possibility to assign 20 technical points to competitors offering:[14]

- paper with FSC, PEFC, Blaue Engel, EU Ecolabel, Nordic Swan or equivalent certification;
- advance notice of delivery by email;
- use of a delivery service with green vehicles assessed through random checks on registration documents;
- use of a delivery service with green pallets (FSC or equivalent certification).

Finally, as clarified in Table 8.3, it is crucial to underline the need for awarding criteria to be designed in such a way as to be non-discriminatory. The related considerations made in discussing participants' selection also apply here.

### *5.3 Measuring the 'greenness' of public procurement: methodologies and further research*

The last issue we are willing to address is related to the need to measure whether public procurement is indeed green or sustainable. This is a challenging task for several reasons, mainly related to the difficulties in providing an objective (e.g. monetary) measure for certain kinds of environmental damages, as well as to the complexities related to the need of disentangling green characteristics from 'non-green' ones. For example, while it is relatively easy to spread the good news about improved energy efficiency and in terms of reduced (estimated) $CO_2$ emissions, it is not as easy to disseminate evidence concerning reduction in life expectancy and the related social losses.

A somewhat different hurdle lies in the very limited amount of available literature on the topic. More precisely, while several papers address the qualitative impacts and the design of public procurement procedures, very little effort has been devoted to the measurement of the degree of 'greenness' of public (as well as private) purchases (Walker and Phillips, 2006). Significant exceptions, however, exist.

The received literature has measured the state of GPP through the use of environmental criteria in tender calls and documents (Bouwer *et al.*, 2005; Kippo-Edlund *et al.*, 2005); most of these contributions are, however, focused on Nordic countries. In a more recent contribution (Palmujoki *et al.*, 2010), the authors focus specifically on the existence and applicability of environmental criteria in the procurement contracts and discuss the comprehensiveness and enforceability of the drafted terms and conditions in the same contracts, highlighting the practices that appear as the most functional and practical from the procuring authorities' point of view. As the authors show, with reference to Sweden and Finland, the application of GPP is increasing over time. However, the inclusion of environmental clauses in procurement contracts is still not widely used. Also, the clauses vary widely in terms of both accuracy and enforceability by the procurement authorities.

The above literature is mainly based on tender calls analysis. As Bouwer *et al.* (2005) underline, such analysis is mainly performed by gathering tender related documents along a chosen time span from a variety of public bodies (local authorities, central government, hospitals, etc.), and by classifying them according to product groups and according to the role played by environmental criteria in the tender documents, technical specification, awarding score and criteria, etc.

Though objective, such a methodology suffers from several limitations, including:

1. Information contained in the tender document has to be complemented by the actual awarding results (winner, value of purchases, etc.).
2. The publication of tenders is compulsory only above a certain tender value (so-called 'above the EU threshold' tenders). On the other hand, very limited information is available concerning smaller tenders.
3. Information on the purchasing body can be crucial in explaining green behaviour and in directing the related policy interventions. On the other hand, such information is in general not included in the tender and difficult to obtain.
4. The willingness to pay for greener public purchases might not be the only determinant of demand for sustainable goods/services by public bodies. Indeed, EU regulation and targets might affect the observed GPP related demand.

These difficulties suggest the need to complement tender documents analysis with interviews that complete the available information, including details both on the public bodies involved in the specific tender and on the final outcome of the tender itself. An online procedure based on questionnaires has been used, among others, by PricewaterhouseCoopers *et al.* (2009), in the report on GPP that was presented in Section 4.1 concerning the EU.

Of course, the use of questionnaires also has limitations, as they can lead to a bias in the respondent's reaction (they can state they are willing to pay for green purchases just to show they act in a socially responsible way, or they can give a distorted view of the purchasing organization they work for). Also, it is more likely that a selection bias takes place, as respondents are likely to come from organizations that are already involved, or more willing to be involved, in GPP.

## 6 Concluding remarks

Green Public Procurement can be (and has proven to be) a potentially very effective tool in the context of environmental policy, leading in some cases to win-win situations where the reduction in environmental impacts of public purchases is coupled with a reduction in the related costs. This is, however, not a general conclusion, so that the opportunity of introducing GPP targets and incentives must be carefully evaluated with sector and country specific analyses. Also, the performance of GPP depends in a crucial way on how it is designed and, specifically, on the degree of centralization and on the way environmental criteria are accounted for along the 'GPP chain'. In the latter respect, the inclusion of environmental considerations in awarding criteria can play a significant role and is, therefore, a sensitive issue for future research.

The main conclusion that stems from our work suggests the need to improve data availability to make GPP design and implementation more efficient. This is straightforward if we look at the Italian case: the building up of comprehensive datasets might be crucial in determining whether the current system is properly designed or if changes in design are needed, for example in terms of a larger degree of centralization. Also, measuring the degree to which GPP is indeed green and/or sustainable needs a substantial systematization of available information on tender calls, value and features of procurement contracts. This is a key issue to measure the state of the art of GPP implementation in Italy, and to suggest directions for future policies in the field.

## Acknowledgements

The authors would like to thank Gian Luigi Albano, Lidia Capparelli and Marco Sparro, from Consip S.p.a., for their helpful suggestions. All errors remain the authors' responsibility.

## Notes

1 Andrea Appolloni – PhD student in Management at University of Rome 'Tor Vergata', Italy. Email: andrea.appolloni@uniroma2.it.
2 Alessio D'Amato – Assistant Professor in Public Economics at University of Rome 'Tor Vergata', Italy. Email: damato@economia.uniroma2.it.
3 Wenjuan Cheng – PhD student in Environmental Economics and Law at University of Rome 'Tor Vergata', Italy. Email: ada.wenjuancheng@gmail.com.
4 For detailed surveys, see the already cited Walker and Phillips (2006) and Brännlund *et al.* (2009).
5 To have an idea of how extensive EU guidance on GPP is, please refer to: http://ec.europa.eu/environment/gpp/index_en.htm.
6 Also, to have specific examples of GPP in EU countries please refer to: http://ec.europa.eu/environment/gpp/case_en.htm.
7 See www.eng.consip.it/on-line/en/Home.html.
8 For details see Capparelli (2011).
9 For this example, please refer to: http://ec.europa.eu/environment/gpp/pdf/news_alert/Issue11_Case_Study27_Consip_Energy.pdf. For details on framework contracts see Albano and Sparro (2010).
10 These two examples are, again, taken from http://ec.europa.eu/environment/gpp/case_en.htm.
11 For other detailed case studies see, for example, http://focus-lab.it/public/Report_GPP_Province.pdf
12 More details on the available solutions can be found, among others, Lewis and Yildirim (2006) and in Anton and Yao (1989).
13 See http://ec.europa.eu/environment/gpp/case_en.htm, Example 15.

## References


AEA (2010) *Assessment and Comparison of National GPP/SPP Criteria and Under-lying Schemes*, AEA/ED47517/Issue 6. Online, available at: http://ec.europa.eu/environment/gpp/pdf/Criteria%20and%20Underlying%20Schemes.pdf.

Albano, G.L. and Sparro, M. (2010) 'Flexible Strategies for Centralized Public Procurement', *Review of Economics and Institutions*, 1: Article 4.

Anton, J.J. and Yao, D.A. (1989) 'Split Awards, Procurement and Innovation', *RAND Journal of Economics*, 20: 538–52.

Baron, D. (1985) 'Non-cooperative Regulation of Non-localized Externality', *RAND Journal of Economics*, 16: 553–68.

Bouwer, M., De Jong, K., Jonk, M., Berman, T., Bersani, R., Lusser, H., Nissinen, A. Parikka, K. and Szuppinger, P. (2005) *Green Public Procurement in Europe 2005 – Status Overview*. Online, available at: http://ec.europa.eu/environment/gpp/pdf/report_facts.pdf.

Brännlund, R., Carlén, O., Lundgren, T. and Marklund, P.O. (2009) 'Samhällsekonomiska konsekvenser av intensivodling, faktaunderlag till MINT-utredningen', *SLU, Rapport* (in Swedish).

Capparelli, L. (2011) 'Consip's Approach to GPP'. Presented at the Workshop 4/4/2011 – E-procurement and energy efficient datacenters. Consip – Rome, Italy.

Clark, G. (2007) 'Evolution of the Global Sustainable Consumption and Production Policy and the United Nations Environment Programme's (UNEP) Supporting Activities', *Journal of Cleaner Production*, 15: 492–8.

COM (2008) 'Public Procurement for a Better Environment, Communication from the Commission to the European Parliament'. The European Economic and Social Committee and the Committee of the Regions, COM (2008) 400.

D'Amato, A. (2006) 'Environmental Issues in Public Procurement: How Much Decentralization?', *Rivista di Politica Economica*, 96(1–2): 209–34.

European Commission (2001) *Green Paper on Integrated Product Policy*. COM(2001)68. Online, available at: http://ec.europa.eu/environment/ipp.

European Commission (2004) *Buying Green! A Handbook on Environmental Public Procurement*. Online, available at: http://ec.europa.eu/environment/gpp/pdf/buying_green_handbook_en.pdf.

European Commission (2008a) *Public Procurement for a Better Environment*. Communication from the Commission to the European Parliament. The European Economic and Social Committee and the Committee of the Regions, COM (2008) 400.

European Commission (2008b) *Green Public Procurement (GPP) Training Toolkit: Green Public Procurement and the European Ecolabel.*

European Commission (2011) Proposal for a Directive of the European Parliament and of the Council on Public Procurement. COM(2011) 896 final, 20/12/2012.

Gunther, E. and Scheibe, L. (2006) 'The Hurdle Analysis. A Self-evaluation Tool for Municipalities to Identify, Analyse and Overcome Hurdles to Green Procurement', *Corporate Social Responsibility and Environmental Management*, 13: 61–77.

Kippo-Edlund, P., Hauta-Heikkilä H., Miettinen H. and Nissinen, A. (2005) 'Measuring the Environmental Soundness of Public Procurement in Nordic Countries'. Tema Nord 2005:505, Nordic Council of Ministers, Copenhagen. Online, available at: http://www.norden.org/da/publikationer/2005-505/

Larsen, K. and Svane, Ö. (2005) 'Routines and Communities of Practice in Public Environmental Procurement Processes'. CESIS Electronic Working Paper Series, Paper 44.

Lewis, T.R. and Yildirim H. (eds) (2006) 'Managing Dynamic Procurement'. In N. Dimitri, G. Piga and G. Spagnolo (eds), *Handbook of Procurement* (pp. 433–45), Cambridge: Cambridge University Press.

Li, L. and Geiser, K. (2005) 'Environmentally Responsible Public Procurement (ERPP) and its Implications for Integrated Product Policy', *Journal of Cleaner Production*, 13: 705–15.

Martimort, D. (1996) 'The Multiprincipal Nature of the Government', *European Economic Review*, 40: 673–85.

Nissinen, A., Parikka-Alhola, K. and Rita, H. (2009) 'Environmental Criteria in the Public Purchases above the EU Threshold Values by Three Nordic Countries: 2003 and 2005', *Ecological Economics*, 68: 1838–49.

OECD (2002) *Recommendation of the Council on Improving the Environmental Performance of Public Procurement*. OECD Act C (2002) 3. Paris, France.

Öko-Institut E.V. and ICLEI (2007) 'Costs and Benefits of Green Public Procurement in Europe'. Online, available at: http://ec.europa.eu/environment/gpp/studies_en.htm.

Palmujoki, A., Parikka-Alhola, K. and Ekroos, A. (2010) 'Green Public Procurement: Analysis on the Use of Environmental Criteria in Contracts', *Review of European Community & International Environmental Law*, 19: 250–62.

Parikka-Alhola, K., Nissinen, A. and Ekroos, A. (2006) 'Green Award Criteria in the most Economically Advantageous Tender in Public Purchasing'. In K.V. Thai and G. Piga (eds), *Advancing Public Procurement* (pp. 257–79), Boca Raton: PrAcademics Press.

Piga, G. and Zanza, M. (2004) 'An Exploratory Analysis of Public Procurement Practices in Europe', *Quaderni Consip*, 3.

PricewaterhouseCoopers, Significant and Ecofys (2009) 'Collection of Statistical Information on Green Public Procurement in the EU'. Online, available at: http://ec.europa.eu/environment/gpp/pdf/statistical_information.pdf.

Tietenberg, T. and Lewis, L. (2009) *Environmental and Natural Resource Economics*, Prentice Hall, 8th edition.

Tukker, A., Cohen, M.J., de Zoysa, U., Hertwich, E., Hofstetter, P., Inaba, A., Lorek, S. and Stø, E. (2008) 'The Oslo Declaration on Sustainable Consumption', *Journal of Industrial Ecology*, 10: 9–14.

Walker, H. and Phillips, W. (2006) 'Sustainable Procurement: Emerging Issues', *International Public Procurement Conference Proceedings*, September.

# 9 The *Lianakis* ruling and good procurement

*Torstein Fjeldet Lunde and*
*Dag Thomas Nybø-Sørensen*

## 1 Introduction

Following the decision of the European Court of Justice (the Court) in C-532/06 (*Lianakis*)[1] the European Public Procurement community has had widespread discussions concerning the distinction between selection and award criteria. The *Lianakis* case has undergone thorough scrutiny both in national complaint boards and courts as well as in legal periodicals.[2]

In short, the core subject in the *Lianakis* case is the separation of the selection and award phase. The Court raised this question as an *obiter dictum*, following remarks regarding the topic from the Commission. In general, selection criteria are criteria the tenderer has to meet to substantiate that he will be able to perform the contract in question. Award criteria are used to identify the best tender, in other words the qualities of the tenders. In *Lianakis* the Court concluded that criteria such as 'the tenderers' experience, manpower and equipment, or their ability to perform the contract by the anticipated deadline' are qualitative selection criteria rather than award criteria.[3]

The aim of this chapter is to discuss the consequences of a strict interpretation of the *Lianakis* decision concerning the separation of the selection and award phase could have for the buyer's possibilities to actually select the most economically advantageous tender from a commercial point of view. In other words, we will discuss if *Lianakis* may have negative consequences for good procurement practice.

We will discuss the *Lianakis* ruling and subsequent rulings in the Court as well as in the Nordic countries and interpretations of *Lianakis* from a commercial point of view. We will concentrate on works contracts and contracts regarding high-tech services as these are procurement areas where the *Lianakis* ruling especially raises concerns.

## 2 On the separation of selection and award criteria

### *2.1 The* Lianakis *case*

In case C-532/06 (*Lianakis*) the Court has created what in hindsight seems to be quite some disturbance considering the distinction between selection and award criteria.

In *Lianakis*, the Court issued an *obiter dictum* concerning the lawfulness of the criteria chosen as award criteria (see paragraphs 22–24).

In paragraphs 29–32 the Court states:

> [29] However, although in the latter case Article 36(1) of Directive 92/50 does not set out an exhaustive list of the criteria which may be chosen by the contracting authorities, and therefore leaves it open to the authorities awarding contracts to select the criteria on which they propose to base their award of the contract, their choice is nevertheless limited to criteria aimed at identifying the tender which is economically the most advantageous (see, to that effect, in relation to public works contracts, Beentjes, paragraph 19; Case C_19/00 SIAC Construction [2001] ECR I_7725, paragraphs 35 and 36; and, in relation to public service contracts, Case C_513/99 Concordia Bus Finland [2002] ECR I_7213, paragraphs 54 and 59, and Case C_315/01 GAT [2003] ECR I_6351, paragraphs 63 and 64).
>
> [30] Therefore, 'award criteria' do not include criteria that are not aimed at identifying the tender which is economically the most advantageous, but are instead essentially linked to the evaluation of the tenderers' ability to perform the contract in question.
>
> [31] In the case in the main proceedings, however, the criteria selected as 'award criteria' by the contracting authority relate principally to the experience, qualifications and means of ensuring proper performance of the contract in question. Those are criteria which concern the tenderers' suitability to perform the contract and which therefore do not have the status of 'award criteria' pursuant to Article 36(1) of Directive 92/50.
>
> [32] Consequently, it must be held that, in a tendering procedure, a contracting authority is precluded by Articles 23(1), 32 and 36(1) of Directive 92/50 from taking into account as 'award criteria' rather than as 'qualitative selection criteria' the tenderers' experience, manpower and equipment, or their ability to perform the contract by the anticipated deadline.

As stated by Steen Treumer:

> The formulation in [32] appears *in general* to rule out the use of the flexible approach, as the Court expressed that 'in a tendering procedure, a contracting authority is precluded by Articles 23(1), 32 and 36(1) of Directive 92/50 from taking into account as "award criteria" rather than as "selection criteria" the tenderers' experience, manpower and equipment, or their ability to perform the contract by the anticipated deadline'.[4]

The Court has not later given any judgments clarifying whether the *Lianakis* decision was meant to rule out the use of the flexible approach in general, as stated by Treumer, or if the Court's *obiter dictum* later has been interpreted as possibly more general than intended.

In C-199/07, *Commission* v. *Greece*, the Greek public entity ERGA OSE AE published a contract notice relating to the carrying out of a study concerning property and electro mechanical projects in connection with the construction of a railway station. The following criteria were used as award criteria:

1 Specific and general experience, in particular design work on similar projects either by consultancy firms or consultants and their scientific staff.
2 Real capacity to conduct a study within the timescale planned together with obligations assumed regarding the carrying-out of other studies and the specific scientific and operational staff proposed to conduct the study in question as well as the equipment in relation to the object of the study.

The Court upheld the strict interpretation laid down in *Lianakis* as the Court stated in paragraph 56 that:

> In the present case, the criteria selected as 'award criteria' by the contracting authority, in point 2 of Section IV of the contract notice in question, relate to the experience and real capacity to ensure proper performance of the contract in question. Those are criteria which concern the tenderers' ability to perform the contract and which therefore do not have the status of 'award criteria'.

### *2.2 Subsequent interpretation*

#### *2.2.1 General overview*

*Public Procurement Law Review* no. 3 (2009) is a special issue dedicated to *Lianakis*. Different authors examined the consequences of *Lianakis* in Denmark, Germany, Belgium, Italy, France, the UK and Norway.

The studies showed that the consequences varied. In most countries the *Lianakis* case seemingly had no dramatic effects in the case-law.

Steen Treumer summarized the studies as follows:

> The common trend after Lianakis is clear. The national courts and complaints boards have generally adopted a narrow interpretation of the ruling and have indirectly rejected the restrictive interpretation that could be based on Lianakis. It is even hard to find any modification of previous national approaches. As a consequence the flexible approach is still accepted by the majority of national courts and complaints boards in the countries considered in our analysis.[5]

### *2.2.2 Interpretation in the Nordic countries*

In Norway the *Lianakis* case has been tried in several cases before the Norwegian Complaints Board for Public Procurement.

In KOFA-case 2008/120, the first decision by KOFA on the distinction between selection and award criteria post-*Lianakis*, KOFA concluded that the *Lianakis* decision does not exclude the possibility for a flexible approach. In paragraph [56] KOFA states:

> The Complaint Board is of the opinion that the decision (Lianakis) has to be understood in such a way that the ability to perform the contract in relation to a defined service must always be considered as a selection criterion that cannot be repeated as an award criterion. Competence and experience can nevertheless, based on the circumstances, be a part of a qualitative comparison between the suppliers' offered service quality where the tender documents do not lock the fulfilment to contract terms about the contents of the services or the delivery time.[6]
>
> (Translation)

This interpretation has later taken precedence in subsequent KOFA-cases. KOFA seems to have a practical view, where the question is whether the criterion in question is actually suitable to distinguish the most economically advantageous tender from the lesser economically advantageous tenders or not.

This Norwegian practice is in principle very much a continuation of the practice from before the decision in the *Lianakis* case. In reality KOFA has had more cases regarding the distinction between selection and award criteria post-*Lianakis*, as the *Lianakis* principles are something complainants often argue in their complaints.

In Sweden there have been quite a few judgments post-*Lianakis* but the situation seems a bit more unclear than in Norway.

In the paper 'Conflicting Swedish approaches – distinction between selection and award criteria' Andrea Sundstrand presents the situation in Sweden as of April 2010.[7] In the paper Sundstrand explains that the Administrative Courts of Appeal in Stockholm, Gothenburg and Sundsvall have all passed judgments regarding the issue without clarifying the situation. The Swedish Supreme Administrative Court has not given any direction in these questions.

Denmark also seems to have adopted a flexible approach to *Lianakis*. Steen Treumer has conducted a thorough examination of Danish case-law.[8]

## *2.3 Potential positive effects of a strict interpretation of* Lianakis *from a commercial point of view*

As mentioned above in the introduction, there are two main approaches to the *Lianakis* case: the strict approach calls for a strict separation between the selection and award phase. The flexible approach indicates 'that the use of what are normally considered criteria and elements of relevance to the selection stage are accepted at the award stage as exceptions and upon certain conditions'.[9]

Our question is if a strict approach in effect will help the public sector in achieving the aim of good procurement practice.

Evaluation of tenders is often a complicated and time-consuming job. Our experience after performing and assisting several hundred public procurement competitions as consultants to the public sector as well as after monitoring contract notices published in the Norwegian system corresponding to TED, Doffin, is that in most purchases, except for purchases of shelf goods, the purchaser chooses to use 'the most economically advantageous tender' as the award method. It is also our experience that in many cases the purchaser wants to somehow adopt criteria such as the tenderers' experience, manpower and/or equipment, or their ability to perform the contract by the anticipated deadline.

The reason for this is a belief that it will be possible to separate tenderers based on criteria such as competence, etc., and that for example the performing team in a service contract will have such an impact on the delivery that such a criterion should be adopted in the award phase. This view is also supported by Mario E. Comba: 'it is possible to say that the bidder *is* the offer, in the sense that the offer is based uniquely on the experience of the bidder, which is at the same time the only criterion for selection of bidders.'[10,11]

In our experience we see that it is often possible for the contracting authority to define the competence necessary and good enough to perform the contract in question to an extent that this absolute level may be stated as a selection criterion. If this is the case, a strict interpretation of *Lianakis* could actually force contracting authorities to perform procurement processes in a more efficient way. Exact competence criteria in the selection phase may lead to more competitions where lowest price only is the award criteria. Hence, the evaluation process will be less time- and resource-consuming. It may also lead to fewer complaints since the room for error in the award phase is reduced.

On the other hand the restriction of competence to the selection phase will possibly lead to a more creative use of requirement specifications in the award phase, where the contracting authorities, to avoid risks, narrow the choices by adding requirements that exclude new or unfamiliar companies from the competition. For example the contracting authority could demand 'extensive experience' instead of 'necessary experience' to ensure that the supplier awarded the contract will definitely perform well.

## *2.4 The* Lianakis *ruling and good procurement practice*

### *2.4.1 Introduction*

According to a strict interpretation of *Lianakis*, criteria such as the tenderers' experience, manpower and equipment, or their ability to perform the contract by the anticipated deadline, should never be used as award criteria.

As mentioned above, the post-*Lianakis* practice tends towards a flexible approach.

It is nevertheless the case that such a flexible approach most often limits the use of such criteria as exceptions and upon certain conditions, and that even if the *Lianakis* case is not interpreted with a strict approach, there are quite strict criteria for when to and when not to use, for example, experience as an award criterion.

### *2.4.2 Norwegian case-law*

An examination of Norwegian case-law from the Norwegian complaints board (KOFA) and the courts shows that the conditions for allowing experience, manpower, equipment, etc., as award criteria are quite strict. To this end see also Kai Krüger: 'The Norwegian Complaint Board … will no doubt adapt to the Lianakis ruling, somewhat restricting earlier practice which might now be said to have been too liberal.'[12]

KOFA-case 2008/120 is the first case where KOFA tries questions related to *Lianakis*. KOFA therefore makes a thorough interpretation of the *Lianakis* case. The case related to a procurement made by the City of Oslo. The scope covered the reconstruction and renovation of a domestic building that was to become a kindergarten. The contract was to be performed as general contracting. 'Competence' was one of the award criteria. Regarding the *Lianakis* case KOFA declared:

> The Complaint Board is of the opinion that the judgement should be understood such that performance ability (oppfyllelsesevne) in relation to a defined service must always be regarded as a selection criterion that cannot be repeated as an award criterion. Competence and experience can nevertheless, based on the circumstances, be a part of a qualitative comparison between the suppliers' offered service quality where the tender documents do not lock the fulfilment to contract terms about the contents of the services or the delivery time.[13]
>
> (Translation)

Regarding the current case, KOFA concluded that the contractor in relation to the award criteria 'competence' had emphasized conditions directed at the offer and the actual implementation of the contract, and that the criteria, when used in this way, could be suitable to identify the economically most advantageous offer (see paragraph 57). However, since the contractor had not properly made clear the distinction between the evaluation subjects in the selection and award phases, the criteria was still found to be illegal.

In KOFA-case 2009/49 the City of Oslo arranged a competition regarding the procurement of climate monitor and various reconstruction works. Parts of the works involved reconstruction work on a preserved building.

In the selection phase one the criterion was 'Competence and experience from similar contracts' (translation). The tenderers were asked to document the manpower for the contract (organization chart) with names and CVs for key personnel for the performance of the contract.

In the award phase 'the offered personnel's experience from equivalent contracts' was listed as a sub-criterion in connection to the award criterion 'project execution and task realization'.

KOFA dismissed the use of the quoted award criterion. This was done with references to the *Lianakis* case and KOFA-case 2008/120, which is the 'precedent' KOFA-case concerning the Norwegian interpretation of *Lianakis*. The reason for the dismissal was that the contract as presented appeared to be an 'ordinary' works contract. However, KOFA did state that the only thing which might be considered to justify an exception for the use of experience as an award criterion was the works connected to the preserved building. KOFA stated that there might be a need to separate the tenders based on how extensive experience the offered personnel had concerning preserved buildings. Since the award criterion was referring not only to the works on the preserved building, and the particular works only constituted a minor part of the total works, KOFA concluded that the award criterion was illegal.

In KOFA-case 2009/260 the City of Bergen had notified a competition regarding noise reducing works on the façade of buildings along a new tramway route. One award criterion was 'Project execution'. Relevant experience for the performing team was stated as a sub-criterion. In the tender documents the following was stated regarding the scope:

> The works consist of replacing windows on the most exposed façades. Additional works such as replacing/installing vents and improving sound isolation, must also be performed in some cases. The installation must be adapted existing constructions/installations; hence large flexibility on the entrepreneur's side is demanded. These conditions are to be clarified with the house owners.[14]
>
> (Translation)

The City of Bergen argued that the execution of the works had a huge impact on the final result considering noise reduction. They also argued that the contract contained special challenges that made the experience of the team performing the contract a factor in considering the economic value for the contractor. The defendant exemplified this referring to the demands to coordinate several trades and coordination with several house owners. It was also stated that noise reduction works were especially challenging.

KOFA concluded that the award criterion was illegal. With reference to KOFA-case 2009/49, KOFA concluded that the works in question should be considered as ordinary works.

In KOFA-case 2010/191 Norges Bank (Norway's central bank) had announced a competition for the procurement of production and distribution of broadcasts of press conferences and speeches on Norges Bank's website. 'The tenderer's named relevant employees experience, competence and references from relevant tasks' was stated as an award criterion. KOFA accepted the use of this award criterion. KOFA stated that: 'The services to be provided demands competence and experience regarding the offered personnel in order to achieve a good result, hence the award criterion is relevant to identify the most economically advantageous tender' (translation).

In KOFA-case 2008/136 the City of Oslo was procuring waste collection services. As an award criterion the contractor had used understanding of the task (oppdragsforståelse). Two sub-criteria were 'competence/certificate of apprenticeship and experience among the personnel to perform the services' and 'measures to recruit, maintain and keep employees and emergency plan' (see paragraph 7). KOFA concluded that the award criterion was not a repetition of similar criteria from the selection phase. KOFA found that the award criterion was illegal, as it concerned the tenderers' ability to perform (see paragraphs 84 and 85).

The subject matter of the case decided by KOFA in case 2008/136 has later been brought before the ordinary courts in Norway. In LB-2010–68992 the Court of Appeal (Borgarting lagmannsrett) has tried the same questions as were brought before KOFA in case 2008/136. Regarding the sub-criterion 'Competence/certificate of apprenticeship and experience among the personnel to perform the services' the Court of Appeal disagreed with KOFA regarding the legality. The Court of Appeal expressed the opinion that the personnel's competence includes more than the strictly practical and technical performance of the renovation services. The Court stated that:

> In their work, the personnel will get in contact with a great number of clients across large areas of Oslo, and their conduct and service attitude in this regard will be an important aspect of the execution of the services.
>
> (Translation)

Therefore the Court of Appeal concluded that the contractor must be allowed to emphasize quality gaps between the tenderers. In LB-2010–68992 the Court also refers to the Supreme Court ruling published in Rt. 2007 p. 1783 (NIDA). Here the Supreme Court accepted reliability on performance as an award criterion. In Rt. 2007 p. 1783 the contractor had a need to ensure that he could award the tenderer who could offer the most reliable tender to secure an accelerated completion of the project.[15] Regarding the sub-criterion 'measures to recruit, maintain and keep employees and emergency plan' the Court of Appeal concurred with KOFA, concluding that the criterion was illegal.

### 2.4.3 *Remarks regarding the case-law*

As shown above, Norwegian case-law does not in principle apply a strict interpretation of *Lianakis*. Still there seems to be quite a narrow window for actually escaping after applying criteria in the award phase concerning 'competence', 'experience', etc.

In the Court of Appeal, as referred from case LB-2010–68992, the Court seems to adopt a slightly more flexible approach than in KOFA, with reference to the Supreme Court decision in NIDA. No cases regarding these issues have been brought before the Supreme Court after the European Court of Justice delivered its judgment in *Lianakis*.

Our concern is that a strict interpretation of the *Lianakis* judgment results in less quality and innovation connected to public procurements and, in the end, less possibilities to ensure that the tenderer with the most economically advantageous tender actually is awarded the contract.

This concern is also raised by Steen Treumer:

> Practitioners are to the author's knowledge now much more reluctant to draft their selection and award criteria in accordance with the flexible approach and many simply avoid the insertion of criteria that could be challenged as not accepting the fundamental distinction between selection and award criteria. Others, often more resourceful contracting authorities, are fully aware of the potential risk of challenge but pursue the flexible approach and take utmost care when drafting the selection and award criteria. It is submitted that this is an unfortunate development.[16]

The consequences of such restraints are incalculable, but possibly the contracting authorities will, more often than they should, select tenders which are not in reality the most economically advantageous tenders. This is due to the consequence of a strict interpretation that the contracting authority will have less room for his own professional assessment during the award phase, and therefore less room to take into consideration in the award phase important inputs the suppliers give in their tenders which the purchaser has not considered at the publication stage.

## 3 Concerns regarding works contracts

As shown above in KOFA-cases 2009/49 and 2009/260 it has become a norm that where contractors arrange competitions concerning contracts covering 'normal works', they cannot assume that award criteria such as 'competence' and 'experience' will be accepted. However, KOFA does not in principle rule out the possibility of using such award criterion, as shown in case 2008/120.

Based on the *Lianakis* decision and the development of Norwegian case-law, we still fear that in reality only works contracts covering both design and construction, as opposed to works contracts covering only construction, will be considered suitable for quality award criteria.

The complainant in KOFA-case 2008/120 seems to base his claim on a separation between contracts based on the tenderer's input commitment (*innsatsforpliktelse*) as opposed to contracts based on the contractor's result commitment (*resultatforpliktelse*), where he claims that competitions concerning contracts with a result commitment to a lesser degree should be allowed on the basis of award criteria like competence, experience, etc.

High demands regarding the implementation and quality in works contracts may sometimes be difficult to ensure if one awards the contract based on the lowest price. Sometimes the contractors do not find it sufficient to include contract clauses regarding performance. The standard-form contracts often used for works contracts are adapted to ordinary works. It will often be desirable and even necessary from a contractor's point of view to use award criteria such as team competence and experience, execution plans, etc., to distinguish the best from the runners up. As an example we may refer to the Norwegian Public Roads Administrations project 'Nasjonale turistveger' ('National tourist routes in Norway').[17] Here projects are developed based on groundbreaking architecture with contributions from top international architects. Even though the works contracts only cover construction, the project demands work of a very high quality and the projects most often involve constructional challenges during the performance phase. Based on our examination of post-*Lianakis* case-law above, there seems to be possible difficulties with including award criteria such as competence and experience in these competitions. Even so, the fact is that in these cases it is of more value to the contractor to make sure that the projects will be performed with the highest possible quality than to have the tenderer that is 'good enough' awarded the contract based on the lowest price.

In this example it will of course be possible for the contractor to include adequate quality demands in the contract as well as in the requirement specification. But to ensure the best possible project, one will have to include relevant criteria to distinguish the tenderers in the award phase.

We may want to construct a reasoning regarding ability to deliver added value as a basis for evaluating competence and experience in the award phase. As shown in the examination of case-law, such an added value argument may be the key to get around the obstacles put forward in case-law regarding the contractor's right to define which criteria to use when the award is made to the tender most economically advantageous. Arguing that award criteria is aimed at distinguishing the tenderer providing the best possibilities for added value in the performance phase, makes it clear that one does not evaluate on the basis of the contract in question, but on the basis of the substantiated ability to deliver better than what the contractor has defined as a minimum performance.

Such an added value argument could be used to turn around the conclusions in KOFA-cases 2009/49 and 2009/260. If the contractor had argued that the tenderers' competence and experience could lead to a more effective performance and better solutions and cooperation throughout the performance period, and if such an added value argument was made visible in the tender documents in connection with the award criterion, it is our belief that KOFA could not have dismissed the argument on the basis of the contracts being 'ordinary' works contracts.

The question is if this argument for added value should really be necessary. In our view criteria such as competence and experience will have a value in almost any works contract. At least it should be the contractor's right to decide if he expects such criteria to represent a value for him regarding the evaluation of which tender is the most economically advantageous. As long as this argument can be justified in factual and reasonable ways, and as long as the award criteria, their contents and the reason for their use is stated clearly in the tender documents, the courts should not interfere.

Such reasoning seems to be supported by Philip Lee, as he states: 'In a construction project, a poor design is likely to lead to additional costs from the contractor. The experience of the design team is critical in ensuring the highest economic advantage to the client.'[18]

## 4 Concerns regarding high-tech services

Regarding service contracts, our view is that many of the same arguments presented regarding works contracts are valid.

In a high-tech service contract it is often critical for the contractor to have the best possible competence. As argued above we would think that in an added value perspective, a team or personnel approach should always be possible in the awarding stages.

For high-tech services, or services where the competence is critical for the outcome, our question is whether the contractor should be allowed to go one step further regarding the award criteria, allowing an evaluation also of company based competence.

In KOFA-case 2008/136 'measures to recruit, maintain and keep employees and emergency plan' was one of the sub-criteria that were deemed illegal.

In our view an award criterion related to the relevant measures to recruit and maintain personnel with at least the same competence as the ones offered for the performance of the contract, could be relevant.

## 5 Conclusions

A strict interpretation of *Lianakis* concerning the separation between the selection and award phase will in our opinion have serious consequences for the contracting authorities' opportunities of good procurement practice. As shown above, even a flexible approach may reduce the contracting authorities' possibilities of ensuring the choice of the most economically advantageous tender.

Especially in procurements regarding works and high-tech services the value of a tender is often strongly linked to the competence and experience of the tenderer, i.e. the person or team of persons which will perform the contract on behalf of the tenderer. As shown above, even a flexible approach may limit the contracting authorities' possibilities to include relevant award criteria concerning competence and experience in unfortunate ways.

The contracting authorities may get around the *Lianakis* principles by focusing on competence and experience related to added value in the award phase, as opposed to performance ability in the selection phase.

## Notes

1 *Emm. G. Lianakis AE* v. *Dimos Alexandroupolis* (C-532/06) [2008] E.C.R. I – 251.
2 For example the *Public Procurement Law Review* released a special issue (issue no. 3 of 2009, pp. 103–64) on the follow-up of the *Lianakis* decision and the distinction between selection and award criteria.
3 See *Lianakis* paragraph 32.
4 Steen Treumer, 'The distinction between selection and award criteria in EC public procurement law – a rule without exemption?', *Public Procurement Law Review*, 2009, pp. 103–11 at p. 104.
5 Steen Treumer, 'The distinction between selection and award criteria in EC public procurement law – a rule without exemption?', *Public Procurement Law Review*, 2009, pp. 103–11 at p. 109.
6 Translation by the author of this article.
7 Andrea Sundstrand, 'Conflicting Swedish approaches – distinction between selection and award criteria', paper presented at the conference Global Revolution V, Copenhagen, September 2010.
8 Steen Treumer, 'The distinction between selection and award criteria in EC public procurement law: the Danish approach', *Public Procurement Law Review*, 2009, pp. 146–54.
9 Steen Treumer, 'The distinction between selection and award criteria in EC public procurement law – a rule without exemption?', *Public Procurement Law Review*, 2009, pp. 103–11 at pp. 105–6.
10 Mario E. Comba, 'Selection and award criteria in Italian public procurement law', *Public Procurement Law Review*, 2009, pp. 122–7 at p. 125.
11 The quote above is taken out of a very specific context, being 'the extreme cases in which the contracting authority is looking for a single professional to supply the service' (see Mario E. Comba, 'Selection and award criteria in Italian public procurement law', *Public Procurement Law Review*, 2009, pp. 122–7 at p. 12). Our understanding is still that Comba does not narrow the use of past performance in the award phase to these extreme cases. Even though one is requiring several persons, the same legislative considerations may apply, depending on the services in question.
12 Kai Krüger, 'Superiority in experience and skills may distinguish a better tender bid! Critical reflections from Norway on the Lianakis ruling', *Public Procurement Law Review*, 2009, pp. 138–45 at pp. 141–2.
13 See KOFA-case 2008/120 paragraph 56.
14 KOFA-case 2009/260 paragraph 5.
15 Kai Krüger, 'Superiority in experience and skills may distinguish a better tender bid! Critical reflections from Norway on the Lianakis ruling', *Public Procurement Law Review*, 2009, pp. 138–45 at p. 140.
16 Steen Treumer, 'The distinction between selection and award criteria in EC public procurement law: the Danish approach', *Public Procurement Law Review*, 2009, pp. 146–54 at p. 153.
17 See www.turistveg.no/en.
18 Philip Lee, 'Implications of the Lianakis decision', *Public Procurement Law Review*, 2010, pp. 47–56 at p. 51.

# Part III

# Re-tendering a contract for breach of procurement rules or changes to contract

# 10 Dialogue

*Hans-Joachim Prieß and Stéphane Saussier*

## 1 Argument by Hans-Joachim Prieß

There are a number of situations which lead to an obligation to re-tender a contract, the main ones that will be discussed here being breach of the procurement rules and changes to the contract. In addition, a brief overview of the procedural rules will be given.

### *1.1 Re-tendering a contract for breach of procurement rules*

Re-tendering a contract may become necessary because of a severe breach of procurement rules that either prevents the public authority from concluding a contract or, if already concluded, leads to the termination of a contract.

If an unsuccessful bidder files a complaint regarding the procurement procedure before the contract has been concluded, the public authority may be forced to cancel the ongoing procurement procedure and to re-tender the contract.

Similarly, a contract that has already been concluded may be cancelled or terminated following a review application by an unsuccessful bidder if the procurement procedure that led to its conclusion violated procurement law.

The Remedies Directives (Directives 89/665, 92/13 and 2007/66) oblige member states to ensure that the contract will be considered to be ineffective in principle in the following cases:

- if the contracting authority has awarded a contract without prior publication of a contract notice in the Official Journal of the European Union without this being permissible; or
- where the mandatory suspensive effect or the standstill period is infringed, and the tenderer has been deprived of the possibility of pursuing pre-contractual remedies and where such an infringement is combined with an infringement of the Procurement Directives, if the latter infringement has affected the chances of the tenderer to obtain the contract.

The consequences of ineffectiveness are provided for by national law which may stipulate retroactive cancellation of all contractual obligations or limit the scope of the cancellation to obligations still to be performed.

Under German law, once the contract has been concluded a challenge of the award decision is in principle no longer possible. However, an aggrieved bidder can claim that the contract was invalid from the beginning if the contracting authority failed to (correctly) inform the unsuccessful bidders about the award or made an illegal de facto award. Such a claim has to be brought within 30 days of becoming aware of the breach of law in question or within 30 days following publication of the contract award in the Official Journal of the EU, and, in any event, at the latest six months after the conclusion of the contract.

## *1.2 Re-tendering a contract for changes to the contract*

There has been a lot of discussion in recent years regarding the possibilities of amending a contract after it has been awarded. In the *Pressetext* (C-454/06) and *Wall AG* (C-91/08) decisions, the CJEU had to deal with changes to the contract and hence clarified the relevant criteria and limitations. The main issues relate to the extension of contracts, amendments and changes to the contractor.

### *1.2.1 Extension of the contract*

The Procurement Directives state that the more flexible negotiated procedure may be used for an 'extension of existing supplies' and the 'repetition of similar works' from or by the same provider. These provisions demonstrate that an extension of an existing contract is generally considered to fall within the scope of the Directives, even though such an extension may in certain circumstances require a new procurement procedure. It is generally accepted, however, that where an extension is already foreseen in the initial contract (and in the contract notice for this contract) and can be exercised by the authority unilaterally, no new procurement procedure is required (CJEU case C-454/06 – *Pressetext*).

### *1.2.2 Amendment of a contract*

It is generally accepted that significant amendments, which are not explicitly foreseen in the original contract, will require a new tender procedure. In *Pressetext*, the CJEU indicated that amendments to an existing contract constitute a new award of a contract under the EU Procurement rules when they are materially different in character from the original contract, and therefore demonstrate the intention of the parties to renegotiate the essential terms of that contract. The CJEU provided the following examples of amendments that would be regarded as material:

- an amendment introducing conditions that, had they been part of the initial award procedure, would have led to applications for admission by tenderers other than those initially admitted or would have allowed for the acceptance of a tender other than the one initially accepted;
- an amendment to the initial (works or supplies) contract that extends the scope of the contract considerably to encompass services not initially covered; and

- an amendment that changes the economic balance of the contract in favour of the contractor in a manner that was not provided for in the terms of the initial contract.

### *1.2.3 Change of contractor*

Only in a very limited number of cases can an existing contract be transferred to another contractor without the need for a new procurement procedure.

As a result of the *Pressetext* decision, an existing contract may be transferred to another contractor without re-tendering only if the transfer cannot be regarded as a renegotiation of essential terms of the initial contract. In this case the CJEU confirmed Advocate General Kokott's statement in her opinion that the transfer of a contract to another contractor without a new procurement procedure can lead to a distortion of competition and undue preference for the new contractor. In the case *Wall AG*, the CJEU held in relation to a service concession that even the change of a subcontractor can under special circumstances be considered to be a material change. Such a material change might even be assumed where the change was provided for in the original contract.

According to the CJEU in *Pressetext*, the sale of a company that has previously obtained a public contract may lead to a relevant change of the contract and therefore make re-tendering necessary. In the case at hand, the contracting company was a stock corporation, where changes in shareholders are not unexpected. Therefore the sale of shares in the company did not lead to a relevant change of contract. Nevertheless, this may be the case in other circumstances, for instance where the company refers to a specific shareholder in the procurement procedure, for example to prove its qualification or for financial reasons. Where the change of shareholders leads to the loss of this qualification or financial strength, it would very likely be considered to be a relevant change.

In Germany, there is a tendency to adopt a broader interpretation of the rules regarding the change of contractor. So, for example, the Higher Regional Court Naumburg (Decision of 29 April 2010, 1 Verg 2/10) held in 2010 that the change of shareholders in a German GmbH (corporation with limited liability) does not always constitute a relevant change of contract. Similarly to the German stock corporation (AG), the GmbH is a company that does not depend on its shareholders. Therefore, it seems to be reasonable to allow changes of the shareholders in a GmbH in the same manner as for stock corporations or any other corporation that is not dependent on its shareholders.

### *1.2.4 Conclusion*

The guidance given by the recent decisions of the CJEU has led to more legal certainty. Nevertheless, as the criteria leave some room for interpretation, the relevance of a change to the contract and the possible need to re-tender have to be assessed in every single case. Generally it is possible to say that there is a broader scope for changes if the original contract includes options or other similar clauses that clearly provide for future changes. But such clauses cannot be without limitation.

The legal discussion of this issue is not over yet because of the CJEU's decisions: in the recently published Green Paper on the modernisation of EU public procurement policy, the European Commission suggests the codification of rules for the change to contract in the Procurement Directives.[1]

### *1.3 Procedural rules – the enforcement of procurement rules*

The enforcement of procurement rules usually takes place at member state level. The Remedies Directives stipulate that first instance review procedures can be conducted by bodies which are not judicial in character. In such a case member states are obliged to provide for procedures whereby any allegedly illegal measure taken by the review body or any alleged defect in the exercise of the powers conferred on it can be the subject of judicial review or review by another body which is a court or tribunal within the meaning of article 267 TFEU. These procedures are only possible within the deadlines set out in the Remedies Directives.

Furthermore, unsuccessful bidders can file a complaint regarding a violation of the procurement rules with the Commission, DG Internal Market. If the Commission decides to take up the case, it usually seeks to clarify and solve the issue in consultation with the member state. If this is unsuccessful, the Commission can bring an action for violation of EU procurement law pursuant to article 258 TFEU against the member state before the CJEU. There is no particular time limit for complaints to the Commission. The complaint does not have an automatic suspensive effect.

In practice there are many differences between the member states. In some member states it is quite common for bidders to file review applications; in others, as for example the UK, this hardly ever happens. The ability to file a complaint with the Commission is not generally perceived to be very effective because of the duration of the Commission's evaluation and of any subsequent necessary CJEU proceedings. In addition, bidders and their advisers are sometimes concerned about losing control over the case. The Commission might, for example, continue to pursue the case after the bidder and the authority have already reached a settlement. For this reason it is not customary for unsuccessful bidders to file complaints with the Commission.

## 2 Argument by Stéphane Saussier

### *2.1 Introduction*

In a world without any transaction costs (i.e. contractual costs), it is costless and easy to specify what you want in a contract and to put in competition private firms in order to obtain a competition price that will not be put into question during the whole life of the contract. But, contracts are often complex agreements signed in an uncertain environment by contracting parties with limited abilities. Procurement contracts do not come as an exception, and give rise to questions concerning the *ex ante* selection of the private partner as well as the *ex post* necessity and mechanisms through which contracts should be adapted. Economists have for long time now recognized those problems.

The question of re-tendering a contract for breach of procurement or changes to contract has not been explored extensively yet. Just to give an example of what issues are at stake, let me give an example: the Mons railway. In 2006 a call for tenders was organized. The objective of the authorities was to preserve the original railway station. Only Santiago Calatrava's initial design fulfilled this requirement. A few months later, his new design evolves to include the destruction of the existing station and the initial budget (37M€) increases to 155M€. The initial object that has been contracted for clearly changed. Should we re-tender the contract? Is it possible? What would be the cost, especially the social costs (delays) for citizens?

I will not provide in this brief note an economic analysis of procurement contracts. Instead, I will give only some thoughts and illustrations.

The main messages I would like to stress are that because of incomplete contracting, there is a need, first, for flexible *ex ante* procurement rules and, second, for adapting *ex post*. Too rigid rules, leading to a re-tendering process, might not always be a good way to increase competition and efficiency. It might also be socially very costly to delay investments and projects.

### *2.2 Incomplete contracting: the need of flexible* ex ante *procurement rules*

Procurement rules are necessary in order to avoid 'procurement failures'. Several award procedures exist at the European level.

Organizing call for tenders in order to foster competition between private candidates to end up with a competition price is not an easy task, however.

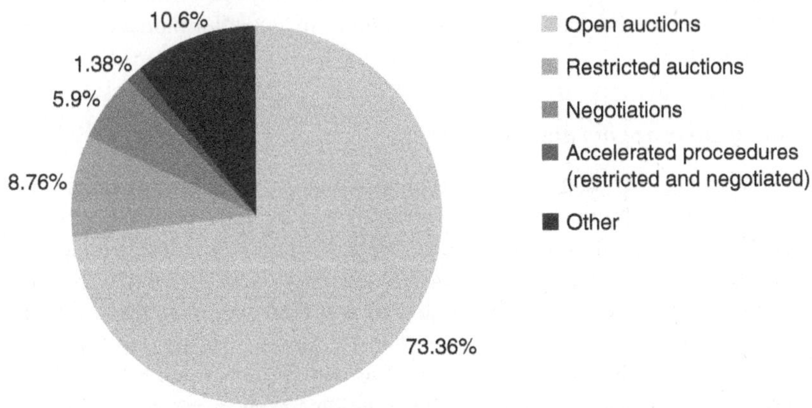


*Figure 10.1* (Small) diversity of award procedures used for public procurement in the EU (source: EU Internal Market Scoreboard, 2009).

Without being exhaustive, the following risks exist:

- The public party might face bidders that choose to cooperate instead of playing the game of competition (i.e. cartels). This is especially true when markets are concentrated and calls for tenders are recurrent.
- Private partners may differ concerning:
  - Their capabilities to renegotiate the contract *ex post*, once signed. Hence, private partners that are more confident in their abilities to achieve this might have aggressive bidding behaviours because they know they will not have to commit to their initial offer and will renegotiate contractual terms at the *ex post* stage, bilaterally, without any further competition.
  - Their information concerning the cost to provide the goods and/or services and their future revenues (if they bear exploitation risk). Hence private partners that are proposing best offers might not be the most efficient ones, but the most optimistic ones, leading to *ex post* enforcement problems and possible bankruptcy and/or renegotiations (winner's curse effect).
  - Some private firms may seek to influence public authorities in order to win call for tenders (this does not exclude cartel behaviours that may exist hand-in-hand with corruption (Lambert-Mogiliansky and Kosenok 2009)).

Procurement rules are put in place in order to foster competition and avoid those limits. One interesting point is that contrary to the lawyers' point of view, which fosters the necessity for procurement rules to place private candidates in equal situations, without one or several candidates being advantaged compared to the others, the economists' point of view differs slightly by fostering the need to have efficient procurement rules, leading to the best possible (and credible) offers for the public parties. In other words, more competition does not necessarily mean rules in order to increase the number of potential bidders receiving equal treatment.

### *2.3 More bidders are not always good*

Economists recognize that the uncertainty about future renegotiations in a incomplete contract should be lower if the buyer and the candidates have already interacted in the past: they may have developed routines, enhanced reciprocal understanding or invested in relationship-specific assets. Several empirical studies suggest that the lower the anticipated coordination costs, the lower the bids (Gil and Marion 2009; Bajari *et al.* 2006). Moreover, in case of imperfect contractibility, it can be shown that interacting with a limited number of suppliers increases the actualized value of the relationship as more businesses are anticipated (Calzolari and Spagnolo 2009; Gil and Marion 2009; Desrieux *et al.* 2012). Firms then have incentives to truthfully reveal their private costs and take into account and enforce the informal dimensions of the contract, in order not to compromise their access to the future contracts.

Thus, the 'shadow of the future' is reinforced by interacting with a limited number of bidders, which enables to solve both adverse selection and moral hazard issues.

All this suggests that efficient procurement rules might be such that public authorities are able to reduce the number of participants and to favour some of them over others.

A good example is provided by urban transport in France and the UK. Both London and France are characterized by an obligation to organize tendering procedures for local public services – this is even called an anti-corruption requirement in France. The French case is interesting because it clearly illustrates that the rules of the game imposed on competitors are crucial and may not foster competition nor prevent anti-competitive behaviour (the three main operators in urban public transport in France were fined more than 12 million euros by the French Competition Commission in July 2005 for collusive strategies). The auction procedure chosen in London is the combination of transparent procedures (to prevent corruption and provide incentives for private operators to bid), discretionary power of the regulator and incentives for private operators to participate (bids are organized on a route-by-route basis in order to encourage the participation of many competitors and hence prevent collusive strategies). Those characteristics of the London tendering procedure are a key determinant of the performance differential observed between France and London and do not focus on the necessity to put all bidders on the same starting line (Amaral *et al.* 2009).

### *2.4 Incomplete contracting: the need to adapt* **ex post**

Changes in contracts are analysed in economics mainly as amendments or renegotiation issues. Contract renegotiation has been the object of much attention in the economic literature, at least at the theoretical level.

Little has been done at the empirical level explaining why the matter of renegotiations in contractual agreements still has not received any clear-cut answer. However, many studies, for a long time now, pointed out the fact that contracts are often renegotiated (Macaulay 1963). Such recurrent empirical observations explain, to a certain extent, the evolution of theoretical developments.

On one side of the spectrum of theoretical analysis, a large part of the contract theory is based on incentive issues in which initial developments insisted on the need for full commitment from contracting parties. In other words, in order to resolve efficiently adverse selection and moral hazard issues, the principal must be able to commit not to renegotiate and to accept *ex post* inefficiencies (i.e. once asymmetric information is resolved, the incentive compatible contract does not lead to the first best anymore) or to frame contracts that are renegotiation-proof.

However, in line with empirical observations, recent developments have been studying the impacts of limited commitment, due for example to imperfect institutions (Guasch *et al.* 2006, 2007, 2008).

On the other side, the incomplete contract theory suggests that renegotiations are unavoidable and useful as soon as parties develop investments that are non-contractible and specific to the relationship (Grossman and Hart 1986; Hart 1995). Renegotiations were then originally viewed as necessary adaptations to fill contractual blanks generating no renegotiation costs.

However, in line with empirical observations pointing out the fact that renegotiation might sometimes be costly, recent developments of the incomplete contract theory (Hart and Moore 2008; Fehr *et al.* 2011) put forward the behavioural hypothesis that parties accept the contract as a reference point and do not feel entitled to outcomes outside the contract, while they may prefer different outcomes within a contract. Renegotiation is thus likely to make one party disappointed, encouraging him to engage in shading.

In between those two views, lies transaction cost economics that has recognized for a long time that contracts are inefficient governance structures that have to be adapted to their evolving environment, mainly because of the complexity of the environment and bounded rationality of economic actors. Renegotiations are thus viewed as a necessary and risky adaptation process that should accommodate potential opportunistic behaviours (Crocker and Masten 1991; Crocker and Reynolds 1993; Saussier 2000).

Hence, there is a consensus in the theoretical literature on the fact that we need to have a nuanced view concerning the effect of renegotiations. But, this literature gives us only very few insights concerning the overall effect of renegotiations on contractual surplus. And it is of no help when it turns to the precise question of what effect we should expect depending on the scope and the kind of renegotiations that occur during contractual agreements. Because contracts are incomplete and economic actors potentially opportunistic, contractual adjustment might reflect the necessity to adapt to new circumstances or the parties' actions to appropriate surplus.

### 2.5 Renegotiations and changes of the contract are not always bad

Because they deal with services of general interest, public–private contracts and their renegotiations are especially under the scrutiny of regulation bodies (Spiller 2008). This does not imply that renegotiations are infrequent.

Many examples of renegotiations in public–private agreements are given by Guasch (2004). Studying more than 1,000 concession contracts signed in Latin American countries, he found that 54.7 per cent of transportation contracts and 74.4 per cent of water and sanitation contracts were renegotiated between the mid 1980s and 2000. He found that renegotiation occurs shortly after the award (on average 2.2 years after the award) and that they often, at first glance, favour the private party. The most common outcomes of renegotiations are delays, tariff increases and reduction in investment obligations. This leads the author to consider renegotiations as having mainly negative impacts, reflecting opportunistic behaviours from private partners and cancelling out the potential advantages of competitive auctions. Renegotiations are often viewed as the consequence of aggressive bids in a context of *ex ante* lack of commitment from the government. Because the government is unable to commit not to renegotiate and because firms learn their type only after they propose a bid, if a firm wins and then discovers it is inefficient (i.e. negative profits), it will be prone to ask for renegotiation (Guasch *et al.* 2006, 2008).

Alternatively, other research deals with government-led renegotiations (Guasch *et al.* 2007) and renegotiations that enable incumbent governments to circumvent budgetary rules before elections. Whoever is at the origin of the renegotiation process, the empirical literature on renegotiations has underlined very contrasting outcomes: they might be viewed as a game in which there are losers and winners (Estache 2006) or as a win-win game (de Brux 2010) depending on contracting parties' behaviour and the reason why renegotiations occur.

However, to the extent of our knowledge, no empirical study collected data in order to assess the impact of renegotiations with the exception of one ongoing study concerning car park contracts in France

### *2.6 The impact of renegotiations: car park contracts in France*

In an ongoing study concerning public private car park contracts in France (de Brux *et al.* 2011), the authors codified the content of every renegotiation in the 295 expired contracts they worked on, and they focused on the probability of the contract being renewed with the same partner. The idea is that if renegotiations are only the result of opportunistic behaviours, they should reduce the contractual surplus and then lead contracting partners to stop their 'cooperation' at the end of the contract, without renewing it.

The paper thus studied the impact of the frequency of renegotiations, the scope of renegotiations, the celerity of renegotiations and the kind of renegotiation on the probability of a contract being renewed. There were several interesting results:

- Traditional procurement contracts are not renegotiated less frequently compared to PPPs, that are longer duration contracts (on average, contracts are renegotiated once every two years).
- No evidence of a relationship between renegotiations and the probability to be renewed in the public procurement subsample.
- In the PPPs subsample characterized by public authorities' discretionary power the study suggests that:
  - The higher the frequency and the scope of renegotiations, the higher the probability to see a contract renewed. This result suggests that renegotiating per se should not be interpreted as a sign of failure of the relationship.
  - Depending on the dimensions that are renegotiated, the impact on the probability to see the contract renewed is different. Indeed, some renegotiations clearly increase the probability to see a contract renewed;

others do not (renegotiations on prices and financial equilibrium of the contract). Hence, results suggest a positive, negative or neutral impact on the contractual surplus depending on the kind of renegotiation that is considered.

## 3 Reply by Hans-Joachim Prieß

### *3.1 General statements*

- I agree that '*ex post* adaptation is necessary and a condition of contract efficiency'; this is even more so if the contract in question is a medium- or long-term contract and not just a one-off supply contract.
- Consequently it is – I believe – also correct that 'rigidities limiting adaptations' have a negative effect on contract efficiency.
- More generally it is also true that the tendering process as such is only a formalized procedural way of selecting a contract partner. This process is based on the assumption that a guaranteed access to public contracts increases participation by bidders which in turn increases competition that consequently leads to lower prices.

It is true, however, that the rigorous formal standards of the procedural framework often lead to exclusions from the tender procedure so that many suitable bidders will be eliminated – with a negative effect on competition and competitive prices. I therefore agree that (1) bidders proposing best offers might not be the most efficient ones and it follows that (2) the award decision will not necessarily be in line with objective market prices but can be a rather random result.

### *3.2 More bidders are not always good?*

- I believe that neither bidders nor contracting authorities are necessarily concerned with 'truthful' costs of providing the required service or of supplying the required goods. Even a below-cost price may be attractive for a bidder in order to gain reputation or cover his fixed costs and likewise a higher than market price may be in the interest of a contracting authority if the identity of the actual supplier matters more to him than the economics (it only spends public money anyway).
- On the other hand I agree that there is a mutual advantage from awarding contracts to the same bidder for the very reasons mentioned: developed routines, enhanced reciprocal understanding, etc. The obvious downside, however, is the development of sloppiness and inefficiencies because this bidder knows that he will be awarded further contracts just because of a past relationship. This invariably affects his efficiency in a negative way as the competitive pressure eases.
- The French example is not very compelling in demonstrating that more bidders are not always good as it is obvious that collusive and/or antitrust violations always affect the economies of a contract in a negative way. The

London example clearly shows that there is an advantage in incentives to bid. Again the question remains whether and how this demonstrates that a smaller number of bidders leads to more efficient (economically advantageous) results.

- I also wonder how the French housing example shows that a smaller number of bidders is a better outcome.

### 3.3 *The need to adapt* ex post

- It is indeed true, I believe, that there is a need for adaptation of longer term contracts and that this need is satisfied by renegotiations. This is positive in allowing a contract to survive changes beyond the control of the parties.
- But renegotiations are not necessarily unavoidable because a well-drafted contract will provide for an adaptation mechanism. Such mechanisms will not lead to a re-tendering obligation but can effect the necessary adaptation within the contractual framework originally conceived.
- In addition, strict re-tendering obligations force the parties to be more careful in the conclusion phase in order to avoid post-contract inefficiencies.
- Procurement law and the *Pressetext* case law specifically aim at preventing the problems described, namely the renegotiation in favour of a private party. Such renegotiation possibilities render the tender procedure inefficient as they give an opportunity (and incentive) to bid aggressively and frivolously. A strict enforcement of the re-tendering obligation can prevent such behaviour as the bidder will understand that he is tied to the terms of the contract as awarded or faces damages claims.
- I agree that renegotiations are not a sign of failure of a contractual relationship. They may be a sign, though, of sloppy drafting.
- In general, I believe that the term of the contract and the complexity of an economic environment are more likely to lead to renegotiations than the distinction between a 'traditional procurement contract' and a 'PPP'.

## 4 Reply by Stéphane Saussier

The provided note is very clear and I have very few comments or questions.

### 4.1 *Concerning procurement rules*

- From a lawyer's point of view, do rules exist to foster competition or to put all potential bidders on an equal footing? Still on this issue, what is the discretionary margin that is allowed for public authorities to choose the winning bid not only on objective but also on subjective criteria? Would such behaviour (from the public authority) constitute a breach of procurement rules?
- From my point of view, economists would consider that to foster competition and to achieve a good tendering result, it is sometimes necessary to let the public authority maintain a part of discretionary power that might not fit

well with the idea that procurement rules are framed in order to give equal chances to all bidders.

### *4.2 Concerning amendments of contracts and rules leading to re-tendering*

- Are they framed in order to reduce the possibility of opportunistic behaviours from private contractor and/or to limit corruption and/or capture?
- Do we observe many cases of contracts that are re-tendered because of amendments? I raise this question because I am not sure how transparent amendments in procurement contracts are, and how and who controls for them.
- When the private operator made investments, did the public authority have to refund the private operator for terminating the contract before the anticipated end? How do we measure a 'fair' amount in this case?
- I raise these questions because many empirical studies pointed out the fact that amendments (renegotiations in the economists' language) are the rule more than the exception.

## 5 Conclusions by Hans-Joachim Prieß

### *5.1 Concerning procurement rules*

- *From a lawyer's point of view, do they exist to foster competition or to put all potential bidders on an equal footing? Still on this issue, what is the discretionary margin that is allowed for public authorities to choose the winning bid not only on objective but also on subjective criteria? Would such behaviour (from the public authority) constitute a breach of procurement rules?*

Answer/comment: the object and purpose of the procurement rules is to implement the fundamental freedoms of the TFEU in the area of public procurement. This means that their function is essentially to rule out discrimination and to ensure equal treatment of bidders, to ensure the necessary transparency (making sure there is equal access to public tender procedures). The competition aspect is less pronounced but still relevant in a subsidiary way: the Court has for example allowed a contracting authority to proceed with an award decision in a case where only one bidder remained in the procedure. But it also stated that there is no obligation to proceed with the award in such a case – so there is a certain margin of discretion as to whether the result reached in the opinion of the contracting authority represents good/fair market value and is the result of a functioning competition.

Subjective criteria (for example the 'quality' of a project/solution description) can play a significant role but the contracting authority must be able to explain the rationale of their use and application as this is reviewed by courts. If a contracting authority cannot explain that/how it applied the subjective criteria in a non-discriminatory fashion the award decision will be overturned.

### *5.2 Concerning amendments of contracts and rules leading to re-tendering*

- *Are they framed in order to reduce the possibility of opportunistic behaviours from the private contractor and/or to limit corruption and/or capture?*

Answer/comment: the primary function of a re-tendering obligation is to prevent a distortion of the tender result. Often, the 'necessary' changes really alter the contract terms in a way that – had they been known at the stage of the tender procedure – additional bidders might have participated (affecting the transparency of the process and the access to the tender) or non-successful bidders may have presented different and probably more successful bids (affecting the equal treatment or non-discrimination principle). As far as a change in the contract partner is concerned, what needs to be prevented is that a public contract is 'acquired' by direct (intransparent/discriminatory) negotiations between the contracting authority, its contract partner and one pre-selected acquirer. The underlying idea is that any such change should occur in a procedure that safeguards transparency and non-*discrimination.*

- *Do we observe many cases of contracts that are re-tendered because of amendments? I raise this question because I am not sure how transparent amendments in procurement contracts are, and how and who controls for them.*

Answer/comment: I believe yes, because contracting authorities are either not well-advised and take the risk for the contract. The only effective means of control is a review proceeding but if the amendment does not leak out into the press how can the competitors of the contractor become aware of what goes on?

- *When the private operator made investments, does the public authority have to refund the private operator for terminating the contract before the anticipated end? How do we measure a 'fair' amount in this case?*

Answer/comment: this is strictly speaking not a procurement law issue but rather one to be dealt with in the contract. As any transfer of the contract requires the consent of the current contractor he normally has a strong negotiating position to ask for and obtain adequate compensation for investments not yet recovered – most probably from the new contractor. The new contractor can then recover this compensation amount over the term of the contract.

- *Those questions because many empirical studies pointed out the fact that amendments (renegotiations in the economists' language) are the rule more than the exception.*

Answer/comment: I agree, in practice most longer term contracts require some adaptation but this can be provided for in the contract through change clauses. These cannot, however, provide for unlimited changes.

## 6 Conclusions by Stéphane Saussier

### *6.1 The need to re-tender the contract*

If we accept that renegotiations are the rule and not the exception, that they often are substantial and do not always lead to a reduction of social surplus, the question of re-tendering renegotiated contracts is not an easy one.

On the one side, it might be justified because renegotiations change the nature of what was put to tender. On the other hand, this would lead to frequent re-tendering processes and may generate high social costs, especially by delaying projects. Another question concerns the fact that such re-tendering process is feasible. To the extent of my knowledge, we observe few cases of contracts that are re-tendered because of amendments. Probably because amendments in procurement contracts are not transparent and carefully controlled. But another issue concerns the situations in which private operators made (specific) investments. In case of re-tendering, the public authority has to refund the private operator for terminating the contract before the anticipated end and the measure of a 'fair' amount might be complex.

### *6.2 Conclusion*

What I wanted to stress in this short note is that as soon as you consider contracts as incomplete coordination mechanisms framed by economic actors with limited abilities, the economic analysis suggests that, first, *ex post* adaptation is necessary and is a condition of contract efficiency and, second, efficient procurement rules might necessitate to give some discretionary power to the public authority in order to reduce the number of bidders and to choose the best offer. It follows that the question of the necessity to re-tender a contract because of *ex post* changes is not obvious and might lead to rigidities limiting adaptations and hence efficiency of contractual agreements. When errors have been made at the bidding stages and the breach of procurement is coming from the public side, economists would advise to fine public authorities instead of considering re-tendering the contract in order to avoid social costs associated with delayed projects.

## Note

1 In the draft new public procurement directives published on 20 December 2011 the European Commission suggests the codification of rules for contract amendments along the lines of the CJEU jurisprudence referred to in this chapter. The proposals also introduce benchmarks at which the modification will not be considered substantial (provided the modification does not alter the overall nature of the contract), for

example where the cumulative value of the amendments is less than 5 per cent of the original contract price.

## References

Amaral, M., Saussier, Stéphane and Yvrande-Billon, A. 2009. Auction procedures and competition in public services: the case of urban public transport in France and London. *Utilities Policy*, 17(2), 166–75.

Bajari, P., Houghton, S. and Tadelis, S. 2006. Bidding for incomplete contracts: an empirical analysis. *NBER Working Paper*.

de Brux, J. 2010. The dark and bright sides of renegotiation: an application to transport concession contracts. *Utilities Policy*, 18(2), 77–85.

de Brux, J., Beuve, J. and Saussier, Stéphane. 2011. The impact of renegotiations on the value of contractual relationships? An empirical investigation. *Working Paper, Chaire EPPP - Sorbonne*.

Calzolari, G. and Spagnolo, G. 2009. Relational contracts and competitive screening. *SSRN eLibrary*. Available at: http://papers.ssrn.com/sol3/papers.cfm?abstract_id=1484466 [last accessed 29 April 2011].

Crocker, K.J. and Masten, S.E. 1991. Pretia ex machina: prices and process in long term contracts. *Journal of Law and Economics*, 34(1), 64–99.

Crocker, K.J. and Reynolds, K.J. 1993. The efficiency of incomplete contracts: an empirical analysis of Air Force engine procurement. *RAND Journal of Economics*, 24(1), 126–46.

Desrieux, C., Chong, E. and Saussier, Stéphane. 2012. Putting all one's eggs in one basket: relational contracts and the provision of local public services. *Journal of Economic Behavior & Organization* (forthcoming).

Estache, A. 2006. PPI partnerships vs. PPI divorces in LDCs. *Review of Industrial Organization*, 29(1), 3–26.

Fehr, E., Hart, O. and Zehnder, C. 2011. Contracts as reference points: experimental evidence. *American Economic Review*, 101(2), 493–525.

Gil, R. and Marion, J., 2009. The role of repeated interactions, self-enforcing agreements and relational [sub]contracting: evidence from California highway procurement auctions. *Unpublished manuscript, University of California, Santa Cruz*.

Grossman, S.J. and Hart, O. 1986. The cost and benefits of ownership: a theory of vertical and lateral intégration. *Journal of Political Economy*, 94(4), 691–719.

Guasch, J.L. 2004. *Granting and Renegotiating Infrastructure Concession: Doing It Right*. Washington, DC: The World Bank.

Guasch, J.L., Laffont, J.-J. and Straub, Stéphane. 2006. Renegotiation of concession contracts: a theoretical approach. Available at: http://neo.univ-tlse1.fr.

Guasch, J.L., Laffont, J.-J. and Straub, Stéphane. 2007. Concessions of infrastructure in Latin America: government-led renegotiation. *Journal of Applied Econometrics*, 22(7), 1267–94.

Guasch, J.L., Laffont, J.-J. and Straub, Stéphane. 2008. Renegotiation of concession contracts in Latin America: evidence from the water and transport sectors. *International Journal of Industrial Organization*, 26(2), 421–42.

Hart, O. 1995. *Firms, Contracts and Financial Structure*. Oxford: Oxford University Press.

Hart, O. and Moore, J. 2008. Contracts as reference points*. *Quarterly Journal of Economics*, 123(1), 1–48.

Lambert-Mogiliansky, A. and Kosenok, G. 2009. Fine-tailored for the cartel-favoritism in procurement. *Review of Industrial Organization*, 35(1–2), 95–121.

Macaulay, S. 1963. Non-contractual relations in business: a preliminary study. *American Sociological Review*, 28(1), 55–67.

Saussier, Stephane. 2000. Transaction costs and contractual incompleteness: the case of Electricite de France. *Journal of Economic Behavior and Organization*, 42(2), 189–206.

Spiller, P.T. 2008. An institutional theory of public contracts: regulatory implications. *NBER Working Paper*, 14152.

# 11 When amending leads to ending

## A theoretical and practical insight into the retendering of contracts after a material change

*Jan M. Hebly and Paul Heijnsbroek*[1]

### 1 Introduction

What is the value of the European procurement procedure if the contract ultimately performed by the successful tenderer is completely different from the public contract that was put out to tender? Leaving aside for a moment the legal aspects (which will be examined later), other tenderers may take exception because they are not given the chance to tender for that contract. The lack of competitive pressure on the tender for the final contract can also be undesirable from a government perspective. The doctrine of 'material change' avoids this problem: material changes may not be made to an agreement formed after a European award procedure. If they are, it creates a new contract which in principle has to be advertised in a European award procedure. The original contract has then been amended to such an extent that it ends.

This doctrine has a significant influence in practice. It is not uncommon for parties to want to amend a contract when circumstances change during its term. If this results in a 'material change', the proposed amendment can be completely undermined. Publishing a fresh invitation to tender could mean a different successful tenderer and it is therefore an absolute precondition for parties to the contract that any amendments made remain within the framework of procurement law.

Despite its practical importance, research on the subject remains limited. Legislation is virtually silent on this issue and there is little ECJ case law:[2] this gives rise to legal uncertainty during the implementation of contracts formed following a European award procedure. We will attempt to shed more light in this chapter on what constitutes a material change and discuss the potential consequences.[3] In doing so, we will also examine actual cases in the Netherlands and extract what we consider to be the most serious obstacles in practice. We will conclude by presenting a number of recommendations on those points.

In this chapter, we will focus primarily on amendments during the term of an agreement. However, to gain a thorough understanding we must first pause briefly to consider existing legislation and regulations, which as we will see focus primarily on the admissibility of amendments prior to implementation.

## 2 EU legislation on amendments

### *2.1 Amendments during the award procedure*

The Council and the Commission incorporated the following general statement on amendments during the award procedure in the amendment of the Works Directive in 1989:[4]

> The Council and the Commission state that in open and restricted procedures all negotiations with candidates or tenderers on fundamental aspects of contracts, variations which are likely to distort competition, and in particular on prices, shall be ruled out; however, discussions with candidates or tenderers may be held but only for the purpose of clarifying or supplementing the content of their tenders of the requirements of the contracting authorities and provided this does not involve discrimination.

It follows from this statement that during the award procedure, amendments of the contract (as a result of negotiations) are not allowed, insofar as the amendments concern fundamental aspects of the contract.

### *2.2 Negotiated procedure*

The existing procurement directives from 2004 (classic and utilities sectors) contain an obligation to invite tenders for public contracts.[5] There are, however, a few exceptional cases in which the award procedures prescribed in the directives (which assume prior publication in the European Official Journal) do not have to be followed.[6] In such cases, therefore, a tender procedure without the mandatory prior notification (a so-called direct award) is permitted.

#### *2.2.1 Unsuccessful award procedure*

One such exception is the open or restricted award procedure in which no tenders, no suitable tenders, or no applications have been submitted.[7] If the procurement procedure is unsuccessful, however, the contracting authority may only award the contract without following a new procedure in accordance with the Directive:[8] 'provided that the initial conditions of contract are not substantially altered'. The Commission indicated in its Guides in 1997 that the condition that the original terms of the contract not be substantially altered is not in any event met in the following cases: changes to the financing conditions, the deadlines for completion, the requirements for acceptance of the works, the construction technique or the technical specifications.[9]

### *2.2.2 Additional works, services or supplies*

Another exception relates to contracts for additional works or services. The prescribed procurement procedures need not be followed:[10]

> for additional works or services not included in the project initially considered or in the original contract but which have, through unforeseen circumstances, become necessary for the performance of the works or services described therein, on condition that the award is made to the economic operator performing such works or services:
>
> - when such additional works or services cannot be technically or economically separated from the original contract without major inconvenience to the contracting authorities, or
> - when such works or services, although separable from the performance of the original contract, are strictly necessary for its completion.
>
> However, the aggregate value of contracts awarded for additional works or services may not exceed 50% of the amount of the original contract.

The Directives contain a similar exception for additional supplies.[11] The negotiated procedure without prior publication may be followed:

> for additional deliveries by the original supplier which are intended either as a partial replacement of normal supplies or installations or as the extension of existing supplies or installations where a change of supplier would oblige the contracting authority to acquire material having different technical characteristics which would result in incompatibility or disproportionate technical difficulties in operation and maintenance; the length of such contracts as well as that of recurrent contracts may not, as a general rule, exceed three years.

The provisions above were already present in the predecessors of the current procurement directives, albeit in a slightly different wording. The Works Directive, Supplies Directive and Service Directive contained similar exceptions for failed invitations to tender, in which case direct award was allowed.[12] The same applied for additional works, supplies and services.[13]

## ***2.3 Competitive dialogue***

What is new in the 2004 Procurement Directive for the classic sectors is the competitive dialogue. The preamble to the Directive establishes that this procedure must not be used in such a way as to restrict or distort competition, particularly by altering any fundamental aspects of the offers, or by imposing substantial new requirements on the successful tenderer, or by involving any tenderer other than the one selected as the most economically advantageous.[14]

This principle is elaborated in Article 29, paragraph 6, of the Directive regarding the contracting authority's entitlement to request tenderers to clarify, specify or fine-tune their tenders: 'However, such clarification, specification, fine-tuning or additional information may not involve changes to the basic features of the tender or the call for tender, variations in which are likely to distort competition or have a discriminatory effect.' Once the most economically advantageous tender has been identified, the contracting authority can request the tenderer to clarify aspects of the tender or to confirm commitments made in the tender. Article 29, paragraph 7 further imposes the condition: 'provided this does not have the effect of modifying substantial aspects of the tender or of the call for tender and does not risk distorting competition or causing discrimination'. Consequently, scope for negotiating with the envisaged successful tenderer is extremely limited.[15] In light of the above statement by the Council and the Commission, it must be assumed that this limited scope also applies to the other award procedures.

The procurement directives do not include a *general* provision imposing limits on changes to the tender documentation in the course of the procurement procedure.[16] The case law of the Court, however, shows that such changes may not extend to the award criteria. The principles of equal treatment and transparency impose an obligation on contracting authorities to apply the same interpretation to the award criteria throughout the entire procedure.[17] It follows from this, according to the Court, that no changes may be made to the award criteria in the course of the procurement procedure.[18] Arguably, the same argument also applies to changes to eligibility requirements and selection criteria.[19]

With regard to changes to the tender itself, the Court has taken as its basic premise that:

> When a contracting entity takes into account an amendment to the initial tenders of only one tenderer, it is clear that that tenderer enjoys an advantage over his competitors, which breaches the principle of the equal treatment of tenderers and impairs the transparency of the procedure.[20]

### 2.4 Interim conclusion

It is clear from the foregoing that although the procurement directives introduce the concept of 'material change', they provide no further elaboration.

All of these provisions set out three situations in which contracts must be put out to tender: after an unsuccessful procurement procedure, in the context of a competitive dialogue, or in the case of additional contracts that must be awarded to the original contractor.

But what are the procedures to follow for any changes that might occur during the implementation of an awarded contract? After all, the procurement procedure has already been concluded and there is often no clearly separate additional contract in such cases or the stringent requirements for additional contracts in the directives are not met. From the late 1990s, the Court has used the doctrine of material change to address this lacuna.

## 3 Changes during the implementation phase

The first indications of the importance of and need for a procurement law framework for changes during the implementation phase can be found in the jurisprudence of the Court (Section 3.1). The Commission has also started to focus on this subject (Section 3.2).

### *3.1 European Court of Justice jurisprudence*

#### *3.1.1 Tögel*

In his opinion on the *Tögel* case, AG Fennelly examines, *inter alia*, the admissibility of changes during the performance of the contract and proposes that only national law determines whether a contract is continued or whether it must be renegotiated,[21] in which case, according to the AG, the procedures of the Procurement Directive must be followed.

#### *3.1.2 Rennes*

However, the Court makes clear in subsequent case law that the admissibility of a change must be assessed under European law. In its ruling in *Rennes*, the Court considers a negotiation process that had started before the relevant Procurement Directive (Directive 93/38/EEC) became applicable.[22] Nevertheless, the question of renegotiation arose subsequently because of the withdrawal of funding for the project. The Court held that it must be determined whether these negotiations:

> were substantially different in character from those already conducted and were, therefore, such as to demonstrate the intention of the parties to renegotiate the essential terms of the contract, so that the application of the provisions of Directive 93/38 might be justified.

However, the Court also held that the Commission had not adequately demonstrated the existence of such justification for applying the Procurement Directive. Whereas the Commission had argued that there were substantial differences in technology and price, the Court held that the difference in technology was linked to development of the equipment and the fact that parties take technical developments into account during lengthy negotiations does not need to be construed as negotiating on the essential terms of the contract. With regard to price, the Court found that the adjustment was based on the correct application of a price revision formula that had been agreed to by the parties in the context of the original negotiations.

### *3.1.3 Succhi di Frutta*

Some years later, the Court gave its ruling in the *Succhi di Frutta* case,[23] which centred on an invitation to tender issued by the Commission. The Court emphasized that a contracting authority must respect the principle of equal treatment of tenderers. The transparency principle follows from the principle of equality. On the grounds of these principles in particular, the Commission must respect its own criteria, not only during the registration process as such, but more generally until the end of implementation of the relevant tender.[24]

The Court held that a contracting authority:

> may not alter the general scheme of the invitation to tender by subsequently proceeding unilaterally to amend one of the essential conditions for the award, in particular if it is a condition which, had it been included in the notice of invitation to tender, would have made it possible for tenderers to submit a substantially different tender.

In this case, the Court held that one of the essential conditions for the award had been the subject of such an amendment, namely the payment terms.

In the *Succhi di Frutta* ruling, the Court also indicated how the Commission could have avoided this breach of the principles of equality and transparency. According to the Court, the Commission could have expressly included scope for adjustment in the notice of invitation to tender, defining the conditions under which adjustments could be made.[25]

### *3.1.4 Commission* v. *France*

Shortly afterwards, in the *Commission* v. *France* ruling, the First Chamber of the Court examined a change to a French procurement procedure for the construction of a sewage treatment plant.[26] The entire project consisted of three phases; an invitation to tender was issued for the first and third phases. The notice for the invitation to tender for the first phase indicated that the successful candidate '[may] be invited to cooperate in the execution of his idea, under a study contract for [inter alia] the provision of assistance to the maître d'ouvrage envisaged in the first and third parts of the second phase'.[27] The contract for these services in the second phase (in which the estimated value exceeded the threshold value) was then awarded to the successful candidate in the invitation to tender for the first phase. The Commission alleged that a new procurement procedure was required and started infringement proceedings.

The Court agreed with the Commission, holding that the principles of equal treatment and transparency require the subject matter of each contract and the criteria governing its award to be clearly defined. The Court continued:[28]

> That obligation exists where the subject matter of a contract and the criteria selected for its award must be regarded as decisive for the purposes

> of determining which of the procedures provided for in the directive is to be implemented and assessing whether the requirements related to that procedure have been observed. It follows that in the present case the mere option of awarding the contract relating to the second phase according to criteria laid down in respect of a different contract, that is the one related to the first phase, does not amount to awarding the contract in accordance with one of the procedures laid down in the Directive.

### *3.1.5 Pressetext*

Almost four years later, the *Pressetext* case gave the Court the opportunity to comment specifically on the impact of changes made during the term of a contract.[29] The Austrian referring court wanted to know the conditions under which changes to an existing contract between the contracting authority and a service provider can be regarded as a new award of a public contract for services within the meaning of the applicable Procurement Directive (Directive 92/50/EEC).

The core of the Court's response is found in the following passage:[30]

> In order to ensure transparency of procedures and equal treatment of tenderers, amendments to the provisions of a public contract during the currency of the contract constitute a new award of a contract within the meaning of Directive 92/50 when they are materially different in character from the original contract and, therefore, such as to demonstrate the intention of the parties to renegotiate the essential terms of that contract.

After citing the *Rennes* ruling discussed above, the Court went on to indicate that an amendment to a public contract during its currency may (in any event) be regarded as being material if:[31]

- a it introduces conditions which, had they been part of the initial award procedure, would have allowed for:
  - i the admission of tenderers other than those initially admitted; or
  - ii would have allowed for the acceptance of a tender other than the one initially accepted;
- b it extends the scope of the contract considerably to encompass services not initially covered; or
- c it changes the economic balance of the contract in favour of the contractor in a manner which was not provided for in the terms of the initial contract.

The alternative under (b), in the opinion of the Court, was confirmed in the restrictions imposed by the applicable Procurement Directive on the extent to which contracting authorities may use the negotiated procedure for awarding services without prior publication of a notice for additional services.[32]

The Court first set out these general terms and then went on to assess a number of specific changes. In none of these cases did the Court accept that there was a material change. The following were some of those changes that the Court did not accept as being material:

- the change of the contracting authority's contractual partner is in principle a material change except in the event of internal reorganization. The same applies to the transfer of shares in the contract or partner to a third party, other than a normal share transfer in respect of a listed company;
- the conversion to euros of prices initially expressed in the national currency constitutes an adjustment to accommodate changed external circumstances and as such is not a material change. A further price adjustment in order to round off the price to the detriment of the contractor will not cause a material change;
- the replacement of the price index by a subsequent index was provided for in the original contract and does not therefore constitute a material change;
- the inclusion of a clause containing a temporary waiver of the right to terminate the contract does not, in the view of the Court, entail a risk of distorting competition to the detriment of potential new tenderers. The Court states as the reason that there is nothing in the case file to indicate that the contracting authority would have actually considered terminating the contract during the currency of that clause. Nor does an increase in the rate of rebates entail distortion of competition to the detriment of potential tenderers. Moreover, that increase does not shift the economic balance of the contract in favour of the contract.

### *3.1.6 Wall*

In the *Wall* ruling, the Grand Chamber of the Court applied the basic principle of the *Pressetext* ruling to service concessions and confirmed the scope for material change described in (a) above:[33]

> In order to ensure transparency of procedures and equal treatment of tenderers, substantial amendments to essential provisions of a service concession contract could in certain cases require the award of a new concession contract, if they are materially different in character from the original contract and are therefore such as to demonstrate the intention of the parties to renegotiate the essential terms of that contract …
>
> An amendment to a service concession contract during its currency may be regarded as substantial if it introduces conditions which, if they had been part of the original award procedure, would have allowed for the admission of tenderers other than those originally admitted or would have allowed for the acceptance of an offer other than that originally accepted.

This case involved the substitution of the subcontractor. According to the Court, a change of subcontractor may constitute a material change in exceptional cases, even if the possibility of change is provided for in the contract: for instance, if the use of a particular subcontractor had been a decisive factor in concluding the contract.

The Court then goes on to outline the potential consequences of a material change. The Court observes that if the referring court concludes that one of the essential terms of the concession contract has been amended, 'all necessary measures must be taken, in accordance with the national legal system of the Member State concerned, to restore the transparency of the procedure, which may extend to a new award procedure'.[34]

### *3.2 The view of the Commission*

At the end of 2002, the European Commission made a decision on possible state aid to the London Underground Public Private Partnership.[35] In that context, the Commission examined *inter alia* whether changes in the contract conditions after the preferred bidder had been selected (by means of a negotiated procedure with prior notice) would have caused discrimination or unequal treatment.[36]

The Commission pointed out firstly that a contracting authority, in particular in a negotiated procedure,

> may include in the contract documents a mechanism which provides for ongoing testing (for example to ensure that performance criteria remain appropriate and provide necessary incentives) or external factors (such as inflation) which allow changes to be made throughout the procedure.

Changes made in accordance with such a system did not, in the view of the Commission, automatically cause discrimination, particularly in complex procurement procedures which are negotiated over a long period of time. This was the case in the London Underground PPP.

Moreover, the Commission observed that the changes in question 'are not so substantial, individually or collectively, as to be likely to have attracted prospective tenderers which did not consider tendering following publication of the original OJEC Notices'.

In the 2004 Green Paper on PPP, the Commission indicated that European procurement law did not generally reject the possibility of making changes to a PPP agreement during its term.[37] For instance, the tender documents may include review clauses which define the precise circumstances and conditions under which the contractual relationship can be adjusted. These provisions, according to the Commission, must always be sufficiently clear to allow the economic partners to interpret them in the same manner during the partner selection phase.

Changes not covered by such clauses call into question the principle of equality of treatment of economic operators, according to the Commission:

> Such unregulated modifications are therefore acceptable only if they are made necessary by an unforeseen circumstance, or if they are justified on grounds of public policy, public security or public health. In addition, any

> substantial modification relating to the actual subject matter of the contract must be considered equivalent to the conclusion of a new contract, requiring a new competition.

In the Commission's interpretative communication on institutionalized PPP in 2008, the Commission expresses its position somewhat differently,[38] proposing that if the contracting authority wishes to be able to change certain conditions, it must expressly formulate the notice or the specifications in such a way as to provide for that possibility and for the manner of implementation. If it does not, a change to the essential terms of the contract will require a new procurement procedure. Examples of this are the subject of the work or the user fee charged by the contractual partner. In a footnote, the Commission reiterates the above scope for justification of a material change, as set out in the 2004 Green Paper.

In the recent Green Paper on the future of European procurement law, the Commission indicates that the problem of successive changes affecting the contract itself and its implementation is a very complex issue.[39] The Commission understands from contracting authorities that the current jurisprudence of the Court is not explicit enough to determine whether a new award procedure is necessary. A possible statutory clarification at EU level could also regulate the *consequences* of a material change. The Commission cites as an example a simplified procedure for the award of the amended contract.

### 3.3 *Interim conclusion*

It follows from the foregoing that with European law as it stands, a change during the implementation of an awarded contract must pass through four phases:

1 What is the nature and extent of the change?
2 Was this change provided for in the tender documentation?
3 If not, is the change a material change?
4 If so, what are the consequences?

#### *3.3.1 Item 1 – nature and extent*

The first question is factual in nature and depends on the circumstances of the case.

#### *3.3.2 Item 2 – provided for in the tender documentation*

For the second question it is important to determine whether the tender documentation expressly specifies that the change may occur and the conditions under which it can then be implemented.[40] The Court of Justice stated this explicitly in the *Succhi di Frutta* ruling and it is also the concept that forms the basis for the examples in the *Pressetext* ruling, which are based on the premise that the change was not mentioned or included in the original procurement procedure or that the shift of economic balance as a result of that change was not envisaged under the terms of the original contract. Like the Court, the Commission seems to be in favour of a strict interpretation and, moreover, feels that any scope for change that is included must be sufficiently clear to allow all economic partners to interpret it in the same manner.

It follows from case law that price adjustments (indexation)[41] and adjustments in the method of payment[42] in particular can be 'incorporated' in advance. The implication of the *Commission* v. *France* ruling is, however, that a change is not foreseen if the tender documentation only provides for the mere possibility of extending the contract to other types of services without describing the services in the award criteria. It is assumed in the literature that in principle a change which requires mutual consent constitutes a new contract, even if the parties knew of the possibility in advance.[43]

### *3.3.3 Item 3 – material change*

Essentially, the Court has applied the same criterion since the *Rennes* ruling: changes must be deemed to be material if, first, they are materially different in character from that of the original contract and, second, are therefore such as to demonstrate the intention of the parties to renegotiate the essential terms of the contract.

The three examples from *Pressetext* elaborate on this basic premise, and form the current criteria. The Court's earlier position in *Succhi di Frutta*, that a material change exists if it has allowed the tenderers to submit a significantly different tender, is narrowed in *Pressetext* to the admission of other tenderers or the choice of an alternative tender. The Grand Chamber of the Court confirmed this interpretation in *Wall*, and it can therefore be assumed that the Court has definitively abandoned the opinion expressed in *Succhi di Frutta*.

The final assessment of whether there is a material change on the basis of the aforesaid criterion will depend to a large extent on the exact facts and circumstances. Nevertheless, it seems that from this it can be inferred that there are several types of change that are not automatically considered material:

- change due to technological developments;
- adaptation to external conditions, such as euro conversion;
- change of subcontractor (only a material change in exceptional circumstances).[44]

The same applies by analogy to the following changes, which actually do as a general rule constitute a material change:

- change to payment terms;
- change of contractual partner;
- change in the scope of work, particularly in the case of major expansion;

- change to the fee which the contractual partner charges third parties (specific to PPP);
- changes to terms relating to:
  - financing;
  - deadlines for completion and delivery;
  - building technology; or
  - technical specifications.

### *3.3.4 Item 4 – consequences*

The Court held in *Pressetext* that a material change constituted the award of a new contract within the meaning of the Procurement Directive. The Court ruled similarly in *Wall*, i.e. that a change to the essential terms of the contract may require, *inter alia*, a new procurement procedure to restore the transparency of the procedure.

The Commission also believes that a material change requires a new procurement procedure. The precise type of procurement procedure would have to be regulated by European law. The Commission cites the possibility of a simplified award procedure.[45]

However, the Commission seems to suggest that a new procurement procedure could be omitted altogether if the change were necessitated by an unforeseen event or on the grounds of public policy, public security or public health.[46] It is unclear whether the Court also concurs with these grounds for justification.

## 4 Dutch jurisprudence

In the Netherlands, changes during the implementation phase are a common occurrence and the courts have made numerous proposals for dealing with such changes from the perspective of procurement law. In this section, we will provide a brief overview of what we consider to be the most important rulings.

### *4.1 Application of ECJ case law in the Netherlands*

For a long time, the guiding case on the subject of changes was the Hague Court of Appeal's ruling of 1996, in which it held that a new invitation to tender is required[47]

> if the changes introduced to the schedule of requirements are such that the group of contractors with a potential interest in the original project differs from the group of contractors with a potential interest in the project after it is modified.

This criterion is very similar to the (much later) criterion (a)(i) from *Pressetext* (see above, p. 169).

In the Dutch jurisprudence since *Pressetext*, that ruling has seldom even been cited, let alone its criteria applied. The same applies to *Wall*. One of the few exceptions is a ruling by the Haarlem Court which contains a comprehensive assessment of the *Pressetext* criteria.[48] The contract involved the construction of a bridge and 200 dwellings and the relocation of a marina. The contract was changed in the course of implementation: the new location of the marina was changed and a further 18 dwellings were added. According to the summary proceedings judge, the extent of the change was minimal and, moreover, the nature of the change was not entirely different, thus the criterion at (a) was not satisfied. With regard to the criterion at (b), the summary proceedings judge applied Article 31, paragraph 4, of Directive 2004/18/EC. In this case, the court held that the additional work could not be technically and economically separated from the original contract without seriously inconveniencing the contracting authority. The inconvenience consisted of: first, a possible claim for compensation by the contractor if the amended contract work awarded to another contractor and, second, the inefficiency of having the 18 additional dwellings built by a third party instead of the contractor who was building the 200 dwellings in the same area. The value of the additional works, moreover, was under 50 per cent of the value of the original contract. With regard to the criterion at (c), the summary proceedings judge held that an unforeseen change in the economic balance had not been adequately demonstrated.

### *4.2 New tender procedure for a materially amended contract*

One subject which has not yet been referred to the European Court of Justice, but which comes up regularly in the Dutch courts, is the situation in which the contracting authority has withdrawn an invitation to tender, changed the contract, and published an invitation to tender for the amended contract.[49] In those situations the question arises whether the amended contract differs from the original contract to such an extent that the annulment of the original award procedure and the following retender are jusitified.

As such, this subject has no connection to the changes discussed here during the implementation phase, but it does relate to the procurement procedure for new contracts (see Section 2.4, with regard to the distinction between the award of a new contract and changes during the implementation of an awarded contract). In light of its minimal relevance in practice and the lack of relevant European case law, legislation and regulations, we believe that this Dutch case law can be dealt with briefly.

Dutch case law does not seem consistent on whether the doctrine of material change under European law is directly applicable in such cases, four of which we will examine below.

In an initial case in 2008 which concerned this type of invitation to tender for an amended contract, the 's-Hertogenbosch Court found that there must be a material change in the specifications of the actual work.[50] The division of the work into two lots[51] and changes to the selection criteria and/or the administrative provisions did not constitute a change to the specifications of the work. Reliance by the contracting authority on *Pressetext* did not affect this finding.

The second ruling relates to renovation work.[52] The Hague Court concurs that an invitation to tender for the amended contract is permissible provided the contracting authority has made material changes to the contract specifications. In this case, the changes consisted of contract variations valued at 25 per cent of the total contract price, which the court considered sufficient for a material change.

Towards the end of 2010, the Amsterdam Court held that a new invitation to tender could only be issued for a materially changed contract and therefore the required change was not limited to the contract specifications.[53] *Pressetext* forms the basis for determining the existence or otherwise of a material change. The court widened the *Pressetext* criterion (b) from just an *expansion* of the contract to include a *restriction* of the contract; the qualification 'significantly' was omitted entirely. The court believes that there is also a material change if the economic balance is shifted, which implies that a shift to the detriment of the contractor can also give rise to a material change.

However, in a very recent ruling the 's-Hertogenbosch Court returned to the 'old' consideration that a new invitation to tender is only permitted in the event of material changes to the contract specifications.[54]

### *4.3 Other noteworthy Dutch rulings*

One noteworthy ruling concerned a case in 2008 in which the rates in a contract awarded after a European tender were amended by a court. The contracting authority argued that this had caused a material change to the contract and that a new invitation to tender was required.[55] According to the court, if it is the contracting authority that initiates the change, the requirement of a new invitation to tender cannot be ruled out. However, a situation in which the court changes a contract is not covered by EU procurement regulations and therefore the municipality's defence failed.[56]

A recent ruling by the Hague Court in a case concerning the award by a municipality of a concession contract for services is also worthy of note. The municipality in question had invited tenders in a sort of beauty contest, in which 'the conditions under which a contract would be concluded with the successful tenderer were not clear in advance'.[57] This scope in the invitation to tender was an important reason for assuming that the operating contract ultimately concluded with the successful bidder did not constitute a material change in relation to the invitation to tender.

## 5 Issues in practice

Current European legislation and case law offer only a limited framework to determine whether a material change exists and, if so, what the consequences are. The paucity of Dutch case law serves to illustrate that the doctrine of material change is certainly not yet fully developed. In our practice we see this ambiguity giving rise to problems, particularly in certain areas which we will discuss below.

### *5.1 Should scope for change be included in tender documentation?*

In some cases, the (often problematic) assessment of whether there is a material change could be largely avoided by incorporating a scope-for-change clause in the tender documentation. For instance, this could include a unilateral option for additional works of the same nature or an objective change mechanism such as price indexation.[58]

In the most extreme cases, the result might be an award procedure for a type of 'outline agreement' that contains only basic premises and makes provision for subsequent elaboration of the exact nature and scope of the contract and the conditions under which it is implemented (cf. the aforementioned beauty contest in the case at the Hague Court). This type of contract would give the contracting authority and the contractor maximum flexibility with respect to future changes.

We believe, however, that such a contract is at odds with the basic principles of procurement law. The nature and scope of the contract put out to tender are not sufficiently precise to afford the tenderers equal opportunities to tender, thereby making room for discrimination and arbitrariness. After all, in that case the final contract as such is not subject to the competition of the procurement procedure and there is also a risk that the contract will be extended for years to come.[59]

Nevertheless, we believe that the nature and scope of the contract that is put out to tender can still be sufficiently defined if the invitation to tender provides for changes that are described in less detail than the unilateral options and objective change mechanisms referred to above. We concur in this context with Arrowsmith's argument that the reasonable expectations of the relevant sector can be important.[60] We also feel that the role, if any, of anticipated changes in the procurement procedure is relevant. In other words, could the possibility of changes be taken into account by tenderers when they formulated their tenders and by the contracting authority when it evaluated those tenders? If it cannot, as in the *Commission* v. *France* ruling, there is no 'foreseen change'. If it can, however, for example because work is based on unit prices which remain the same in the event of a change to the nature or scope of the work, it is our opinion that the doctrine of material change need not be applied. Moreover, we feel that the extent of the anticipated change in relation to the original contract is far less relevant in that context.[61]

### *5.2 Aggregation?*

The issue of potential changes to a contract is one which can be expected to arise more than once during its implementation. However, the scope for these changes is limited, namely to the level where the changes are considered essential.

In that context, it would seem self-evident that changes during implementation should be added together and assessed as a whole against the criteria of a material change. The most obvious point of reference for such a proposition is the provision in Article 31, paragraph 4(a), of Procurement Directive 2004/18/EC: the *total* value of contracts awarded for the additional work may not exceed 50 per cent of the value of the initial contract.

However, this sort of aggregation can lead to practical problems, particularly in longer-term contracts. Not only is scope for change increasingly limited over time as a result of each change, but in order to act lawfully it is required that such changes must be recorded properly so that they can be assessed as a whole to determine whether they (then) constitute a material change.

In our view, the basic principle should therefore be that each change should be judged on its merits under procurement law. In other words, whenever a change occurs, it must be assessed as such by reference to the doctrine of material change. The only circumstances in which this would vary would be if the effectiveness of European procurement law were jeopardized, in which case it might be necessary to consider two distinct (and chronologically separate) acts as a single legal act.[62] This might occur, for instance, if it were a foregone conclusion that certain changes will be made in phases, purely so that each individual change does not constitute a material change, whereas they would constitute a material change if taken as a whole.

### *5.3 Relationship between material change and additional contracts?*

A corollary to aggregation is the question of how the assessment of whether there is a material change relates to the limited scope which the public procurement directives provide for additional contracts. If the conditions of the applicable procurement directive are not met with respect to an additional contract, is the change a material change by definition? We do not believe it should be, particularly if the scope remains under the 50 per cent limit.[63] In our view, the doctrine of material change provides a framework for all types of changes, including additions. It is already established within that framework that additions that meet the conditions of the relevant procurement directive for additional contracts may be awarded directly to the existing contractor (as a new contract), in which case a substantive assessment to determine whether there is a material change can be omitted. In our view, that does not automatically imply that there is a material change if those conditions are *not* met: the addition in question must be assessed on its own merits on the grounds of the criteria developed by the Court.

A question which arises frequently in practice is whether additional contracts that can be granted to the original contractor on the grounds of the applicable procurement directive must be aggregated with the other changes for the purpose of determining whether they constitute a material change to the contract. As indicated above, we feel that the answer to this is 'no' unless European procurement law is circumvented.

### *5.4 Should a new procurement procedure be waived in the event of a material change?*

In principle, a new procurement procedure is required as soon as there is a material change. However, in certain circumstances this can be very unwelcome for the contracting authority, the original contractor and possibly the public interest.

The broadest grounds for justification are apparently those proposed by the Commission: a procurement procedure may be omitted if the change is necessitated by an unforeseen event. In such cases, however, the most obvious course is to primarily invoke the provisions of the applicable procurement directive relating to additional contracts, certainly if the terms can be interpreted as broadly as they were interpreted by the Haarlem Court in the ruling cited above (a potential claim for damages by the original contractor and inefficient performance constituted sufficient justification). Moreover, the interests of third parties might also be involved.[64]

At the moment, such grounds for justification have no sound basis in European legislation or case law. In our opinion, however, the waiver of a procurement procedure following a change is justifiable if it is likely that the original contractor will be the successful tenderer in a procurement procedure. During this process, the costs of the procurement procedure and the risks of another (second) contractor must also be taken into account.[65] The principle that a procurement procedure can be omitted if the successful tenderer can be indicated in advance is also to be found in the procurement directive in the justification for the negotiated procedure without prior notification for additional contracts, or alternatively in the event of technical or artistic reasons or for the protection of exclusive rights.[66]

### *5.5 Invitation to tender in the event of material change?*

If an invitation to tender is apparently unavoidable following a material change and 'amending' therefore leads to 'ending', this begs the question of what precisely must be included in the new invitation to tender, how it should be issued and when.

We believe that the basic principle should be that the invitation to tender for the amended contract is issued at the earliest opportunity and in accordance with one of the normal procurement procedures that would also apply in the event of a new contract rather than as a consequence of a material change. The earliest opportunity would then be determined by the effective date of the new contract. This date will depend first on the termination of the work already being performed under the original contract (the contract must be 'transferable') and second on the time required for a procurement procedure and an implementation period for the new contract. The contracting authority's potential liability for damages to the original contractor on account of termination of the contract would not then, in our opinion, play a role.

The amended contract would then have to be assessed in itself under procurement law to determine the type of procurement procedure required. For instance, it is conceivable that if the amendment occurs at the end of the original period of implementation, the estimated value of the amended contract will not exceed the threshold, in which case we do not feel that a European award procedure is required. In the further absence of a clear cross-border interest, the amended contract can be awarded directly to the original contractor.[67] In such circumstances, terminating the original contract and awarding the amended contract directly to the same contractor is highly artificial and unnecessarily complex. In our view, it should then therefore be possible to continue the contract after the material change.

To the extent that an invitation to tender is required for the amended contract, we see no automatic justification to allow the use of a different, simplified award procedure than that applied in respect of the original contract.[68] In some cases, a more flexible system could create an opportunity to circumvent the (new) obligation to invite tenders.[69]

### 5.6 Penalty

In the event of an illegal direct award, there is a risk of the contract becoming ineffective. Under the remedies directives as amended by Directive 2007/66/EC,[70] Member States must ensure that a contract resulting from an illegal direct award must be considered ineffective, where ineffectiveness is ascertained by or is the result of a decision of a review body that is independent of the contracting authority. Member States may limit the period within which a third party can claim ineffectiveness to six months.[71]

This was recently implemented in Dutch national legislation, which allows the contract entered into to be set aside (i.e. retroactively).[72] Given that this is a recent legislative amendment, it remains to be seen how often this heavy penalty will be sought and applied in practice.

## 6 Conclusion

The current legislation and regulations discussed in this chapter provide a framework for dealing with changes during the award procedure. The scope for implementing changes in such cases is limited by the goal of ensuring a fair and transparent procurement procedure: the changes must not undermine the importance of a fair invitation to tender in which the best tender is successful.

In our opinion, this framework is not adequate for changes made during the implementation phase. Despite gradual developments in recent years on this type of change in both case law and in legislation and regulations, the scope for change during the implementation phase and the possible consequences of a material change are still not clear. Any assessment is confronted with a conflict between the limited scope for changes during the award procedure on the one hand and on the other the need to amend an existing contract to take account of changed circumstances, where the best and most efficient implementation of the contract is in the interests of the principal (i.e. the contracting authority) and the contractor. This could be impaired if there were not enough scope for change. The interests of third parties (citizens) also play a role, particularly in the implementation of public works.[73] For instance, citizens are the ultimate users of public works such as a road and it is they who are inconvenienced by delays resulting from a new award procedure for the modified work, and bear the costs in their taxes.

To do justice to the differences between the procurement and the implementation phase, we advocate more scope for making changes during the implementation phase. We have made a number of concrete suggestions for ensuring that a change does not easily constitute a material change.[74]

However, we believe that if a material change is made at any time during implementation, it must result in a new invitation to tender in accordance with a normal award procedure.

## Notes

1 Jan M. Hebly and Paul Heijnsbroek are procurement lawyers at Houthoff Buruma, one of the leading law firms in the Netherlands. Jan Hebly is a partner in the firm, heads the 'Procurement Law Group' (PLG), and is a Professor of Construction and Procurement Law at the law faculty of Leiden University. Paul Heijnsbroek, an associate, is also a member of the PLG, and is an external doctoral candidate at the law faculty of Utrecht University.

2 See also A. Brown, 'When Do Changes to an Existing Public Contract Amount to the Award of a New Contract for the Purposes of the EU Procurement Rules? Guidance at Last in *Pressetext Nachrichtenagentur GmbH* (Case C-454/06)' (2008) 17 PPLR, NA253, Chapter 4, and AG Kokott in her opinion delivered on 13 March 2008 in case number C-454/06 (*Pressetext*), para. 42. The Commission describes it as a 'particularly complex issue' and points out that according to contracting authorities, case law is not explicit enough about some types of amendment; see 'Green Paper on the Modernisation of EU Public Procurement Policy. Towards a More Efficient European Procurement Market', COM(2011)15, p. 27.

3 In this chapter, our focus is on EU law. However, the issue of amending a contract formed after an award procedure is also dealt with in international regulations. See for example the Agreement on Government Procurement (1994) (GPA), signed in Marrakesh on 15 April 1994, Articles IX(10), XIII(1)(b), XIV(4)(b), XIV(4)(c), XV(1)(d) and XV(1)(f). The text can be found at www.wto.org/english/tratop_e/gproc_e/gp_gpa_e.htm; see on this subject: S. Arrowsmith, *Government Procurement in the WTO*, The Hague: Kluwer Law International, 2003, pp. 256–63. See also UNCITRAL Model Law on Procurement of Goods, Construction and Services ('UNCITRAL 1994'), Article 34 paragraph 1 (a), and Appendix 3, para. 9. The text of the UNCITRAL 1994 is available at www.uncitral.org/uncitral/en/uncitral_texts/procurement_infrastructure/1994Model.html. Both regulations are currently under revision, in which process explicit attention is paid to amendments in the context of procurement procedures. Regulations on this subject can also be found in the World Bank, Guidelines: Procurement of Goods, Works, and Non-Consulting Services under IBRD Loans and IDA Credits & Grants dated January 2011, para. 2.24–2.25, 2.46, 2.61–2.64, and 3.7 (a), as well as Appendix 1, para. 3.

4 OJEC 1989, L-210/22.

5 Directive 2004/18/EC, OJ 2004, L-134/114 and Directive 2004/17/EC, OJ 2004 L 134/1, both dated 31 March 2004.

6 Directive 2004/18/EC, Article 31.

7 Directive 2004/18/EC, Article 31(1)(a) and Directive 2004/17/EC, Article 40(3)(a).

8 The Directive contains a similar provision 'in the event of irregular tenders or the submission of tenders which are unacceptable under national provisions compatible

with Articles 4, 24, 25, 27 and Chapter VII'. In those circumstances, the negotiated procedure *with* prior publication may be used. See Directive 2004/18/EC, Article 30(1)(a).

9 Guide on Public Works Contracts, p. 25; Guide on Procurement of Services, p. 24.

10 Directive 2004/18/EC, Article 31(4)(a). Directive 2004/17/EC contains a very similar provision (Article 40(3)(f)), which however lacks a limitation to the value of the additional works or services.

11 Directive 2004/18/EC, Article 31(2)(b) and Directive 2004/17/EC, Article 40(3)(e). The latter provision does however not contain the 3-year limitation.

12 Directive 71/305/EEC, Article 9(a); Directive 77/62/EEC, Article 6(1)(a); Directive 92/50/EC, Articles 11(2)(a) and (11)(3)(a).

13 Directive 71/305/EEC, Article 9(f); Directive 77/62/EEC, Article 6(1)(e); Directive 92/50/EC, Article 11(3)(e).

14 Directive 2004/18/EC, recital 31. See also Jan M. Hebly, *European Public Procurement, Legislative History of the 'Classic' Directive 2004/18/EC*, Alphen aan den Rijn: Kluwer Law International, 2007, pp. 205–16.

15 See also the Commission's Explanatory note on competitive dialogue, p. 9.

16 This arises regularly in Dutch case law. See *inter alia* Interlocutory District Court of Haarlem, 6 August 2009, LJN: BJ6775 and Leeuwarden Court of Appeal, 15 May 2009, LJN: BI5096, in which the Leeuwarden Court of Appeal holds that no more stringent framework applies to such changes than that applicable to changes during implementation.

17 ECJ 18 October 2001, C-19/00 (*SIAC*), Pt. 43.

18 ECJ 4 December 2003, C-448/01 (*EVN and Wienstrom*), Pt. 93. According to the Court, dropping an award criterion constitutes such a change. The same applies to a change in the weighting of an award criterion, see ECJ 18 November 2010, C-226/09 (*Commission* v. *Ireland*), Pt. 62.

19 See also E.H. Pijnacker Hordijk, G.W. van der Bend and J.F. van Nouhuys, *Aanbestedingsrecht* [Procurement Law], The Hague: SDU Publishers, 2009, p. 288.

20 ECJ 25 April 1996, C-87/94 (*Walloon Buses*), Pt. 56.

21 Opinion of the AG dated 2 April 1998, Case C-76/97 (*Tögel*), para. 63 et seq. See the critique in S. Arrowsmith, *The Law of Public and Utilities Procurement*, London: Sweet & Maxwell, 2005, para. 6.10.

22 ECJ 5 October 2000 Case C-337/98 (*Rennes*), Pt. 42 et seq.

23 ECJ 29 April 2004, C-496/99 P (*Succhi di Frutta*).

24 ECJ 29 April 2004, C-496/99 P (*Succhi di Frutta*), Pt. 115.

25 ECJ 29 April 2004, C-496/99 P (*Succhi di Frutta*), Pt. 118–26.

26 ECJ 14 October 2004, C-340/02 (*Commission* v. *France*).

27 ECJ 14 October 2004, C-340/02 (*Commission* v. *France*), Pt. 11.

28 ECJ 14 October 2004, C-340/02 (*Commission* v. *France*), Pt. 35–6.

29 ECJ 19 June 2008, C-454/06 (*Pressetext*). See also A. Brown, op. cit.

30 ECJ 19 June 2008, C-454/06 (*Pressetext*), Pt. 34.

31 ECJ 19 June 2008, C-454/06 (*Pressetext*), Pt. 35–7. The AG noted in particular the criterion at (a), see AG Kokott in her opinion of 13 March 2008, Case C-454/06 (*Pressetext*), para. 49.

32 ECJ 19 June 2008, C-454/06 (*Pressetext*), Pt. 36.

33 ECJ 13 April 2010, Case C-91/08, Pt. 37–8. See also A. Brown, 'Changing a Subcontractor Under a Public Service Concessie: *Wall AG v Stadt Frankfurt am Main*' (2010) 19 PPLR, NA160.

34 ECJ 13 April 2010, Case C-91/08, Pt. 42.

35 State aid No N 264/2002, C(2002)3578.

36 Para. 86 et seq.

37 Green Paper on Public-Private Partnerships and Community Law on Public Contracts and Concessions, COM(2004)327, p. 16 et seq.

38 Commission interpretative communication on the application of Community law on Public Procurement and Concessions to institutionalised PPP (IPPP), OJ EU 2008 C-91/4.

39 'Green Paper on the Modernisation of EU Public Procurement Policy. Towards a More Efficient European Procurement Market', COM(2011)15, pp. 27–8. Moreover, the Commission recently concluded infringement proceedings against Spain which related to Spanish legislation. The Commission alleged that that legislation afforded contracting authorities almost unlimited scope for changing essential terms of the contract after its award. In a response to the Commission's objections, the Spanish adopted new legislation which limited that scope. See IP/11/430 of 6 April 2011. For other recent infringement procedures with regard to material amendments, see also IP/10/500 and IP/10/1244.

40 In this light, see also AG Bot in his opinion of 27 October 2009 in case C-91/08 (*Wall*), para. 65 and A. Brown, 'Changing a Sub-contractor Under a Public Service Concessie: *Wall AG v Stadt Frankfurt am Main*' (2010) 19 PPLR, NA160, para. 3.1.

41 See *Rennes* and *Pressetext* and *London Underground.*

42 See *Succhi di Frutta.*

43 Arrowsmith, op. cit., para. 6.9. According to Arrowsmith, foreseen changes can also give rise to a new contract if the changes in question are 'substantial changes'.

44 Adopted in the Netherlands by the Summary Proceedings Judge, The Hague Court, 30 November 2010, LJN: BO9252.

45 2011 Green Paper, op. cit., para. 2.5.

46 See in that context: Arrowsmith, op. cit., para. 6.7.

47 The Hague Court of Appeal, 19 February 1996, BR 1996/531.

48 The Summary Proceedings Judge, Haarlem Court, 30 March 2009, LJN:BH9057.

49 See also L. Sueters, 'Wezenlijke wijziging van een opdracht bij heraanbesteding' ['Material Change to a Contract upon Issue of New Invitation to Tender'] Tender Newsletter number 4, June 2009.

50 The Summary Proceedings Judge, 's-Hertogenbosch Court, 11 December 2008, LJN: BH2904.

51 For a similar opinion, based on national contract law, see the Summary Proceedings Judge, Rotterdam Court, 8 October 2008, LJN: BG3796.

52 The Hague Court, 16 June 2010, LJN: BN4842.

53 The Summary Proceedings Judge, Amsterdam Court, 8 December 2010, LJN: BO8420. See in the same context the Summary Proceedings Judge, Rotterdam Court, 10 March 2009, LJN: BH5386, and Summary Proceedings Judge, The Hague Court, 20 May 2011, LJN: BQ5311.

54 The Summary Proceedings Judge, 's-Hertogenbosch Court, 3 February 2011, LJN: BP2974.

55 The Summary Proceedings Judge, Alkmaar Court, 24 April 2008, LJN: BD0487; follow-up to Summary Proceedings Judge, Alkmaar Court, 3 April 2008, LJN: BC8558.

56 We believe this to be a controversial ruling, since the question of who initiated the amendment is not relevant to the effect of that amendment on the principle of equal treatment of the other tenderers. However, this ruling might be explained by the fact that it predates *Pressetext.*

57 The Hague Court, 18 August 2010, LJN: BN4777.

58 See also Arrowsmith, op. cit., para. 6.8.

59 See also Arrowsmith, op. cit., para. 6.9. In *Pressetext* the Court considered that the practice of concluding a public service contract for an indefinite period is in itself at odds with the scheme and purpose of the Community rules governing public contracts; see ECJ 19 June 2008, C-454/06 (*Pressetext*), Pt. 73.

60 See Arrowsmith, op. cit., para. 6.9.

61 Alternatively: Arrowsmith, op. cit., para. 6.10.

62 Cf. AG Mengozzi in his Opinion of 17 November 2009 in Case C-451/08 (*Müller*), para. 103–107 and ECJ 10 November 2005, C-29/04 (*Mödling*).

63 See also J.M. Hebly and M.B. Klijn, 'Wezenlijke wijziging van een overheidsopdracht', TBR 2008/157.

64 See for instance Summary Proceedings Judge, The Hague Court, 21 May 2010, LJN: BM5875. That case concerned the supply and installation of drainage channels in a shopping area which involved deviation from the terms of the tender documentation. In its opinion, the court also weighed the interests of retailers and residents in the area in the speedy completion of the work.

65 See in a similar sense Arrowsmith, op. cit., para. 6.6 and Hebly and Klijn, op. cit.

66 See for example P. Trepte, *Public Procurement in the EU. A Practitioner's Guide*, Oxford: Oxford University Press, 2007, para. 7.59 and 7.66.

67 ECJ 21 February 2008, C-412/04 (*Commission* v. *Italy*). We also believe that it is not inconceivable for a direct award to be allowed, even where there is a clear cross-border interest. This would arise if the specific circumstances of the case constituted an objective justification for the omission of a prior obligation of transparency.

68 See the Commission discussion of the issue raised above in its recent Green Paper.

69 For further detail, see the response of the Houthoff Buruma procurement working group to the Green Paper which is accessible via http://ec.europa.eu/internal_market/publicprocurement/modernising_rules/consultations/index_en.htm.

70 OJEC 2007, L-335/31.

71 Assuming that the contracting authority has not published the amendment.

72 For more information on the enforcement of EU public procurement rules, as well as the state of law in a number of other Member States, see Steen Treumer and Francois Lichère (eds), *Enforcement of the EU Public Procurement Rules*, Copenhagen: DJØF Publishing, 2011.

73 The public interest can also play a role in the context of whether or not an (amended) contract resulting from an illegal direct award should be declared ineffective: see Directive 2007/66/EC, Article 2d, para. 3.

74 Another suggestion that we have not developed further in this chapter would be to fix a de minimis to determine the shift of economic balance in favour of the contract, as provided for in *Pressetext* criterion (c).

# 12 Strengthening the level of integrity of public procurement at the execution phase

## Evidence from the Italian National Frame Contracts

*Gian Luigi Albano and Roberto Zampino*

### 1 Introduction

It is a widely shared view that corrupt practices undermine the main objectives of procurement processes. The problem is admittedly more widespread than what emerges for the hard evidence gathered by means of investigations or whistleblowing.[1] However intuitive to the layperson, the word 'corruption' may have so many, often misleading, shades so that an operational definition is needed. According to Transparency International (2006), 'corruption' describes 'the misuse of entrusted power for private gain', where 'private gain' should be interpreted widely, including 'gains accruing i.e. to an economic actor's close family members, political party and in some cases to an independent organization or charitable institution in which the economic actor has a financial or social interest'.[2]

Being a dysfunctional trait of any organization, corruption scandals especially in the public sector often trigger the temptation to 'overregulate', that is, to add more and more constraints to the choice of procurement officials. That legal rules matter is hardly questionable, but 'good economics' would teach that they ought to be designed in a way to provide 'correct' economic incentives to those who are involved in procurement processes.

The 'incentive approach' to minimize the risk of corruption in public procurement hinges on two founding observations. First, irrespective of the institutional and legal background, public procurement looks like a three-tier hierarchy where a *principal* – the government and, ultimately, the taxpayers – needs specific goods/services/civil works; an *agent* – procurement official(s), agency or any other office – implements the process to procure them; *firms* compete to provide them.[3] Second, when opening up the 'Pandora's box' of public procurement processes, we broadly observe quite a standard cycle: identification of needs and resources allocation, design and preparation of tender documents, tendering procedure, evaluation and contract award, contract management.

The two perspectives above become useful to characterize the potential contribution of an economic analysis of the integrity of public procurement process.

Since the degree of precision of rules and regulation is limited at least by unforeseeable contingencies, multiple choices available at each stage of the decision process will always create room for manipulation. Consequently, the allocation of precise responsibilities in the organization, and a consistent system of incentives and 'checks and balances' are needed to minimize the risk of corruption in public procurement processes.

In this chapter, we focus on one specific phase of the public procurement process which is arguably the most vulnerable to the lack of integrity: contract management (or contract execution). As we argue in more detail in the remainder of our work, there exist several reasons to worry about the contract execution phase. First, and perhaps foremost, regulatory frameworks mostly prescribe the 'rules of the game' until the contract award. Second, the contract execution concerns mainly two actors – the awarding authority and the contractor – interacting often for a long period of time outside of the reach of possible watchdogs such as the losing bidders.[4] Third, demand aggregation by means of framework agreements awarded by a central purchasing body (CPB) might put public authorities, purchasing goods and services through those framework agreements, in a more passive role than other public buyers that carry out the whole procurement cycle on their own.

The latter circumstance motivates our investigation. We exploit data from a quality auditing mechanism used to assess the degree of compliance with contractual clauses set in 11 National Frame Contracts[5] that were awarded in 2006–7 by Consip S.p.A. (Consip henceforth), the Italian Public Procurement Agency. Some of the studied National Frame Contracts are mandatory for central government, while local government has always the choice to use them or to carry out its own procurement process.

The extent of contract mismanagement looks daunting. Out of 743 inspections, 481 cases of breach of contract were collected, but only in 2.49 per cent of such cases penalty clauses were enforced by purchasing entities. Contract mismanagement seems to be less acute in low-service contracts, suggesting that when a contractor's performance is easily describable and verifiable (as, say, for the delivery of IT equipment) contract management may become an easier task. Moreover, local government performs better than central government as a contract manager, which is coherent with lower individual incentives in monitoring the contractor's performance in bigger public organizations such as ministries.

Worrisome as it may appear, widespread contract mismanagement does not provide evidence of corrupt practices per se. The difficulty of disentangling corruption from other explanations of contract mismanagement does not make the problem less severe as it jeopardizes the main objective of competitive procurement processes, that is, the best value-for-money measured when performance is delivered and not when tenders are submitted.

The remainder of our work is organized as follows. In Section 2 we survey the most pressing (economic) reasons on the integrity risks at the contract execution stage, and in particular when the award and post-award stages of a (public) procurement process are managed by two different authorities. Section 3 contains the main descriptive statistics on the quality monitoring system put in place to support those Italian public bodies using the National Frame Contracts awarded by Consip. In Section 4, we gather our main empirical results. Section 5 concludes.

## 2 The risk of integrity at the contract management stage of public procurement

Although the awarding stage is a critical link in the procurement chain, in principle all the efforts to assure competition, transparency and objective criteria in decision-making – that are instrumental to an efficient allocation of social resources – ought to be assured throughout the entire cycle of the public procurement procedure, from its inception until the completion of the execution of the contract. Yet, after the award, the public buyer may accept or suffer a different (that is, worse) performance. There are several reasons why we should be particularly concerned about the lack of integrity during the contract execution phase. First, the contract management phase stretches typically over a longer period than the contractor selection phase. While such time imbalance between the pre- and the post-award phase may be moderate in the procurement cycle of high-obsolescence goods such as IT equipment, it becomes more striking in the case of the procurement of infrastructures such as highways, bridges and tunnels. The longer the contract execution phase the more likely unlawful relations arise between the contractor and the contract manager(s). Indeed, the repeated nature of the interaction may give rise to cooperative strategies whereby profits arising from lower-than-promised levels of performance are shared between the contractor and the contract manager(s). Second, lack of integrity at the contract management stage may jeopardize de facto the competitive procedure leading to the contractor selection. As Racca *et al.* (2011) maintain, any violation, modification or worsening of the quality during the execution phase entail undue profit for the winner, thus giving rise to a change in the conditions set in the award, and consequently in the contractual equilibrium set therein. This leads to a violation of the competition principle as applied in the selection and in the award of the contract, which infringes the rights of losing bidders. Put differently, any substantial modification of the contractual terms during the contract execution is *as if* the contractor's quality-price tender had become *ex post lower* than the one submitted at the award stage. Consequently, the contractor does not guarantee, from an *ex post* perspective, the best value-for-money to the buyer.

More generally, integrity concerns about contract management are more likely to arise when the contract-awarding public authority does not coincide with that (or those) using the contract for making purchasing orders. This may occur when public procurement is centralized, at least to some extent, through a Central Procurement Agency (aka Central Procurement Body – CPB – in the European Directive 2004/18/CE), awarding framework agreements on behalf of other public authorities.[6] Such a separation of roles may generate low(er than efficient) contract management efforts simply because of imperfect knowledge of contractual clauses (i.e. penalty clauses and termination of the contract).[7]

Moreover, as a consequence of the just-mentioned problem, the much debated phenomenon of 'abnormally low bids' may occur because of bidders' 'rational' choice of recovering their additional 'investment' (i.e. lower mark-ups) at the bidding stage by delivering lower-than-promised performance levels.

In the remainder of the chapter, we will show that there exists at least some evidence that contract mismanagement is quite widespread, thus paving the way for possibly corrupt practices. We exploit the structure of the National Frame Contracts (NFCs) which are managed by Consip as part of the broader Italian programme for the rationalization of public spending in goods and services (the Programme henceforth). The NFCs consist of a set of contracts whereby competitively selected contractors undertake to accept – *at given conditions and prices* – orders from public administrations, up to a predetermined monetary amount or quantity of goods or, in any case, until the expiry date of the framework contract. Administrations send their online orders for supplies (fax orders are still possible) directly to the companies that have been awarded the contracts. All public administrations can make use of the NFCs. However, while central government (mainly ministries) are mandated to use NFCs, other authorities (regions, provinces, municipalities, school and health sectors) can use NFCs if they wish. However, whenever a NFC is active all other authorities have to meet-or-beat the quality-price ratio set by the standing NFC if they wish to perform a procurement process of their own.

According to the Italian legal system, the NFCs' life-cycle can be depicted as shown in Figure 12.1.

The whole procurement process may be split into two main phases. Consip is in charge of designing and managing most of the procurement process, that is, demand analysis (i.e. public buyers' needs), tender and contract documentation, supplier(s) selection and, when the case arises, litigation with claimant(s). Hence, Consip's mission is constrained by existing laws to the first part of the national NFCs process, whereas the second part – that is, contract management – is not *strictu sensu* within the scope of its mission.

## 3 Strengthening contract management in the system of the Italian National Frame Contracts

Since the beginning of the Programme, it was a shared view that, while potentially benefiting from lower unit price – due to demand aggregation – and

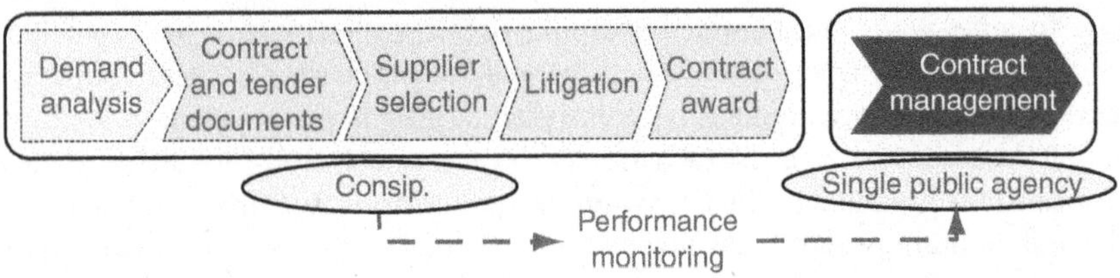


*Figure 12.1* The NFCs' life-cycle according to the Italian legal system.

procurement process simplification, public administrations making use of the NFCs might become progressively less active users as managerial efforts had to be focused on the management of a procurement contract they have played only an indirect role in designing. In order to lower the risk of contract mismanagement, in 2006 Consip designed and implemented a 'monitoring system' to provide assistance to public administrations' efforts at the management stage of the NFCs. The system consists in sending a number of inspectors/auditors all over the country to verify whether anything at the contract management stage has gone wrong, that is, whether any contractor has not performed in compliance with contractual terms.[8] An unbiased efficient monitoring system requires a reliable selection mechanism of inspectors/auditors. Only when a *random* selection mechanism is used – that is, each inspector is allocated to one particular geographical area but the sample of inspectors that actually go and visit public buyers is picked randomly – it is possible to gather high-quality data from inspections in order to carry out potentially insightful statistical analysis.

### *3.1 The sample of inspections*

Thanks to this mechanism, we built a reliable dataset of inspections carried out in 2008 within a number of NFCs. The sample comprises 11 NFCs, including seven mandatory and four non-mandatory NFCs.[9] As already mentioned, central government bodies must purchase through NFCs, whereas other public agencies can choose to use them if they wish or, alternatively, purchase on their own provided that they meet or beat the quality-price benchmark set by the NFCs.[10] Furthermore, our sample of NFCs can be split into six 'low-' and five 'high-service' components, according to the degree of potential complexity of contract management.[11] The results from 743 inspections draw a picture of how many and which types of public agencies were concerned (see Figure 12.2). Most inspections were conducted on local administrations (330, roughly 44.5 per cent), followed by central bodies (226, roughly 30.5 per cent), health and education bodies[12] (respectively, 96 and 91, that is, 13 per cent and 12 per cent). The location of inspections is more concentrated in the North of Italy for 48.5 per cent of cases (360), rather than in the South (214) and in the Centre (169).

The inspections aimed mainly at measuring some performance indicators related to objective quality dimensions concerning the execution of purchases/orders (before public buyers get the item), and those related to other dimensions such as the delivered (intrinsic) quality of goods and post-purchase services (after public buyers have received the item). Each dimension is measured by a 'compliance score' evaluated on a 1–5 scale, where quality increases from 1 to 5. Basically, these compliance scores were based on five quality dimensions, capturing different aspects of the overall supply:

1 the order execution process;
2 the intrinsic quality of the goods/services;
3 the administration services related to the supply;

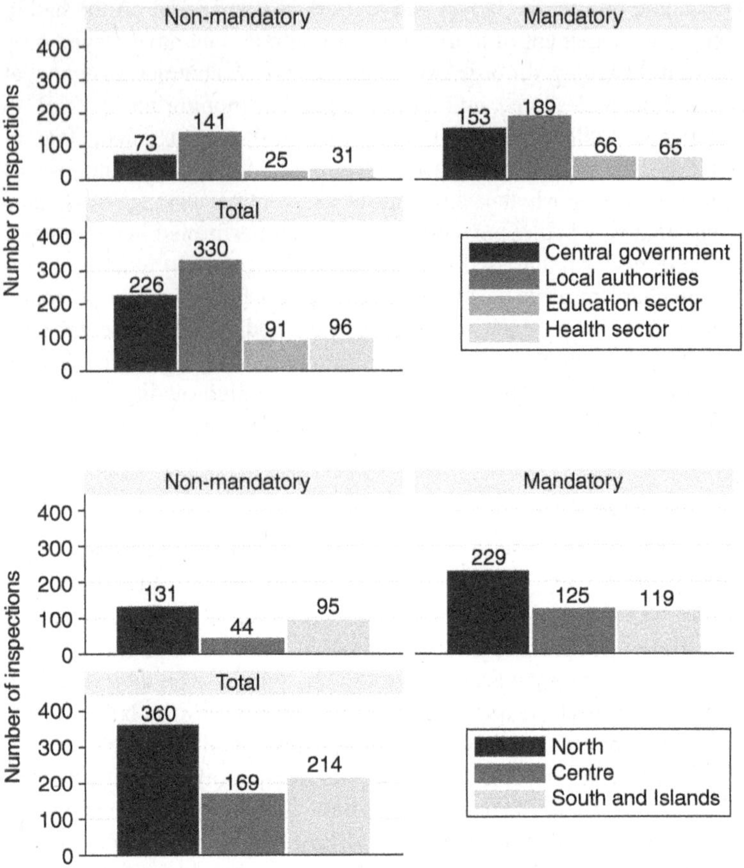


*Figure 12.2* Number of inspections by nature of the public bodies and geographical location.

4 the supplier's call centre services (e.g. average waiting time and/or accuracy of the information provided);
5 the supplier's post-purchase technical support (supply ancillary services).

The average total performance index (*avg_TPI*) summarizes all compliance scores for each inspection. In Table 12.1, we provide a list of the considered variables: besides the reference variable (*avg_TPI*) for the total performance index, which is information originally included in our sample, we construct a series of dummy variables (equal to 1 if true, and 0 otherwise) from the descriptive information referred to each inspection contained in our dataset. These variables represent the covariates included in our empirical analysis.

From a legal point of view, all evaluated quality dimensions are associated to contractually agreed penalty clauses to be levied when minimum levels of

*Table 12.1* Summary statistics of sample and constructed variables

| *Variable* | *obs.*[1] | *Mean* | *Std. Dev.* | *Min.* | *Max* |
|---|---|---|---|---|---|
| avg_TPI | 692 | 3.978195 | 1.361909 | 1 | 5 |
| mandatory NFCs | 692 | 0.640173 | 0.480297 | 0 | 1 |
| non-mandatory NFCs | 692 | 0.359827 | 0.480297 | 0 | 1 |
| central bodies | 692 | 0.300578 | 0.458841 | 0 | 1 |
| local authorities | 692 | 0.449422 | 0.497795 | 0 | 1 |
| education sector | 692 | 0.117052 | 0.321715 | 0 | 1 |
| health sector | 692 | 0.132948 | 0.339764 | 0 | 1 |
| north area | 692 | 0.498555 | 0.50036 | 0 | 1 |
| centre area | 692 | 0.223988 | 0.417216 | 0 | 1 |
| south area | 692 | 0.277457 | 0.448068 | 0 | 1 |
| low-service components (goods) | 692 | 0.536127 | 0.499054 | 0 | 1 |
| high-service components (services) | 692 | 0.463873 | 0.499054 | 0 | 1 |

Note

1 Here are presented the summary statistics concerning the reduced sample of inspections, that is 692 cases out of 743, coherently with the sample basis of statistics tests.

performance are not fulfilled (i.e. delivery time, etc.).[13] Table 12.2 suggests the extent of two opposite set of circumstances: those situations in which contract performance was almost close to perfect compliance (1,083); those in which (low) performance could have triggered the use of remedies (481). In spite of the sizeable set of non-compliances (30.75 per cent), figures show that only in 12 out of 481 cases (2.49 per cent) contractual remedies were effectively used (see Table 12.2). This simple observation might be reinterpreted as the probability that a bad-performing supplier (in relation to the agreed quality levels) gets caught and punished by the public buyer.

Why is contract mismanagement so severe? In principle, there might exist several (possibly coexisting) explanations:

1 *lack of knowledge*: one might reasonably argue that if contracting officers purchasing through NFCs play no role in drafting the latter (Consip is in charge of drafting NFCs), the same officers might not be as knowledgeable about all relevant contractual details as when the contract is drafted by the purchasing authority itself;

*Table 12.2* Sample of performance dimensions and measures of contract enforcement

| | |
|---|---|
| No. of cases of compliance | 1,062 |
| No. of cases of compliance with remarks | 21 |
| No. of cases of low non-compliance | 41 |
| No. of cases of mild non-compliance | 39 |
| No. of cases of high non-compliance | 401 |
| *Total no. of cases* | *1,564* |
| *Total no. of cases of non-compliance (NC)* | *481* |
| *No. of enforced penalty clauses (PC)* | *12* |

2 *lack of incentives*: contracting officers have to pay a positive cost in enforcing the contract but do not necessarily foresee any concrete benefit;
3 *in-kind compensations*: renegotiations between public buyers and suppliers, especially in case of more complex projects, might take place in that bad performance on one dimension might be compensated by the contractor's additional effort on another task;
iv finally, *corruption*: public officers might simply exert low effort in exchange for personal gains.

## 4 Main results

### *4.1 Descriptive statistics*

The analysis aims at identifying those potential factors able to affect the level of provided *ex-post* quality as well as the public buyer's satisfaction, mainly associated with both the nature and/or the mandatory scheme of provision and the public sector or geographical region of public buyers. The availability of exogenous variables (coming from the set of inspections carried out in 2008) and the random sample property allow us to conduct a rigorous analysis on inferred levels of contractual management. We run a number of individual *t-tests*[14] on the average levels of delivered (intrinsic) quality, which suggest that central government (30 per cent of total public buyers included in the sample) performs worse in terms of contract enforcement – with an average TPI of 3.84 – relative to local (45 per cent of total buyers), educational and health administrations, together achieving an average TPI of 4.70. One possible interpretation is that, in bigger organizations, contract management might be spread over a large number of officers, thus generating a free-riding problem, whereas at the local level it is more likely that contract managers interact on a day-by-day basis with suppliers and that administrations face tighter budget constraints. Our results on the central government's post-award behaviour (contract management) seem to be in line with those referring to the pre-award phase found by Bandiera *et al.* (2009). Nearly 48 per cent of inspections in central bodies resulted in non-compliance (the highest percentage, followed by the education system, 47 per cent), whilst penalty clauses have been enforced only in 2.78 per cent of cases (only the education system displays a lower performance). Table 12.3 shows the percentages of contractually agreed penalty clauses enforced by different sectors of public administrations against verified non-compliances.

Local authorities display a lower ratio of contractual non-fulfilments than those observed for other sectors (35 per cent) as well as the highest proportion of enforced penalty clauses (nearly 6 per cent). These findings are confirmed also by the distribution of values based on the classification between mandatory and non-mandatory contracts. Although the latter display the highest level of unsatisfactory performance (over 50 per cent),[15] the preponderance of local authorities in the sample (141 inspected non-mandatory contracts vs. 73 related to central bodies, 25 and 31 respectively referred to the education and the health sector)

*Table 12.3* Distribution of non-compliances and enforced penalty clauses by nature of public bodies

| *Non-compliances* | *Central bodies* | *Local authorities* | *Education sec.* | *Health sec.* |
|---|---|---|---|---|
| 0 | 118 | 213 | 48 | 57 |
| *1* | *57* | *94* | *37* | *37* |
| *2* | *10* | *15* | *1* | *1* |
| *3* | *17* | *6* | *3* | *1* |
| *4* | *18* | *1* | *1* | *0* |
| *5* | *5* | *1* | *1* | *0* |
| *6* | *1* | *0* | *0* | *0* |
| Total NC | 108 | 117 | 43 | 39 |
| % (on inspections) | 47.79% | 35.45% | 47.25% | 40.63% |
| Enforced penalty clauses | Central bodies | Local authorities | Education sec. | Health sec. |
| No | 223 | 323 | 91 | 94 |
| *Yes* | *3* | *7* | *0* | *2* |
| % (on NC) | 2.78% | 5.98% | 0.00% | 5.13% |

may again be associated with a better contractual management, as proved by the highest ratio of enforced penalty clauses (7.30 per cent, see Table 12.4).

Public buyers located in the North – roughly 50 per cent of the sample – do slightly better (being the average TPI equal to 4.61), in terms of contract enforcement, than those located in the rest of Italy (4.16); moreover, the Southern administrations (28 per cent of total) do better than the Central ones. The counterfactual analysis based on the distribution (by geographical location) of non-compliances and the resulting figures on enforced penalty clauses confirm both a lower level of unsatisfactory performance (40 per cent of inspections) and higher share of enforced penalty clauses (5.56 per cent, see Table 12.5) in the Northern regions.

*Table 12.4* Distribution of non-compliances and enforced penalty clauses in the two classes of NFCs

| *Non-compliances* | *Mandatory* | *Non-mandatory* |
|---|---|---|
| 0 | 303 | 133 |
| *1* | *139* | *86* |
| *2* | *13* | *14* |
| *3* | *6* | *21* |
| *4* | *9* | *11* |
| *5* | *3* | *4* |
| *6* | *0* | *1* |
| Total NC | 170 | 137 |
| % (on inspections) | 35.94% | 50.74% |
| Enforced penalty clauses | Mandatory | Non-mandatory |
| No | 471 | 260 |
| *Yes* | *2* | *10* |
| % (on NC) | 1.18% | 7.30% |

*Table 12.5* Distribution of non-compliances and enforced penalty clauses by geographical areas

| *Non-compliances* | *North* | *Centre* | *South and Islands* |
|---|---|---|---|
| 0 | 216 | 94 | 126 |
| *1* | *119* | *39* | *67* |
| *2* | *12* | *6* | *9* |
| *3* | *10* | *9* | *8* |
| *4* | *3* | *16* | *1* |
| *5* | *0* | *4* | *3* |
| *6* | *0* | *1* | *0* |
| Total NC | 144 | 75 | 88 |
| % (on inspections) | 40.00% | 44.38% | 41.12% |
| Enforced penalty clauses | North | Centre | South and Islands |
| No | 352 | 166 | 213 |
| *Yes* | *8* | *3* | *1* |
| % (on NC) | 5.56% | 4.00% | 1.14% |

Finally, let us have a look at the relation between the levels of contract enforcement and the degree of complexity of the purchased goods/services. Intuitively, we would expect higher levels of performance for standardized supplies, that is, the ones with low-service dimensions. Indeed the data support our intuition (the average TPI being equal to 4.97 vs. 3.09 in the case of high-service dimensions). Figures on non-compliances are also consistent with the previous consideration since the share of non-compliances in the case of high-service components is roughly 2 per cent higher than the one for low-service components. Surprisingly, however, the fraction of enforced penalty clauses in the latter case is fairly higher than in the case of high-service (5.06 per cent vs. 2.68 per cent) suggesting a simpler/less costly process for levying penalties in low-service contracts.

*Table 12.6* Distribution of non-compliances and enforced penalty clauses by contract complexity

| *Non-compliances* | *Low-service* | *High-service* |
|---|---|---|
| 0 | 234 | 202 |
| *1* | *149* | *76* |
| *2* | *8* | *19* |
| *3* | *1* | *26* |
| *4* | *0* | *20* |
| *5* | *0* | *7* |
| *6* | *0* | *1* |
| Total NC | 158 | 149 |
| % (on inspections) | 40.31% | 42.45% |
| Enforced penalty clauses | Low-service | High-service |
| No | 384 | 347 |
| *Yes* | *8* | *4* |
| % (on NC) | 5.06% | 2.68% |

### *4.2 Regression analysis*

We run the estimation of a very simple regression model (standard OLS), where the total performance index (*avg_TPI*) is the dependent variable and a vector of binary variables[16] (equal 1 if true, and 0 otherwise) represents the independent ones. This empirical strategy allows us to address a number of more sophisticated questions related to the potential effect of both the nature of the NFCs and the type of public buyer on the suppliers' performance. The estimated model is as follows:

$$y_i = \beta_0 + d'_{i,k} \cdot \beta_k + \varepsilon_i \,, \tag{1}$$

where $k = 1,\ldots K$ indexes all explanatory dummy variables in the vector ***d'***, while $i = 1,\ldots N$ indexes the observation units: cross-section estimations are carried out on 692 inspections (see Table 12.7).

Geographical location has very little effect on suppliers' performance, which appears scattered in a similar non-statistically significant way both in the Centre and in the South of Italy, even if the direction of effects would confirm a higher TPI average in the North. Local administrations, instead, are more effective in terms of contract management. Indeed, a strong positive correlation might corroborate the idea that smaller public agencies respond better to incentives generated by contracts in which they are likely to play a more active role as well as to more stringent budget constraints. Estimated coefficients show a negative correlation with the non-mandatory feature of NFCs, but raise a further counterintuitive negative effect for the low-service NFCs which conflicts with the most immediate insights of descriptive statistics.

A more careful look at the data suggests, however, that the observations are to be considered as censored, where L=1 is the lower (or left) cut-off, and U=5 is the upper (or right) cut-off point. This hypothesis is confirmed by the distribution of the average TPI, depicted in Figure 12.3. Basically, there are more cases with scores of 1 and even more with scores of 5 than one would expect looking at the rest of the distribution. This evidence suggests to consider an alternative estimation method such as the Tobit regression model for censored data, rather than the OLS regression which would not yield consistent estimates since the censored sample will not be representative of the population.

It is worth emphasizing that, in using the Tobit regression, the observed dependent variable $y_i$ in (1) will be related to the latent variable $y_i$* through the following observation rule

$$y = \begin{cases} U & \text{if} \quad y^* \geq 5 \\ y^* & \text{if} \quad L < y^* < U \\ L & \text{if} \quad y^* \leq 1. \end{cases}$$

As a consequence, we run this model to yield the truncated mean, or expected value, of $y_i$ for the non-censored observations, that is, when the value of the average TPI is more than 1 or less than 5. As a matter of fact, the distribution of

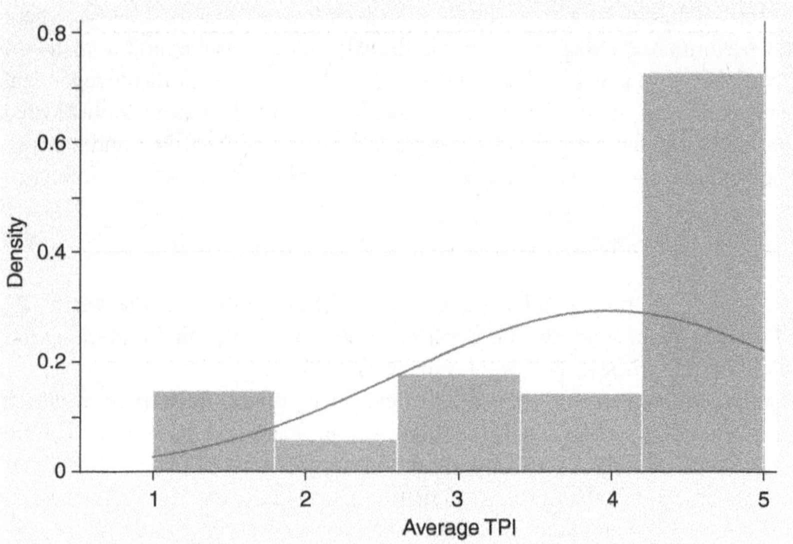


*Figure 12.3* Histogram of the distribution of the dependent variable (average TPI).

the variable of interest is heavily right-censored, as 370 observations out of 692 take the value of the upper threshold, while it is slightly left-censored with 70 observations on the lower cut-off. It is worth noticing that the Tobit regression confirms the results of the OLS regressions while reinforcing the magnitude of the most relevant relations. More specifically, the intensity of both the non-mandatory feature of NFCs and the dummy for local administrations increase with respect to the previous OLS model. The direction of effects is also confirmed. The first two covariates, related to the institutional nature of the NFCs and the type of public bodies, are therefore confirmed as factors of primary importance in explaining in which direction our response variable moves. At the same time, the low-complexity feature of NFCs becomes less significant.

The estimated regressions reveal, therefore, that the average TPI is strongly and negatively affected by the non-mandatory feature of NFCs. These estimations, that are also consistent with the descriptive statistics in Table 12.4 – where the percentage of non-compliances (50.7 per cent) is higher than that observed for mandatory contracts (35.9 per cent) – suggest to deepen the analysis by investigating the factors that are most likely to explain the probability of enforcing penalty clauses if a lower quality performance is observed.

The last column of Table 12.7 illustrates which covariates mainly influence the use of contractual remedies by estimating a Logit regression, according to the following model:

$$\Pr(y=1 \mid d)=\frac{e^{d'\beta}}{(1+e^{d'\beta})'} \tag{2}$$

*Table 12.7* Regression analysis based on OLS, Tobit and Logit models

| | *OLS* | | | *TOBIT** | *LOGIT* |
|---|---|---|---|---|---|
| Dependent variable | (Avg. TPI) I. | (Avg. TPI) II. | (Avg. TPI) III. | (Avg. TPI) | (Enforced Penalties) |
| d_non_mandatory | –0.5780*** (–5.43) | –0.6002*** (–5.65) | –0.6002*** (–5.65) | –1.6515*** (–5.79) | 2.1101** (2.55) |
| d_local_administration | – | 0.2840*** (2.67) | 0.2840*** (2.67) | 0.8220*** (2.87) | 0.5236 (0.75) |
| d_central_adminitration | –0.1283 (–1.08) | – | – | – | – |
| d_low_service | –0.2161** (–2.05) | –0.2520** (–2.41) | –0.2520** (–2.41) | –0.4817* (–1.73) | 0.6905 (0.91) |
| d_north_location | 0.1852 (1.38) | 0.1650 (1.26) | – | – | – |
| d_sud_location | 0.1536 (1.05) | 0.1338 (0.92) | –0.0312 (–0.26) | –0.1243 (–0.39) | –1.5761 (–1.46) |
| d_centre_location | – | – | –0.1650 (–1.26) | –0.3636 (–1.06) | 0.5039 (0.63) |
| Constant | 4.205*** (29.91) | 4.08*** (33.83) | 4.247*** (39.92) | 5.836*** (19.25) | –5.074*** (–4.93) |
| N. obs. | 692 | 692 | 692 | 692 | 307 |
| F-test (5, 686) | 7.20 | 8.44 | 8.44 | – | – |
| LR Chi2(5) | – | – | – | 43.14 | 14.73 |
| $R^2$ | 0.049 | 0.058 | 0.058 | – | – |
| Pseudo – $R^2$ | – | – | – | 0.022 | 0.145 |

Notes

Parameters statistically different from zero at 1% (***), 5% (**) and 10% (*) confidence level; t-statistic and z-score in parenthesis, respectively, for OLS/Tobit and Logit regressions.

* In the Tobit regression, 70 observations are left-censored at avg. TPI $\leq 1$ and 370 observations are right-censored at avg. TPI $\geq 5$. The dependent variable avg. TPI is almost symmetrically distributed and has negligible non-normal kurtosis, that is skewness = -1.07 and kurtosis = 2.81.

where all our explanatory dummy variables are in the vector $\boldsymbol{d'}$, while $y$ is a binary variable equal to 1 if penalty clauses have been enforced, and 0 otherwise. The model is estimated on a reduced dataset of 307 observations concerning only those cases of verified non-compliances.

Unsurprisingly, the only significant covariate is the one corresponding to non-mandatory NFCs. As already emphasized in the descriptive statistics depicted in Table 12.4, penalty clauses were enforced in 7.30 per cent of the non-compliance cases. On the other hand, the same percentage in case of mandatory non-compliant NFCs drops to 1.18 per cent. The low statistical representativeness of this phenomenon in the sample (12 cases of enforced penalty clauses out of 307 inspections affected by 481 non-compliances) does not provide further elements to assess the explanatory power of the remaining exogenous variables.

## 5 Conclusions

Our empirical findings raise serious concerns. Not only does contract mismanagement imperil the principle of competition of the whole procurement process, but when correctly anticipating the lack of contract enforcement competing firms may 'rationally' react by submitting more 'aggressive' price-quality schedules in order to get the contract, and then recover extra profit margins at the execution stage. As a result, seemingly abnormally low bids might just reveal to the awarding authority – a central purchasing body in our case – that, at least to some extent, firms fight ruthlessly to 'buy the option' of implicitly renegotiating contracts at a later stage, thus undermining the whole purpose of selecting the highest value-for-money tender at the selection stage.

Both the nature and the quality of data do not allow us to draw any conclusion as to why contract mismanagement is so endemic in the National Frame Contracts system. This phenomenon represents in fact a kind of contract renegotiation. Whether such renegotiation is explicit – as in the case of in-kind compensations that might be beneficial to both contracting parties – or implicit – as in the case of a contract manager accepting a gift for 'turning a blind eye' while monitoring the contractor's performance – would certainly require a closer investigation of the monitoring process at the purchasing authority's level.

## Acknowledgements

This work grew up from a short paper drafted for the 'OECD High Level Seminar on e-Procurement, Efficiency and Integrity: Challenges and Good Practices', jointly organized with Consip S.p.A. on 17–18 June 2010. The authors are grateful to G. Castaldi for valuable research assistance. The usual disclaimer applies.

Dr Gian Luigi is Head of R&D, Consip S.p.A., the Italian Public Procurement Agency, via Isonzo 19/e, 00198 Rome, Italy. Email: gianluigi.albano@consip.it.

Dr Roberto Zampino is an economist at the R&D Unit, Consip S.p.A., the Italian Public Procurement Agency, via Isonzo 19/e, 00198 Rome, Italy. Email: roberto.zampino@consip.it.

## Notes

1 In the 2011 report, the Italian Court of Audits estimated the cost of corrupt practices in the Italian public sector at approximately €60 billion.
2 Transparency International (2006: 14).
3 This hierarchical structure is also explicitly adopted by the OECD (2010: 24):

> *Corruption* involves a vertical relationship between one or more bidders and the procurement official. It is first and foremost a principal-agent problem where the agent (the procurement official) enriches himself at the expense of his principal, the government purchaser (or the public more generally).

4 Racca *et al.* (2011).
5 (National) Frame Contracts can be thought of as framework agreements concluded with one economic operator and all (contractual) conditions laid down.
6 Yukins (2008) and Soudry (2008).
7 Racca (2010).
8 Inspectors/auditors are in fact employed by an 'auditing firm' which is selected by Consip itself by means of a competitive process.
9 As defined by the 23 January 2008 Decree of the Italian Ministry of Economy and Finance.
10 The product/service categories in the mandatory NFCs comprise the acquisition of software, photocopier rental services, laptop and desktop computers, printers and local network services; the ones in the non-mandatory NFCs comprise the purchase of cars, real estate and video-communication services.
11 The nature of provision has been used as a proxy of contractual complexity. In particular, commercial/standardized items – those for which the delivery of physical goods was the most relevant component (the purchase of cars, the acquisition of software licences, laptop and desktop computers, printers) – are those characterized by low-service components. On the other hand, there are supplies based on high-service components, where contractors are required to provide effective and flexible teams of professionals, technological solutions to best fit various needs of the buyers as, for instance, the acquisition of photocopier rental services and local network services, the purchase of real estate and video-communication services.
12 The education sector refers to the school and university national system; the health sector refers to the national health care system.
13

> Penalty clauses are terms of contracts that seek to impose upon a party to the contract the obligation to pay a sum of money in the event that the contract has been breached, and the terms of the contract cannot be properly classified as a liquidated damages clause. Sums specified as being payable under penalty clauses are not recoverable, as opposed to liquidated damages, which are. The commercial purpose of such clauses is to relieve the party not in breach of having to prove their damage: the contract specifies the sum payable and in practice reduces the instances of money claims proceeding to court to be litigated.
>
> (Retrieved from www.gillhams.com/articles/326.cfm)

14 Statistical significance of test is very high: up to 1 per cent. The tests have been run on a reduced sample of inspections, that is 692 cases out of 743, the largest sub-set of data for which all inspection results (for each quality dimension) were available.
15 This might be most likely due to a self-selection bias of low-skilled public buyers in purchasing from non-mandatory FCs rather than using different and autonomously driven procurement options.
16 The explanatory (dummy) variables include the dimension of mandatory vs. non-mandatory types of contracts, the classification of administrations by sector (local

administrations vs. non-local ones) and by geographical location (the Northern public buyers vs. the rest), the supplies based on low-service components vs. high-service.

## References

Albano, G.L., Dini, F. and Zampino, R. (2009). 'Bidding for Complex Projects: Evidence from Italian Government's Acquisitions of IT Services'. *Lecture Notes in Computer Science*, Electronic Government, 5693: 353–63. DOI: 10.1007/978-3-642-03516-6.

Bandiera, O., Prat, A. and Valletti, T. (2009). 'Active and Passive Waste in Government Spending: Evidence from a Policy Experiment'. *American Economic Review*, 99(4): 1278–308.

OECD (2010). *Competition Policy Roundtables. Collusion and Corruption in Public Procurement*. Retrieved from www.oecd.org/dataoecd/35/19/46235884.pdf.

Racca, G.M. (2010). 'Collaborative Procurement and Contract Performance in the Italian Healthcare Sector: Illustration of a Common Problem in European Procurement'. *Public Procurement Law Review*, 119: 130–1.

Racca, G.M., Cavallo Perin, R. and Albano, G.L. (2011). 'Competition in the Execution Phase of Public Procurement'. *Public Contract Law Journal*, 41(1): 89–108.

Soudry, O. (2008). 'A Principal-Agent Analysis of Accountability in Public Procurement', in G. Piga and K.V. Thai (eds), *Advancing Public Procurement: Practices, Innovation and Knowledge-sharing*, Boca Raton: PrAcademics Press, 433 and 441–2.

Transparency International (2006). *Handbook for Curbing Corruption in Public Procurement*, Berlin: Transparency International.

Yukins, C. (2008). 'Are IDIQs Inefficient? Sharing Lessons with European Framework Contracting'. *Public Contract Law Journal*, 37(3): 545–68.

# 13 Retendering or sale of contract in case of bankruptcy of the contractor?

## Different solutions in an EU and comparative perspective

*Mario Comba*

### 1 Introduction

The issue addressed in this chapter is a quite specific and technical one, having to do with the consequences of bankruptcy on the execution of the public procurement contract.

When deepening the approach to the problem, however, one realizes that it is placed at the crossroads between two very general legal topics – public procurements and bankruptcy – whose interactions are very difficult to assess in a short chapter such as this. It is however necessary to settle some general considerations in order to frame the problem in the correct perspective and, before exploring the result of the interaction between public procurement law and bankruptcy law, it seems appropriate to pick out separately the relevant rules of public procurements and bankruptcy applicable to this case. This short analysis will be done in Section 2 (for public procurement) and Section 3 (for bankruptcy).

Once the features of the two sets of rules applicable to the public procurement contract after bankruptcy of the contractor have been clarified, Section 4 will tackle the interaction between these rules, first in the perspective of European law and then through a comparative approach, with reference to Italian and French law.

### 2 The perspective of public procurement law (and of state aid law)

From the perspective of European public procurement law, it is not easy to find the applicable rules to the bankruptcy of the economic operator after the award of the contract, because public procurement in EU legislation does not impose regulations during the contract execution phase. The subject matter of the European Union Directives on public procurements is in fact only the contract award, which implies that they do not impose regulations about what happens after the award.[1] It follows that, in principle, there are no EU rules regulating the public procurement after the award of the contract.

It is however possible, in a few cases, to talk about ultra-activity or 'expansive force'[2] of European Union directives relating to public contracts, as their effect spreads even during the executive phase of contracts, mainly through the creation of case law by the Court of Justice of the EU (CJEU). This is typically the case when the contracting authority wants to change the essential terms of public contracts: the CJEU – with the decision *Pressetext*[3] – has recently ruled that in this situation public procurement directives apply because the change of essential terms of a contract is to be considered equivalent to the implicit cancellation of the original contract and followed by the stipulation of a new contract and therefore it requires a new procedure under Directives 17 or 18/2004.

The *Pressetext* decision is widely analysed in other chapters of this book and therefore will not be discussed here, but suffice it to say that one of its main points consists in affirming that the change of the contractor represents the change of an essential term of the contract. In particular, according to the Court of Justice:

> 40 As a rule, the substitution of a new contractual partner for the one to which the contracting authority had initially awarded the contract must be regarded as constituting a change to one of the essential terms of the public contract in question, unless that substitution was provided for in the terms of the initial contract, such as, by way of example, provision for sub-contracting.

It seems that the reference to sub-contracting as an example of the change of contractual partner is a kind of mistake because sub-contracting does not imply the change of the original contractor, but only the 'delegation' of some activities to a third party, after which the original contractor is still responsible for the complete execution of the contract with the contracting entity.[4] But the main point in this exception relates to the specificity required for the transfer clause to be provided for in the initial contract: is it necessary to specify the name of the subject to whom the contract will be transferred, or is it enough to insert a standard clause stating that the contract could be transferred to third parties with the consent of the contracting authority?

It is obvious that in the latter case the rule stated by the Court can be easily bypassed, by inserting in all public procurement contracts such a standard clause, while if the exception admitted by the *Pressetext* judgment follows the stricter interpretation, it will be applicable almost never because it is very difficult to know in advance who is the potential buyer of the public contract, especially if it is a very long contract (in the *Pressetext* case it was a permanent concession). And it is even more difficult to conceive of a clause stating that, in case of bankruptcy of the contractor, the contract will be transferred to a third company, which practically excludes the applicability of this exception to the case of bankruptcy of the contractor.

Nor the other possible exception to the *Pressetext* rule seems applicable to a case of bankruptcy of the contractor. According to *Pressetext*, the contract transfer is allowed also when it is to the advantage of a company where 100 per cent of the capital is owned by the original contractor, as in such a case there is only an internal reorganization of the contract counterparty. It is a kind of in-house relationship between the original contractor and the company to whom the contract has been transferred. But this exception implies some difficulties in its practical application, since it can happen that the original contractor, after having transferred the contract to a 100 per cent owned subsidiary, transfers to a third party a percentage of the shares of the subsidiary: in this case, according to *Pressetext*, the change in the original contract becomes essential and therefore a new procedure is necessary. The CJEU, however, does not specify if the transfer of a single share is essential or if there is a threshold above which the transfer of shares becomes essential, which leaves another important issue open to interpretation.

We cannot discuss this exception extensively here, but suffice it to say that it is hardly applicable to a case of bankruptcy of the contractor, since usually companies owned 100 per cent by the bankrupt company are involved in the bankruptcy as well and are therefore in the same position as the original contractor.

The execution of public procurement contracts is subject to another piece of EU legislation, that is the state aid rules. In a 2002 decision, the EU Commission[5] stated that the modification of a public contract in the phase of execution can be considered as an illegal state aid if it alters the initial economic equilibrium of the contract in favour of the contractor. It is a situation which overlaps the *Pressetext* rule, because the modification of the economic equilibrium of the contract also falls in the category of the essential modifications of the contract. As it may well be understood, the difference between applying public procurement or state aid rules is not irrelevant under many aspects, first of which the fact that under public procurement the national judge is competent, while for state aid violations only the EU Commission and the Court of Justice can intervene.

It is not possible here to deepen the interactions between public procurement and state aid rules in the execution of the public contract, but suffice it to say that the contracting authority, during the execution phase of the public procurement contract, is not allowed to act in a private law capacity, but is subject to a set of rules stemming both from public procurement law and state aid law.

This conclusion suggests a comparative consideration about the legal nature of the relation between the contracting authority and the economic operator in public procurement contracts – particularly in the execution phase – which will be shortly explained because it influences the answer to the questions about the destiny of the contract after the bankruptcy of the contractor.

There are different theories about the classification of the legal nature of public procurements in EU Member States. All of them use as a classification criterion the distinction between the public/private nature of the contract and all of them recognize the dualism between the French model and the British one.[6] In the French model, the *contrats publics* have a special nature and are therefore subject to specific legislative regulations, not applicable to contracts pertaining to private law. This particular model, introduced also in Spanish law, has been developed in France principally through case law. In the British model, on the contrary, the contract stipulated by contracting authorities coincides with civil law and therefore it is not given an independent status. Likewise it is not subject to jurisdiction different to the standard one.

At this point, the two reconstruction theories begin to diverge: according to some scholars,[7] the Italian, German and Dutch model represent a third autonomous model, where the principle is in force which establishes that the contract is a means of private law, but it is subject to a wide variety of special regulations when it is utilized by public bodies, which makes one doubtful about whether it is an exception or whether it is the rule. But the principle will always remain that, whenever specific regulations are lacking, the ones pertaining to civil law are enforced. According to other scholars,[8] there is not a third model, but the Italian situation is just an evolution of the French, being more public than private, while the German and the Dutch are referable to the British one, being more private than public.

The distinction between the dualist and the three-tier doctrines is not relevant for the purposes of this chapter, but it is mentioned in order to point out that the stress is about the public/private nature of the contract or, more specifically, about the public/private nature of the relationship between the contracting authority and the economic operator during the execution phase. It is also to be added that the distinction between these models tends to be reduced, largely due to the influence put into practice by EU law that has regulated the selection phase of the contracting party with a public law model.[9] In the United Kingdom, a debate has arisen about the opportunity to introduce general rules applicable to public contracts and a general permission has been given to public bodies to conclude contracts, while previously a specific legislative permission was necessary on a case-by-case basis. Above all, the judicial review of public contracts was increased in order to guarantee a better protection of public interests.[10]

When we come to the execution phase of the contract, the comparative analysis[11] demonstrates that – contrary to what one may expect – the models are very similar. All of them in fact recognize similar powers of the contracting authority mainly to terminate and modify contracts, which are much wider than the powers normally awarded to private parties even if they are however limited in order to abide by the competition rules. This also happens in the British 'private law' model, the only difference being that the public powers are recognized not through a law but through a circular or a contract model which the contracting authorities impose on private contractors.

Therefore, the result is almost similar in all the EU Member States. The contracting authorities can terminate or modify the contract without the consent of the private contractor. Under the French model this occurs pursuant to a legislative provision. Conversely, under the British model this occurs according to contract clauses which are imposed by the contracting authority on private contractors.

But if in the execution phase of the contract the contracting authority is not acting in its private law capacity since it still has public powers, then it follows that the same contracting authority is subject to controls and limitations typical of the administrative activity. Hence the consequence that it cannot sell or dispose of the contract at its discretion, during the execution phase, but is still subject to strict rules.

As one can see, European case law about the execution phase of the public procurement, as stated in *Pressetext*, is not too different from what the comparative analysis tells us about national legislation of member states, at least on a macro-comparison level. In fact, both recognize that also in the execution phase some public law rules are applicable with the consequence that the contracting authority is not acting as a private economic operator and, subsequently, that in the case of bankruptcy of a public procurement contractor, bankruptcy law rules must be reconciled with public procurement (and state aid) rules pertaining to the execution phase of public procurements.

## 3 The perspective of bankruptcy law

From the standpoint of bankruptcy law, the main difficulty consists in the fact that there is not a European law on bankruptcy, not even a shared definition of bankruptcy among Member States, with the consequence that the expression 'bankruptcy of the contractor' can have different meanings in different Member States.

At the level of European law, regulation 2000/1346 EC of 29 May 2000 does not employ the word 'bankruptcy', but states in its title that it deals with 'insolvency procedures', which can be considered similar to bankruptcy. However, it gives a very light common definition in art. 1: 'The Regulation shall apply to collective insolvency proceedings which entail the partial or total divestment of a debtor and the appointment of a liquidator.'

The regulation is very careful in stressing that the discipline of bankruptcy procedures does not fall within the competence of the EU but of Member States and the regulation itself has only limited scope to solve problems usually arising in case of cross-border insolvency procedures. In fact the scope of the regulation is 'confined to provisions governing jurisdiction for opening insolvency proceedings and judgments which are delivered directly on the basis of the insolvency proceedings and are closely connected with such proceedings. In addition, this Regulation should contain provisions regarding the recognition of those judgments and the applicable law which also satisfy that principle' (whereas n. 6) and thus it does not 'introduce insolvency proceedings with universal scope in the entire Community' (whereas n. 11) leaving to any single State its own substantial procedure.[12]

In article 2, regulation 2000/1346/EC distinguishes between 'Insolvency procedures' as defined in art. 2.a and 'Winding up procedures' defined in art. 2.c and in both cases it remands to Annexes where a list of national definitions is provided. Annexes are thus a precious source of information as to what are in Member States insolvency procedures which can be considered similar and can therefore be compared as of the consequences on the execution of the public procurement contract. For example, Annex A (insolvency proceedings) list for Italy 'fallimento, concordato preventivo, liquidazione coatta amministrativa, amministrazione straordinaria, amministrazione controllata' and for France 'liquidation judiciaire and redressement judiciarie avec nomination d'un administrateur', while Annex B (winding up procedures) lists for Italy 'fallimento and liquidazione coatta amministrativa' and for France 'liquidation judiciaire'. A first analysis of the list shows that in Italy and in France respectively 'fallimento and liquidazione coatta amministrativa' and 'liquidation judiciaire' are both insolvency procedures and winding up procedures because the liquidator can decide, according to the situation of the company, whether to try a bailout of the company or to wind it up.

It follows that, when exploring the consequences of bankruptcy in relation to public procurements, while the definition of public procurement is shared at a European law level, because it is defined in Directive 17/2004/CE and 18/2004/CE (art. 1, para. 2.a), the definition of bankruptcy has to be looked for in every single national legal system. The recourse to a comparative method is hence inevitable, in order to assess the consequences of bankruptcy – or of insolvency procedures – on the public procurement contract, because the same definition of bankruptcy can vary.

It is however possible to identify the common scope of insolvency procedures, at least from an economic point of view, in two features:

> The first is that it should maximize the ex post value of the firm, while the second is that it should ensure that the bonding role of debt is preserved. The latter means that the bankruptcy procedure should not create incentives for debtors to resort to bankruptcy.[13]

In addition, EU Member States' legislations on bankruptcy usually pursue also the scope to guarantee an equal treatment to all creditors (the so-called '*par condicio creditorum*').

There is thus a public interest underlying any bankruptcy procedure, which explains why a Court is usually implied through the appointment of a liquidator, according to the definition of regulation 2000/1346/EC. Hence comes the similarity with the execution phase of the public procurement contract, addressed in the previous paragraph: in both cases a public interest is pursued, which means that when the contractor of a public procurement goes bankrupt, the liquidator appointed by the Court is not free to act as a private economic operator, but is bound to follow one or more public interests set forth by the law, and the same obligation is pending on the contracting authority, which is still acting (also) in its public law capacity.

The point is to see if those public interests (the public procurement one and the bankruptcy one) coincide or diverge, and what happens in the latter case, which is the topic of the following section.

## 4 The consequences of bankruptcy on public procurement contracts before and after the award of the contract

It is now possible to address directly the problem of interconnections between bankruptcy and public procurement contracts.

Public procurement directives mention bankruptcy as a possible cause of exclusion of the economic operator from the awarding procedure: article 45, para. 2, Directive 18/2004 states that any economic operator *may* be excluded from participation in a contract where he:

> (a) is bankrupt or is being wound up, where his affairs are being administered by the court, where he has entered into an arrangement with creditors, where he has suspended business activities or is in any analogous situation arising from a similar procedure under national laws and regulations; (b) is the subject of proceedings for a declaration of bankruptcy, for an order for compulsory winding up or administration by the court or of an arrangement with creditors or of any other similar proceedings under national laws and regulations.

As a first consideration, one may notice that the cause of exclusion seem to be wider than the definition of insolvency procedures given by regulation 2000/1346/EC because it includes not only bankruptcy (here probably the wording 'bankruptcy' is to be intended as equal to 'insolvency procedure') and winding up procedures, but also another number of cases where there is a public (judicial) intervention in the managing of the company in order to guarantee creditors. However, if one examines more accurately the cause of exclusion listed in article 45, para. 2, it may be found that they are almost all included in what are considered, in Members States' legislations, the insolvency and winding up procedures as listed in Annex A and B of regulation 2000/1346/EC.

According to article 45, para. 2, Member States may decide that an economic operator who falls under one of those categories cannot participate in a bid for a public procurement contract. It follows that, if bankruptcy happens after the award of the contract, national legislations can provide for the automatic termination of the contract.

As we have seen in para. 3, insolvency procedures in Member States can be divided in two different categories:

1 insolvency procedures *stricto sensu*, where the liquidator appointed by the Court may decide to go on with the economic activity of the bankrupt company, with the perspective to redress it and sell it on the market; and
2 winding up procedures, where the only scope of the liquidator is to wind up the company, sell the assets and pay the creditors.

In the case of winding up procedures, the contract cannot be continued with the bankrupt company by definition and thus the alternative arises between retendering or sale of contract; in the case of insolvency procedure *stricto sensu*, the contract could be continued by the bankrupt company, unless the national legislation of the specific Member State provides for the contrary, applying the principle of article 42, para. 3 Directive 2004/18/EC also to the execution phase of the public procurement.

A quick comparative survey shows that on this point Member State legislation can differ widely. For example, in Italy the Consiglio di Stato stated that a bankrupt company cannot carry on a public procurement contract, even if the liquidator and the contracting authority would be ready to do so, the only admissible solution being retendering.[14] In France, on the contrary, art. 46 of the Cahier des clauses administratives generals (CCGA) states that in case of *liquidation judiciaire* and *redressement judiciarie*, the contracting authority can notify the liquidator of its intention to continue the execution of the contract and, if the liquidator does not accept, can terminate the contract.

We have now reached the core problem of this chapter: in case of bankruptcy of the contractor, the Court-appointed liquidator who does not want to, or cannot (like in the Italian case), carry on the public procurement contract, can sell it to another company, or on the contrary, the contract is automatically terminated and the contracting authority has to retender it.

In the absence of specific European statutory or case law rules, one could think that this case falls under the *Pressetext* rule and therefore the sale of the contract after bankruptcy is forbidden and the contract should be retendered by the contracting authority, with the two exceptions mentioned in Section 2 of this chapter.

The application of *Pressetext* rule to the sale of contract after bankruptcy seems however very poor in efficiency terms: the insolvency procedure loses an economic asset, which is the public procurement contract itself, and therefore reduces the possibility to satisfy creditors and the contracting authority has to start a new public procedure for the award of the contract which implies at least a loss of time, but perhaps also of money, if market conditions offered are worse than those incorporated in the initial contract.[15]

In order to avoid these inefficiencies, one has to ask whether the sale of contract after bankruptcy can constitute an exception to the *Pressetext* rule.

There is also another consideration which underlines the importance of the question and is connected to the increasing use of performance bonds for guaranteeing the good result of the execution of the procurement, particularly in works procurements.[16] The structure of a performance bond is such that the insurance company is obliged to choose a new company for the execution of the contract if the original contractor is bankrupt or for any reason cannot carry on the contract. Therefore the strict application of *Pressetext* to the sale of contract after bankruptcy will prevent the use of performance bonds where they are mostly useful, that is in case of bankruptcy of the original contractor.

In order to prove that *Pressetext* is not applicable to the sale of contract after bankruptcy two arguments can be used.

The first argument is that bankruptcy is not a predictable event and therefore it is highly unlikely that an economic operator decides to go bankrupt just so it can sell the public procurement contract. The sale of the contract is thus simply an ancillary event of bankruptcy which excludes the intention of circumvention of EU rules from the economic operator. Put in other words, since bankruptcy is an extraordinary event, it cannot be ruled under *Pressetext* case law which refers only to ordinary cases of sale of contract.[17]

The second argument can start considering that *Pressetext* referred to a case in which a private company had transferred the public procurement contract to another private company and that was considered – as a general rule, even if not in the specific case – a distortion of the market because a private company could be favoured over the others by receiving the transfer of the public procurement contract, even if the economic conditions were not changed.

But in the case of bankruptcy or winding up procedures, a liquidator is generally appointed by a Court[18] because the whole insolvency procedure is carried out under the control of a public (judicial) authority in order to pursue the public interest. As a general rule, the liquidator cannot sell the assets of the bankrupt company without following a sort of public procedure or, at least, without choosing the buyer with impartial criteria, even if of course the rules can vary widely from Member State to Member State.

Under this perspective, the transfer of the contract is not carried out by the bankrupt company, but by the liquidator appointed by the Court and this can give sufficient guarantees of an impartial procedure – even if it not exactly with the procedure provided by Directives 17 and 18/2006 – likely to avoid distortions of the market and circumvention. In other words, if the transfer of the contract is carried out by a liquidator appointed by the Court and not by a private company, and if the economic conditions of the contract are not materially changed, then one can argue that a distortion of the market does not occur and therefore the transfer of the contract after bankruptcy should be allowed under EU law.

The latter argument needs a deeper analysis particularly under the perspective of comparative law, because it can be greatly strengthened if it can be proved that national legislations on bankruptcy provide for public and impartial procedures for the sale of the goods and contracts of the bankrupt company.

## Notes

1 The main reason for EU regulation of public procurements is to bring their markets parallel to the operation of private markets on the demand side – that is the public side – which can be altered because it pursues the public interest instead of the maximization of profits: C.H. Bovis, *EU Public Procurement Law*, Cheltenham: Elgar, 2007, pp. 11–16. This is why it only focuses on the award phase, because only in this phase the pursuit of the public interest can alter the market equilibrium. See also: G. Morbidelli and M. Zoppolato, 'Appalti pubblici', in M. Chiti and G. Greco (eds), *Trattato di diritto amministrativo europeo*, II edn, Milan: Giuffré, parte speciale, tomo I, pp. 535–6.

2 This is the wording used by E. Ferrari, 'Introduzione- I contratti della pubblica amministrazione: dalla ricerca del mercato alla ricerca delle regole', in E. Ferrari (ed.), *I contratti della pubblica amministrazione in Europa*, Turin: Giappichelli, 2003, pp. XX–XXI.

3 C-454/06, Judgment of 19/06/2008, Pressetext Nachrichtenagentur (ECR 2008, p.I-4401).

4 R. Nogellou, 'La Cour de justice prend une position de principe restrictive sur les cessions de marchés, puisqu'elle admet que celles-ci constituent, sauf si elles ont été prévues dans le marché initial, un changement de l'un des termes essentiels du marché, appelant par là une mise en concurrence', *Droit administratif*, 10, October 2008, notes: 'la Cour donne l'impression de confondre deux mécanismes pourtant juridiquement distincts, la sous-traitance et la cession de contrat'.

5 Decision C (2002)3578 fin, of 2 October 2002 – State aid n. 264/2002 – *United Kingdom London Underground Public Private partenership.*

6 J.B. Auby, 'Comparative approaches to the rise of the contract in the public sphere', *Public Law*, I, 2007, pp. 46–8; M. Fromont, *Droit adminsitratif des Etats européens*, Paris: PUF, 2006, p. 297–324 and R. Noguellou and U. Stelkens, 'Propos introductifs', in R. Noguellou and U. Stelkens (eds), *Comparative Law on Public Contracts Treatise/Traité de droit comparé des contrats publics*, Brussels: Bruylant, 2010, pp. 1–26, point 3.1.

7 Auby, *Public Contracts*, p. 46.

8 M. Fromont, *Droit adminsitratif des Etats européens*, pp. 297–324 and Noguellou and Stelkens, 'Propos introductifs', pp. 1–26, point 3.1.

9 This is due not only to Directives 17/2004/EC and 18/2004/EC but also to the remedies directive 66/2007/CE: see M. Comba, 'La direttiva ricorsi (2007/66/CE) e le sue conseguenze a livello sistematico: l'imposizione del modello francese di "contrat administratif"', in M. Comba (ed.), *Il recepimento della direttiva 2007/66/CE. Il rito speciale degli appalti nel nuovo codice del processo amministrativo e le sue conseguenze sul processo di aggiudicazione*, Turin, IUSE Working Papers, 2011, 62 (www.workingpapers.iuse.it).

10 Auby, *Public Contracts*, pp. 53–5. See also A.C.L. Davies, *Public Law of Government Contracts*, Oxford: Oxford University Press, 2008, pp. 180–3.

11 M. Fromont, 'L'évolution du droit des contrats de l'administration – differences théoriques et convergences de fait', in R. Noguellou and U. Stelkens (eds), *Comparative Law on Public Contracts Treatise/Traité de droit comparé des contrats publics*, Brussels: Bruylant, 2010, pp. 263–80, para. 4.

12 The difficult compromise reached by regulation 2000/1346/EC between national sovereignty and the quest for an efficient regulation of international bankruptcy cases is adressed in: F. Duina, 'Between efficiency and sovereignity: transnational actors, the European Union and the regulation of bankruptcy', *Comparative European Politics*, 2006, pp. 1–22. For some technical comments on regulation 2000/1346/EC see: J.L. Vallens, 'La mise en oeuvre du règlement communautaire sur les procedures d'insolvabilité: question de procédure', *Le Dalloz*, 2003, cahier droit des affaires, pp. 1421–7; R. Damman, 'L'application du règlement CE n. 1346–2000 après les arrêts "Staublitz-Schreiber" et "Eurofood" de la CJCE', *Le Dalloz*, 2006, pp. 1752–1756.

13 J.P. Thomas, *Bankruptcy Procedures for Soverign State Insolvency*, in United Nations University, Discussion Paper n. 2002/109, 2002, p. 2.

14 Consiglio di Stato, commissione speciale, parere 22 gennaio 2008, n. 4574/07, commented by M.L. Beccaria in *Urbanistica e appalti*, 2008, pp. 624–9. There is however an exception, only for public works (public contracts code, art. 140), consisting in the possibility for the contracting authority, if the original contractor has gone bankrupt, to transfer the contract to the company which ranked at the second place in the awarding procedure and, if it does not accept, to offer it to the third company and so on until the fifth ranked, always at the same conditions offered by the original contractor.

15 Similar considerations can be found in S. Treumer, 'Changes of concluded contracts and its implications in the EU context: sale of contracts after bankruptcy', in *Papers*

*for International Public Procurement Forum II (2010)*, hosted by Central University of Finance and Economics (Beijing, China) and Xinjiang University of Finance and Economics (Xinjiang, China), pp. 149–53.

16 In Italy performance bonds are compulsory for work procurements over 100 million euros (public procurement code, art. 129.3) and for all work procurements where a general contractor is operating (public procurement code, art. 176.13).

17 This is the main argument by Treumer, 'Changes of concluded contracts'. In Italian law this is the reason why it is forbidden to sell public procurement contracts, but it is allowed to transfer public procurement contracts along with extraordinary corporate operations, like the incorporation of two companies or the sale of a branch of a firm to another (art. 116 of Italian public procurement code).

18 I refer to the terms 'liquidator' and 'Court' as defined in Reg. 2000/1346 EC, art. 2.

# Part IV

# Set-asides for small and medium firms, as in the US system with the Small Business Act that reserves shares of tenders to SMEs only

# 14 Dialogue

*Christopher Yukins and Gustavo Piga*

## 1 Argument by Christopher Yukins

*Background*: the US government spends approximately US $500 billion per year through procurement. Of that amount, by statute at least 23 per cent, or roughly $115 billion, are supposed to go to *small* businesses (15 U.S.C. § 644(g)(2)).

('Medium-sized' businesses are not defined or protected in the US federal system; the internationally recognized term 'SME' thus is not used in US federal procurement.) These preferences for small (and disadvantaged) businesses stretch far beyond 'set-asides', to include preferences and supports that include the following (see, e.g., www.poh.usace.army.mil/DB/SBPGuide.pdf):

- HUBZone businesses (small businesses in designated, historically underdeveloped, geographic areas) are to receive 3 per cent of federal procurement dollars.
- Section 8(a) of the SBA Act sets aside procurements for small and disadvantaged businesses; disadvantage is often defined by ethnic or racial background of the business owner(s), and, for example, many of those who immigrate from around the Pacific rim and the Indian subcontinent may qualify as disadvantaged.
- Women-owned small businesses are to receive 5 per cent of all federal procurement.
- Veteran-owned small businesses enjoy procurement preferences.
- Service-Disabled-Veteran-owned small businesses are to receive 3 per cent of procurement.
- Native-American-owned small businesses have procurement support.
- Alaska Native Corporations are tribal businesses which may establish affiliates, through which they may enjoy significant preferences in federal procurement.
- Native-Hawaiian-owned small businesses enjoy procurement preferences.
- Small Business Innovation Research (SBIR) is a programme through which federal agencies with large research and development budgets must set aside a portion of their funds for small businesses.
- Questions regarding small businesses' contractor qualifications ('responsibility')

will be referred from a contracting officer to the SBA for a 'Certificate of Competency'.

- Prime contractors must set their own goals for subcontracting with small businesses.

See, for example, www.sba.gov/category/navigation-structure/contracting/working-with-government/small-business-certifications-audiences; 13 C.F.R. § 121.401 (listing programmes).

Question:
*Do SME preferences tend to proliferate over time? Once in place, are they immutable?*

These preferences do *not* work merely through rigid set-asides. It is true that some smaller contracts technically must *always* be set aside for small businesses, and *presumptively* larger contracts must be set aside, at least in part, for small businesses if two or more small businesses are expected to compete (see Federal Acquisition Regulation Subpart 19.5, 48 C.F.R. Subpart 19.5). As a practical matter, however, agencies tend to act in a more ad hoc and *outcome-oriented* manner, steering contracts to small businesses on an opportunistic basis in order to meet the 23 per cent annual goals, which are *set* and *judged* on an agency-by-agency basis.

See, for example, www.sba.gov/content/small-business-goaling; www.fpdsng.com/downloads/top_requests/FPDSNG_SB_Goaling_FY_2009.pdf (sample report). Agencies – and administrations – that do not meet the 23 per cent goal are open to serious political criticism. See, for example, Press Release, Office of Senator John Kerry ('It's big business as usual in the Bush Administration's Department of Energy', said Kerry … 'When nine out of 10 dollars for contracts can't even be touched by small firms, it's evidence that the Bush Administration continues to reward their big business supporters at the expense of America's entrepreneurs') (11 April 2006).

Questions:
*How should SME preferences be implemented? Would European procuring entities themselves meet SME goals? If not, what accountability measures are best?*

*Purpose for small business preferences*: the Small Business Act sets forth, in 15 U.S.C. § 631(a), some of the congressional purpose behind the small business preferences:

> The essence of the American economic system of private enterprise is free competition. Only through full and free competition can free markets, free entry into business, and opportunities for the expression and growth of personal initiative and individual judgment be assured. The preservation and expansion of such competition is basic not only to the economic well-being

> but to the security of this Nation. Such security and well-being cannot be realized unless the actual and potential capacity of small business is encouraged and developed. It is the declared policy of the Congress that the Government should aid, counsel, assist, and protect, insofar as is possible, the interests of small-business concerns in order to preserve free competitive enterprise, to insure that a fair proportion of the total purchases and contracts or subcontracts for property and services for the Government … be placed with small-business enterprises… and to maintain and strengthen the overall economy of the Nation.

Questions:

- *Is fostering SMEs essential to economic strength and national security?*
- *Do SME preferences meet a European vision of a dynamic free market?*
- *Do SMEs preferences restore competition in public procurement markets? Put differently, do large businesses otherwise tend to crowd out SMEs in public procurement?*

*Defining small businesses*: 'Small' businesses are generally defined by *annual revenues* or by *numbers of employees*. The methodology used by the Small Business Administration (SBA) in establishing these standards is explained in a 2009 white paper, www.sba.gov/sites/default/files/size_standards_methodology.pdf. The SBA described the guiding considerations as follows:

> In establishing size standards, the Act and its legislative history highlight two considerations. First, *size standards should vary to account for differences among industries*. Second, the policies of the Agency should *assist small businesses as a means of encouraging and strengthening their competitiveness in the economy*. These two considerations are the basis for the SBA current methodology for establishing small business size standards.
>
> … As a starting point, SBA presumes $7.0 million [in annual revenues] as an appropriate size standard for the services, retail trade, construction, and other industries with receipts based size standards; 500 employees for the manufacturing, mining and other industries with employee based size standards; and 100 employees for the wholesale trade industries. These three levels, referred to as 'anchor size standards,' are not minimum size standards, but rather benchmarks or starting points. To the extent an industry displays 'differing industry characteristics,' a size standard higher, or in some cases lower, than an anchor size standard is supportable.
>
> (Emphasis added)

The white paper was the first step in a broader effort by the SBA to update size standards, which had been essentially frozen for many years (see www.sba.gov/content/what%E2%80%99s-new-with-size-standards). In some cases, those efforts to adjust (generally, increase) size standards to account for changes in industry have been met with vigorous criticism from the small business community.

Questions:

- *Should size standards be based on annual receipts (revenues) or employee headcount, or on other factors, such as net worth or net income? Do the relatively narrow and rigid bases for defining small businesses in the US system (and the way those standards tend to 'freeze' over time) reflect agency inertia, transaction costs concerns or political fears?*
- *Do small business preferences ultimately punish the successful and so constrain growth? How could such a constraint be remedied?*

*Impact on international trade*: in practice, it is almost impossible for foreign firms, even if small, to qualify for US small business preferences (see 13 C.F.R. § 121.105) (a small business is 'a business entity organized for profit, with a place of business located in the United States, and which operates primarily within the United States or which makes a significant contribution to the U.S. economy through payment of taxes or use of American products, materials or labor').

The small business preference is, in the eyes of many foreign observers, a domestic preference.

This preference exists despite the United States' general commitment, under the WTO Agreement on Government Procurement (GPA), to open the federal procurement market to the plurilateral members of that agreement. The United States has exempted only the following from the GPA, under its General Notes: 'set asides on behalf of small and minority businesses'. As the discussion above reflects, however, in fact the US preferences for small businesses extend far beyond formal set-asides for small and minority businesses.

Questions:

- *Are international agreements an effective means of constraining small business preferences and other socioeconomic initiatives in procurement?*
- *Should international standards regarding SMEs be harmonized?*
- *Who is likely to enforce international commitments to limit preference programmes – signatory nations or vendors enforcing their remedy rights?*

## 2 Argument by Gustavo Piga

Several countries[1] characterized by a substantially market-oriented approach to industrial policy subsidize small and medium firms in government procurement. The European Union does not, the issue being either considered contrary to the current EU Directives or even against the principles of the European Treaty itself.[2] Understanding this diverse approach to public procurement might be considered worthwhile for several reasons: first, for the large amounts involved as for example, in the United States, a target amount of 23 per cent of total federal expenditure is considered for set-asides for small firms; second to obtain a rigorous methodology to review possible changes in the legislation like, in the EU, the recent Public Consultation by the European Commission on Public Procurement that mentions set-asides as a possible reform.[3]

Subsidies lower the offer that a subsidized firm will be considered for given its bid for which it will be paid. Subsidies at times can be so high that they deter any participation by large firms, that would consider it too costly to try to enter the competition under those conditions. In this case the bidders that participate are the same as the ones that would be involved when the government explicitly forbids such an entry by non-designated bidders ('set-aside'). Under 'softer' schemes the subsidy is not so high to deter/forbid entry by non-subsidized firms.

We know by now enough regarding the potential benefits of such subsidies. If they allow entry of non subsidized-firms they might make the latter bid more aggressively than in the absence of a subsidy, if and only if, that is, the subsidy is granted to the weakest bidders. If they do not allow/permit entry of non-subsidized firms they make participation of the weakest bidders more likely compared to a non-subsidized or open tender and they make large firms more aggressive in their pricing in the (fewer) procurement tenders that are left open to them. In the process, subsidies might end up pushing government spending for procurement *down* (notwithstanding the fact that it might appear that they actually raise it by not awarding the contract to firms – the non-subsidized ones – that have declared through their bid to be happy with an even lower payment for their services than the one that will be paid to subsidized firms, the final price paid turning out to being lower than what it would have been without set-asides), even if efficiency (the total value added deriving from the transaction between winner and supplier) goes down when the contract is awarded to the firm that does not have the lowest cost for providing the good or service to the Public Administration.[4]

There are other advantages from subsidizing weaker bidders. The first are related to making cartels (usually functioning best across large firms[5]) less effective and also, as a consequence, making corruption between bureaucrats and firms less profitable and harder to sustain. Second, insofar as the lack of competitiveness of small firms with respect to large firms is due to discrimination in credit markets (including as a consequence of delays of payment by governments), inefficiencies from subsidies are reduced. Third, dynamic competition may make these inefficiencies vanish over time as subsidies today – that encourage small firms to sustain fixed costs and try to enter the public market by participating to tenders – increase the likelihood of unsubsidized entry tomorrow by stronger candidates (SMEs that have become large/successful firms).

To understand the rather isolated EU position against subsidies and set-asides for small firms one might try however to imagine why subsidies and set-asides might be the wrong instrument to be used in procurement. Several arguments can be thrown into the arena.

First of all, one of fraud. Indeed one might claim that 'fake' (small) corporations might be created only for the purpose of being awarded the procurement contract at a higher price. Or else, large companies might redefine their structure to participate as small ones and obtain the advantage. This argument should hold true for both the European Union and other countries that currently adopt subsidies, unless one is to argue that the EU is more prone to fraud than elsewhere. Controls might indeed be set up so as to verify the statements of participants and stiff penalties introduced for misreporting true status. Overall, as we are not aware of large complaints on this issue in countries where such subsidies exist, we would not stress this argument too much.

Second of all, centralization (or bundling) that might appear as the other side of the coin of the difference in policies in the EU compared to the rest of the world. Bundling has been given a formal status of relevance in the Directives through the insertion of Central Purchasing Bodies (CPBs). The latter often tend to award larger contracts, subdividing when necessary the procuring needs into a given amount of lots that is often similar to the number of large actors present in the market, encouraging collusion. Set-asides in this context would make collusion harder to sustain by making large firms compete among themselves for fewer lots. But as this danger does not seem to be relevant in the minds of European policy-makers (as CPB are seen as fostering competition and not hampering it) so it looks only logical that set-asides cannot be used as a panacea.

Third, it is well-known that subsidizing small firms can be successful if and only if: a) there is an insufficient number of bidders and more competition needs to be stimulated and b) it is evident to identify in small firms a weak class of bidders compared to large firms. While b) is recognized even by the EC as a relevant issue[6] (that needs however, according to the dominant approach, to be solved with instruments different from set-asides), it could well be that the European authorities do not sense that competition is lacking in EU tenders. Indeed their main focus so far on the single issue of cross-border participation and the functional separation of the two relevant EC Directions (Competition Internal Markets…) might explain such a lack of attention.

Overall, summing up, it is hard to find a strong reason for the stubborn resistance of the European Union to refusing to allow subsidies to small firms in public procurement, whose benefits seem to largely outweigh the risks. The small amount of data available suggest indeed that the issue of the scarce openness of public markets to small firms is still a relevant problem in the EU: 'In terms of estimated total contract value secured, SMEs accounted for between 31% and 38% of public procurement while their overall share in the economy, as calculated on the basis of their combined turnover is 52%'.

Amazingly, the very recent Public Consultation by the EC mentioned above is instead rather determined into considering the issue of subsidies and set-asides for other actors/themes rather than with respect to small firms: local or regional suppliers[7] (a much clearer case of violation of the principle of discrimination in the Treaty), jobseekers or person with disabilities,[8] non-profit organizations for social service contracts.[9] Would these 'affirmative action' moves be more commendable than the ones suggested above for small firms?

As mentioned by Ayres and Cramton (1996), in the United States government affirmative action must have a 'compelling governmental purpose' and must not be narrowly tailored to reach that goal, i.e. there must not exist other less restrictive ways to achieve the same goal. We are tempted to exclude favouritism for local and regional suppliers from our analysis, since it appears to be against the principle of non-discrimination embedded in the Treaty, and we would like to do the same for non-profit organizations, for which little compelling purpose can be found. One might, however, consider the case of subsidizing firms that engage jobseekers or persons with disabilities, in light not so much of their (to be proven) productive disadvantage but the (likely) potential discrimination against those persons. In such case one could see a compelling EU purpose in subsidizing firms in procurement that hire these workers.

But would large firms that employ jobseekers or persons with disabilities be considered as 'weak' candidates in a tender, so that subsidizing them would enhance revenue and minimize losses in terms of efficiency? It is not evident. Furthermore, there could be a risk of even stronger manipulations to qualify as a firm to be subsidized than the fraud potential we saw above for small firms, since jobseekers and persons with disabilities could be hired by strong large firms at little cost to the organization only to obtain a subsidy, generating a negative expenditure effect from the subsidy programme, since large firms would win the tender more easily, discouraging even further participation by small firms.

What is to be recommended for the European Union then? Subsidies in procurement or not? The truth of the matter is that (possibly to their own surprise) governments in Europe are already subsidizing bidders to reduce the possibility that firms extract most of the gains from trade in the public market. They do so by allowing public procurement offices to set base prices at a lower level than the maximum price they would be willing to pay for the services of suppliers. Like in a subsidy, such a move increases the chances that the 'wrong' (i.e. not the least cost) supplier wins the contract (in this case the procurement office itself would be the winner if no one shows up at the tender to bid) but it also decreases (if there is participation) the expenditure for the procurement contract by pushing firms to bid more aggressively (i.e. below the more aggressive base price).

If the principle is there, there seems to be little reason to obstinately deny the possibility to achieve opportunities for lower public expenditure through competition-enhancing mechanisms such as subsidies for weaker bidders like small firms. Increasing competition might well be a compelling EU purpose, for which, at least in procurement, no other method but subsidies seems to have worked.

## 3 Reply by Christopher Yukins

Professor Piga's section raises a number of interesting points.

*Why don't the Americans view their small business programmes as 'subsidies'?* As was noted in my opening section, the US federal procurement system supports an extraordinary array of small business programmes, and the (vigorously enforced) annual target is for at least 23 per cent of overall federal procurement spending (approximately $500 billion) to go to small businesses (see, e.g., www.sba.gov/about-offices-content/1/2986). Probably no one in US policy circles, however, would call this a 'subsidy'.

*Labelling the small business programmes as 'subsidies' would be politically explosive*, partly because many of the benefits flow to firms owned by ethnic and racial minorities in the United States. Subsidies to firms owned by ethnic and racial minorities are, in some quarters, deeply controversial in the United States. It is important to stress that where preferences for small and disadvantaged businesses are *race-based*, as a matter of constitutional law those preferences will receive *closer judicial scrutiny* (the preference must be shown to be narrowly drawn to accomplish a compelling state interest) (see, e.g., US Commission on Civil Rights, 'Federal Procurement After *Adarand*' (September 2005), www.usccr.gov/pubs/080505_fedprocadarand.pdf). Broader preferences – such as general preferences for small businesses – receive much more deferential review under the US constitution.

*Calling the small business programmes 'subsidies' would make small businesses look weak.* As a practical matter, US proponents of small business programmes argue vigorously that small businesses are the 'engine' of growth in the US economy.

Proponents point to the enormous numbers of small businesses that emerge every year (see, e.g., U.S. Census Bureau, www.census.gov/econ/smallbus.html; *Business Week*, www.businessweek.com/smallbiz/news/coladvice/ask/sa990930.htm (discussing statistics on starts and failures of small businesses)).

*Because the small business programmes cannot be termed 'subsidies', it is difficult to target support for the 'weak'.* Instead, the support programmes tend to focus on *categories* of contractors (Native American-owned, women-owned, veteran-owned, etc.), rather than on specific firms that are most in need of support.

The small business support programmes have no theoretical or practical basis for supporting the 'weakest' firms; instead, the small business programmes have a broader economic goal, of enhancing competition in procurement and integrating entire classes of entrepreneurs (women, Native Americans, veterans, etc.) into the mainstream of US business.

*US small business programmes are probably founded on Professor Piga's intuition that large businesses tend to dominate public procurement.* In the US federal system there is an abiding concern that the largest contractors are too 'cozy' with public officials (see Farewell Address of President Eisenhower (January 1961) (discussing 'grave' implications of the US 'military-industrial complex'), www.youtube.com/watch?v=8y06NSBBRtY). There has clearly been concentration in the US defense industry (see, e.g., Stockholm International Peace Research Institute (SIPRI), www.sipri.org/research/armaments/production/researchissues/concentration_aprod), and the largest firms tend to dominate the federal information technology market, as well. This concentration may be due to risk aversion on the part of purchasing officials, or to the largest firms' advantages in anticipating government requirements, or perhaps on a desire by government officials to establish good relations with the likeliest future private sector employers (though this last point is roundly repudiated in policy discussions). Whatever the cause, this perceived bias towards the largest contractors has helped fuel popular support for small business programmes.

*To achieve their goals, small business programmes are not structured as 'subsidies', but as preferences or set-asides*. Beyond the central goal of ensuring that 23 per cent of federal procurement dollars flow to small businesses, US procurement rules are laced with other preferences for small businesses. Small businesses, for example, enjoy a stronger price preference if a domestic firm is competing against foreign firms under the Buy American Act. In another example, the Defense Department recently issued an interim rule calling for all possible efforts to speed payments to small businesses on contracts, despite the (longer) fixed payment periods already set by statute for *all* contracts, under the Prompt Payment Act. 76 Fed. Reg. 23505 (27 April 2011). The Defense Department has thus essentially sacrificed any prompt payment discounts it could otherwise negotiate with small businesses.

*Because the goals are not clear, needed levels of support for small business are unclear*. As is discussed above, it is not clear what the goals of the US small business programmes are: to assist businesses disadvantaged by social prejudices? To boost dynamic growth in the small business sector? To counterbalance large businesses' undefined advantages in public procurement? Because the political and economic goals are unclear, the needed levels of support are unclear, and so the statutory and regulatory structure that surrounds these programmes has fluctuated substantially over the years.

*Landscape is complicated by a hidden political agenda behind small business programmes – to deliver political benefits, quickly.*

The policy discussion is complicated by an apparent political goal in the small business programmes, a goal which cannot be fully acknowledged in the policy debate: politicians' desire to build political support by nurturing small businesses in their political districts. For politicians on relatively short re-election cycles – members of the US House of Representatives, for example, come up for election every two years – it is vitally important to be able to point to material benefits to the district, brought in quickly. Because capital and work can flow much more quickly in the small business community, small businesses can bring jobs and projects to a congressional district much more quickly than many large contractors. While large contractors can play the same tactical game – large weapons systems companies will, for example, spread their contracting and subcontracting across a staggering number of states and congressional districts – small businesses are often a quicker, easier path to securing votes.

*Accomplishing social and political goals means establishing bureaucracy*: the costs of establishing small business programmes are, however, quite steep. The state must erect means of assessing and approving small- and medium-sized businesses, of diverting procurements to small- and/or medium-sized firms, of policing the contractors that assert entitlement, and of ensuring that enterprises do not seize opportunities without being duly qualified. This may mean establishing a substantial adjudicative and monitoring bureaucracy – a cost that must be factored into any plan for small business procurement programmes.

## 4 Reply by Gustavo Piga

I do find very many stimuli in Prof. Yukins' list of issues that need to be tackled when facing set-asides or rather, as he correctly reminds us, when facing the wide array of types of preferences that are granted not only to small firms per se but to a more complex set of actors, at least in the United States.

The first issue I wish to respond to is the one as to whether 'ethnic or racial background of the business owner(s) of … Women-owned … Veteran-owned … Service-Disabled-Veteran-owned … Native-American owned … Alaska Native Corporations owned.… Native Hawaiian owned small businesses' and also innovation research should enjoy set-asides. I do not think I have the credentials to judge whether such affirmative action responds to a 'compelling governmental purpose'. However, if 'remedying past discrimination or … furthering diversity' (which was what Cramton and Ayres suggested) is such purpose, then one might argue that all but innovation fit this first criterion. Actually one would want to add current discrimination to the list, insofar as a relevant part of the economic literature (see for example the survey of Ravina) seems to argue that taste-based discrimination is still relevant today.[10]

As for furthering innovation, which could indeed be a compelling purpose, I believe it is predominantly an empirical question. I see in principle no specific reason as to why favouring small firms would necessarily achieve this goal, as large firms could very well be more capable of reaching it. If on the other hand small firms are weak but more innovative, innovation set-asides for SMEs could be a good substitute for innovation policies.

Wouldn't we run the risk that for those different types of minorities, by 'remedying past discrimination or … furthering diversity' through set-asides in procurement, there could exist other less restrictive ways to achieve the same goal that we neglect? The example of South Africa, for example, where empowerment of black people can be obtained (in the new ideated system of Broad-Based Black Economic Empowerment, BEE) in other ways than in reserving procurement to small firms owned by black people – for example a firm, whether black-owned or white-owned, is ranked higher in procurement if it increases the extent to which it buys goods and services from BEE-compliant suppliers – seems to confirm this risk. Other ways one could imagine could be those of favouring networks and/or consortia of SMEs in procurement.

The second issue raised by Prof. Yukins which I would like to comment on is if 'SME preferences tend to proliferate over time and if, once in place, they are immutable'. A question that denotes, I believe, an understandable fear of big government becoming bigger.[11] As for what happened in the United States since the 1953 establishment of the Small Business Act, this is eminently an empirical question that deserves a rapid enquiry that goes beyond our space here. Let me just state that I am not aware of any SBA study that verifies whether SMEs helped by the SBA policies on procurement have actually grown, closed or simply stayed put, and this lack of research is quite astonishing as it reduces the accountability of the work of the SBA. The issue remains as to whether the European Union would be able to show the same restraint once the gates are opened for set-asides, but there seems to be no reason to argue in one sense or the other. My feeling would be that while the number of minorities interested in the SBA has increased, the size of the pie available for them (i.e. the 23 per cent) has tended to remain the same: everyone gets a piece of the same pie, just a smaller one. Finally please note that the South African example cited above seems to underscore the fact that preferences schemes can change and possibly be improved over time.

In asking whether 'fostering SMEs (is) essential to economic strength and national security' Prof. Yukins reminds me of a critical issue that I did not address in my first section (see above, pp. 218–221), which is for which compelling purpose 'should (we be) helping SME in procurement'. Let me tackle the issue for the European Union only. If such compelling purpose were to be the EU principle of 'equal treatment (non-discrimination/fairness)' of equals and different treatment for different situations it is evident that SMEs deserve to be subsidized to a certain extent in procurement: SBA studies point out that 'at the aggregate level, regulatory compliance costs per employee appear to be at least 36% higher in small firms than in medium size and large firms'. Credit market imperfections biased against small firms have similar implications. How could anyone argue that today's tenders in the EU provide for equal treatment (yes) of equal situations (no)? On the other hand – and at a higher political level – one could argue that small firms are intrinsically local: favouring them means hindering a European single market formation and Europe with it. If external trade fosters peace, so the argument goes, establishing set-asides for small firms should not pass the 'compelling purpose' test. Keeping in mind that we are discussing a European SBA that would not prevent a small French firm to be favoured in German procurement, one could nonetheless argue that a more united Europe is one that is capable of preserving its local traditions and customs and that large firms 'dominating' the trading landscape of Europe could soon enough lead to unrest and a temptation to break up the Union.

'Do SME preferences meet a European vision of a dynamic free market?'. Now this is another relevant question that should be tackled. I am not aware of such dynamic vision of competition in the European Union. A very large and competitive tender today that puts all the public demand in the hands of a sole supplier (the winner) could end up becoming a monopoly tomorrow once other firms have abandoned the market as a consequence of their defeat in the original tender and of the lock-in that the winner has been able to induce with respect to the public sector end-users of the good or service sold. However Central Purchasing Bodies, with their tendency to foster bundling and being pushed by the new EU Directives as a tool that promotes competition, often may end up doing just that; and no mechanism is in place today in the European Union (contrary to the United States) to stop this. So I would reverse the question of Prof. Yukins and ask whether 'The European vision of competition meets the continued participation of small firms to public markets'.

Finally there is the decisive policy issue of international trade agreements, once more raised by my colleague. There is little doubt in my mind that the 'small business preference is … a domestic preference', but one that treats large firms, whether national or foreign, symmetrically. There is indeed a distortion against small foreign firms, but how many of them would venture overseas to fight for small contracts against a small US firm anyway? However one should also keep in mind that 'a domestic preference is not a small business preference' and that we should be much more worried about fighting the possibility of domestic preferences (like the Buy American Act) that are bound to be largely more damaging.

## 5 Conclusions by Christopher Yukins

The colloquy with my distinguished colleague, Professor Gustavo Piga, has highlighted several issues in procurement preferences for small- and medium-sized enterprises (SMEs), which are well-established in US federal procurement and are under active consideration in the European Union.

### *5.1 Existing international free trade regimes do not stop sweeping SME preferences*

As the World Trade Organization (WTO) points out, government procurement is generally exempted from the WTO's normal legal requirements regarding national treatment:

> [G]overnment procurement has been effectively excluded from the application of the main multilateral trade rules under the GATT and the WTO. In the General Agreement on Tariffs and Trade, originally negotiated in 1947, government procurement was explicitly excluded from the key national treatment obligation. More recently, government procurement has also been excluded from the main market access commitments of the General Agreement on Trade in Services.
>
> (www.wto.org/english/tratop_e/gproc_e/overview_e.htm)

This means that SME preferences must be addressed under the WTO's plurilateral Government Procurement Agreement (GPA).

As noted, the United States' reservation of rights in the GPA to use SME preferences is, in fact, very limited: it covers only 'set asides on behalf of small and minority businesses'. These few words have been used, in practice, to exempt an enormous array of preferences for small businesses, reaching far beyond traditional 'set-asides'. There is, it seems, little will amongst the GPA members to constrain the use of SME preferences through traditional WTO/GPA enforcement mechanisms. Any constraint on the EU member states probably must, therefore, come from within the EU itself.

### *5.2 Considering why SMEs should receive a preference*

There appear to be several possible reasons to grant preferences to SMEs:

- To subsidize SMEs.
- To encourage growth in SMEs.
- To correct structural defects in the economy, sometimes caused by racial, ethnic or sexual discrimination.
- To correct structural defects (e.g. by increasing competition) in procurement markets.
- To ensure domestic sources of supply.
- To build political support.

To sort out whether SME preferences should be implemented, the EU and its member states will have to determine *why* SME preferences are a good idea.

### *5.3 How SME preferences can be structured*

The exchange with Professor Piga suggests that SME preferences can be structured in several different ways:

- Changes in procurement regimes, to facilitate competition by SMEs.
- Direct subsidies to SMEs.
- Price and/or technical preferences in procurement evaluations.
- Set-asides of specific procurements for SMEs.

## 6 Conclusions by Gustavo Piga

I agree with Prof. Yukins that semantics are key to our discussion. Economists often use the term 'subsidy' when they see one without measuring the devastating legal and political economy implications of handling such definitions with some lightness.

I am no lawyer, but this is what I found on the Web. If one adopts the definition (www.wto.org/english/tratop_e/scm_e/subs_e.htm) of what constitutes a subsidy, provided by the World Trade Organization's SCM Agreement, it

> contains three basic elements: (i) a financial contribution (ii) by a government or any public body within the territory of a Member (iii) which confers a benefit. All three of these elements must be satisfied in order for a subsidy to exist.

Government purchases are explicitly named as subsidies. We should add that WTO rules would seem to regard a subsidy to small firms or minority-owned firms as 'specific', a precondition for being prohibited or actionable if I understand correctly. Interestingly, in the 'WTO Trade Policy Review: Malaysia (WT/TPR/S/31, 3 Nov. 1997, para. 122)'[12] one finds in the WTO declaration that:

> government procurement preferences accorded to Malaysian firms constitute government assistance to these firms. Selected state-owned enterprises are required by public procurement regulations to follow similar practices. These preferences not only restrict competition among suppliers, thereby impairing economic efficiency, but also raise the cost to the Government and state-owned enterprises of procuring goods and services. The competitiveness of state-owned enterprises is, in turn, hampered insofar as they are forced by preferential procurement regulations to purchase their inputs from relatively high-cost local suppliers.

The California Department of Transportation (Caltrans) implements the preference in the form of a 5 per cent bid discount. In determining the winner of a project, Caltrans reduces the bids of qualified small businesses by 5 per cent, up to a maximum of $50,000, when comparing them to the remaining bids.[13]

Having said this, whether small firms preferences are a formal subsidy or not, what matters here is if we are dealing with a helpful policy move or a damaging one for a country as a whole. And so the real issue we should probe relates to the goals of preference programmes for small firms, which as Prof. Yukins correctly points out, are unclear. Yet he seems to identify them when he says that 'the small business programmes have a broader economic goal, of enhancing competition in procurement and integrating entire classes of entrepreneurs (women, Native Americans, veterans, etc.) into the mainstream of US business'.

Interestingly enough, 'enhancing competition' would often be (see for example the above quoted citation of the WTO regarding Malaysia) the reason to deny the desirability of set-asides. The dramatic differences in defining and coming to an agreement on what constitutes competition across the two sides of the Atlantic remains in my view a key obstacle to a mutual agreement on the optimal use of preferences.

Another important point mentioned by Prof. Yukins relates to the 'needed level of support'. Athey *et al.* demonstrate how in general subsidy policies improve over set-asides for small business.[14] This is mostly due to the intrinsic difference between the two programmes: the set-aside precludes the possibility for non-favoured firms to participate in the auction, while subsidies favour small firms without precluding big ones from competing. Still, efficiency losses from set-asides may be minimized if a careful market analysis precedes the programme implementation, that is when the relative strength of targeted and non-targeted bidders is taken into account. We would expect (as proven by data on timber auctions) that the relative strength varies with the size of the contract: in large sales, small firms bid substantially less than big ones, therefore set-asides should be limited or, preferably, a subsidy should be introduced. In the opposite case, for the smallest contract the difference in bidding between the two groups of firms may be relatively less important therefore allowing small firms to win will increase revenues for them (distributional goal) at relative low inefficiency losses.

One last point. Prof. Yukins seems in his final considerations to raise concern regarding, first, the pork barrel potential and, second, the bureaucratic dimension of these programmes. It is a warning that should be appropriately considered especially in Europe, where the programme could quickly become burdened by special interests and red tape because of the lack of a favourable culture and understanding of these programmes. In this regard, the presence in all large procurement organizations of a Procurement Representative that monitors the inefficient bundling of contracts, like in the United States, could be very beneficial in promoting such a mutual understanding of the needs and capabilities of small firms, thereby contributing to their subsequent capacity to take-off, on their own, in the competitive global arena.

## Notes

1 The United States is not alone: South Africa, Canada and Brazil have equally relevant programmes for SME-biased procurement.

2 We do not naturally refer to national legislation that promotes set-asides reserved for single member state SMEs, as this would obviously infringe the principle of non-discrimination, but to set-asides for EU-based small firms.

3 English version of the Public EC Consultation:

> One idea, for instance, might be to *set targets for SME shares* in overall procurement. Such a system would not involve reserving specific contracts for SMEs, but they would simply provide an incentive for contracting authorities to make the best possible use of the available instruments for SME-friendly procurement.

The Italian and French version of the same document speak of setting *targets for SME participation*, not shares, betraying some ambiguities in the approach to be followed.

4 In reality inefficiencies from set-asides/subsidies are reduced when they generate lower expenditure. This is because (distortionary) taxes are lower and allocative efficiency from using inputs at a lower cost increases.

5 I. Ayres and P. Cramton, 'Deficit reduction through diversity: how affirmative action at the FCC increased auction competition', *Stanford Law Review* 48(4): 761–815, 1996.

6 See the recent EC Green Paper, European Commission, *Green Paper on the Modernisation of EU Public Procurement Policy: Towards a More Efficient European Procurement Market*, EC COM(2011) 15 final (Brussels, 27 January 2011), available at: http://ec.europa.eu/internal_market/consultations/docs/2011/public_procurement/20110127_COM_en.pdf. It is however an empirical issue. Some small firms might indeed be more competitive than large ones. In this case subsidizing them would be damaging.

7 'Do you see cases where a restriction to local or regional suppliers could be justified by legitimate and objective reasons that are not based on purely economic considerations?', EC, *Green Paper*.

8 'Do you consider that the link with the subject matter of the contract should be loosened or eliminated at the award stage in order to take other policy considerations into

account (e.g. extra points for tenderers who employ jobseekers or persons with disabilities)?'

9 'Should the Directives allow the possibility of reserving contracts involving social services to non-profit organizations/should there be other privileges for such organizations in the context of the award of social services contracts?'

10

> Understanding the mechanisms behind the gap in wages and access to credit faced by minorities is very important to design effective economic policies. If the reason why they are disfavoured by firms is that their human capital and creditworthiness are worse along unobservable dimensions, like statistical discrimination theories would suggest, then the best policy is to improve their access to education and other tools to increase their human capital. If, on the contrary, minority applicants are intrinsically the same as the other applicants and their worse performance is due to animus, like taste-based discrimination theory postulates, then anti-discriminatory and affirmative action policies might be more effective.

11 On the other hand it might simply mean that certain minorities have grown in their capacity to 'voice' their existence, which might in itself be good news.

12 Quoted in Christopher McCrudden and Stuart G. Gross, 'WTO Government Procurement Rules and the Local Dynamics of Procurement Policies: A Malaysian Case Study', *The European Journal of International Law*, 17(1), 2006.

13 See Elena Krasnokutskaya and Katja Seim, 'Bid Preference Programs and Participation in Highway Procurement Auctions', *American Economic Review*, 101(6): 2653–86.

14 Susan Athey, Dominic Coey and Jonathan Levin, 'Set-asides and Subsidies in Auctions', NBER Working Paper No. 16851 (March 2011).

# 15 Public procurement and SMEs – an approach to increased participation

*Paul Davis*

## 1 Purpose of the chapter and literature addressed

The purpose of the chapter is to illustrate the process involved in the development of a procurement of innovation policy for the Irish public sector. The initial research work was undertaken between September 2008 and June 2009, and culminated in the publication of the '10 Step Guide to Smarter Procurement'[1] by the Irish government.

## 2 Background

The European Union (EU) is described as an economic and political union of 27 Member States. It is underpinned by a series of Treaties, which set broad policy goals for all Member States to adhere to. The Treaties also empower certain institutions with the necessary legal authority to implement those policy goals. As a member of the EU, Ireland is obliged to abide by the laws enacted under it. This includes the endorsement of any policies and best-practice initiatives that might be highlighted as areas of concern or areas for prioritized action.

The Lisbon Strategy was agreed at the Lisbon Council of 2000.[2] The vision agreed at that time was 'To make the E.U. the most competitive and dynamic knowledge-based economy in the world capable of sustaining more and better jobs and with greater social cohesion, by 2010'. According to the European Anti-Poverty Network (2011), the Lisbon Strategy is a practice of describing the more immediate priority objectives of the EU. The Lisbon Strategy was relaunched by the European Council in 2005 to include a narrower focus on important goals such as growth and jobs. Progress on meeting the agreed visions or objectives is annually reported on at the EU Spring Council through National Reform Programmes. It is decided at the Spring Council what key factors need to be addressed or followed up on as priority.

Due to the financial downturn of economies a lot more emphasis has been placed on creating jobs and in particular it has been recognized that innovation is an area where many jobs might potentially be created.

According to Enterprise Ireland (2011),[3] 'innovation is about doing something new, that has a positive effect and which delivers improvements to a business in terms of cost savings or increased value'. In other words, 'innovation' is a method of seeking out new and better products or services or even new ways to structure processes within an organization which might otherwise have gone unnoticed by an organization and from which benefits can be derived. These products, services or processes should ultimately create better value for money and generate cost savings for an organization.

A report called 'Creating an Innovative Europe' (The Aho Report 2006),[4] which called on the governments to 'use public procurement to drive demand for innovative goods, while at the same time improving the level of public services', was presented to the European Commission prior to the Spring Council in (2006). Upon consideration of the recommendations contained within the report, it was decided by the Council to introduce a broad-based innovation strategy, including the promotion and diffusion of eco-innovations, to be rolled out to all Member States.

The Commission, later in 2006 and also in 2007, presented further strategic communication documents relating to innovation. These outlined a number of priority actions for innovation policy within the EU. One such document was a Commission staff working document called 'A Guide on Dealing with Innovative Solutions in Public Procurement: 10 Elements of Good Practice' (2007).[5] This document focused on public procurement as part of a broader innovation strategy and it explained how public procurement can motivate innovation. Member States were encouraged by the European Commission to embrace these guidelines into the public procurement environs of each individual country.

## 3 SME participation – definitions of micro enterprises

There is no single definition of a small firm, mainly because of the wide diversity of businesses. The methodology to define what constitutes a small firm may trace its roots to the Bolton Committee (1971).[6]

The Commission proposed an economic definition and suggested that small firms meet the following criteria:

- they have a relatively small share of their marketplace;
- they are managed by owners in a personalized way, and not through the medium of a formalized management structure;
- they are independent of a larger enterprise.

The Bolton Committee, in its *Report of the Committee of Enquiry on Small Firms*, also suggested that the best description of the key characteristics of a small firm is that it is an independent business, managed by its owner or part owners and having a small market share. The report also adopted a number of different statistical definitions. The Commission recognised that size is relevant to sector. That is, a firm of a given size could be small in relation to one sector where the market is large and there are many competitors; whereas a firm of similar proportions could be considered large in another sector with fewer players and/or generally smaller firms within it.

In similar vein Storey (1994)[7] argues that there is no uniformly acceptable definition of a small firm and suggests that in an industry like petrochemicals a small firm is more likely to have much higher levels of capitalization, sales and possibly employment than a small firm in the car repairs trade. Accordingly he suggested that definitions

> that relate to 'objective' measures of size, such as number of employees, sales turnover, profitability, net worth etc., when examined at sectoral level, mean that in some sectors all firms may be regarded as small, while in other sectors there are possibly no firms which are small.

It remains the case that there is no generally accepted definition of what constitutes small and medium enterprises. According to the European Commission (2003),[8] enterprises are defined as follows:

> An enterprise is considered to be any entity engaged in an economic activity, irrespective of its legal form. This includes, in particular, self-employed persons and family businesses engaged in craft or other activities, and partnerships or associations regularly engaged in an economic activity.

Enterprises are further defined according to their headcounts and either according to the amount of the annual turnover or the annual balance sheet.

There are substantial variations in international definitions of what constitutes an SME (including different sectoral definitions). There is no internationally accepted reporting framework for data relating to this area. However in 1996, the European Union (EU) standardized the term 'SME' and redefined it. Thus, the quantitative upper limits of the SME were companies that have less than 250 workers; a maximum of a 40 million euro annual turnover and a maximum 27 million euro annual balance-sheet total. These figures have since been revised.

For the purposes of this chapter the definitions will follow that of Article 2 of the Annex of the European Commission Regulation 361/EC:

> The category of micro, small and medium sized enterprises (SMEs) is made up of enterprises which employ fewer than 250 persons and which have an annual turnover not exceeding 50 million euro, and/or an annual balance sheet total not exceeding 43 million euro.
>
> (European Commission 2003)[9]

Within that definition Medium-sized Enterprises (MEs) are regarded as entities that have between 50 employees and 249 employees and have either an annual turnover not exceeding €50m or an annual balance-sheet total not exceeding €43m. Small Enterprises (SEs) are those that have fewer than 50 employees and have either an annual turnover and/or an annual balance-sheet total not exceeding €10m. This definition is critical in establishing which companies may benefit

*Table 15.1* European Commission definition of SMEs

| *Enterprise category* | *Headcount* | *Turnover* | *Balance sheet total* |
|---|---|---|---|
| Medium-sized | <250 | ≤ € 50 million | ≤ €43 million |
| Small | <50 | ≤ € 10 million | ≤ €10 million |
| Micro | <10 | ≤ € 2 million | ≤ €2 million |

from EU programmes aimed at SMEs and from certain policies such as SME-specific competition rules. This is represented in tabular form in Table 15.1.

The Single European Act of 1993 allowed the free movement of goods, capital, services and labour and gave legal standing to a union of Western European countries. At that point there were 17 million enterprises in the private and non-private sector of the EU. According to ESNI (1994)[10] some 99.9 per cent were SMEs whose combined workforce totalled 68 million people. Within those figures there were 18 million self-employed and 50 million employees. In the UK, according to the Glover Report (2008),[11] 'Small and Medium Enterprises (SMEs) constitute 99.9 per cent of businesses in the UK, employing 59 per cent of the private sector workforce and making up 52 per cent of business turnover'. More recently and nearer to home Europa (2008)[12] states that there are 20 SMEs for every 1,000 people in Ireland and gives a total figure of 84,412. This figure is at variance with data, which the DKM[13] survey, *The Economic Impact of Small Business in Ireland*, compiled on behalf of Forfás established. They noted:

> we are left with a wide variation of estimates of the number of businesses in Ireland. There does appear to be general agreement that the vast bulk of businesses (roughly 97%) are small, i.e. they have fewer than 50 persons engaged. The estimates fall into two broad camps: on the one hand are the CSO and IDS figures, in the region of 230,000. On the other hand are the estimates that derive directly or indirectly from the Revenue Commissioners, which vary from 274,000 (registered employers plus an estimate of non-employers) to 346,000 (tax returns issued to individuals and companies).

Within Ireland there are some 187,000 non-construction small businesses according to the Tax Strategy Group (TSG)[14] information paper of 2006. They state that 664,000 people worked in small businesses, which is 46 per cent of the total private sector non-agricultural workforce. The workforce of small enterprises has increased by 90 per cent from 1995. With regard to legal form 70 per cent of small businesses are sole traders, 18 per cent are limited companies and 12 per cent are partnerships. They note that for an economy in transition, domestic demand rather than the external side of the economy becomes the main source of economic growth and, with the decline in construction, it is important that other sectors, such as SMEs, become an increasing source of economic growth. The group noted the problems highlighted repeatedly by SMEs and their representative bodies as being:

- costs of doing business;
- access to finance;
- regulatory burden.

SMEs play an increasingly important role in many economies. They are multifarious and distinct in character from large firms. The unique characteristics of SMEs do not always bestow them with great influence in their markets but nevertheless it must be recognized that their size can give them competitive advantage. It is clear that organizational structures in small firms are much less rigid, sophisticated or complex as in large firms. The flexibility of arrangements that exist in small firms contributes to their fluidity and creativity, traits that are necessary for continued success. However, IBEC (2008)[15] stated:

> Given the importance of small and medium enterprises (SMEs) to the Irish economy, a level playing field is needed for all economic operators wishing to participate in public tendering. The benefits of higher SME participation in the public procurement process are twofold: first, it would promote competition for public contracts; second, it would allow companies to innovate.

The Glover Report (2008) notes that:

> Although there is much good practice in both local and central government, with some real progress being made since the 2003 report, it quickly became clear from the evidence gathered that small firms still face substantial hurdles to compete on an equal footing with larger enterprises in the public sector procurement market place. This means that they lose out and that Government also misses the opportunities for innovation and better value for money small firms can provide.

## 4 The procurement process

Procurement itself in the public sector differs from the private sector in a number of ways, the most notable being that it is more highly regulated and politically constrained than the private sector (Ferlie 1992;[16] Boyett *et al.* 1996;[17] Bryntse 1996[18]). Van Weele (2004)[19] goes further and states that the purchasing decision-making is often intertwined with political objectives and issues. Second, the budget system used within public sector bodies does not provide sufficient incentives for budget holders to actively strive for the best value for money. Usually budgets should be spent in the year they have been assigned. Third, most countries still favour a nationalist and protectionist approach when it comes to placing orders of supplies. In most cases, local suppliers are favoured for a variety of reasons.

In developing an approach for identifying how to develop innovation and get access for SMEs, it was decided to base any structure around an agreed and researched procurement process. Davis (2010)[20] had identified in working papers

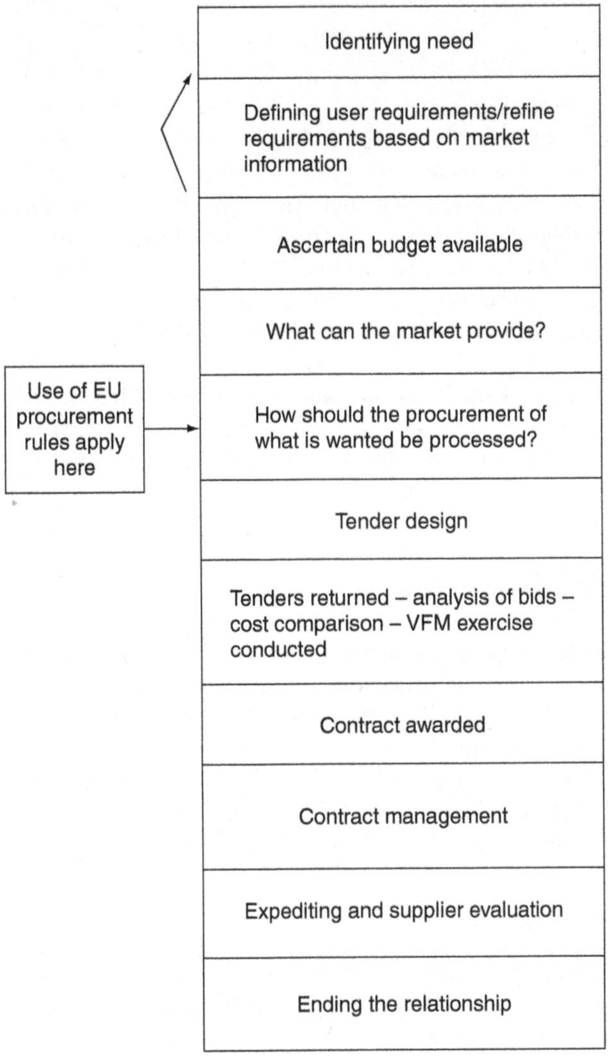


*Figure 15.1* Model of procurement (Davis 2010).

a common procurement process that could be adopted for the proposals. Figure 15.1 illustrates the model.

Many factors are particular to public as opposed to private sector procurement decision-making (Harland *et al.* 2000).[21] Although public procurement can be differentiated from the private sector, the purchasing process is similar in that there are sets of core or common routines. The decision-making process is different in terms of outcomes or factors that have to be taken into consideration, but the performed activities are similar. Both public and private sector procurement start with a problem that needs to be solved: a buying need that has to be fulfilled. To fulfil this need certain activities need to be performed either formally or informally, explicitly or implicitly, comprehensively or selectively. These activities constitute the purchasing process.

It is common to divide the procurement process into a number of different stages. Differences between these accounts emerge at the level of detail, specifically the number of stages that are described.

Traditionally purchasing was managed as a three-stage process (Lysons and Gillingham 2003).[22] This was the Identification Phase, the Ordering Phase and the Post-ordering Phase. They go further by stating that the inefficiencies of these traditional procedures include

- a sequence of non-value adding clerical activities;
- excessive documentation;
- excessive time in processing orders both internally and externally;
- excessive cost on purely clerical work.

With Porter's (1985)[23] Value Chain came a questioning of what value-adding activities needed to be done and more importantly how did they need to be done. Reck and Long's (1988)[24] purchasing development model suggested that this traditional approach was in the passive phase. Yet the development of supplier relationships and the shift of focus to external performance indicators (Harwick 1997)[25] suggested that a more process-oriented view of purchasing needed to be adopted.

Procurement is now seen as the process that includes all activities required to get an item (be that product or service) from the supplier to the final destination, e.g. customer (Brenner and Hamm 1996).[26] This encompasses the traditional purchasing steps but also very clearly encompasses the roles of supply management.

Van Weele (2004) defines it very specifically as: 'obtaining from external sources all goods, services, capabilities and knowledge where necessary for running, maintaining and managing the company's primary and support activities at the most favourable conditions.' Further definitions can be found in the literature, and Table 15.2 illustrates some commonality in the models found.

Procurement then is seen as including all the activities required in order to get the product from the supplier to the final destination. It encompasses the purchasing function, stores, traffic and transportation, incoming inspection, and quality control and invoicing. Some organizations would also include salvage and environmental issues as well. Procurement spans the supply chain as defined and the management of procurement in a modern organization encompasses logistics management as well.

*Table 15.2* Models of procurement

| Novak and Simco (1991)[1] | Gershon (1999)[2] | Archer and Yuan (2000)[3] | Van Weele (2004)[4] | Caldwell *et al.* (2007)[5] |
|---|---|---|---|---|
| Identify or re-evaluate needs | What is it that is wanted? | Information gathering (search for suppliers that can satisfy requirements) | Determine the specification of goods and services that need to be bought | Specification phase |
| Define and evaluate user requirements | | | | |
| Decide to make or buy – identify type of purchase | How should the procurement of what is wanted be processed? | | | |
| Conduct market analysis | What can the market provide? | | | |
| Identify all possible suppliers | | Supplier contact (request for quotes are advertised or direct contact made with suppliers) | | |
| Pre-screen all suppliers | | Background review (e.g. references are checked) | | |
| Evaluate remaining supplier base | | | Identify most suitable suppliers | Selection phase |
| Choose supplier | | Negotiation | Preparing and conducting negotiations | Contracting phase |
| Deliver product/perform service | Making the purchase | Fulfilment | Placing an order with selected supplier | Ordering |
| Post-purchase/make performance evaluation | Achieving the desired outcome | Consumption, maintenance and disposal (evaluation of performance) | Monitor and control the order | Expediting and supplier Evaluation |
| | | Renewal | After-care and evaluation | Follow-up and procurement evaluation |
| | Ending the relationship | | | |

Notes

1 Novak, R.A. and Simco, S.W. (1991) The industrial procurement process: a supply chain perspective, *Journal of Business Logistics* 12 (1), 145–67.

2 Gershon, P. (1999) Review of Civil Procurement in Central Government. Available from: www.hmtreasury.gov.uk/Documents/Enterprise_and_Productivity/Public_Enterprise_Partnerships/ent_pep_gershon.cfm [accessed 28 January 2007].

3 Archer, N.P. and Yuan, Y. (1995) Comparing telephone-computer interface designs: are software simulations as good as hardware prototypes? *International Journal of Human Computing Study* 42 (2), 169–84.

4 Van Weele, A. (2004) *Purchasing and Supply Chain Management, Analysis, Strategy, Planning and Practice*, 4th edn, London: Thomson.

5 Caldwell, N., Bakker, E. and Read, J. (2007) The purchasing process in public procurement, in L. Knight, C. Harland, J. Telgen, K. Thai, G. Callender and K.

## 5 Ireland – a case study

Developing an innovation-driven economy was and still is crucial for Ireland's competitiveness. In the Strategy for Science Technology and Innovation 2006–2013 (SSTI)[27] the vital role of technological innovation was highlighted. Procurement for innovation is the purchase of goods and services that do not yet exist, or need to be improved and hence require research and innovation to meet the specified user needs.

When considering how best to implement a guidance document to include 'innovation' within the public sector, department officials decided to set up a cross-functional group of experienced representatives from all sectors of the economy, namely, government, business organizations and academia, to work on all related issues.

On 30 July 2008, the Procurement for Innovation Group was convened. Innovation in public procurement has been outlined in the government publication 'Innovation in Ireland'[28] as one of the key drivers in promoting the agenda and of strategic importance to the changing Irish economy.

The group comprised all the major stakeholders from the relevant government departments and agencies, large public sector authorities and business representatives. It was proposed to develop a series of focus group sessions to create networks of learning for capturing best-practice examples of the procurement of innovative solutions and products and to examine where possible procurement practices associated with these. It was planned to run these on a regional basis and as such there were six sessions planned, including a pilot session. These were carried out between 6 October 2008 and 15 December 2009.

These focus groups included both public sector buyers and users and involved different sectoral interests within the public sector.

The objectives of the focus groups were to:

- involve the public sector buyers and users in the key data-gathering phase;
- the collection of information relevant to the primary objective of identifying best-practice procurement;
- to analyse the information collected to explore and obtain findings to support best-practice procurement.

A series of case studies were developed from the research. These were presented as best-practice examples for the procurement of innovation in Ireland.

When implementing the guidance documents, both 'A Guide on Dealing with Innovative Solutions in Public Procurement: 10 Elements of Good Practice' (2007)[29] and 'Buying Green – A Handbook on Environmental Public Procurement' (2004)[30] were considered to be very relevant and insightful resources of information by the Procurement Innovation Group. As such, many of the elements identified in both documents were incorporated into the final report and subsequent guide produced by the Procurement Innovation Group.

The incorporation of a structured step guide linked to the procurement process enabled discussions to be had with buyers about where interventions could be made without overreliance on the application of the Directives. This was important step in engaging buyers in pre-commercial procurement, and in particular in encouraging them to engage with small local suppliers.

This guide was titled 'Buying Innovation – The 10 Step Guide to SMART Procurement and SME Access to Public Contracts'.[31] The then Tánaiste and Minister for Enterprise and Employment, Ms. Mary Coughlan T.D., published it in July 2009. The publication of the '10 Step Guide to Smarter Procurement' was the first policy document from the Irish government examining the role of procurement.

## 6 Discussion

Recommendations from the 10 Step Guide included breaking contracts into lots.

The very fact that contracts are bundled together or aggregated means that there are fewer contracts for SMEs or small indigenous suppliers (SISs) to bid for, reducing the chance of an SIS winning public sector contracts. It follows that aggregated contracts will tend to attract only larger organizations and makes it difficult to compare performance between contractors since there will be fewer in the market. The scrutiny of the contract negotiated centrally but operated locally will doubtless make it difficult to monitor, control and evaluate since the contract negotiators will for the most part be at arm's length from the operation of the contract.

Decreasing the number of opportunities to compete will actively discourage further take up by all but the largest SMEs. Given the results of a recent survey[32] though it seems that over 51 per cent of companies competing for public procurement business in Ireland employ less than ten people. It has been suggested in recent discussions that the opportunity to increase the number of contracts open to SMEs can gain momentum by the public sector divesting itself of much of its non-core activity through outsourcing. This move to outsourcing of activities and yet and more centralized procurement seems contradictory and needs to be investigated further.

There are perceived purchasing tensions seen through the centralized procurement policies adopted in straitened circumstances. These policies play to the strategic aim of securing lower costs but at the detriment of encouraging SME participation. In this the procurement function has, unwittingly or otherwise, moved from being a localized clerical activity to one of corporate strategy. It seems to the author that the fundamental objective of securing value for money and reduced costs, under the spotlight of the overbearing demand to find savings, must sacrifice the alternate policy of the development of a benevolent approach to SMEs.

SMEs that compete and win centralized public sector contracts during the current depressed circumstances will likely be well placed when less aggressive markets emerge.

During the research for the procurement of innovation report the literature identified the very high cost of engaging in a tendering process. The author strongly concurs with the Glover Report's recommendation and advocates the early adoption of similar action by the centralized bodies where they state: 'Qualification criteria that are not specific to a sector should be standardized and incorporated in all pre-qualification questionnaires so that businesses do not need to repeatedly submit the same core information in different formats'.

Many SMEs stated that they would value more face-to-face contact with procurers to develop relationships and learn about upcoming opportunities. They expressed concern that dedicated procurers of centralized contracts may not have the level and depth of familiarity with the goods and services being procured compared to the knowledge embedded within the downstream operators themselves. In the Winning in Tendering[33] project this approach is being encouraged through the adoption of mentor practices for buyers. Early adoption will confer dual benefits on both those tendering and the buyers. For businesses it will clarify whether the very substantial investment is worthwhile and for the buyers there will be greater insight into the market.

SMEs must compete with larger organizations to offer the best goods and services at competitive prices, delivering cost savings to the taxpayer. The barriers created by the inequality of the administrative burden can mean that SMEs are not always able to compete on an equal footing for public procurement opportunities with larger entities. Not taking action to minimize the bureaucratic overhead will cause the government and public sector to continue to miss out on the real benefits of a fully competitive market for procurement.

The public sector has formidable purchasing power and can drive business competitiveness, improve productivity and obtain improved goods and services. This can secure better value for money and lead to an improvement in public services over the long term. However, if public sector demand is fragmented, and if different public sector bodies act in un-coordinated ways there may not be any public sector buyer power. If SMEs are to be encouraged to participate in seeking public sector business a sea change in approach will be necessary. This concept follows that view in the 2002 OECD[34] Report, where it is stated:

> Co-ordination failures occur when information is available and is understood, but is not acted upon because disparate actors cannot organize themselves to act in concert. It often is difficult for small and medium sized firms to organize joint activities. They might lack the capacity or the trust necessary to act in concert. Even if they do not, it is often difficult to find a forum and a neutral facilitator to aid inter-firm co-ordination. In many instances, potential joint gains simply fail to materialize.

SMEs will need to view competition with larger entities from a strategic rather than an operational standpoint, whilst the activity of the consortia may well be operational. They will need to plan towards developing consortia capable of matching the input and power that larger companies have; they will need to develop skills or secure consultancy advice on approaches to tendering. This aspect was reported in a survey undertaken by Campbell (2010[35]) where it was concluded 'that SMEs and the private sector require more up-skilling on public sector procurement procedures'. They also note that 'It is easy to understand from this sample survey how many SMEs make simple mistakes when tendering for public sector contracts based on a lack of knowledge'.

It appears that many SMEs do not participate in the tendering process since they can only provide one aspect of a solution. However, by forming a consortium with like-minded suppliers, they have the potential to respond to a greater range of opportunities by amalgamating their combined strengths. A caveat on this approach is that it is most time-consuming to build relationships with erstwhile competitors and this can be more onerous for resource constrained SMEs. Most frequently the lead-time to respond to requests for tenders does not allow for such an approach, thereby unconsciously eliminating or restricting participation in tenders by SMEs. It may be that business organizations could play a part by monitoring upcoming tenders and giving advance notice to their members or by facilitating their coming together.

In July 2004 Sir Peter Gershon[36] called for an efficiency drive within departments. He suggested that aggregating and reorganizing other functions offers the promise of savings in procurement, buildings and facilities and argued the case for aggregating demand into a smaller number of contracts. His aim was to free up contract managers through the reduction of procurement noise and ensure greater value for money was gained through economies of scale.

## 7 Main contribution

The report of the working group has been used to influence industrial policy in Ireland, in particular the approach to SME participation in public procurement. It has led to further research in this area, in particular the funding success of the Winning in Tendering (WIT) project, an Interreg IV €3.2 million research project examining the role of public procurement on small indigenous suppliers. One of the key areas that has come under focus is the micro-enterprise sector, which has not been dealt with in many of the EU policies. In the recent National Surveys of Public Procurement in Ireland, over 51 per cent of companies bidding for business employed between one and nine people, and over 45 per cent only competed for business within 120 km of where they were located. For the Winning in Tendering project these were identified as small indigenous suppliers (SISs).

The design of WIT's complementary and innovative targeted training and education interventions tackle SIS and public buyer skills gaps so SISs are not unfairly disadvantaged in public tendering and can realistically compete for public sector work. This will significantly contribute to greater competitiveness and sustainable growth via development of innovative businesses with high growth potential and will provide greater levels of employment and better jobs, improving the region's overall social, economic and environmental well-being. WIT will address common skills issues for SMEs and develop skills in the changing economy.

WIT's development of an On-line Diagnostic Educational Tool will raise awareness and knowledge of the changing nature of public sector buyer requirements (e.g. the increasing emphasis on compliance and sustainability, reducing carbon footprint in product delivery miles, etc.), helping SISs prepare for the changing economy's current and future needs.

The 'Barriers to Procurement Opportunity Report',[37] WAG, March 2009, shows SISs expend vast resources completing tendering pre-qualification questionnaires, yet with low prospects of winning. The development of a common education programme focusing on SISs taking advantage of lower value procurement (and including a sustainable development/procurement module), jointly delivered, is of strategic importance and is hoped to build a sustainable economy in the region.

WIT is in conjunction with national agencies, organizing cross-border SIS graduate placements, also facilitating the utilization of WIT's On-line Diagnostic Tool by SISs. Graduates will in turn gain the benefit of cross-border work experience and practical training.

The two large-scale surveys, mentioned previously (run through the Irish e-tenders system) were carried out in December 2011 and have had responses in excess of over 4,000 suppliers and over 600 procurers. These surveys will also enable an assessment to be carried out of the impact of the policy documents published, and to create an effective benchmark against which to measure further policy interventions. There has been to date no large-scale national surveys produced in public procurement in any European jurisdiction, which would enable multiple jurisdictions to be compared over success of policy intervention.

Although there is much work still to be done, it was the combination of grounded research and the application of the research, which led to the development of a structured policy for public procurement interventions for SMEs. Further, this research allowed the development of further research such as the Winning in Tendering project and now the large-scale surveys, where grounded data is being gathered and used by the policy-makers to ensure greater participation by SMEs.

## Notes

1 www.djei.ie/publications/trade/2009/buyinginnovation.pdf.

2 The European Anti-Poverty Network (2011) *The Lisbon Strategy: A General Overview* [Online]. Available from: www.eapn.eu/en/what-we-do/issues-we-focus-on/europe-2020-strategy/258-the-lisbon-strategy-a-general-overview [accessed 5 January 2012].

3 Enterprise Ireland [Online]. Available from: www.enterprise-ireland.com/en/ [accessed 6 January 2012].

4 http://ec.europa.eu/invest-in-research/pdf/download_en/aho_report.pdf.

5 European Commission (2007) *A Guide on Dealing with Innovative Solutions in Public*

*Procurement: 10 Elements of Good Practice*. Luxembourg and Belgium: Office for Official Publications of the European Communities.

6 Bolton Committee (1971) *Report of the Committee of Enquiry on Small Firms*. London: HMSO.

7 Storey, D.J. (1994) *Understanding the Small Business Sector*. London: Routledge.

8 European Commission (2003) *Commission Recommendation concerning the definition of micro, small and medium-sized enterprises (C (2003) 1422))*.

9 European Commission Regulation (2003) Definition of Small and Medium Sized Enterprises. 2003/361/EC. Available from: http://ec.europa.eu/enterprise/policies/sme/facts-figures-analysis/sme-definition/index_en.htm.

10 ENSI – The European Network for SME Research (1994) *European Observatory for SMEs: Second Annual Report*. The Netherlands: ENSI.

11 Glover, A. (2008) *Accelerating the SME Economic Engine: Through Transparent, Simple and Strategic Procurement*. HM Treasury. Available from: www.hm-treasury.gov.uk/d/pbr08_economicengine_2390.pdf.

12 Europa (2008) *Small Business Act Fact Sheet*. Available from: http://ec.europa.eu/enterprise/policies/sme/files/craft/sme_perf_review/doc_08/spr08_fact_sheet_ie_en.pdf.

13 DKM survey (2006) *The Economic Impact of Small Business in Ireland*.

14 Tax Strategy Group Paper (2006) *The SME Sector in Ireland*.

15 IBEC, 2010, Agenda. Issue 9. Available from: http://agenda.ibec.ie/17tk0ytsms5.

16 Ferlie, E. (1992) The creation and evolution of quasi markets in the public sector: a problem for strategic management, *Strategic Management Journal* 13, 79–97.

17 Boyett, I., Robinson, P., Brown, A. and Finlay, D. (1996) Supplier – purchaser relationships within a quasi-market: the case of British Rail and British steel track products, *Journal of Academy of Marketing Science* 23, 236–45.

18 Bryntse, K. (1996) The purchasing of public services: exploring the purchasing function in a service context, *European Journal of Purchasing & Supply Management* 2 (4), 193–201.

19 Van Weele, A. (2004) *Purchasing and Supply Chain Management, Analysis, Strategy, Planning and Practice*, 4th edition. London: Thomson.

20 Davis, P. (2010) Development of a framework for the assessment of the role and impact of technology on the public procurement process – an Irish health sector study. PhD Thesis, DIT.

21 Harland, C., Gibbs, J. and Sutton, P. (2000) Supply strategy for the public sector: framing the issues, IPSERA, 9th Annual Conference.

22 Lysons, K. and Gillingham, M. (2003) *Purchasing and Supply Chain Management*, 6th edition. London: FT Prentice Hall.

23 Porter, M. (1985) *Competitive Advantage; Creating and Sustaining Superior Performance*. New York: The Free Press.

24 Reck, R.F. and Long, B.G. (1988) Purchasing: a competitive weapon, *International Journal of Purchasing and Materials Management* 24 (3), 2–8.

25 Harwick, T. (1997) Optimal decision making for the supply chain, *APICS – The Performance Advantage* 7 (1), 42–4.

26 Brenner, W. and Hamm, W. (1996) Information technology for purchasing in a process environment, *European Journal of Purchasing and Supply Management* 2 (4), 211–19.

27 www.djei.ie/science/technology/sciencestrategy.htm.

28 www.djei.ie/publications/science/innovationpolicystatement.pdf.

29 www.eurosfaire.prd.fr/7pc/bibliotheque/consulter.php?id=589.

30 http://ec.europa.eu/environment/gpp/pdf/buying_green_handbook_en.pdf.

31 www.djei.ie/publications/trade/2009/buyinginnovation.pdf.

32 National Procurement Service (Ireland) 1st Annual Survey – results pending.

33 www.winningintendering.eu.

34 OECD (2002) *Local Partnership, Clusters and SME Globalisation*; Queensland Government (2002) *Procurement Management Development Project: Purchasing Processes and Efficiencies*.
35 Campbell, V. (2010) *The National Procurement Service – A Case Study*. DCU, p. 68. Available from: www.winnningtendering.eu/_fileupload/Dublin_City_University_Business_School_thesis_vs_15.pdf.
36 Gershon, P. (2004) *Releasing Resources for the Frontline: Independent Review of Public Sector Efficiency*. HM Treasury. Available from: www.hm-treasury.gov.uk/d/efficiency_review120704.pdf.
37 http://wales.gov.uk/docs/dpsp/publications/valuewales/barrierstoprocurementopportunity/090520barrierstoprocurement2en.pdf.

# 16 Socio-economic programmes in public procurements

## Are preferences fair and effective for all?

*Fernand A. Lavallée*[1]

A distinctive, if not unique, characteristic of federal public procurement in the United States is the national commitment to socio-economic goals, and the methods in which the federal government attempts to meet or exceed these goals. The concept of socio-economic policies and goals is not itself unique to the United States. The European Union, and many of the European Union member states, for example, have established policies for, and to promote, small businesses, and like the United States, are signatories to the Organization for Economic Cooperation and Development's (OECD) Bologna Charter on Small and Medium-Sized Enterprises (SME) Policies.[2]

What is quintessentially American – and unique to the United States – is the confluence of economic, historical, legal, philosophical, social and cultural forces and influences that have shaped, and continue to animate, American socio-economic policies and programmes. In the United States, unlike anywhere else in the world, socio-economic policies and programmes in federal procurement are a manifestation of an ongoing American conversation, started in the era of the formation of the country. This national conversation continues today as the United States strives to make a cohesive and unifying sense of the diverse peoples, cultures, disparate situations and visions that at times compete, stand in tension, but constantly seek to resolve into a cohesive and functioning synthesis of American pluralism.

This chapter provides a concise interdisciplinary assessment of several major socio-economic programmes in US federal public procurement, explores the economic impacts and consequences of these programmes, and seeks, with brevity, to offer lessons learned from, and suggestions on, effective socio-economic programmes in public procurements.

### 1 Economic, philosophic and social impacts of small business in the United States: the predicates for socio-economic preferences in federal public procurements

The United States is widely regarded as a country that is hospitable to business.[3] Historically there was no doubt of the importance of small businesses to the health and vitality of the US economy. Innumerable treatises and commentaries are dedicated to the history of businesses in the United States, most noting that, by necessity, prior to 1880, the vast majority of businesses were small.[4] Even today, small businesses are a crucial and compelling component of the US economy, as evident from oft-cited, and equally often debated, statistics from the United States Small Business Administration (SBA) including:

- Small businesses represent 99.7 per cent of all employer firms.
- Small businesses employ just over half of all private sector employees.
- Small businesses pay 44 per cent of total US private payroll.
- Small businesses have generated 64 per cent of net new jobs over the past 15 years.
- Small businesses create more than half of the nonfarm private gross domestic product (GDP).
- Small businesses hire 40 per cent of high-tech workers (such as scientists, engineers and computer programmers).[5]

These statistics alone provide proof for the argument that small businesses continue today to have a substantial economic impact on the multi-trillion dollar economy of the United States. For example, a consideration that is as critical from a domestic political perspective as it is economically is the contribution of small businesses to employment. As illustrated in Figure 16.1, in the United

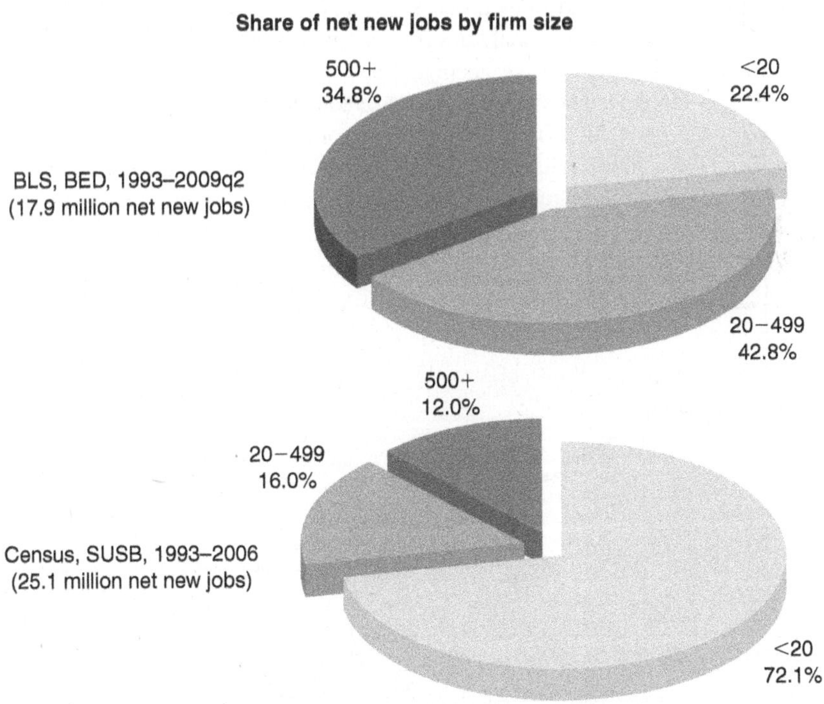


*Figure 16.1* Share of net new jobs by firm size.

States small businesses have accounted for approximately 65 per cent to 90 per cent of the private-sector net job creation over the past 15 years, depending on which US federal government statistics are used.[6]

Moreover, these statistics underscore the sophistication of US small businesses. In particular, the statistics on the employment of individuals who are typically highly educated and skilled, such as scientists, engineers and other high-tech workers, demonstrates that small businesses have the human resources to deal with complex technical challenges and are a substantial source of employment for highly skilled individuals.

Economically, and in the context of the recession from which the United States economy is slowly emerging, the current outlook for small business is optimistic.[7] The most recent Small Business Quarterly Bulletin issued by the US Small Business Administration for the fourth quarter of 2010 suggests that small businesses, too, are recovering. For example, demand for loans by small businesses is increasing (see Figure 16.2).

The number of small businesses that are expanding is outnumbering those that are shrinking (see Figure 16.3).

And small businesses are leading in private-sector employment gains (see Figure 16.4).

Additional recent US small business data can be seen in Table 16.2.

What these statistics do not fully reflect or reveal are an inherently interdisciplinary set of relationships and value propositions that is a consequence of US federal socio-economic programmes, including procurement preferences for small businesses. This is because there are economic and non-economic impacts of socio-economic programmes that cannot easily be reduced to mathematically precise metrics but which nonetheless provide economic and non-economic benefits to the economy and the country. Such contributions importantly include the consequences such socio-economic preference programmes have in lessening racial divides,

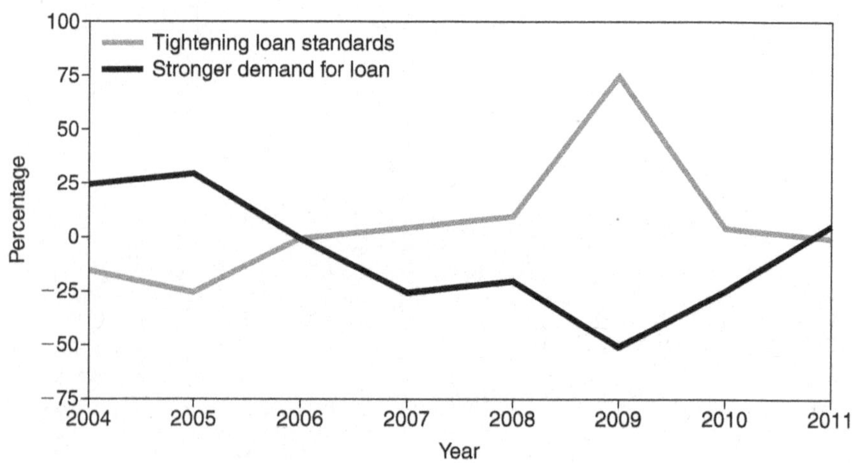


*Figure 16.2* Small business bank lending.

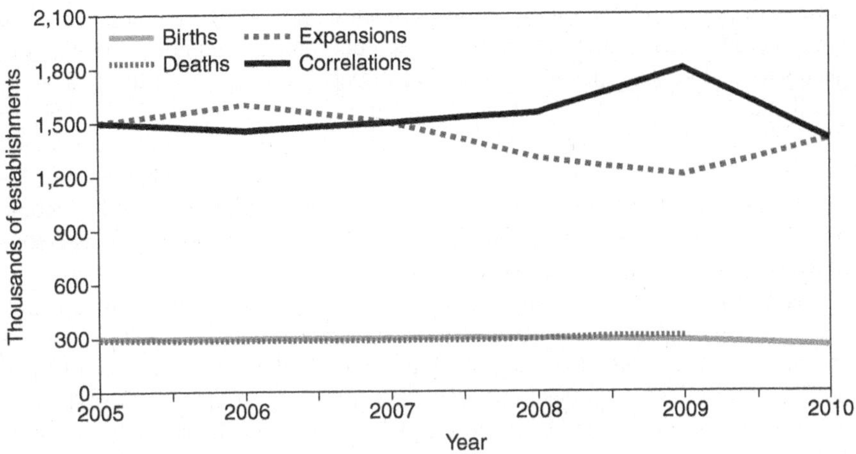


*Figure 16.3* Establishment dynamics (thousands, seasonally adjusted).

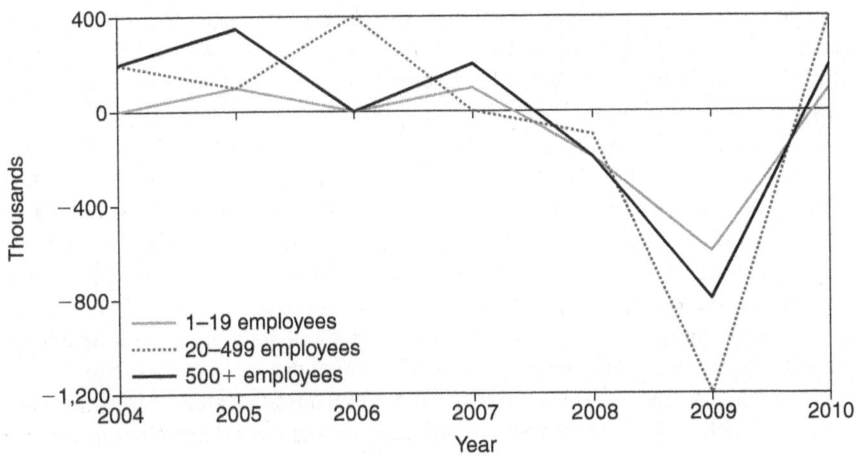


*Figure 16.4* Employment change by size of firm (thousands, seasonally adjusted).

promoting national unity and assisting the American polity in defining who Americans are as a people. To be sure, such impacts promote productivity and overall favourable economic activity – generally good consequences, and glimpses of which may be captured, at least partially, in certain traditional economic metrics – but these impacts are not necessarily ones that can be neatly measured with precision. This is a point that President Coolidge's assessment of the business of America expressly acknowledged: that is, there are many other things that Americans want 'very much more' than monetary wealth. Socio-economic preferences in federal public procurement have helped Americans secure wealth as well as the 'other things wanted very much more' than wealth.

The theme of how small business has always been viewed favourably by the American populace, not solely for its economic and 'monetary' importance to both the individual and the body politic, but perhaps equally for its non-pecuniary value, is a theme that readily emerges in treatises on the history of small business in the United States.[8] Small business is integrally tied to the American psyche, an embodiment of American reverence for independence and self-reliance, an unifying factor akin to a common spoken language in this 'nation of immigrants'[9] that cultivates – and values – pluralism, and a people who embrace the ideal of the United States as a land of opportunity for persons of every national origin, ethnicity and creed.[10]

Many Americans view small business as contributing meaningfully to the safeguarding of the republic, as a line of defence for democracy.[11] This is not to suggest that the American public does not place great value on the economic value of small business. Rather, it seems that Americans take a very broad view as to what comprises total economic value, willing to look beyond the quantifiable contributions of small businesses to the employment statistics, the percentage of Gross National Product, and other standard metrics, satisfied with the perception of small businesses' unparalleled contributions to innovation in all manner of products and services.[12]

There is also anecdotal evidence that American small businesses contribute to positive international perceptions of American ingenuity, efficiency and even social responsibility. For example, Center Rock, Inc. and Zephyr Technology Corporation were among two US small businesses which made noteworthy efforts and contributions to the rescue of the Chilean miners trapped in the catastrophic collapse of the San Jose Mine in Copiapo, Chile, in 2010.[13] The contributions of these small companies were noteworthy amidst the heroic Chilean rescue efforts of many other US and non-US companies, including the United Parcel Service (UPS) which delivered within 48 hours much of the drilling equipment, including items that weighed over 13 tons alone, and the Layne Christensen Company, which worked the drills and machinery used to reach the miners, and to enlarge the holes to ultimately effect the successful rescue.

Center Rock, Inc. (CRI), a small US-based business located in Berlin, Pennsylvania, with only 75 employees, manufactures and distributes a complete line of air drilling tools and products. CRI's products and services support the construction, foundation drilling, oil and gas, water well/blast hole, mining/quarry, geothermal, utility and renewable energy industries. CRI manufactured the 28 inch wide canisters that functioned as the 'drill bit' on the successful rig which drilled the shafts used to extricate the miners trapped approximately 2,070 feet below the surface at the San Jose mine.[14] Each CRI canister is advanced technology and contains an innovative array of four air hammers and four drill bits that operate in tandem to quickly drill through rock.[15]

The Zephyr Technology Corporation is a small US-based business headquartered in Annapolis, Maryland. Zephyr, a leader in the Health, Defense, First Responder, Training and Research markets, designs and manufactures real-time physiological and biomechanical monitoring technologies and devices, more widely referred to as Physical Status Monitoring (PSM) solutions. Zephyr's PSM technology, including specifically the Zephyr BioHarnesses™, was used by the Chilean government to monitor the health of the trapped miners.[16] The Zephyr PSM technology was used to record remotely the miners' vital signs, pulse, heart rhythm and breathing. These small biometric monitors, mounted on chest belts, were sent down to the miners to help keep track of their physical condition and to prepare for their follow-on medical care following their rescue. Zephyr is a US federal government contractor with at least a US General Services Administration (GSA) Multiple Award Schedule contract. Although it is not apparent that Zephyr has received any federal 'set-aside' contract awards, it does self-identify as a small business on its GSA Schedule contract.

## 2 Socio-economic preferences in US federal public procurement[17]

### *2.1 The purpose of federal socio-economic preferences*

The federal statutes that establish socio-economic preferences in US federal procurement contracting expressly state the purpose and aspirations for such preferences. The statutory purpose is to set the policy that the federal government will advance the interests of small business when practicable.[18] To effectuate this policy, federal government agencies are required to follow two guiding principles:

1. Provide the 'maximum practical opportunity' for small businesses to participate in contracts let by federal agencies, including subcontracts for subsystems, assemblies, components and related services for major systems.[19]
2. Place, or incentivize the placement of, a 'fair proportion' of their procurements, including direct or 'prime' contracts and subcontracts (to the extent that such subcontracts are necessary for the performance of the federal prime contracts, even though there is no privity of contract between the federal government and the subcontractor), with small business concerns.[20]

Accordingly, there is a statutory mandate for federal executive agencies to take steps to ensure that small businesses will secure a fair portion of federal contract work by having the maximum practicable opportunity to compete for contracts to the extent consistent with the government's needs.[21]

A key method used by the US federal government to implement the principle of providing a fair portion of the total purchases and contracts or subcontracts for property and services for the federal government is through contracting and subcontracting goals established by Congress, the federal executive agencies and the US Small Business Administration. In turn, to facilitate achievement of these contracting and subcontracting goals, federal law has established preferences, including specifically the 'set-aside' or restriction of certain federal public procurements to small businesses, or to a specific type of small business such as a Women-Owned Small Business or a Service-Disabled Veteran-Owned Small Business.

Table 16.1 summarizes major socio-economic preferences and the eligibility requirements for each.

*Table 16.1* Major US federal socio-economic preferences

| *Category/type of business* | *Eligibility* |
|---|---|
| Small Business ("SB") | • Is a "small" business concern under its industry specific North American Industry Classification System ("NAICS") code threshold which defines size either in terms of the average number of employees over the past 12 months, or average annual receipts over the past three years. Typically service businesses are defined using the three-year average annual receipts threshold while manufacturing businesses use the number of employee threshold.<br>• is organized for profit;<br>• has a place of business in the United States;<br>• operates primarily within the United States or makes a significant contribution to the US economy through payment of taxes or use of American products, materials or labour;<br>• is independently owned and operated; and<br>• is not dominant in its field on a national basis. |
| 8(a) Business Development Programme, Small Disadvantaged Business ("SDB") | • The business must be a small business concern;<br>• the business must demonstrate a potential for success (generally by being in business for, at least, two years);<br>• the business must be unconditionally owned and controlled by:<br>1. one or more socially or economically disadvantaged individuals who<br>2. are US citizens and who<br>3. are of good character. |
| Woman-Owned Small Business ("WOSB") | • The business must be a small business concern that is at least 51 per cent unconditionally and directly owned and controlled by one or more women who are US citizens.<br>• Have a woman manage the day-to-day operations, make long-term decisions for the business, hold the highest officer position in the business and work at the business full-time during normal working hours.<br>• To be an eligible EDWOSB, a company must be at least 51 per cent owned by one or more women who are "economically disadvantaged"; and, have an economically disadvantaged woman manage the day-to-day operations, make long-term decisions for the business, hold the highest officer position in the business and work at the business full-time during normal working hours.<br>For both WOSB and EDWOSB, the 51 per cent ownership must be unconditional and direct. |

| | |
|---|---|
| HUBZone Small Business ("HUBZone") | • The business must be a small business concern.<br>• It must be owned and controlled at least 51 per cent by US citizens, or a Community Development Corporation, or an agricultural cooperative or an Indian tribe.<br>• Its principal office must be located within a "Historically Underutilized Business Zone", which includes lands considered "Indian Country" and military facilities closed by the Base Realignment and Closure Act. A principal office is the location where the greatest number of employees at any one location are performing work, with the exception of the construction and service industries.<br>• At least 35 per cent of its employees must reside in a HUBZone. Reside means to live in a primary residence at a place for at least 180 days, or as a currently registered voter, and with intent to live there indefinitely. |
| Service-Disabled Veteran-Owned Small Business ("SDVOSB") | For the SBA Program[1]:<br>• The business must be a small business concern.<br>• The business must be owned by a veteran; meaning a person who served in the active military, naval or air service and was discharged under conditions other than dishonorable. 38 U.S.C. § 101(2).<br>• The veteran owner must have a disability that is service connected, i.e. a disability that was incurred or aggravated in the line of duty in the active military, naval or air service. 15 U.S.C. § 632(q); See also 38 U.S.C. § 101(16).<br>• A concern must be at least 51 per cent unconditionally and directly owned by one or more service-disabled veterans. 13 C.F.R § 125.9. Ownership must be direct. In the case of a limited liability company, at least 51 per cent of each class of member interest must be unconditionally owned by one or more service-disabled veterans.<br>• The business must be controlled by one or more service-disabled veterans (or in the case of a veteran with permanent and severe disability, the spouse or permanent caregiver of such veteran). Under the SBA regulations, control means both:<br>1. Both long-term decision-making and day-to-day management are performed by a service-disabled veteran (or in the case of a service-disabled veteran with permanent and severe disability, the spouse or permanent caregiver of such veteran).<br>2. A service-disabled veteran (or in the case of a service-disabled veteran with permanent and severe disability, the spouse or permanent caregiver of such veteran) holds the highest officer position in the concern (usually President or Chief Executive Officer) and has the requisite experience to run the business concern. 13 C.F.R. § 125.10(a)-(b). |

Note

1 The Department of Veteran's Affairs maintains a separate Veteran-Owned Small Business and Service-Disabled Veteran-Owned Small Business programme that entails a formal (instead of self-) certification.

The central figure in carrying out the federal government's socio-economic policies is the US Small Business Administration (SBA). The SBA is the federal agency that supervises and controls the small business programmes. The SBA establishes small business size standards, determines Small Disadvantaged Business (SDB) status and 'SBA 8(a) programme' eligibility, rules on size appeals, and alone is authorized to make a determination that a small contractor is not responsible to receive and perform a specific contract.

## *2.2 Overview of significant federal socio-economic designations/ programmes*

### *2.2.1 The 8(a) Business Development programme*

The 8(a) programme was the first and perhaps the best known of the SBA's contracting-related certification programmes. This nine-year programme provides business development assistance to all its participants. Programme participants may also compete for federal contracts reserved for the 8(a) programme through sole-source or limited competition awards.

Generally, a business concern meets the basic requirement for admission to the 8(a) programme if it is a small business which is unconditionally owned and controlled by one or more socially and economically disadvantaged individuals who are of good character and citizens of the United States, and which demonstrates potential for success. United States citizenship is a requirement for participation; permanent resident alien status is insufficient.

Socially disadvantaged individuals are those who have been subjected to racial or ethnic prejudice or cultural bias within American society because of their identities as members of groups and without regard to their individual qualities. There is a rebuttable presumption that the following individuals are socially disadvantaged: Black Americans; Hispanic Americans; Native Americans; Asian Pacific; Subcontinent Asian Americans; and members of other groups designated from time to time by SBA. An individual must demonstrate that he/she had held himself/herself out, and is currently identified by others, as a member of a designated group if SBA requires it.

An individual who is not a member of one of the groups presumed to be socially disadvantaged must establish individual social disadvantage by a preponderance of the evidence. Evidence of individual social disadvantage must be presented.

Economically disadvantaged individuals are socially disadvantaged individuals whose ability to compete in the free market has been impaired due to diminished capital and credit opportunities as compared to others in the same or similar line of business who are not socially disadvantaged.

### *2.2.2 Small Disadvantaged Business (SDB) programme*

While the 8(a) programme offers a broad scope of assistance to socially and economically disadvantaged businesses, SDB certification strictly pertains to benefits in federal procurement. All 8(a) businesses automatically qualify for SDB certification.

In order for a concern to represent that it is an SDB it must:

1 be a current participant in the SBA's 8(a) programme;
2 have been certified by the SBA within three years of the date it seeks to certify as a SDB;
3 have received certification from the procuring agency that it qualifies as a SDB; *or*
4 have submitted an application for SDB certification to the procuring agency and must not have received a negative determination regarding that application.

US citizenship is a requirement for participation in the SDB programme; permanent resident alien status is insufficient.

### *2.2.3 Historically Underutilized Business zone (HUBzone) programme*

The HUBzone programme provides contracting assistance to small businesses located in economically underutilized communities, referred to as historically underutilized business zones or HUBzones, to promote job growth, capital investment and economic development in these areas, including Indian reservations.

In order to qualify for the HUBzone programme, a business (except tribally-owned concerns) must:

1 be a small business by SBA standards;
2 be owned and controlled at least 51 per cent by United States citizens, a Community Development corporation, an agricultural cooperative, or an Indian tribe;
3 have its principal office located within a 'historically underutilized business zone', which includes lands considered 'Indian Country' and military facilities closed by the Base Realignment and Closure Act; and
4 have at least 35 per cent of its employees reside within a HUBzone.

US citizenship is a requirement for participation; permanent resident aliens are specifically excluded from eligibility.

Computer mapping software available on the SBA's website allows businesses to search a database to determine whether they are located in a qualified HUBzone (www.sba.gov/hubzone). Existing businesses that choose to move to qualified areas are eligible for the HUBzone programme. To satisfy the requirement that 35 per cent of a HUBzone business' employees reside in a HUBzone, the employees must have a primary residence within a HUBzone for at least 180 days or be a currently registered voter in a HUBzone.

### 2.2.4 Service-Disabled Veteran-Owned Small Business (SDVOSB)

A SDVOSB is defined as a business that is at least 51 per cent owned by one or more eligible veterans or, in the case of a publicly owned business, at least 51 per cent of the stock is owned by one or more veterans. These veterans must also control the firm's management and daily business operations. It appears that SDVOSB eligibility is not contingent on US citizenship. None of the regulatory or statutory provisions reviewed expressly provide for such a restriction.

### 2.2.5 Women-Owned Small Business (WOSB)

The Women-Owned Small Business (WOSB) Federal Contract programme authorizes contracting officers to set aside certain federal contracts for eligible Women-Owned Small Businesses or Economically Disadvantaged Women-Owned Small Businesses (EDWOSB). To be an eligible WOSB, a company must:

1 be a small business that is at least 51 per cent unconditionally and directly owned and controlled by one or more women who are US citizens; and
2 have a woman manage the day-to-day operations, make long-term decisions for the business, hold the highest officer position in the business and work at the business full-time during normal working hours.

To be an eligible EDWOSB, a company must:

1 be a WOSB that is at least 51 per cent owned by one or more women who are 'economically disadvantaged'; and
2 have an economically disadvantaged woman manage the day-to-day operations, make long-term decisions for the business, hold the highest officer position in the business and work at the business full-time during normal working hours.

A woman is presumed economically disadvantaged if she has a personal net worth of less than $750,000 (with some exclusions), her adjusted gross yearly income averaged over the three years preceding the certification less than $350,000, and the fair market value of all her assets is less than $6 million.

For both WOSB and EDWOSB, the 51 per cent ownership must be unconditional and direct.

There are over 300 6-digit North American Industry Classification System (NAICS) codes that are eligible for federal contracting under the WOSB Program. The URL to the current listing is: www.sba.gov/sites/default/files/files/gc_wosb_naics_grids.pdf.

Federal contracting officers may set aside a requirement for WOSBs if:

1 the NAICS code is in an industry in which SBA has designated that WOSBs are substantially underrepresented;

2 the contracting officer has a reasonable expectation that two or more WOSBs will submit offers;
3 the anticipated award price of the contract does not exceed \$6.5 million in the case of manufacturing contracts and \$4 million in the case of all other contracts; and
4 the contracting officer believes the contract can be awarded at a fair and reasonable price.

Federal contracting officers may set aside a requirement for EDWOSBs if the NAICS code is in an industry in which SBA has designated that WOSBs are underrepresented.

### *2.2.6 Service-Disabled Veteran-Owned Small Businesses*

There are two distinct SDVOSB programmes. The best-known, and longest running, is the SBA's SDVOSB programme. The SBA has issued detailed regulations implementing this programme.[22] The Department of Veteran's Affairs (VA) has also established a Veteran Owned Small Business programme. The SBA SDVOSB programme is summarized below, along with details on the VA's programme. The SBA SDVOSB eligibility requirements are: a SDVOSB concern is a concern that is at least 51 per cent unconditionally and directly owned by one or more service-disabled veterans; the management and daily business operations must be controlled by one or more service-disabled veterans, or in the case of a service-disabled veteran with permanent and severe disability, the spouse or permanent caregiver of such veteran. Of course, the business must be defined as small in accordance with the SBA's size regulations.[23]

Specifically, the SDVOSB must meet the following requirements:

1 the business must be owned by a veteran; meaning a person who served in the active military, naval or air service and was discharged or released under conditions other than dishonourable;[24]
2 the veteran owner must have a disability that is service connected, i.e. a disability that was incurred or aggravated in the line of duty in the active military, naval or air service;[25]
3 a concern must be at least 51 per cent unconditionally and directly owned by one or more service-disabled veterans.[26] Ownership must be direct. As such, a concern owned principally by another business entity that is in turn owned and controlled by one or more service-disabled veterans does not meet the requirement. In the case of a limited liability company, at least 51 per cent of each class of member interest must be unconditionally owned by one or more service-disabled veterans;
4 in addition to proper ownership, the business must be controlled by one or more service-disabled veterans (or in the case of a veteran with permanent and severe disability, the spouse or permanent caregiver of such veteran). Under the SBA regulations, control means:

i both long-term decision-making and day-to-day management are performed by a service-disabled veteran (or in the case of a service-disabled veteran with permanent and severe disability, the spouse or permanent caregiver of such veteran); and

ii a service-disabled veteran (or in the case of a service-disabled veteran with permanent and severe disability, the spouse or permanent caregiver of such veteran) holds the highest officer position in the concern (usually President or Chief Executive Officer) and has the requisite experience to run the business concern.[27]

The service-disabled veteran (or in the case of a veteran with permanent and severe disability, the spouse or permanent caregiver of such veteran) need not have the technical expertise or possess the required licence to be found to control the concern if the service-disabled veteran can demonstrate that he or she has ultimate managerial and supervisory control over those who possess the required licences or technical expertise. In such case, the Small Business Administration Office of Hearings and Appeals often looks to see whether the service-disabled veteran has the managerial experience of the extent and complexity needed to run the business. Additionally, in the case of a limited liability company, one or more service-disabled veterans must serve as managing members, with control over *all* decisions of the limited liability company,[28] and

5 the business concern must be small within the size standards of the NAICS code assigned to the contract. This size requirement must be met at the time of the contract offer.[29]

Under the SBA SDVOSB programme, an SDVOSB 'self-certifies' that it meets the requirements of the SDVOSB programme when it bids on an SDVOSB contract. Specifically, an SDVOSB concern must submit the following representations with its initial offer on a specific contract, self-certifying that it:

1 is a SDVOSB concern;
2 is small under the NAICS code assigned to the procurement;
3 will meet the percentage of work requirements set forth in 13 C.F.R. § 125.6;
4 is an eligible joint venture (if applicable); and,
5 is an eligible non-manufacturer (if applicable).[30]

In addition to these basic requirements, other requirements may apply to a service-disabled veteran business depending on the business type and how the SDVOSB contract is performed.

## 3 Lessons learned and special considerations for utility for EU procurements

A critic might assert that the US policy of advancing the interests of small businesses is irreparably in conflict with, and contradictory to, the federal government's primary goal that the public procurement process operate to provide the United States with the high quality goods and services that it needs on a competitive and best value, if not lowest cost, basis.[31] The critic will no doubt observe that preferences that restrict a procurement competition to certain small business firms are, by definition, antithetical to the fundamental concept of competition, not to mention the US federal procurement mandate for 'full and open competition'. Indeed, socio-economic preferences appear to be wholly unrelated to the goal of acquiring the best value for the government, and ultimately the US taxpayers.

Such a critique could expand to question the 'fairness', and even public ethics, of preferences that discriminate against individual human beings, and the business enterprises that they own and control, based on their gender, or their ethnic and national origins, as opposed to merits or individual achievements. The critic asks, in the context of the historical American dialectic, whether the zeal with which the body politic has been vigilant against the 'tyranny of the majority' has resulted in a form of an equally undesirable 'tyranny of the minority'?

The critic, though, misses fundamental structural aspects of the US socio-economic policy. For example, the statutes establishing the policy and programmes frame the preferences as promoting competition.[32] In the short term this is accomplished by the 'Rule of Two'[33] and the requirement for competition amongst responsible small businesses within the category for which the set-aside or restriction is intended. In the long term, full and open competition is achieved by having removed the barriers to entry for small businesses and having the most meritorious succeed and grow. At all times, full and open competition is supported by the benefits to the country, and businesses of all sizes, of the innovation of small businesses, and the diverse employment provided by small businesses, among other tangible economic benefits. When viewed from this perspective, socio-economic preferences are not anti-competitive, but rather are intrinsic to achieving the ideal of true full and open competition.

It is important to note that in the United States socio-economic preferences do not artificially bolster small businesses that do not have the ability to compete. For example, even a restricted or set-aside federal procurement includes a 'responsibility determination' regarding the awardee. Similarly, small businesses are subject to the vast array of regulatory 'checks-and-balances' and ethics requirements for public contractors. Finally, there are reviews and assessments of the small businesses to ensure they are viable for the long term.

The key lessons learned are that, when it comes to socio-economic preferences, the government must be vigilant to ensure that the appropriate groups are targeted for eligibility in the programmes. As in all aspects of public procurements, transparency is fundamental. A well defined and meaningful system for protests and challenges to the government's solicitation and evaluation process and decisions is crucial. Ultimately, to be successful, the benefits and value of the socio-economic preferences must give due consideration to the non-economic objectives of the nation.

*Table 16.2* Small business quarterly bulletin

| | *Trend* | *Quarterly data* | | | | | | | | | | *Annual data (or year end)* | | | | | | | |
|---|---|---|---|---|---|---|---|---|---|---|---|---|---|---|---|---|---|---|---|
| | | *2008* | | *2009* | | | | *2010* | | | | | | | | | | | |
| | | *Q3* | *Q4* | *Q1* | *Q2* | *Q3* | *Q4* | *Q1* | *Q2* | *Q3* | *Q4* | *1995* | *2000* | *2005* | *2006* | *2007* | *2008* | *2009* | *2010* |
| Self-employed (000)*† unincorporated | – | 10,126 | 9,585 | 9,910 | 10,079 | 9,959 | 9,622 | 9,632 | 9,977 | 9,680 | 9,309 | 10,482 | 10,214 | 10,464 | 10,586 | 10,413 | 10,080 | 9,831 | 9,681 |
| Incorporated | + | 5,777 | 5,814 | 5,640 | 5,316 | 5,368 | 5,520 | 5,446 | 5,254 | 5,036 | 5,263 | na | 4,459 | 5,254 | 5,499 | 5,735 | 5,784 | 5,466 | 5,191 |
| Businesses, turnover establishments (000) births | = | 192 | 188 | 172 | 176 | 169 | 184 | 172 | 172 | | | 751 | 826 | 867 | 870 | 845 | 786 | 701 | |
| Deaths | – | 223 | 240 | 235 | 226 | 216 | – | – | – | – | – | 651 | 759 | 737 | 763 | 804 | 901 | – | – |
| Business bankruptcies* | – | 11,504 | 12,901 | 14,319 | 16,014 | 15,177 | 15,020 | 14,607 | 14,452 | 13,957 | 13,030 | 51,959 | 35,472 | 39,201 | 19,695 | 28,322 | 43,546 | 60,837 | 56,282 |
| Employment nonfarm payroll (millions) | + | 136.31 | 134.38 | 132.04 | 130.49 | 129.73 | 129.32 | 129.44 | 129.98 | 129.84 | 130.23 | 117.30 | 131.79 | 133.70 | 136.09 | 137.60 | 136.79 | 130.81 | 129.82 |
| Net private-sector job creation (000)total‡ | + | -966 | -1,814 | -2,741 | -1,604 | -900 | -228 | -311 | 728 | | | 2,378 | 1,905 | 2,148 | 1,737 | 735 | –3,575 | –5,473 | |
| <20 employees | + | -234 | -464 | -628 | -302 | -270 | -112 | -188 | 110 | – | – | 487 | 275 | 479 | 321 | -33 | -1,043 | -1,312 | – |
| 20–499 employees | + | -340 | -760 | -1,154 | -530 | -309 | -141 | -11 | 412 | – | – | 1,088 | 772 | 756 | 801 | 370 | -1,212 | -2,134 | – |
| 500+ employees | + | -460 | -659 | -870 | -903 | -398 | -53 | -71 | 166 | – | – | 830 | 905 | 910 | 508 | 304 | -1,475 | -2,224 | – |
| Finance and income tightening | | | | | | | | | | | | | | | | | | | |
| lending standards§ | + | 65.3 | 74.5 | 69.2 | 42.3 | 34.0 | 16.1 | 3.7 | 0.0 | -9.1 | -7.1 | -1.8 | 27.3 | -5.3 | -1.8 | 9.6 | 74.5 | 16.1 | -7.1 |
| Demand for loans§ | – | -15 | -7 | -58 | -64 | -55 | -36 | -30 | -9 | -4 | -21 | 7.2 | -12.8 | 8.9 | -13.0 | -7.7 | -7.4 | -35.7 | -21.4 |
| C&I loans outstanding ($billion) | + | 1,503 | 1,494 | 1,433 | 1,365 | 1,275 | 1,222 | 1,185 | 1,172 | 1,175 | 1,186 | 674 | 1,086 | 1,086 | 1,215 | 1,439 | 1,494 | 1,222 | 1,186 |
| Proprietor's income ($billion) | + | 1,112 | 1,073 | 1,019 | 1,001 | 1,006 | 1,022 | 1,031 | 1,050 | 1,060 | 1,081 | 516 | 818 | 1,070 | 1,133 | 1,090 | 1,102 | 1,012 | 1,055 |
| Economy (percent) real GDP change† | + | -4.0 | -6.8 | -4.9 | -0.7 | 1.6 | 5.0 | 3.7 | 1.7 | 2.6 | 2.8 | 2.5 | 4.1 | 3.1 | 2.7 | 1.9 | 0.0 | -2.6 | 2.8 |
| Chained CPI† | + | 0.8 | -15.8 | 4.1 | 5.5 | 0.7 | -0.5 | 3.2 | 0.3 | 0.5 | 1.4 | na | 2.0 | 2.9 | 2.9 | 2.5 | 3.7 | -0.5 | 1.5 |
| Unemployment rate | – | 6.2 | 7.3 | 8.6 | 9.5 | 9.8 | 9.9 | 9.7 | 9.5 | 9.6 | 9.4 | 5.6 | 4.0 | 5.1 | 4.6 | 4.6 | 5.8 | 9.3 | 9.6 |

Sources: US Small Business Administration, Office of Advocacy, from data provided by the US Bureau of Labor Statistics (Business Employment Dynamics), Administrative Office of the US Courts, Federal Reserve Board of Govenors (Senior Loan Officer Survey), US Bureau of Economic Analysis and Federal Deposit Insurance Corporation.
From the US Small Business Administration Office of Advocacy, Small Business Quarterly Bulletin, Fourth Quarter 2010, prepared by Brian Headd, Economist, available at: www.sba.gov/sites/default/files/SBQB_2010q4.pdf.

Notes
* Not seasonally adjusted.
† Annualized quarterly figures, from last month of quarter where applicable.
‡ Totals may not add because indeterminate firm sizes.
§ Percent of responses.

The US Department of Veterans Affairs (VA) administers the Veterans-Owned Small Business programme and has issued regulations implementing the programme.[34] Vendor Information Pages (VIP) is a database of businesses eligible to participate in the VA's Veteran-Owned Small Business programme, and can be accessed online at www.VetBiz.gov.

The eligibility requirements for the VA programme have several features in common with the SBA requirements. A SDVOSB concern is a concern that is at least 51 per cent unconditionally and directly owned by one or more service-disabled veterans. The management and daily business operations must be controlled by one or more service-disabled veterans, or in the case of a service-disabled veteran with permanent and severe disability, the spouse or permanent caregiver of such veteran. The VA's Center for Veterans Affairs (CVE) applies the small business concern definition established by 48 C.F.R. §2.101; i.e. small in accordance with the SBA's size regulations at 13 C.F.R. §125. The VA programme is available for VOSBs and SDVOSBs.

The VA SDVOSB must meet the following requirements:

1 the business must be owned by a veteran, meaning a person who served on active duty with the US Army, Air Force, Navy, Marine Corps or Coast Guard for any length of time and who was discharged or released under conditions other than dishonorable. Reservists or members of the National Guard called to federal duty or disabled from a disease or injury incurred or aggravated in the line of duty or while in training status also qualify as a veteran;[35]
2 the veteran owner must have a disability rating letter issued by the Department of Veterans Affairs establishing a service-connected rating between 0 and 100 per cent, or a disability determination from the Department of Defense;
3 a concern must be at least 51 per cent unconditionally and directly owned by one or more service-disabled veterans.[36] Ownership must be direct. As such, a concern owned principally by another business entity that is in turn owned and controlled by one or more service-disabled veterans does not meet the requirement. Ownership must not be subject to conditions precedent, conditions subsequent, executory agreements, voting trusts, restrictions on assignments of voting rights or other arrangements causing or potentially causing ownership benefits to go to another (other than after death or incapacity). In the case of a limited liability company, at least 51 per cent of each class of member interest must be unconditionally owned by one or more service-disabled veterans. Additionally, one or more service-disabled veterans must be entitled to receive at least 51 per cent of the annual profits paid to the LLC applicant;
4 the business must be controlled by one or more service-disabled veterans (or in the case of a veteran with permanent and severe disability, the spouse or permanent caregiver of such veteran). Under the VA regulations, control means both long-term decision-making and day-to-day management are

performed by a service-disabled veteran. The service-disabled veteran must also hold the highest officer position in the firm (usually President or Chief Executive Officer) and have the requisite experience to run the business concern.[37] A veteran need not have the technical expertise or possess a required licence to be found to control the entity if he/she can demonstrate that he/she has the ultimate managerial and supervisory control over those who possess such expertise. However, where a critical licence is held by a non-veteran having an equity interest in the participant firm, the non-veteran may be found to control the firm. In the case of a limited liability company, one or more service-disabled veterans must serve as managing members, with control over *all* decisions of the limited liability company. On 18 February 2011, the VA issued a final rule rescinding the requirement that an owner work full-time for the participant firm;

5 the CVE applies the small business concern definition established by 48 C.F.R. §2.101. The business concern must be small within the size standards of the NAICS code assigned to the contract; and
6 the VA regulation expressly provides that VetBiz verified businesses must have good character. Debarred or suspended concerns or concerns owned or controlled by debarred or suspended persons are ineligible for VetBiz VIP Verification.

Under the VA programme, an SDVOSB must go through a *formal* certification process. The process involves *verification* of the veteran's status and *examination* of the applicant. Each VetBiz VIP applicant submits the electronic forms and attachments required by CVE. These forms include, but are not limited to, financial statements, federal personal and business tax returns, payroll records and personal history statements.[38]

The VA certification process takes about two to three months to complete. Verification of the veteran's status typically takes two to three weeks. Once the veteran's status has been verified, the VA will request business documents from the concern and review the completed application. This phase of the certification may take up to 60 days.

## Notes

1 Fernand Lavallée is a partner resident in the Washington, DC, USA law offices of DLA Piper LLP (US). Mr Lavallée holds an A.B. in Government from Georgetown University and a Doctor of Jurisprudence from the College of William & Mary Law School. *Chambers USA: America's Leading Lawyers for Business* lists Mr Lavallée as a leading national practitioner in public contracts law.
2 OECD, The Bologna Charter on SME Policies, 15 June 2000, available at: www.oecd.org/document/17/0,3343,en_2649_34197_1809105_1_1_1_1,00.html. For an excellent comparison of small business contracting in the United States and Europe, see Max V. Kidalov, Small Business Contracting in the United States and Europe: A Comparative Assessment, *Public Contract Law Journal*, Volume 40, No. 2, Winter 2011, 443.
3 The quip that '[t]he business of America is business' famously is attributed to Calvin

Coolidge, the 30th President of the United States. The quote is often cited for the proposition that the federal government should interfere as little as possible with business and with individuals. Ironically, though pithy, this is a misquote of the president's actual words from a speech titled 'The Press Under a Free Government'. In the speech, given before the American Society of Newspaper Editors in Washington, DC, on 17 January 1925, President Coolidge said 'After all, the chief business of the American people is business. Of course the accumulation of wealth cannot be justified as the chief end of existence'. See *The Press Under a Free Government*, Address before the American Society of Newspaper Editors, 17 January 1925, available at: www.calvin-coolidge.org/html/the_press_under_a_free_governm.html. The last paragraph in President Coolidge's speech reveals a more profound appreciation of the ultimate ends of American's 'chief business':

> We make no concealment of the fact that we want wealth, but there are many other things that we want very much more. We want peace and honor, and that charity which is so strong an element of all civilization. The chief ideal of the American people is idealism. I cannot repeat too often that America is a nation of idealists. That is the only motive to which they ever give any strong and lasting reaction.

4 See, e.g., Mansel G. Blackford, *A History of Small Business in America*, 2nd edn, Chapel Hill: The University of North Carolina Press, 2008. See also Christopher Conte, Small Business in U.S. History, *eJournal USA*, January 2006, p. 6 (For the first century of its existence virtually all businesses in the United States were small by necessity: 'Transportation was slow and inefficient, keeping markets too fragmented to support large scale enterprise. Financial institutions also were too small to support big business. And productive capacity was limited because wind, water, and animal power were the only sources of energy.')

5 US Small Business Administration, Frequently Asked Questions, How Important are Small Businesses to the US Economy, citing the US Dept. of Commerce, Bureau of the Census and International Trade Admin.; Advocacy Funded Research by Kathryn Kobe, 2007; CHI Research, 2003; and the U.S. Dept. of Labor, Bureau of Labor Statistics, available at: www.sba.gov/advocacy/7495/8420.

6 Brian Headd, An Analysis of Small Business and Jobs, U.S. Small Business Administration Office of Advocacy, Release Date: March 2010, available at: www.sba.gov/sites/default/files/files/an%20analysis%20of%20small%20business%20and%20jobs(1).pdf. The difference in the statistics is based on the methodology of the source. The US Bureau of Labor Statistics' Business Employment Dynamics (BED) is produced quarterly and with only a six- to nine-month lag, but does not have diverse business or geographic coverage. The Bureau's Statistics of US Businesses (SUSB) is produced annually, but with a two-to-three year lag. Finally, the SUSB's method of size classification is 'start year sizing' whereas the BED utilizes 'dynamic sizing'.

7 US Small Business Administration Office of Advocacy, Small Business Quarterly Bulletin, Fourth Quarter 2010, prepared by Brian Headd, Economist, available at: www.sba.gov/sites/default/files/files/SBQB_2010q4.pdf.

8 Blackford, *A History of Small Business in America*, p. 74.

9 John Fitzgerald Kennedy (ed. Robert F. Kennedy), *A Nation of Immigrants*, New York: HarperCollins, 1964.

10 Interestingly, statistics suggest that until the 1990s, small business ownership offered fewer opportunities for members of minority ethnic groups in the United States than for Caucasians (Blackford, *A History of Small Business in America*, p. 180). For example, while the number of minority-owned concerns more than doubled in the decade between 1972 and 1982, the participation rate of minorities in business ownership by the late 1970s was only one-fifth that of non-hispanic Caucasians. However, between 1987 and 1992, the number of black-owned businesses increased by 46 per

cent, about the same rate of increase as non-black businesses in the United States (Blackford, *A History of Small Business in America*, pp. 180–1).

11 Some commentators explain this common belief solely by pointing to factors like the decentralizing effect of small businesses on the concentration of wealth; the diversity in workplaces and cultures that small business inherently accommodates, if not drives; and the civic virtues that many ascribe to small business such as industriousness, character and healthy ambition. There is also, though, a cultural-political force that reaches deep in both American history, political philosophy and the social dialectic that continues to this day. Though perhaps not overtly articulated in the same terms, small businesses bolster the American ideals of democracy in a republic by providing a practical mechanism to diffuse the 'tyranny of the majority', perhaps most notably cautioned against by Alexis de Tocqueville in his epic tome *Democracy in America*, but also addressed by the Framers of the American Constitution, including in the Federalist Papers. See, e.g., Federalist Paper No. 51. Certainly, a 'tyranny of the majority' is not an original American concept, harkening at least to Voltaire's '*tyrannie de plusiers*' ('tyranny of the many') in his Philosophical Dictionary of 1764.

12 US Small Business Administration, Frequently Asked Questions, How Important are Small Businesses to the US Economy, available at: www.sba.gov/advocacy/7495/8420. US SBA statistics indicate that US small businesses produce 13 times more patents per employee than large patenting firms. Moreover, the innovations patented by small businesses are twice as likely as large firm patents to be among the 1 per cent most cited.

13 In fact, small businesses made up 97.3 per cent of all identified exporters and produced 30.2 per cent of the known export value for the United States in FY 2007. While it is not clear what portion of this success for American small businesses in international trade can be fairly attributed to US federal socio-economic programmes in public procurements, the implications have not all been positive. The European Commission, for example, has suggested a link between US federal small business socio-economic preferences and barriers for European Union contractors to the US public procurement market. See Kidalov, Small Business Contracting in the United States and Europe, pp. 443, 445, notes 1 and 2 (citing European Union successive annual complaints that US small business set-aside schemes are discriminatory measures that limit bidding opportunities for European Union contractors contained in the European Commission's U.S. Barriers to Trade and Investment Reports such as the Report for 2008, at 15 (July 2009), available at: http://trade.ec.europa.eu/doclib/docs/2009/july/tradoc_144160.pdf).

14 See Center Rock, Inc. – Rescue 33, available at: www.centerrock.com/chilean-mine-rescue.

15 *Ibid.* CRI is a small business under US Small Business Administration size standards. It is not known whether CRI has done contracting with the US federal government, or has participated in any federal socio-economic preference programme.

16 See Press Release, ZEPHYR'S PSM MONITORS CHILEAN MINERS' HEALTH & FITNESS, 6 October 2010, available at: www.zephyr-technology.com/wp-content/uploads/2010/12/ZEPHYR'S-PSM-MONITOR-CHILEAN-MINER'S-HEALTH-FITNESS-FINAL.pdf.

17 In the United States, due to federalism, the states each maintain their own systems for public procurements. This chapter focuses on the separate federal procurement system at the national level, and the policies utilized by the federal government.

18 15 United States Code (U.S.C.) § 631(a); see *Baird Corp.* v. *United States*, 1 Cl. Ct. 662 (1983).

19 *Ibid.*, § 637(d)(1).

20 41 U.S.C. § 252(b); 15 U.S.C. § 631(a); Federal Acquisition Regulation (FAR), 48 C.F.R. 19.201(a).

21 15 U.S.C. §§ 631, 631(a); FAR 48 C.F.R. 19.202–1.

22 13 C.F.R. §§ 125.8–125.29.
23 13 C.F.R. §125.11.
24 38 U.S.C. § 101(2).
25 15 U.S.C. § 632(q); see also 38 U.S.C. § 101(16).
26 13 C.F.R § 125.9.
27 13 C.F.R. § 125.10(a)–(b).
28 13 C.F.R. § 125.10(d).
29 13 C.F.R. § 125.11(a).
30 13 C.F.R. § 125.15(a).
31 See generally Competition in Contracting Act, 41 U.S.C. Sec. 253a(a)(1)(A)(civilian agencies) and 10 U.S.C. Sec. 2304(a)(1)(A)(Department of Defense agencies).
32 See generally 15 U.S.C. § 631(a)(Full and free competition is the essence of the American economic system of private enterprise).
33 The Rule of Two requires federal executive agencies to set aside any contract above $100,000 USD if there is a reasonable expectation of receiving fair-priced offers from two or more small businesses. See, e.g., Delex Sys., Inc., B-400403, 2008 CPD ¶ 181.
34 13 C.F.R. §§ 125.8–125.28.
35 38 C.F.R. § 74.1.
36 38 C.F.R. § 74.3.
37 38 C.F.R. § 74.4.
38 38 C.F.R. § 74.12.

# 17 Contested terrain

## Analysis of minority-owned construction firms selling goods and services to government clients in the United States

*Timothy Bates*

### 1 Contested terrain

Small firms owned by persons of African or Asian ancestry – as well as those of Hispanic heritage – are popularly known in the United States as minority-owned businesses (MBEs). Historically, MBEs have been uninvolved in the contracting and procurement activities of government agencies and authorities, yet this changed rapidly in the 1970s as the political power of African American voters was demonstrated in municipal elections in many of America's largest cities. While the majority of the population in Atlanta, Georgia, in 1973 was African American, black-owned firms received less than a tenth of 1 per cent of the city's procurement contracts in that year. Yet 1973 was noteworthy because of the election of Atlanta's first African American mayor, and soon after, Atlanta enacted a preferential procurement programme designed to expand the presence of MBEs in public-sector contracting. During the first full year of the city's new procurement programme, the MBE share of procurement spending rose to nearly 20 per cent (Boston, 1999).

Following the lead of Atlanta, many cities headed by black mayors aggressively sought to steer city contracts to minority-owned businesses. Atlanta's preferential procurement programme served as the model, widely copied by large cities where minority voters had political influence, and later emulated by the federal government and numerous state governments. By the late 1980s, many billions of procurement dollars were being earmarked annually for MBEs at all levels of government. As this multi-billion dollar market opened up, employment in the impacted MBE industry sectors soared, and most of the new employees were themselves minorities. Expanded access to public procurement clearly encouraged widespread creation and expansion of minority-owned small businesses (Bates, 1997). From the standpoint of the sponsoring government entities, minority-targeted preferential procurement programmes were designed to remedy the effects of past and present discrimination and disadvantage by giving MBEs greater opportunities to participate in public-sector procurement. The related objective was to use the procurement powers of government as a tool for generating growth of minority businesses. Exactly how these objectives were put into practice varied widely.

There is a dark side to the MBE success story in government procurement: the facade of statistical success often rested on a foundation of misinformation and fraud. MBE fraud in public-sector procurement came in many varieties but one element was normally present – the fraudulent MBE contract recipient was not performing any commercially useful function. One common variety was the front company, an arrangement whereby the MBE contract recipient received a small fee for permitting the non-minority firm actually doing the work to use its name. Structural deficiencies built into many public-sector preferential procurement programmes in fact often encouraged the proliferation of front company abuses. While some preferential procurement programmes effectively functioned as valuable local economic development programmes fostering minority business growth and job creation, others promoted MBE fronts that sold their government contracts to other firms and covered their tracks by maintaining fictional paper trails (Bates and Williams, 1995).

## 2 Background

Government procurement contracts are won most often by construction firms, by supplier firms producing and distributing goods, and by certain providers of skilled services, including law firms and engineering service companies. The minority business community in the United States, as it entered into the 1970s, was made up largely of very small firms concentrated in personal services and retailing. Minority entrepreneurs typically struggled to make a living running marginal businesses. From its origins, the MBE community was constrained by limited access to credit, limited opportunities for training and education, and white stereotypes about suitable roles for minorities in society (Bates, 1997).

The immediate difficulty created by the sudden appearance of opportunities to participate in government procurement in the 1970s was the mismatch between the needs of government for specific goods and services and the industry distribution and limited capacity of most MBEs. Most were in the wrong lines of business and lacked, as well, the necessary expertise, working capital, and bonding capacity contractors needed to complete successfully all but the smallest government procurement tasks. A dose of historical context puts this dilemma – exploiting new business opportunities amidst traditional constraints – into focus. Scholars studying the historical development of minority-owned businesses in the United States are unanimous on at least one issue: minority self-employment patterns only make sense when viewed in the context of prevailing constraints and opportunities (Waldinger *et al.*, 2006).

US census data indicate that MBE owners nationwide in 1960 had, on average, 7.6 years of formal education and mean self-employment earnings of $1,812; their earnings lagged behind those of minorities working as employees (Bates, 1987). Distinct traces of a caste system shaped both minority business ownership and employment opportunities. Highly educated members of minority groups were particularly trapped. According to a Stanford University official, 'It is almost impossible to place a Chinese or Japanese of either the first or the second generation in any kind of position in engineering, manufacturing, or business. Most firms have general regulations against employing them' (Ichihashi, 1932, in Bonacich and Modell, 1981, p. 86). Self-employment was thus a common refuge.

The career choices of college-educated minorities have long been hemmed in by attitudes of the dominant society about occupations appropriate for Asian Americans, African Americans and Hispanics. Thus, 73 per cent of all black Americans graduating from college and universities nationwide between 1912 and 1938 became either preachers or teachers in racially segregated schools (Holsey, 1938). The few entering professional fields served an all-black clientele. Caterers, shoe shiners, even barbers, might serve white clients, but black professionals did not. Merit still mattered in this American variant of the caste system, but the career choices open to entrepreneurially inclined minorities were greatly narrowed (Bates, 1997). The nature of the minority business community was thusly circumscribed.

The case of Chinese Americans was typical. Prior to the 1970s, self-employed Chinese were heavily concentrated in only two lines of business, restaurants and laundries. Entrepreneurial Chinese did not by nature gravitate into these fields: operation of laundries and restaurants was tolerated by the dominant society because few native-born whites chose to own these kinds of businesses. Whites 'raised no barrier to Chinese in the laundry trade, since this occupation was not one in which white males cared to engage' (Light, 1972, p. 7). Ironing shirts, preparing meals – minorities providing these services to white customers were acting the way the dominant society expected them to act. Since business opportunities in the broader marketplace were limited to fields viewed by white society as appropriate for their inferior status, minority entrepreneurs often chose, instead, to create ventures catering to fellow racial/ethnic-group members. Growing twentieth-century urbanization and ghettoization of minorities strongly encouraged this emerging market orientation (Bates, 1997).

In retrospect, it is clear that the traditional minority business community of barber shops, laundries, restaurants, shoe-shine stands and the like entered the 1970s as a fading relic of a declining era. By the late 1960s, civil rights activism, path-breaking reform legislation, and the subsequent broad but slow weakening of traditional discriminatory barriers were creating new opportunities for minorities, one of which was the opening of public-sector procurement opportunities. A new age was dawning, an age not only of growth but also of qualitative improvement for minority entrepreneurship in the United States.

## 3 The challenge of exploiting emerging opportunities

Not all segments of US society were pleased by the combination of declining discriminatory barriers and rising opportunities available to minorities. The case of the construction industry is instructive. Skills specific to running construction firms are typically acquired through work experience in the industry, often in conjunction with apprenticeship training programmes. Craft unions often restricted minority entrance into training programmes in the skilled construction trades, particularly in northern cities where union presence was strong. The greatest single barrier to MBE progress in the construction was the limited access minorities faced when they sought employment and training in the industry.

The primary mechanism limiting MBE presence in construction was (and still is) the old-boy network, which frustrated not only minority business access to major construction projects, but acquisition, as well, of skills in select special trades like plumbing and sheet-metal work (Waldinger and Bailey, 1991; Bates and Howell, 1998). The fact that such exclusion was illegal after 1965 often had little immediate impact on entrenched industry practices. Beneath the laws, regulations and the union contracts governing industry practices lies a reality of personal contacts and informal networks limiting minority participation. 'A high proportion of skilled workers report having fathers or relatives in the trades' (Waldinger and Bailey, 1991, p. 299). Construction is dominated by small firms hiring and promoting through informal mechanisms. Even skills acquisition did not solve the problem of old-boy networks, where work is parcelled out to in-group members, few of whom are minorities.

Large US cities electing black mayors in the 1970s – Atlanta, Philadelphia, Los Angeles, Detroit, Newark and many others – spent their procurement dollars largely on construction projects, and their aggressive efforts to involve MBE contractors in public procurement quickly raised numerous operational difficulties. Construction was the single major US industry most resistant to admitting minorities into its ranks, either as employees or as independent contractors. Exclusion was never absolute. White-owned construction firms often willingly hired minorities for temporary positions as unskilled labourers. Minorities working in certain skilled trades, as well, were often employed by mainstream construction firms, although their involvement in skilled positions was typically common only in trades where work was stigmatized as dangerous, hot, dirty, or all of the above: thus, asbestos removal and roofing were often minority jobs. Chicago, for example, was a union town; although skilled minority employees were tolerated in some skilled construction trades, minorities were almost nonexistent in 11 of the city's unionized 19 skilled trades in 1970. Contractors working on public-sector construction projects typically used skilled union workers exclusively (*Builder's Association of Greater Chicago* v. *City of Chicago*, 298 F. Supp. 2d 725 – U.S. Dist., 2003).

Pioneering efforts by cities like Atlanta, Los Angeles and Detroit sought to break traditional patterns of minority exclusion from participation in government procurement contracting and skilled construction employment as well, using two tools to combat entrenched construction industry practices. First, all recipients of government construction contracts were required to employ minimum percentages of skilled minorities on public-sector jobs (a 25 per cent requirement was common); second, firms receiving prime contracts were required to grant a fixed percentage of the subcontracts (30 per cent was common) to MBEs. Recipients of prime government construction contracts, in response, often went to great lengths to circumvent these requirements. They preferred to stay within their own old-boy networks of subcontractors and to hire skilled workers through traditional craft-union channels.

Within construction-firm networks, members know each other, trust each other, and function effectively together. Network outsiders were resisted for many reasons; MBEs seeking to work as subcontractors on major projects were resisted by prime contractors determined to stay within their embedded networks. Working with network insiders – other established white-owned firms – minimizes risk, which is particularly important on large and complex jobs involving many subcontractors and operating within tight time constraints. As newcomers and outsiders, MBEs seeking to work with established prime contractors were resisted precisely because they were not members of the embedded networks: their inclusion was risky. Why should primes take the risk? Even if MBE subcontractors were low bidders, they were typically rejected in favour of trusted insiders (Bates and Howell, 1998; Bates, 2006).

Faced with the necessity of agreeing to hire MBE subcontractors to compete successfully for contracts, resistant mainstream construction firms acted predictably. Most sought to win government contracts with promises of broad participation of both MBE subcontractors and minority construction workers, but once contracts were in hand, they attempted to minimize minority involvement in the actual work. Numerous creative strategies were employed. Use of MBE front firms was initially a common response to requirements for minority involvement, but such outright flaunting of government policy intent was risky and often illegal. Some government entities tolerated front company abuses and some did not. The same objectives – appearing to meet government requirements of substantial minority participation while in fact not complying – were most often achieved indirectly.

One popular approach among primes was to require that their MBE subcontractors on government projects hire only those employees that the prime contractor specified. The prime contractors then proceeded to place their own employees on the payrolls of their MBE subcontractors. Absent strict government monitoring of contracts covered by requirements of minority vendor involvement, compliance by prime contractors was spotty at best. Yet governments seeking to award prime construction contracts directly to MBEs faced a reality of small minority-owned firms lacking both the experience required for successfully managing large-scale projects and many of the necessary resources, including working capital lines of credit and bonding capacity. Particularly in the early years of preferential procurement efforts, MBE vendors typically had the capacity to handle only small-scale construction jobs, a problem that eased only gradually as successful MBEs built capacity. Large contracts were nonetheless sometimes awarded to MBEs that did not have the capacity to complete the required work successfully. The outcome was often the failure of the MBE vendor to meet contract requirements completely and on a timely basis, which in turn frequently resulted in the firm's going out of business (Bates and Williams, 1995).

## 4 Creative government policy responses to challenges confronting preferential procurement programmes

Impacts of government programmes and policies for expanding MBE participation in public procurement contracting vary widely but a simple generalization clarifies the important issues: programme impact depends upon how government agencies administer procurement programmes. Preferential procurement programmes effectively expand MBE presence in government procurement when top government officials make programme effectiveness a key priority. If subordinates are given the authority and resources necessary to make the programmes work *and* they understand that programme effectiveness is demanded by those in charge, then preferential procurement policies indeed effectively expand the share of procurement dollars received by minority contractors. MBE contractors genuinely having the capacity to fulfil their contract obligations, furthermore, often grow and prosper in this environment of supportive government preferential procurement programmes.

By the 1980s it was apparent that the nation's ambitious and innovative preferential procurement programmes operated most often in cities like Atlanta where black mayors presided. The discretion granted to mayors over local government procurement contracts gave them the opportunity to reward constituents, and MBEs owned by constituents were direct beneficiaries. Political power was generating economic benefits: the actions of black mayors were producing positive minority business development impacts to such a degree that empirical measurement verified those positive impacts. Using census data on small businesses, Bates and Williams (1993) demonstrated statistically that among MBEs in industries where government contracting was common, firms in cities with black mayors had higher revenues and lower rates of failure than otherwise identical firms in cities where the mayor was white. The obvious question was how did they do it?

Long-term tenure expands a mayor's ability to promote effective preferential procurement policies. Procurement decisions are typically decentralized, with special districts controlling spending and contracting decisions in many areas. Placing proponents of preferential procurement into positions of authority takes time. Between 1973 and 1980, 'the black share of administrators rose from 14 to 35% in Atlanta and from 12 to 41% in Detroit' (Eisinger, 1984, p. 252). Procurement opportunities resulting from these realignments of local political control benefitted existing MBEs and encouraged new firm formation. Preferential procurement packaged with complementary assistance was the mode of operation for effectively aiding MBE recipients of government contracts.

Seven specific types of assistance were often used:

1 MBE procurement was handled by a staff having the specific responsibility of assisting MBE vendors.

2. Working capital assistance – including short-term loans and quick-pay provisions – was provided to successful MBE contract recipients.
3. On small- and medium-size contracts traditionally requiring vendor bonding, bonding requirements were waived for MBE vendors.
4. Large contracts were unbundled and downsized to increase their accessibility to MBE bidders.
5. MBEs eligible for assistance were subjected to rigorous certification processes designed to weed out front firms and sham operations.
6. Significant penalties were imposed on MBE contract recipients that circumvented contracting regulations through such actions as fronting for white-owned firms.
7. MBEs receiving contracts were required to generate significant value added; MBE brokers carrying no inventories and not servicing their products, for example, were disallowed.

To test the hypothesis that the nature of the preferential programme determined whether MBE vendors benefitted, the Joint Center for Political and Economic Studies in 1992 collected detailed profiles of preferential procurement programmes operated by 28 large cities in 26 metro areas of the United States. These data were combined with census data describing 1,085 MBE vendors operating in the 26 metro areas that actually sold products to state or local government clients, and these firms were tracked from 1987 through late 1991 to identify those going out of business. Controlling statistically for firm and owner characteristics, logistic regression analysis of MBE vendor survival revealed that three types of assistance – waiver of bonding requirements; provision of working-capital assistance; and rigorous certification – were positively associated with enhanced MBE vendor survival to a statistically significant degree (Bates and Williams, 1995; Bates and Williams, 1996). Among the 28 cities under consideration, only 30 per cent actually provided bonding waivers to MBEs; 63 per cent provided working capital assistance; and 67 per cent undertook rigorous certification of MBE vendors. Impacts of contract unbundling and downsizing also appeared to benefit MBE vendors, but the near universality of this type of assistance made it impossible to investigate econometrically the impact of such assistance on vendor longevity.

Cities with black mayors commonly provided more types of assistance to MBE vendors than others, but there were exceptions. These three types of assistance benefitted MBE vendors because they addressed specific barriers keeping minorities from benefitting from their involvement in public-sector contracting. Causes of MBE vendor failure and firm closure are well known. MBEs, on balance, are younger, smaller, more credit-constrained firms than other vendors selling products to government clients. They typically entered into government procurement as subcontractors on large projects. Overly large contracts, hostile prime contractors and slow payment of invoices by government agencies were among the more common problems that MBE vendors struggled to cope with (Bates, 1997).

Weak firm capitalization and limited access to short-term credit, particularly bank loans, made it difficult for expanding MBEs to finance current operations. The discriminatory lending practices of commercial banks complicated MBE efforts to exploit business opportunities when they become available (Blanchflower *et al.*, 2003; Bates, 2011). While government contracts were potentially a path to growth and greater profitability, large contracts often exacerbated illiquidity problems for MBEs. Quick payment of invoices by government, along with working capital assistance, expanded the capacity of MBEs to perform successfully on procurement contracts. Difficulties obtaining adequate bonding and insurance further frustrated MBEs seeking to capitalize upon public-sector opportunities. The bottom line was that seemly attractive procurement contracts – absent properly tailored assistance – could be a trap for ill-prepared MBEs. 'Successful' minority contract recipients often struggled with procurement contracts and governments frequently did nothing to ease the barriers that sometimes destroyed those vendors (Bates, 2009).

## 5 Post-Croson preferential procurement policy setbacks and innovations

Pragmatic policies for designing effective preferential procurement programmes generated a counter-attack from mainstream contractors in the form of hundreds of lawsuits charging local and state governments with practicing racially discriminatory policies harming white-owned construction companies. Richmond, Virginia, operated a preferential procurement programme requiring recipients of construction contracts to award at least 30 per cent of each contract to MBE subcontractors. This was challenged in federal court, culminating, in January 1989, in the US Supreme Court ruling (*Richmond* v. *Croson*) that Richmond's programme violated the equal protection clause of the US constitution. The City of Richmond argued that it sought only to remedy forms of past and present discrimination, specifically the exclusion of blacks from construction union apprentice programmes and union membership in skilled construction trades. The Court's response was that a generalized assertion of discrimination in an entire industry was unacceptable as a justification for legislation remedying discrimination. Highly detailed statistical proof, in conjunction with other evidence of precise discriminatory processes, was needed before a government entity could even begin to craft a legal remedy for alleviating the discriminatory barriers harming MBE construction companies (Boston, 1999). Hundreds of cities and special-purpose districts abolished preferential procurement programmes in the wake of the *Croson* decision.

For many, the Supreme Court's ruling provided a convenient justification to abolish ineffective programmes that were little more than superficial political gestures to minority constituents. For others, net effects of court-imposed rigorous evidence-based requirements were sometimes actually beneficial, resulting in new well-thought-out preferential procurement programmes benefitting MBE vendors. One traditional practice of government entities has been to use procurement targeted to MBEs as a payoff for favoured MBEs that had political clout. Some governments nonetheless actually instituted genuine broad-based reforms in response to judicial restraints demanding programme reconfiguration, opening up procurement opportunities to a wider group of MBE vendors. As always, policies designed to expand procurement opportunities for MBEs were likely to be effective only when the government entities administering such programmes genuinely sought to aid minority entrepreneurship by reducing explicit discriminatory barriers thwarting MBE creation, viability and growth.

The federal government, in response to judicial constraints on preferential procurement programmes, chose to substitute for 'minority' the concept of 'disadvantaged business enterprises' (DBEs). MBEs, by definition, were DBEs with one exception: net-worth caps were imposed, disqualifying minority owners with personal net worth exceeding $750,000. The logical connection between the defense of affirmative action in the form of preferential procurement and imposition of net-worth caps was never spelled out. When the Clinton Administration first imposed net worth caps of $750,000 on DBE owners seeking to participate in preferential procurement, it was obvious to close observers that they had simply pulled the $750,000 number out of thin air (Bates, 2009).

Yet, owner net-worth caps are not a requirement imposed on preferential procurement policies by the judiciary. According to the March 2000 decision in the case, *Concrete Works* v. *County of Denver*, procurement programmes should be narrowly tailored to encourage large MBEs, not penalize them by revoking their eligibility for preferential treatment.

> This size limitation does not bear a rational relationship to the remedying or avoiding of discrimination. On the contrary, it may inhibit the ability of MBEs ... to grow and develop sufficient capacity to become prime contractors to the City and develop their own network of MBE subcontractors and suppliers.
>
> (2000 WL 266307, D. Colo, p. 37).

Owner net-worth caps explicitly cut out MBEs from procurement in industry groups where large-scale operation is essential both for firms to operate efficiently and to undertake the large contracts that typify most available procurement opportunities. In heavy construction, for example, mean sales of non-minority-owned small firms listed in 2006 in the federal government's central contractor registry (CCR) were $4.0 million. Among MBEs in heavy construction (roads, bridges, sewer lines), in contrast, mean sales among CCR registrants were under $2.4 million, less than 60 per cent of the non-minority average (Euquant, 2007). As large-scale MBEs have increased in number, size and scope in recent decades, net-worth caps have increasingly disqualified those most likely to possess the capacity to handle large tasks. Million-dollar contracts – prime and sub alike – require firms possessing the capacity to handle such jobs, and procurement spending has increasingly been concentrated in very large contracts. In this context, the rationale supporting public-sector preferential procurement programmes is in dire need of re-examination.

Racially discriminatory practices of private businesses continue in the twenty-first century to be the primary obstacles to MBE viability and growth (Bates, 2011). Yet government entities themselves engage in a variety of internal operating procedures that effectively limit the ability of MBEs – indeed most small firms – to participate successfully in their procurement opportunities. Paradoxically, these public entities often encourage and undermine MBE access to government procurement contracting opportunities simultaneously. Procurement policies adopted by the Metropolitan Pier and Exposition Authority (MPEA) – a Chicago-area public-sector agency operating major public amenities – typify twenty-first century types of pragmatic government responses to both the legal constraints shaping preferential procurement programmes in the United States and the very real need to lessen the constraining effects of lingering discriminatory practices thwarting MBE development and growth. Gone is the language of 'preferential procurement'; instead, the MPEA's procurement policies seek to achieve fundamental fairness – a 'level playing field' – in which all vendors, minority and non-minority alike, are equally able to compete for government contracts. To operationalize this objective, the MPEA proceeded by identifying and quantifying the barriers vendors face when they seek government contracts. Predictably, this exercise revealed that MBE vendors faced higher barriers than others (Bates, 2009).

The MPEA – like the federal government, state governments, and indeed most local cities and public authorities – often awards large contracts beyond the reach of small businesses generally. MPEA's prime contractors similarly award large subcontracts most small firms lack the capacity to handle. The MPEA in 2005 conducted a survey, the objective of which was to permit its vendors to identify explicit barriers restricting their ability to sell products to the MPEA. Vendors were asked, 'Which, if any, of the following changes in the MPEA's procedures or requirements would help you to get additional work from the agency?' In a similar vein, vendors working as subcontractors were asked to describe working relationships with their prime contractors. The surveyed vendors, by a wide margin, most often identified 'an unbundling of large contracts' as the policy change that would enable them to participate more actively in MPEA procurement opportunities. Policy changes that would enhance procurement opportunities are listed below, along with the percentage of all vendors responding 'yes':

1 an unbundling of large contracts, 68.9 per cent;
2 prompt payment of invoices, 44.7 per cent;
3 a longer bid lead time, 38.1 per cent;
4 a waiver or a lowering of bonding requirements, 35.1 per cent;
5 a waiver of insurance requirements, 24.7 per cent.

The large, bundled contract barrier came closest to being a universal concern among the surveyed vendors. Other changes – longer bid times, prompt payment, bonding waivers and insurance waivers – assisted a wide variety of businesses in their efforts to sell products to the MPEA. They were barriers to procurement opportunities generally rather than barriers that solely handicap MBEs, yet their reduction would disproportionately benefit minorities. The unifying theme among all five of these MPEA procurement procedures is that each represented a strategy to reduce a barrier that held down vendor participation in public procurement. Contract unbundling increases the ability of small firms to bid for work; large, bundled contracts have the opposite effect. Prompt payment disproportionately assists the undercapitalized vendors, particularly those experiencing restricted access to loans; slow payment discourages their participation (Bates and Williams, 1996).

Minority vendors participating in Chicago-region public-sector procurement generally – and MPEA procurement specifically – are an elite subset of minority businesses: average firm size is large; owners are often college graduates. Among the active MBE vendors selling products to the MPEA, nearly 70 per cent of them reported annual sales exceeding $1,000,000 (Bates, 2009). Yet, relative to vendor firms owned by non-minorities, they displayed traditional disadvantages: they were smaller, younger, more credit-constrained businesses facing entrenched insider networks dominating market niches in fields like construction. These relatively higher barriers are the crux of what is being addressed when the concept of a 'level playing field' is proposed in the public procurement realm. One concrete measure of a level playing field is whether MBEs and their non-minority small-business counterparts face equal barriers. If minorities reported higher barriers, then access to procurement opportunities is more widely accessible to non-minority small-business vendors than to minorities.

For every one of the barriers summarized above, minority vendors were more likely to be adversely impacted than white-owned firms. Particularly concerning prompt payment, bonding and insurance barriers, minorities were more severely impacted than non-minority vendors. Regarding changes in MPEA procedures or requirements that 'would help you get additional work' from the MPEA, the following percentages of minority and white non-minority vendors responded affirmatively (see Table 17.1).

Among surveyed MBEs selling products to the MPEA, 47.5 per cent worked as subcontractors, a higher proportion than the 39.4 per cent figure describing

*Table 17.1* Incidence of barriers limiting small business participation on MPEA procurement (%)

| | *Minority* | *Non-minority* |
|---|---|---|
| Prompt payment of invoices | 58.3 | 42.5 |
| A waiver or lowering of bonding requirements | 49.2 | 31.9 |
| A waiver of insurance requirements | 39.2 | 20.7 |

Note
These differentials describe a playing field that is not level.

non-minorities. Because minority subcontractors are imposed upon resistant primes as a condition for winning MPEA contracts, relations would logically be more contested between primes and minority subs, relative to primes and non-minority subs. After all, entrenched business networks are resistant to outsiders by their very nature (Granovetter, 1985). Since entrenched networks are an important barrier thwarting MBE access to customers, mandatory subcontracting requirements are the obvious tool used by government agencies to assist MBEs in overcoming this barrier. Among the surveyed minority subcontractors, 32.2 per cent described their working relationships with prime contractors as contested; the corresponding percentage of non-minority white subs was 12 per cent. Absent requirements of MBE participation, this evidence indicates prime contractors would be strongly inclined to work more often with non-minority subs rather than MBE subcontractors (Bates, 2009). On the positive side, the fact that 67.8 per cent of the MPEA's minority subcontractors reported harmonious relations with their prime contractors reflects huge progress, relative to past decades when preferential procurement opportunities were unavailable.

## 6 Concluding observations

Explicit barriers limiting small-business involvement in public procurement contracting, when quantified, provide concrete measures of the degree to which the existing playing field is or is not level for MBE vendors. Achieving fundamental fairness – a level playing field – entails alleviating the barriers disproportionately retarding MBE involvement in procurement activities. Some of these barriers are rooted in prime contractor/subcontractor relationships; some are directly under the control of the procurement staff working in government agencies. As relative newcomers, MBEs seeking public-sector procurement contracts face predictable barriers. As outsiders to entrenched networks, problems of small MBE firm size, credit constraints and low bonding capacity are compounded. Limited access to capital has always complicated the efforts of MBEs winning procurement contracts to deliver on these contracts. Major contracts require substantial working capital financing and MBEs frequently lack access to this working capital. The slow payment of vendors often typifying government is particularly destructive: minority vendors expand output, deliver to government, wait for payment, and often encounter liquidity problems if payment is slow. Such liquidity problems may destroy otherwise viable MBEs, but they can also cause MBEs to default on their contract obligations, producing delays and added expenses in the procurement process.

Restricted MBE market access interacts, as well, with low capitalization, lessening firm size and scope, often resulting in small firms lacking the capacity to compete for large contracts that typify most public-sector procurement opportunities. Moving toward a level playing field means downsizing and unbundling contracts, quick payment of MBE invoices, and selective easing of bonding and insurance requirements. Relations between prime and subcontractors must be monitored and sources of conflict must be addressed. On balance, the uneven record of preferential procurement programmes in the United States is one of gradually declining barriers that have permitted MBEs to expand in size and scope and to claim growing shares of government procurement spending in many – but not all – areas of the nation. Capacity built by serving government clients has enabled many MBEs to expand their penetration of mainstream markets, and sales to businesses, including major corporations, now account for greater aggregate sales revenues than MBE sales to government clients. The gradual decline of discriminatory barriers throughout the US economy has been highly beneficial; future prospects for MBEs will be heavily shaped by evolving barriers, which may either decline or reassert themselves in new and ever changing circumstances.

## References

Bates, T. (1987). Self-employed minorities: traits and trends. *Social Science Quarterly* 68: 539–51.

Bates, T. (1997). *Race, Self-Employment, and Upward Mobility* (Baltimore: Johns Hopkins University Press).

Bates, T. (2006). Discrimination in the Chicago-area construction market handicaps minority-owned firms. *Review of Black Political Economy* 33: 7–26.

Bates, T. (2009). Utilizing affirmative action in public-sector procurement as a local economic development strategy. *Economic Development Quarterly* 23: 180–93.

Bates, T. (2011). Minority entrepreneurship. *Foundations and Trends in Entrepreneurship* 7: 151–311.

Bates, T. and D. Howell (1998). The declining status of African American men in the New York construction industry. *Economic Development Quarterly* 12: 88–100.

Bates, T. and D. Williams (1993). Racial politics: does it pay? *Social Science Quarterly* 74: 507–22.

Bates, T. and D. Williams (1995). Preferential procurement programs do not necessarily benefit minority-owned businesses. *Journal of Urban Affairs* 17: 1–17.

Bates, T. and D. Williams (1996). Do preferential programs benefit minority business? *American Economic Review* 86: 294–8.

Blanchflower, D., P. Levine and D. Zimmerman (2003). Discrimination in the small business credit markets. *The Review of Economics and Statistics* 85: 930–43.

Bonacich, E. and J. Modell (1981). *The Economic Basis for Ethnic Solidarity* (Berkeley: University of California Press).

Boston, T. (1999). *Affirmative Action and Black Entrepreneurship* (London: Routledge).

Eisinger, P. (1984). Black mayors and politics of racial advancement. In H. Hahn and C. Levine, eds, *Readings in Urban Politics: Past, Present, and Future* (New York: Longmans).

Euquant (2007). *Increasing the Capacity of the Nation's Small and Disadvantaged Businesses*. Report to the Congressional Black Caucus Foundation (October).

Granovetter, M. (1985). Economic action and social structure: the problem of embeddedness. *American Journal of Sociology* 91: 481–510.

Holsey, A. (1938). Seventy-five years of Negro business. *Crisis* 45: 241–2.

Light, I. (1972). *Ethnic Enterprise in America* (Berkeley: University of California Press).

Waldinger, R. and T. Bailey (1991). The continuing significance of race: racial conflict and racial discrimination in construction. *Politics and Society* 19: 291–323.

Waldinger, R., H. Aldrich and R. Ward (2006). *Ethnic Entrepreneurs:Immigrant Business in Industrial Society* (Newbury Park: Sage).

# 18 SMEs and public contracts

## An EU based perspective

*Marta Fana and Gustavo Piga*

### 1 Introduction

Small and medium sized (as well as minority owned) firms are the actors that today receive the greatest attention from policy-makers when dealing with procurement design. More specifically, SMEs are a type of social and institutional actor that permeates, with its numbers, the political and economic processes of any country. While looked at with a high degree of attention by policy-makers and politicians as SMEs might represent a powerful engine of innovation and growth and at the same time of electoral advantage, they are also potentially downplayed by the same actors for their size. It should therefore not come as a surprise that a large debate and an impressive series of policy initiatives have taken place over the years and over countries to reconcile these two contrasting dimensions through a 'social' use of public procurement meant to protect in some ways SMEs' performance and even existence.

Almost all over the world support to SMEs through procurement is ensured through bid preferences, set-asides and liquidity support. These practices are in stark contrast with the European Union approach according to which

> the EU is not in favour of reserving markets to specific undertakings. Such actions would also be in contradiction with the principle of equal treatment of tenderers, a fundamental pillar of the EU public procurement regime anchored by the Court of Justice in the Treaty freedoms.[1]

In the following we will try to highlight whether equal treatment is at risk once preferences are introduced, or if, on the contrary, they can help policy-makers to reduce unequal treatment already in place.

The chapter is organized as follows: Section 2 discusses the theme of protection applied to procurement; in Section 3 we briefly discuss the main differences between EU and US approaches to government preferential procurement. Section 4 contains concluding remarks.

## 2 Protection and procurement: the anti-discrimination link

### *2.1 Protection rationale*

Most of the time it is possible to see a common pattern of reasoning when considering the issue of preferential treatment to one particular seller/supplier of the public sector. It is the one of an exogenous, pre-existing asymmetric treatment that disfavours one type of firm to the (presumably unfair) advantage of another; where the need is felt to fix such an asymmetry, indeed, through protection or preferences. Preferences, the argument implies, might therefore end up generating an immediately higher expenditure for the procurement entity than if it had not chosen to extend them, trading it off with what can be generated by an act of fairness (less social tensions, greater future participation, more dynamism...). The question then arises naturally of whether a discrimination rationale truly exists or it only reflects a politician's concern to satisfy specific lobbies' requests. Where is the discrimination against small firms, when it comes to procurement that might justify the extension of preferences to the latter, become thus a very relevant question to answer. The question seems to be justified, as small and large firms are apparently subject nowadays to the same legislation and therefore apparently to the same level of red tape and costs. In reality this is not the case, in fact, at the aggregate level, costs per employee due to regulation appear to be at least 36 per cent higher for small firms than for medium size and large firms, a disproportion in compliance costs that especially arises in the manufacturing sector (even if varying across type of regulation).[2]

Procurement activity is thus stranded with fixed costs that by and large impact disproportionately on the unitary costs of small firms, hampering their competitiveness from the start against large firms.

Table 18.1 shows for example the series of problems faced by different sized EU bidders relative to large firms. The column of totals displays on average which portion of firms interviewed answered 'always' or 'often'. We have normalized to 1 the share of large firms that report having a problem with the specific issue mentioned in the rows.

As you can see, while some problems that arise in procurement are common to all firms, some of them seem to affect small firms and micro firms much more: administrative burden, long delays in payment, disproportionate financial criteria and unfair evaluation of bids are among these.

In absolute value, 40 per cent (38 per cent) of respondents perceive long payment terms (late payment) as a problem 'always' or 'often' encountered. If one looks at micro firms, the share rises to 52 per cent for long payment terms and 47 per cent for late payments. Figure 18.1 shows these variables for the year 2009, when credit constraints are likely to have been more binding for those firms and delays graver in their impact. As Bates (2009) puts it, 'prompt payment disproportionally assists undercapitalized vendors, particularly those experiencing restricted access to loans; slow payment discourages participation'. These constraints are reinforced in the case of subcontracts (likely to be taken by small

*Table 18.1* Problems facing European bidders in the procurement process

| *Potential problems* | *Micro* | *Small* | *Medium* | *Large* | *TOTAL (%)* |
|---|---|---|---|---|---|
| Over-emphasis on price | 1.1 | 1.0 | 0.9 | 1 | 1.0 |
| Long payment terms | 1.4 | 1.2 | 1.1 | 1 | 1.1 |
| Late payments | 1.3 | 1.0 | 1.1 | 1 | 1.0 |
| No debriefing | 1.2 | 1.0 | 0.9 | 1 | 1.0 |
| Administrative burden | 1.5 | 1.1 | 1.2 | 1 | 1.1 |
| Lack of clarity | 1.4 | 1.0 | 1.0 | 1 | 1.1 |
| Limited options for interaction | 1.4 | 1.0 | 0.9 | 1 | 1.0 |
| Disproportionate financial criteria | 2.0 | 1.2 | 1.1 | 1 | 1.2 |
| Insufficient time to bid | 1.4 | 1.2 | 0.7 | 1 | 1.0 |
| Lack of information on opportunities | 1.4 | 1.3 | 1.1 | 1 | 1.1 |
| Tenders not evaluated fairly | 5.3 | 4.7 | 8.7 | 1 | 6.3 |
| Disproportionate technical criteria | 1.4 | 1.4 | 1.1 | 1 | 1.2 |
| Large contract value | 22.0 | 22.0 | 5.0 | 1 | 7.0 |
| Joint fulfilment of criteria note allowed | 2.0 | 2.0 | 1.5 | 1 | 1.3 |

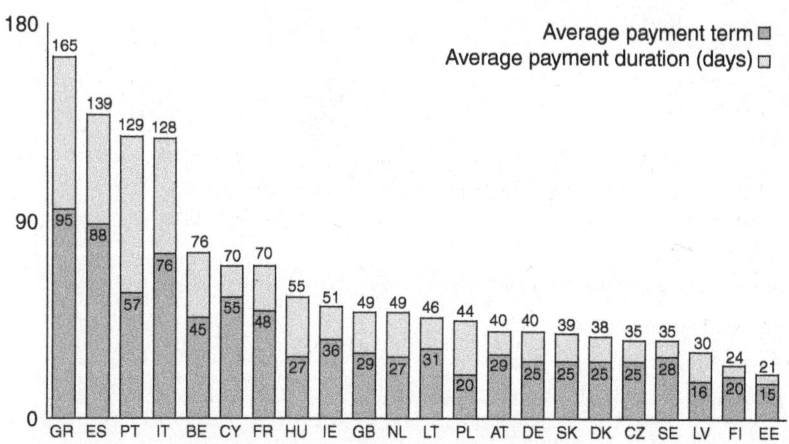


*Figure 18.1* Average payment terms and duration in Europe.

or minority owned firms) that are highly vulnerable to slow payment. A subcontractor can perform the assigned task on schedule and according to specification and yet be driven out of business by mere slow payment for completed work.

Most of all, however, Table 18.1 shows that large contract values seem to affect small and micro firms much more than large firms. If one considers that centralization in the European Union (allowed and encouraged by the last approved Directives) is on the rise, one must feel a growing fear that asymmetric treatment against small firms will slowly increase over time if not tackled with appropriate instruments. Indeed, during the period 2006–8, while the portion of SMEs among companies that won public contracts (in terms of number of contracts) above EU threshold was 60 per cent on average, in terms of estimated contract value SMEs account for only 34 per cent on average (see Figure 18.2).

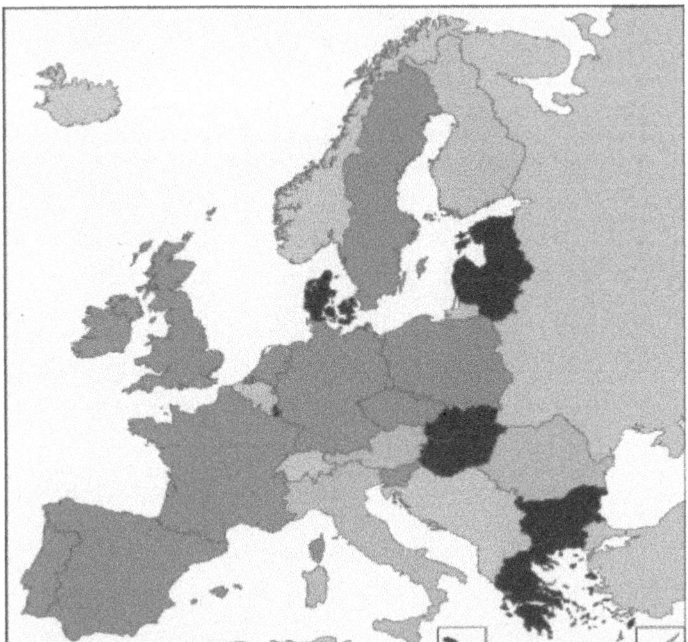


*Figure 18.2* Share of SMEs in the total value of contracts awarded, by Member State (average for 2006–8) (source: GHK calculations based on TED data).

Note that their overall share in the European economy is on average 18 per cent higher (52 per cent).There is thus a tendency for SMEs to win contracts with lower value than large firms and to be under-represented in public markets. Micro enterprises account for 6 per cent of the contract value in public procurement and 17 per cent of total turnover in the European economy, confirming the impression that SMEs are an under-represented group in EU public contracts.[3]

Another European Union study[4] tried to identify the factors influencing SMEs' share in winning public contracts. The larger the contract value the lesser the likelihood that an SME will win that contract, confirming the above-mentioned survey. In addition to this, the division of a contract into lots increases SMEs' success rate, even above the evident effect of smaller contract values. However, European policies do not seem to work even in this direction, in fact centralization (or bundling) has been given a formal status of relevance in the European Directives through the insertion of Central Purchasing Bodies (CPBs). The latter often tend to award larger contracts, subdividing when necessary the procuring needs into a given amount of lots that is often similar to the number of large actors present in the market, encouraging collusion. Set-asides for small firms in this context would make collusion harder to sustain by making large firms compete among themselves for fewer lots. That many small firms are hardly capable of competing in a highly competitive environment is confirmed by the fact that if the procurer is a local entity, the higher the probability for SMEs to win a public contract. Finally, the use of the MEAT (most economically advantageous tender) criteria, that adds discretion to the awarding mechanism, decrease their chance of winning by about 9 per cent, hinting again at a possible impact of favouritism being biased towards larger firms. Another interesting result is that in terms of value, SMEs do better in open procedures than negotiated or restricted ones, in the latter case SMEs more often end up winning less possibly either for reasons related to reputation or for risk-aversion of the contracting authority.

This evidence echoes what Table 18.1 shows, i.e. that unfair evaluation of bids seems to be the second most important factor affecting small firms rather than large firms. While being an apparently highly subjective issue, the literature points out how small firms suffer more from corruption and risk-aversion by procurers. In addition Bates (2009) indicates that subcontracting is often driven by old network logics, where large firms of a given race prefer to subcontract to either large firms or small firms of the same race, increasing the potential for distortions away from efficiency in the absence of a preferential policy for small or minority-owned firms.

We should stress that while small firms may have – as we have shown – structurally higher unitary costs not due to their lack of ability but to the procurement context, this issue is not always confined to situations of firm size. Indeed, structurally higher costs due to factors that are not under the control of the (subsequently) protected firms explain the disabled workers' favouritism clauses in legislation worldwide. In addition, the example of the favourable West German treatment of firms based near the border with the DDR or located in

Berlin during the Cold War, repealed at the end of 1990, confirms that the cause of protection is based on exogenous cost differentials not due to variables that are under the control of the protected firm, but, rather, are imposed on it. In this latter case higher transportation costs and a possibly tougher business environment could not be attributed to the incompetence of firm owners.

## *2.2 Protection and procurement: the boundaries*

When is a given country's juridical framework bound to tolerate preferences? As mentioned by Ayres and Cramton (2001), in the United States government affirmative action must have a 'compelling governmental purpose' and must not be narrowly tailored to reach that goal, i.e. there must not exist other less restrictive ways to achieve the same goal. A slightly similar approach can be found in the European Union, where the principle of proportionality is meant to ensure that 'any action by the Community shall not go beyond what is necessary to achieve the objectives of this Treaty'.[5]

Would preferences in procurement for small, minority owned or other types of firms always pass this joint test?

Compelling purposes in procurement are common across countries. Minorities, disabled and racially-disadvantaged individuals that own firms are often subsidized/protected in public procurement (among others, the United States, Brazil and South Africa stand out as relevant examples), on the basis of the compelling relevance of remedying past discrimination or in furthering diversity. Fighting discrimination seems therefore an evident and compelling purpose to be redressed through public procurement favouritism of some kind, including preferences or set-asides.

Several problems arise in tackling such discrimination via public procurement. For one, the identification of the relevant group to be helped.

Second, differential treatment against potentially discriminated actors is not always due to discrimination itself but rather to other characteristics of those actors. Understanding the sources of differential treatment for specific categories that argue in favour of protection is therefore essential. Enrichetta Ravina (2008) argues for example that:

> understanding the mechanisms behind the gap in wages and access to credit faced by minorities is very important to design effective economic policies. If the reason why they are disfavored by firms is that their human capital and creditworthiness are worse along unobservable dimensions, like statistical discrimination theories would suggest, then the best policy is to improve their access to education and other tools to increase their human capital. If, on the contrary, minority applicants are intrinsically the same as the other applicants and their *worse performance is due to animus*, like taste-based discrimination theory postulates, *then anti-discriminatory and affirmative action policies might be more effective.* The empirical evidence on the issue provides supports for both theories, depending on the market and the

> specific personal characteristics analyzed ... New market settings ... as well as carefully designed audit studies, help address part of these issues and *seem to tilt the evidence in favor of taste-based discrimination.*
>
> (Italics added)

Does discrimination affect small firms too? If SMEs are discriminated against in public procurement we would have enough of a compelling purpose to advance in our reasoning in favour of preferences for small firms.

Discrimination in procurement against small firms can occur for a variety of reasons. First of all, small firms may be discriminated against in credit markets for no reason related to their riskier profile but simply for the risk-aversion of bank officers.[6] Higher rates charged to SMEs make the starting line to compete for government contracts unequal and therefore this situation deserves to be redressed in some way, possibly through set-asides or preferences or competitive loans. Negative discrimination may arise from other sources: corruption and risk-aversion. Corruption has often been shown to derive from political networks and collusion and both are likely to either exclude or be more costly to enter into for SMEs. Corruption is shown to often occur hand in hand with collusion, as long as there exists the possibility to bribe the bureaucrat in charge of the procurement process. In this context, since competition moves from price to bribe, small-sized competitors may not have the capacity to offer a competitive bribe and so they will be excluded from the auction (see Compte *et al.* 2005). In addition, there is ample evidence (Bos-Harrington 2010) that small firms' participation in cartels is scarcer and less convenient. Since non-cartel members produce at capacity and cartel members produce below capacity, firms find it optimal not to join the cartel when their capacity is sufficiently low, because the effect of their membership on price is trivial but, at the same time, it experiences a nontrivial reduction in its output. Thus, we should not expect a cartel to include very small firms.

Risk-aversion that discriminates against SMEs arises through ignorance (according to the EU survey 'asking public procurers what current barriers prevent their organization of undertaking additional activities to favor SMEs, most Contracting Authorities (CAs) mentioned risk-aversion') or via routines that are costly to change (minimum size of revenues, etc.). Small firms do not face a level playing field, even if efficient, due the relevance of fixed costs in procurement which impact on their unitary costs and thus on their competitiveness.

Let us presume now that such discrimination in procurement against small firms exists. Would there be other less restrictive ways to achieve the same goal, i.e. aren't we, by setting up a programme of preferential procurement in favour of small firms, not too narrowly tailoring it to reach the goal of eliminating discrimination against them? For example, in Korea, discrimination in credit markets against SMEs is tackled not through set-asides nor preferences but liquidity provision.

The European Union recently issued its 'EU Small Business Act',[7] where several proposals are put forward to help SMEs in procurement. However, and contrary to the US Small Business Act, this new Act explicitly excludes the possibility of set-asides or preferences in public procurement. The EU approach is heavily oriented towards simplification policies to reduce the burden for SMEs of participating in tenders. A number of other public procurement interventions have been aimed at creating or protecting national/regional development effects, e.g. during the financial crisis, the EU introduced the 'accelerated procedure' to enable public money to be spent faster for certain types of procurement, and the UK introduced a ten-day maximum payment rule for SME invoices to ensure that SMEs supporting public entities did not suffer from the credit crunch. If compliance costs in procurement are a source of discrimination, tackling red tape could indeed be a better way to help SMEs than favouring them through preferences and/or set-asides.[8] However we should not consider, as often done, these two instruments as substitutes. It could very well be that, once red tape has been minimized, there are nevertheless some small firms that would not be able to compete, because still relatively inefficient, against larger firms. Should we think of protecting them and why? There exists little empirical literature on this issue, so it is hard to credibly take a side in the debate.

A possible way of getting out of this conundrum is to consider whether there are other compelling purposes that support SMEs' protection, beside sheer discrimination. For example, could *reducing procurement costs* via a procurement programme of small firms' preferences be considered such a compelling purpose at a quasi-constitutional level? While we agree that the case might appear as less evident than the one that arises from the goal of remedying discrimination, some countries consider deficit reduction an important quasi-constitutional goal (see for example the Maastricht Treaty requirements on public debt and deficit to GDP ratios).[9,10] How would helping SMEs in procurement be the most appropriate way to achieve the same goal of expenditure reduction? We see two relevant cases.

Take first the case in which both types of firms (small and large) are equally technologically efficient (same unitary costs) in public procurement participation. Since survival rates are traditionally shown to be higher for large rather than small firms, if a small firm is awarded a contract in the present that allows it to survive and grow and not abandon the relevant market, such a firm, everything else equal, will also be able to participate in the future to tenders without preferences, generating more participation, competition and expected savings.[11] This dynamic competition effect is likely to be the rationale for the US SBA preference programme.[12]

There is however a more likely case. Often the possibility of reducing government costs in procurement in set-asides is strictly related to the capacity of finding a group of 'clearly inefficient' firms to be targeted with preferential procurement. It could in theory be the case that, if small firms in a specific sector were to be clearly identified as the more efficient ones and large firms the inefficient ones, a specific protection should be granted to the latter and not the former.[13] This example however sounds extreme and unrealistic. While it is hard to identify a group of 'clearly inefficient firms in a given sector', we argue that a

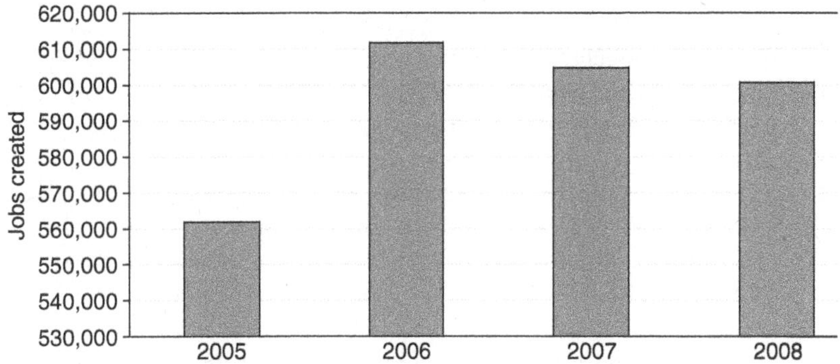


*Figure 18.3* Number of jobs created/retained that the SBA reports as result of its prime contracting and subcontracting assistance programmes alone.

small firm, possibly simply because of its size, is likely to be the one with the highest unitary costs due to regulation.

Finally, the rationale behind preference in procurement in favour of SMEs could be related to other other socio-economic goals, above all the job creation rate, heavily characterizing small firms' activity.[14] As shown in Figure 18.3, the number of jobs created by small firms as result of prime contracting and subcontracting assistance programmes in public procurement displayed a 9 per cent increase between 2005 to 2006 and a slow decline (2 per cent) between 2006 and 2008.

Again, little is known about the dynamic impact of preference policies in terms of growth of targeted firms. If long-term participation of initially small firms is what is desired in terms of goal from a preference scheme, then more data should be gathered in order to establish whether preference schemes have a significant impact on protected firms' chances of survival and growth.

## 3 Governments and preferential procurement policy: a brief EU vs. US comparison

### *3.1 United States*

While the European Union forbids any form of preferential treatment in the light of the non-discriminatory principle[15] for its above threshold tenders,[16] countries worldwide explicitly adopt such policies. For example, this philosophy is in stark contrast with that of the United States.

The US federal preferential procurement, stated in the Federal Acquisition Regulation[17] (FAR) directly refers to the participation of small businesses, historically underutilized business zones (HUBZ),[18] small disadvantaged businesses,[19] service-disabled veteran-owned small businesses,[20] women-owned small business concerns and contracts stipulated under the 8(a).[21] These programmes refer to entities which base their economic activity mostly in the United States and contribute to the US economy through payment of taxes and/or use of American products, material and/or labour, etc. and comply with the above-mentioned business categories.

In particular, the SBA negotiates with each agency mutually acceptable prime and subcontract goals for each small business category. The SBA must ensure that the mutually established cumulative goals for all agencies meet or exceed the government-wide 23 per cent (in dollar shares) small business goal (see Figure 18.4). Moreover, all other categories are subsets of the SB category, that is:

- 5 per cent of prime and subcontracts for women-owned small businesses;
- 3 per cent of prime contracts for HUBzone small businesses;
- 3 per cent of prime and subcontracts for service-disable veteran-owned small businesses.

A procurement can be additionally counted in more than one subset category, as applicable, except 8(a) and small disadvantaged business (SDB) that are reported separately, but together form the SDB government-wide achievement. Contracting authorities alone or jointly with a SBA representative may choose the most appropriate procurement tool in each particular situation. In fact there is not a hierarchical order among those programmes (nor in the choice of not applying set-asides), but the FAR explicitly prescribes that if a preferential scheme is not adopted this decision has to be exhaustively justified. For example, a justification for not using a preference scheme such that a large percentage of previous contracts for the required item have been awarded using small business concerns

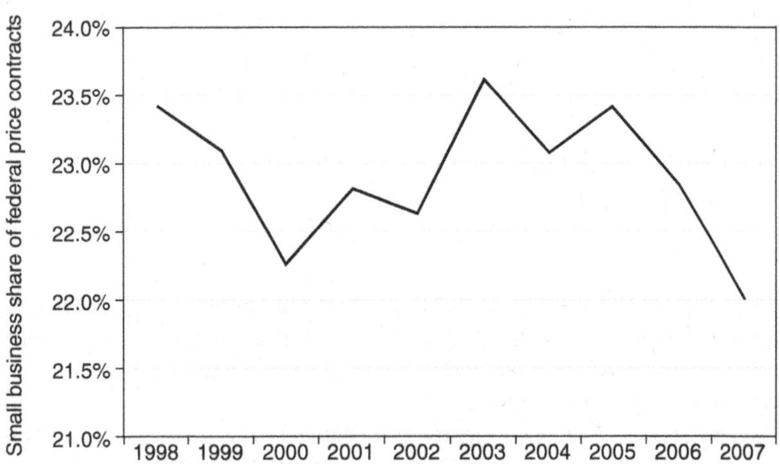


*Figure 18.4* Small business share of federal prime contracts, 1998 to 2007 (source: Europe Economics, data from SBA reports and Federal Procurement Data System).

or that SMEs have already received a fair portion of the overall agency's contracts would not be accepted.[22]

At the same time, even if there exists a strong preference towards the adoption of preferential programmes, the FAR maintains that there should be cases in which set-asides should not be applied. This is the case when there is a presumption that there is little competition, in either a total set-aside or a partial set-aside with lots. For example when only a large and a small firm may participate in the tender, the award with partial set-aside would imply a likely direct award to the only small firm and the only large firm in each respective lot. So in such a case, any kind of preference should not be applied, according to US Federal Regulation.[23]

Something to be noted which makes the administrative procedure of US preferential procurement different from the other ones is that each contracting authority at the local level works in cooperation with the SBA Procurement Centre Representative (PCR). These are representatives of the US Small Business Administration in the various large Procurement Agencies. Their function and powers are summarized in Box 18.1.

**Box 18.1 The Procurement Centre Representative**

Procurement Centre Representatives (PCR) work in SBA area offices and other federal purchasing centres located in the United States contributing practically to the implementation of the Small Business Administration policies by the purchasing agencies. PCRs have both operative and consultancy/training tasks. In particular, as stated by the American Federal Regulation (section 19.4) 'The duties assigned by SBA to its procurement center representatives include the following:

1 Reviewing proposed acquisitions to recommend: (i) The setting aside of selected acquisitions not unilaterally set aside by the contracting officer; (ii) New qualified small business sources, including veteran-owned small, service-disabled veteran-owned small, HUBZone small, small disadvantaged, economically disadvantaged women-owned small, and women-owned small eligible under the Woman-Owned Small Business Program; and (iii) Breakout of components for competitive acquisitions.
2 …If the SBA procurement center representative (or, if a procurement center representative is not assigned, see paragraph (a) of this section) believes that the acquisition, as proposed, makes it unlikely that small businesses can compete for the prime contract, the representative shall recommend any alternate contracting method that the representative reasonably believes will increase small business prime contracting opportunities. The recommendation shall be made to the contracting officer within 15 days after receipt of the package.
3 Recommending concerns for inclusion on a list of concerns to be solicited in a specific acquisition.
4 Appealing to the chief of the contracting office any contracting officer's determination not to solicit a concern recommended by the SBA for a particular acquisition, when not doing so results in no small business being solicited.

5 Conducting periodic reviews of the contracting activity to which assigned to ascertain whether it is complying with the small business policies in this regulation.

6 Sponsoring and participating in conferences and training designed to increase small business participation in the contracting activities of the office.'

In order to comply with the duties stated by the regulation, 'contracting officers shall give the PCRs access to all reasonably obtainable contract information that is directly pertinent to their official duties'. PCRs support the contracting officers in all aspect of the procurement process, therefore they also review proposed small business subcontracting plans and may recommend to the contracting officer various small business goals and various subcontracting options. Finally, PCRs relying on their professional skills and experience provide training, outreach and research.

US federal policy includes also bid preference (price adjustment), but this second tool is reserved only for small disadvantaged and service-disable veteran-owned businesses. Under this scheme, bids submitted by the mentioned enterprises are adjusted by a 5 per cent discount, in order to allow them to compete against more efficient bidders. As long as, given the discount, a favoured offer equalizes or is lower than the best bid submitted, the contract is awarded to the preferred bidder. Even if this policy and associated discount level works at the federal level, each state can use the bid preference scheme in accordance with the SBA office in order to reach the goal of 23 per cent contract value awarded to SMEs and minority businesses, keeping in mind that bid preferences cannot be cumulated to set aside.

### *3.2 The 'new' European perspective*

The Green Book recently issued by the European Commission contained a series of recommendations and issues for a reform of public procurement in the EU. It also contains a reference to set-asides. In its English format it states 'one idea, for instance, might be to set targets for SME shares in overall procurement'.[24] It is however further stated that 'such a system would not involve reserving specific contracts for SMEs, but they would simply provide an incentive for contracting authorities to make the best possible use of the available instruments for SME-friendly procurement'. All references to this issue have anyway disappeared from the EC proposal of a new Procurement Directive.

The Green Book was followed by the summing up of the replies received from the various stakeholders. Unfortunately, no separate answers of SMEs were listed so as to get a sense of the problems these firms face in public procurement. Nonetheless from the summary we identified as relevant problems for SMEs (beside the usual 'simplification of documentation') the issue of transparency and fairness ('with the exception of citizens and, to a certain extent, SME representatives, all stakeholder groups favour *more negotiation* in award procedures for all types of contracts and contracting authorities' (italics added)), aggregation of demand ('stakeholders are in general in favour of a stronger and more generalised aggregation of demand … (which) may hinder SME access to public contracts'), disproportionate technical criteria ('a large majority of respondents from all stakeholder groups except for civil society organisations fear that abandoning the link with the subject matter might create serious problems for SMEs, which may not be able to meet the various societal requirements') and disproportionate financial criteria ('a majority of business and public authorities – but not Member States – think that additional measures are needed to strengthen the innovation capacity of SMEs, recommending for instance financial support schemes and compensation of bidding costs').

Notwithstanding the fact that the Green Paper had already excluded some relevant topics from discussion (like set-asides) and that the comments from SME stakeholders were not gathered in a coherent way to truly get a sense of their issues, the following proposal by the European Commission of a new Public Procurement Directive reduced even further the number of reforms that are to be taken to the European Council. We counted four of them.[25] Some of these reforms in our opinion will turn out to be either counterproductive or irrelevant in helping SMEs, making the final proposal fall short of the expectations that were raised by the previous Green Paper. Also importantly many of these are not specifically related to SMEs per se.

1 Simplification of information obligations.

> The general simplification of information obligations in procurement procedures will greatly benefit SMEs. The proposal provides for the mandatory acceptance of self-declarations as prima-facie evidence for selection purposes. The actual production of documentary evidence will be facilitated by a standardised document, the European Procurement Passport which is a means of proof for the absence of grounds for exclusion.

This help applies to all firms, both small and large, reducing only moderately the competitive advantage that information obligations in general give to large firms compared to small ones.

2 Division into lots.

> Contracting authorities will be invited to divide public contracts into – homogeneous or heterogeneous – lots to make them more accessible for SMEs. If they decide not do so, they will be obliged to provide a specific explanation.

Division into lots is often an instrument to make cartels work more smoothly, and small firms are typically excluded from cartels. Not only is this approach not useful for SMEs but it can also backfire for taxpayers.

3 Limitation on requirements for participation.

> To avoid unjustified barriers in the way of participation by SMEs, the proposed Directive contains an exhaustive list of possible conditions for participation in procurement procedures and states explicitly that any such conditions shall be restricted 'to those that are appropriate to ensure that a candidate or tenderer has the … capacities and … abilities to perform the contract to be awarded'. Turnover requirements which are frequently a formidable obstacle to access by SMEs are explicitly limited to three times the estimated contract value, except in duly justified cases. Finally, any conditions for participation by groups of economic operators – an instrument of particular relevance for SMEs – must be justified by objective reasons and proportionate.

Participation requirements limited (non-mandatory) to three times the estimated contract value (which might be useful not only for small firms) do represent a novelty in the de facto policies or practices of some countries and might make participation to tenders slightly more likely for some SMEs in these countries, but do not reduce the average competitive disadvantage that SMEs have when entering into a tender.[26]

4 Direct payment of subcontractors.

> In addition, Member State can provide that subcontractors may request for direct payment by the contracting authority of supplies, works and services provided to the main contractor in the context of the contract performance. This offers subcontractors which are often SMEs an efficient way of protecting their interest in being paid.

Direct payment of subcontractors, while useful, is also not directly and uniquely meant to support SMEs. Furthermore, when we speak of support to SMEs we often mean to prime contracting, since subcontracting is usually considered by SMEs as a condition of low bargaining power that reduces SMEs' benefit from public procurement.

Overall, this proposal does not manage in a meaningful way to reduce the large disparities that small firms in the European Union face compared to other countries, as we document in this chapter.

## 4 Conclusions

'Open competition is the basis for efficient public procurement' World Bank Guidelines state. We could not agree more. But what is competition in public procurement? Is it 'competition today' ensured by a powerful struggle between, for example, only two large firms (a de facto duopoly), possibly ending up with the failure of the losing vendor and the long-term perspective for government of being locked-in with only one supplier (a de facto monopolist) for the foreseeable future? Or is competition a more dynamic concept, which feeds on an ever larger field of participants, many firms, large or small, domestic or foreign, ready to satisfy public demand for goods or services or infrastructure?

Public procurement is filled with barriers to entry. Bates (2009) describes these barriers having in mind minority-owned firms but we believe our chapter has shown that this reasoning can be extended at least also to small firms:

> applicable barriers limit access to financial capital and product markets; access to skills and work experience that facilitate firm formation are sometimes limited ... Barriers often result in overly small and less viable firms.... The greater incidence of marginal firms, in turn, causes heightened failure rates.
>
> (Bates 2009)

Public procurement can be a powerful tool to reduce those barriers if used with knowledge and pragmatism according to the specific situation. We have argued that while many possible actions exist, including the ones typically recommended in the European Union like reducing red tape in public procurement, no other tool can be as powerful in revamping participation and destroying barriers than the one of extending preferences, in the form of set-asides or price subsidies, to SMEs.

We believe that these schemes cannot be too prolonged in time for any given firm, that they must reduce the incentives for targeted firms not to reduce their costs, and must be carefully monitored for fraud prevention. But precautions must also be taken to monitor if Contracting Authorities are unduly favouring large firms, whether for risk-aversion, incompetence or corruption. Additional use of public employees like Procurement Centre Representatives in the United States can help vastly in shifting procurement tenders towards equal opportunities.

Whether the cost of subsidizing the 'wrong' firms is higher than the benefit of having protected some 'good' firms that would have not survived without the subsidy is an empirical question that has yet to find a solution. However we would strongly doubt that the answer would be at one of the two extremes, 'no protection' or 'only protection', and we encourage policy-makers to enter into the realm of making public procurement a field of social and local experimentation while protecting citizens from political and administrative abuse.

## Notes

1 See the Green Paper of th European Commission at http://eur-lex.europa.eu/LexUriServ/LexUriServ.do?uri=COM:2011:0015:FIN:EN:PDF.

2 The Impact of Regulatory Costs on Small Firms, N. Crain and M. Crain for SBA, 2010.

3 This stylized fact is not merely European. Another recent empirical study by Bates (2009) on preferential procurement in the Chicago area shows through a survey the types of barriers minority business enterprises (MBEs) and small firms more generally face with respect to non-minority and large firms in their quest to become viable

entities. Results do not differ from their European counterpart: '70.5% of surveyed MBEs responded that unbundling large contracts would help them access ... procurement opportunities versus 69.0% of the nonminority small-business vendors.'

4 Evaluation of SMEs access to public procurement markets in the EU, DG Enterprise and Industry, September 2011.

5 Article 5 European Community Treaty – Treaty establishing the European Community.

6 Local firms are often, however, favoured by local banks. This is one case in which the parallel between small and local firms fails.

7 Communication from the Commission to the Council, the European Parliament, the European Economic and Social Committee and the Committee of the Regions, *'Think Small First' A 'Small Business Act' for Europe*, COM(2008) 394 final.

8 Some of these policies could be: skills assessment and development programmes, business mentoring or coaching, training in commercial tendering, small business advice, simplification of bidding documents and questionnaires, translation of documents into local language, lowering or rationalization of pre-qualification criteria, reduction in costs of bidding, e.g. payment for bidding documents, lowering of barriers to entry, e.g. compulsory industry registrations, access to additional or cheaper forms of business financing and investment, more transparent publication of business opportunities, communication programmes.

9 Some political strategies of high relevance, like the recently launched Europe 2020, specifically mentions it as a goal.

10 However, the EC's recently published Green Paper discussed the possibility of favouring in public procurement local and regional suppliers, and also non-profit organizations, a possible decision for which little compelling purpose can be found. One might however consider the case of subsidizing firms that engage jobseekers or persons with disabilities, in the light not so much of their (to be proven) productive disadvantage and inefficiency but their (likely) potential discrimination against. In such a case one could see a compelling EU purpose in subsidizing firms in procurement that hire these workers. But would large firms that employ jobseekers or persons with disabilities be considered as 'weak' candidates in a tender, so that subsidizing them would enhance revenue and minimize losses in terms of efficiency? It is not evident. Furthermore, there could be a risk of even stronger manipulations to qualify as a firm to be subsidized than the fraud potential for small firms (see Section 3), since jobseekers and persons with disabilities could be hired by strong large firms at little cost to the organization only to obtain a preference, generating a negative expenditure effect from the targeting programme, since large firms would win the tender more easily, discouraging even further participation by small firms.

11 Bates (2009) argues however that small firms serving mainly government are more likely to fail than small firms that sell more to the private sector. True enough, but this does not change the fact that an increase in government business, everything else equal, should have a positive effect on the firm's survival rates.

12

> The essence of the American economic system of private enterprise is free competition ... The preservation and expansion of such competition is basic not only to the economic well-being but to the security of this Nation. Such security and well-being cannot be realized unless the actual and potential capacity of small business is encouraged and developed. It is the declared policy of the Congress that the Government should aid, counsel, assist, and protect, insofar as is possible, the interests of small-business concerns in order to preserve free competitive enterprise, to insure that a fair proportion of the total purchases and contracts or subcontracts for property and services for the Government (including but not limited to contracts or subcontracts for maintenance, repair, and construction) be placed with small business enterprises.
>
> (Small Business Act, USA 1953)

13 Naeglen and Mougeot (1998) and Morand (2003).

14 In the United States, over a 4–5 year period, 75–80 per cent of new jobs came from small firms, the Small Business Administration reports. About 30–40 per cent of these new jobs came from the birth of new firms (Office of Advocacy Report 1998). Fitzgerald and Ribar (2001) demonstrate that small firms play a crucial role in creating a low-skilled job opportunities. Neumark *et al.* (2011) estimate that small firms and small establishments create more jobs than large businesses, net of the job destruction rate, both in the manufacturing and in the service sector.

15 Art. 18 TFEU. http://eur-lex.europa.eu/LexUriServ/LexUriServ.do?uri=OJ:C:2008:115:0047:0199:EN:PDF.

16 A further note is required to better analyse the European legislation. As said, for all contracts above the European threshold any kind of preferential scheme is forbidden; however, below the same threshold there is no clear-cut regulation. Member States can adopt their national regulations on public procurement and are constrained only by those principles stated in the Treaty: non-discrimination and proportionality principles should always apply. In particular, non-discrimination can be advocated once there could exist an economic interest, for a non-favoured group or firm, violated by the preferential treatment. A EU-wide set-aside should anyway concern EU SMEs, not national ones. Change of Directives or change of Treaty to switch to set-asides is another open issue. Some lawyers argue that a set-aside, mandated by Directives without going against the Treaty, could be passed as long as it does not imply discrimination on the basis of nationality. The Treaty (Court of Justice jurisprudence) refers to the principle of 'equal' treatment so as to treat differently different situations or equally the same situations. A set-aside, one could argue, would not go against equality of treatment if one were to prove that small firms are not equal to large ones.

17 www.acquisition.gov/far/. The reader will find in Chapters 16 and 17 of this volume a more complete and accurate description of the US preference programme.

18 The programme applies to qualified small business concerns located in historically underutilized business zones, in an effort to increase employment opportunities, investment and economic development in those areas. Subpart 19.3, FAR.

19 A small disadvantaged business (SDB) is a small business that is at least 51 per cent owned by one or more individuals who are both socially and economically disadvantaged. The SBA defines socially disadvantaged groups as those who have been, historically, subjected to 'racial or ethnic prejudice or cultural bias' within the larger American culture. Identified groups include: African Americans, Asian Pacific Americans, Hispanic Americans, Native Americans and Subcontinent Asian Americans. Members of other groups may qualify if they can satisfactorily demonstrate that they meet established criteria.

20 A service-disabled veteran is a person who served in the active military, naval, or air service, and who was discharged or released under conditions other than dishonourable, and whose disability was incurred or aggravated in line of duty in the active military, naval or air service. Source: US Department of Defense.

21 8(a) is a programme that authorizes the Small Business Administration (SBA) to enter into all types of contracts with other agencies and let subcontracts for performing those contracts to firms eligible for programme participation. The SBA's subcontractors are referred to as '8(a) contractors'. Subpart 19.8 – Contracting with the Small Business Administration (the 8(a) Program), FAR.

22 Section 19.502–5 Insufficient causes for not setting aside an acquisition, FAR.

23 19.502–2 Total small business set-asides.

(a) Each acquisition of supplies or services that has an anticipated dollar value exceeding $3,000 … but not over $100,000…, is automatically reserved exclusively for small business concerns and shall be set aside for small business unless the contracting officer determines there is not a reasonable expectation of obtaining offers from two or more responsible small business concerns that are competitive in terms of market prices, quality, and delivery. If the contracting officer does not proceed with the small business set-aside and purchases on an unrestricted basis, the contracting officer shall include in the contract file the reason for this unrestricted purchase. If the contracting officer receives only one acceptable offer from a responsible small business concern in response to a set-aside, the contracting officer should make an award to that firm. If the contracting officer receives no acceptable offers from responsible small business concerns, the set-aside shall be withdrawn and the requirement, if still valid, shall be resolicited on an unrestricted basis.

(b) The contracting officer shall set aside any acquisition over $100,000 for small business participation when there is a reasonable expectation that (1) offers will be obtained from at least two responsible small business concerns offering the products of different small business concerns (but see paragraph (c) of this subsection); and (2) award will be made at fair market prices. Total small business set-asides shall not be made unless such a reasonable expectation exists (but see 19.502–3 as to partial set-asides). Although past acquisition history of an item or similar items is always important, it is not the only factor to be considered in determining whether a reasonable expectation exists. In making R&D small business set-asides, there must also be a reasonable expectation of obtaining from small businesses the best scientific and technological sources consistent with the demands of the proposed acquisition for the best mix of cost, performances, and schedules.

19.502–3 Partial set-asides.

(a) The contracting officer shall set aside a portion of an acquisition, except for construction, for exclusive small business participation when:
  (1) A total set-aside is not appropriate (see 19.502–2);
  (2) The requirement is severable into two or more economic production runs or reasonable lots;
  (3) One or more small business concerns are expected to have the technical competence and productive capacity to satisfy the set-aside portion of the requirement at a fair market price;
  (4) The acquisition is not subject to simplified acquisition procedures; and
  (5) A partial set-aside shall not be made if there is a reasonable expectation that only two concerns (one large and one small) with capability will respond with offers unless authorized by the head of a contracting activity on a case-by-case basis. Similarly, a class of acquisitions, not including construction, may be partially set aside. Under certain specified conditions, partial set-asides may be used in conjunction with multiyear contracting procedures.

(b) When the contracting officer determines that a portion of an acquisition is to be set aside, the requirement shall be divided into a set-aside portion and a non-set-aside portion, each of which shall (1) be an economic production run or reasonable lot and (2) have terms and a delivery schedule comparable to the other. When practicable, the set-aside portion should make maximum use of small business capacity.

24 In its French and Italian version however it mentions ‘global goals in terms of participation for SMEs’ and not of shares. The Green Paper also discusses the possibility of preferential procurement for local or regional suppliers (a potentially much clearer case of violation of the principle of discrimination in the Treaty), jobseekers or persons with disabilities and non-profit organizations for social service contracts.

25 We do not include in this group the implications of the fact that ‘contracting authorities shall not establish specific conditions for participation of … groups in procurement procedures which are not imposed on individual candidates’ might also make

asymmetric treatment of group formation (barring groups of large firms while not barring groups of small firms) more unlikely, reducing the use of a pro-competitive instrument that could indeed help SMEs. Nor do we stress the potential dangers that would arise in the new Directive as proposed arising from the fact that more negotiations might make 'unfair' evaluations more likely at the expense of smaller players. Finally we note that demand aggregation is not forbidden unless gains can be proven, as in the United States: we only get that 'the aggregation and centralisation of purchases should be carefully monitored in order to avoid excessive concentration of purchasing power and collusion, and to preserve transparency and competition, as well as market access opportunities for small and medium-sized enterprises'.

26 Furthermore, a policy of this kind might be sub-optimal as it might restrict the discretionary power of smart procurers that, for a given specific market and tender, would correctly need a higher turnover requirement to obtain value for money.

## Bibliography


Anderson R.D. and Kovacic, W.E., Competition Policy and International Trade Liberalisation: Essential Complements to Ensure Good Performance in Public Procurement Markets. *Public Procurement Law Review* 18(2): 67–101, 2009.

Athey, S., Coey, D. and Levin, J., Set-aside and Subisidies in Auctions. Working Paper 2010.

Ayres, I. and Cramton, P., How Affirmative Action at the FCC Auction Decreased the Deficit. In I. Ayres (ed.), *Pervasive Prejudice? Unconventional Evidence of Race and Gender Discrimination*, Chicago: Chicago University Press, 2001, p. 315.

Bandiera, O., Prat, A. and Valletti, T., Active and Passive Waste in Government Spending: Evidence from a Policy Experiment. *American Economic Review* 99(4): 1278–308, September 2009.

Bates, T., Why do Minority Business Development Programs Generate so Little Minority Business Development? *Economic Development Quarterly* 9(1): 3–14, February 1995.

Bates, T., Utilizing Affirmative Action in Public Sector Procurement as a Local Economic Development Strategy. *Economic Development Quarterly* 23: 180–92, 2009.

Bolton, P., The Public Procurement System in South Africa: Main Characteristics. Public Contract Law Journal 37(4): 719, 2008.

Bolton, P., An Analysis of the Preferential Procurement Legislation in South Africa. Public Procurement Law Review 16(1): 36, 2007.

Bos, I. and Harrington Jr., J.E., Endogenous Cartel Formation with Heterogeneous Firms. *RAND Journal of Economics* 41(1): 92–117, 2010.

Compte, O., Lambert-Mogiliansky, A. and Verdier, T., Corruption and Competition in Procurement Auctions. *RAND Journal of Economics* 36(1): 1–15, 2005.

Crain, N. and Crain, M., The Impact of Regulatory Costs on Small Firms, SBA, 2010.

DG Enterprise and Industry, Evaluation of SMEs' Access to Public Procurement Markets in the EU, Final Report, 2010.

European Commission, *A Report on the Functioning of Public Procurement Markets in the EU: Benefits from the Application of EU Directives and Challenges for the Future*, 3 February 2004.

European Commission, Concerning the Definition of Micro, Small and Medium Sized Enterprises, *Official Journal of the European Union*, 2003/36/EC, May 2003.

European Commission, European SMEs under Pressure, Annual Report on EU Small and Medium-Sized Enterprises, 2009.

Europe Economics, the US Small Business Administration, A Report by Europe Economics for the Enterprise Trust, December 2010.

European Network on Debt and Development, Procurement and Development Effectiveness, a Literature Review, 2009.

Federal Acquisition Regulation, United States of America.

Fitzgerald, J.M. and Ribar, D.C., *Does a Rising Tide of Small Business Jobs Lift All Boats?* (prepared for the Small Business Administration Office of Advocacy under contract number SBAHQ-00-M-0574). Washington, DC: Small Business Administration, July 2001.

Kidalov, M.V., Small Business Contracting in the United States and Europe: A Comparative Assessment, 40 *Pub. Cont. L.J.* 443, 2011.

Linarelli, J., The Limited Case for Permitting SME Procurement Preferences in the WTO Agreement on Government Procurement, in Sue Arrowsmith and R.D. Anderson, *The WTO Regime on Government Procurement: Challenge and Reform*, Cambridge University Press, 2011.

McAfee, R.P. and McMillan, J., Auction and Bidding. *Journal of Economic Literature* XXV: 699–738, June 1987.

McCrudden, C., *Buying Social Justice: Equality, Government Procurement, & Legal Change*. Oxford University Press, 2007.

McCrudden, C. and Gross, S.G., WTO Government Procurement Rules and the Local Dynamics of Procurement Policies: A Malaysian Case Study. *European Journal of International Law* 17: 151–85, 2006.

Morand, Pierre-Henri, SMEs and Public Procurement Policy. *Review of Economic Design* 8(3): 301–18, 2003.

Naegelen, F. and Mougeot, M., Discriminatory Public Procurement Policy and Cost Reduction Incentives. *Journal of Public Economics* 67(3): 349–67, 1998.

Neumark, D., Wall, B. and Zhang, J., Do Small Businesses Create More Jobs? New Evidence for the United States from the National Establishment Time Series. *The Review of Economics and Statistics* 93(1): 16–29, 2011.

OECD-DAC Methodology for Assessment of National Procurement Systems (User's Guide Version 4.0, dated 17 July 2006).

Ravina, E., Love & Loans: The Effect of Beauty and Characteristics in Credit Markets. Working Paper, Columbia University, July 2008.

Report of the Policy Board for Financial Services and Regulation, *South Africa 2001*.

Ribeiro Soriano, D. and Roig Dobon, S., Linking Globalization of Entrepreneurship in Small Organizations. *Small Business Economics* 32: 233–9, 2009.

The US Small Business Administration, A Report by Europe Economics for the Enterprise Trust, December 2010.

Watermeyer, R., The Use of Targeted Procurement as an Instrument of Poverty Alleviation and Job Creation in Infrastructure Projects. *Public Procurement Law* 5: 226–50, 2000.

# Index

Page numbers in *italics* denote tables.